DATE DUE

The Soul of
Latin America

The Soul of Latin America

THE CULTURAL AND
POLITICAL TRADITION

HOWARD J. WIARDA

Yale
University
Press

New
Haven
&
London

Designed by James J. Johnson and set in E+F Swift types
by Integrated Publishing Solutions.
Printed in the United States of America by Sheridan Books, Chelsea, Michigan.

Library of Congress Cataloging-in-Publication Data

Wiarda, Howard J., 1939–
The soul of Latin America: The cultural and political tradition / Howard J. Wiarda.
p. cm.
Includes bibliographical references and index.
ISBN 0-300-08257-6 (alk. paper)

1. Political culture—Latin America. 2. Latin America—Politics and government.
I.Title.
JL960.W52 2001
320.98—dc21 00-061447
A catalogue record for this book is available from the British Library.

The paper in this book meets the guidelines for permanence and durability
of the Committee on Production Guidelines for Book Longevity
of the Council on Library Resources.

1 2 3 4 5 6 7 8 9 10

Contents

Preface   vii

Chapter 1. Foundations of Contrast:
            The United States and Latin America   1

Chapter 2. Origins: Greece, Rome, the Bible,
            and Medieval Christianity   19

Chapter 3. Medieval Iberia: The Distinct Tradition   50

Chapter 4. Spain and Portugal in America:
            The Colonial Heritage   76

Chapter 5. Liberalism and the Latin American
            Independence Movements   112

Chapter 6. Positivism: A Philosophy of Order
            and Progress   145

Chapter 7. Nationalism   175

Chapter 8. Marxism   212

Chapter 9. Corporatism   246

Chapter 10. The Conflict Society, 1930s–1980s   281

Chapter 11. Transitions to Democracy—or Something
            Less Than That?   309

Chapter 12. Which Way Latin America?   344

Notes   359
Bibliography   391
Index   411

Preface

Americans have a hard time understanding Latin America. As James Reston of the *New York Times* once wrote, "The United States will do anything for Latin America except read about it." As an author, I hope, naturally, that Reston's admonition doesn't apply to *my* book; in fact I wrote it precisely to try to help North Americans understand Latin America.

There are a lot of stereotypes about Latin America that get in the way of such understanding. The classic ones, largely derived from old movies and *New Yorker* cartoons, include mustached men-on-horseback galloping in and out of the presidential palace in comic-opera "revolutions," peasants in big sombreros taking siestas under coffee trees, and women with bananas and pineapples on their heads dancing gaily in the streets. In the newer stereotypes the sleepy peasant has become a daring guerrilla with a *bandolero* over his shoulder, a fabulously wealthy narco-trafficker who produces drugs for the U.S. market, or perhaps a Harvard-educated, buttoned-down *técnico* ostensibly seeking to bring U.S.-style democracy and free markets to Latin America. But neither the old nor the new stereotypes are very accurate; further, they often do a disservice to efforts to understand the area in all its complexity.

Along with stereotyping, something else gets in the way of understanding Latin America: a refusal to understand it on its own terms. North Americans tend to view North American society as superior, more developed, a model for others to emulate. America is viewed as a beacon, a "city on a hill," and Americans as a chosen people. Americans persist in viewing Latin America and Latin Americans as little children who need to be educated in proper democratic and economic behavior. Latin America is seen as wanting to be just like the United States and as "developing" toward the U.S. model, presumably liberal, democratic, pluralist, and oriented toward free enterprise. To be successful, Latin America must emulate the United States so it can catch up with its level of development politically, socially, and economically; like Woodrow Wilson, John F. Kennedy, Jimmy Carter, Ronald Reagan, and countless other figures in U.S. history, Americans seek to teach Latin America about good government, social justice, and economic efficiency. Such ethnocentrism (seeing others through one's own eyes, refusing to understand them on their own terms) has been pervasive in American attitudes toward Latin America throughout history and continues to be so today; it is *the* fundamental reason North Americans are unable to comprehend Latin America.

But more is operating here than just stereotypes and ethnocentrism; strong prejudices are also involved—by that I mean more than just ethnic or racial prejudice. For the fact is that Latin America was founded on a feudal, oligarchic, authoritarian, and elitist basis. Latin America was a product of the Counter-Reformation, of medieval scholasticism and Catholicism, of the Inquisition, and of frankly nonegalitarian, nonpluralist, and nondemocratic principles. Many of these early characteristics, now obviously modified, updated, or "modernized," are still present today, embedded in cultural, social, and political behavior and in the area's main institutions. Most Americans are frankly uncomfortable with these traits, with a society not only based on inequality but—at least in private—unapologetically and unabashedly so. Thus the missionary attitude: either the United States must teach Latin Americans how to do things its way, or it must view the area as developing inevitably toward U.S.-style institutions. Because the alternative—an inegalitarian, inquisitorial, and undemocratic society—is simply unacceptable. These myriad biases, prejudices, and misconceptions as well as missionary attitudes prevent Americans from dealing with Latin America on its own terms, through the workings of its own institutions, and without the imposition of deep-seated North American values and beliefs.

This book treats Latin America as a distinct *culture area* or *civilization*. In it I examine the region through its culture, languages, and institutions, not through the rose-colored glasses of North American preferences. I recognize the changes, evolution, and development of Latin America as well as the impact of outside influences, including the profound effect the United States has had on the area. But I also attempt to identify why and how Latin America differs from the United States, why its politics, society, and economies are at such variance from the

American. I look at the founding bases of Latin American civilization, tracing their evolution over time, and show how they operate both historically and currently in ways that are very different from those of the United States. (Note that I say "different," not "emerging," "less developed," or "backward.") I try here to explain how Latin America functions as a distinct society, what its internal norms and operating principles are, what is unique and particular about Latin America, and how and why it is at some degrees of variance from U.S. civilization. While attempting to comprehend Latin America according to its own internal dynamics, I try to hold my own views in abeyance.

But the book has larger purposes than contributing to a better understanding of Latin America—worthy though that is. It also has comparative and theoretical aspirations. That is, people in the United States often assume that John Locke, James Madison, and Thomas Jefferson are the philosophic founders of American pluralist, representative democracy. But whom would one identify as the philosophic founders of Latin America? The answer must include Saint Thomas Aquinas, the architect of medieval Catholicism; Francisco Suárez, the Jesuit neoscholastic who rationalized Spain's system of state-building royal authority and colonialism; Jean-Jacques Rousseau, who justified a top-down and organic form of democracy that often led to authoritarianism; and Auguste Comte, the founder of positivism, who designed an elite-directed model of progress that Latin America quickly assimilated and still follows today. The contrast between these two philosophic traditions, the North American and the Latin American, is enormous and goes a long way toward explaining the comparative divergences between the two parts of the Americas. But both these conceptions, the Lockean and the Aquinas-Suárezian, are currently in trouble, as are the societies founded on their principles; both may be outdated, and both are facing crises of legitimacy. So at one level this book focuses on Latin America, but at another it is a comparative study that examines the formative principles of both the United States and Latin America and asks if either set of principles is relevant to today's complex societies, both north and south.

A word about the approach of the book—although these themes are elaborated in the introductory chapter. First, I place great emphasis on the history of ideas and political culture of Latin America—a theme that is often ignored in contemporary socioeconomic and institutional treatments but which I believe to be of critical importance. Second, I seek to relate these political and sociological ideas to the realities of social structure, class relations, and the operation of domestic political institutions as well as international pressures and forces and to weave a complex tapestry of multicausality that is closely tied to the operating features of Latin America. Third, after spending many years studying the two areas, I am convinced that one cannot understand Latin America without also understanding the principles and institutions carried to the region by the Iberian mother countries of Spain and Portugal. Indeed, my perspective is to treat Iberia and Latin America as a unified, distinct culture area, as opposed to seeing them as parts of separate geographic areas, even while recognizing both the disparities between Iberia and Latin America as well as the impact of other outside influences (for example, Europe and the United States, respectively). Of course, each country in Latin America and Iberia is unique in many ways and deserving of detailed separate treatment; but here the focus is on the big picture, the commonalities, Iberia and Latin America as a distinct civilization.*

This is an unusual book in many ways; almost no one writes on Latin American political theory or political tradition any more; the last comprehensive book on this theme was published almost thirty years ago and is no longer in print. Moreover, most books on Latin American political thought begin with the independence period, thereby ignoring the pivotally important colonial epoch with which Latin America is still struggling. Furthermore, not one of them pays any attention to the crucial feudal and medieval roots of Latin America in Spain and Portugal of the Middle Ages. So far as I know, no book on the political theory of Latin America has treated that subject systematically as part of the larger political culture of the area or tried to relate it to broader socioeconomic and developmental issues. Both the book and its approach are fresh and distinctive and explore important themes that are often ignored; it is also a provocative book and likely to stir discussion and debate.

The book was written both for general readers interested in Latin America and as a text or supplemental reading in courses or seminars on Latin America, comparative politics, political theory, and development issues. The original chapter outline contained twenty-two subjects—too many for a one-semester course; the present organization of twelve chapters enables a teacher to spend one week on each major subject or to subdivide them further depending on time and interest.

---

*The term "civilization" as used here is roughly comparable to its use by Samuel P. Huntington, *The Clash of Civilizations* (New York: Simon and Schuster, 1996)

This book is the product of some forty years of living and working in, studying, and writing about Iberia and Latin America. As an undergraduate at the University of Michigan in the late 1950s and early 1960s, I took my first courses on Latin America and Spain; that was followed by graduate school and then an academic as well as policy-related career devoted to the region. I began my academic career in the 1960s as a student of Latin America, but the more time I spent in the region and the more countries I studied, the more I became convinced that in order to understand their common features I had to go back to the origins in Spain and Portugal. That led to extended research in Iberia during the tumultuous decade of the 1970s (the Portuguese revolution of 1974, Generalissimo Francisco Franco's death in 1975, and transitions to democracy in both countries) and to writing about Iberia and Latin America as well as the connections between them in the 1980s and 1990s. During those four decades, both Iberia and Latin America have changed tremendously, but in my mind the continuities of social structure and political ideas and behavior—including those earlier formative periods and founding principles that I write about here—remain equally impressive.

Over this forty-year period, the debts and obligations I have accumulated are numerous. Among the foundations and funding agencies that have supported my research are the Rockefeller Foundation, the Fulbright Program, the National Endowment for the Humanities, the Labor Relations and Research Center, the University of Massachusetts, the Mershon Center, the National Institutes of Health, the Social Science Research Council–American Council of Learned Societies, the American Philosophic Society, the Tinker Foundation, Mellon Foundation, Pew Foundation, Smith Richardson Foundation, Citibank, Brazilinvest, the Twentieth Century Fund, the Foreign Policy Research Institute, and the United States Institute of Peace. The institutions that I have called home over this long period and that have been very supportive of my research efforts (as well as generous with their leave policies) include the University of Massachusetts, Amherst, the Mershon Center for National Security Policy, the Center for International Affairs at Harvard University, the American Enterprise Institute for Public Policy Research, the Foreign Policy Research Institute, the National War College, and the Center for Strategic and International Studies.

The following persons have read or commented on all or parts of the manuscript: Margaret Mott, Iêda Siqueira Wiarda, Jorge Domínguez,

Richard Morse, Paul Sigmund, David Scott Palmer, and anonymous reviewers for Yale University Press. Solid editorial advice was proffered by John S. Covell, my editor at Yale University Press, while Doris Holden did her usual masterful job of word processing and editing. Iêda Siqueira Wiarda has been my partner and companion for thirty-six of the forty years I have spent studying the subject. Sometimes my travels and needs for assistance have impinged on her career, but that has not prevented her from giving unsparingly of her time and good judgment, while also serving as the world's best mom, wife, friend, scholar, teacher, and professional colleague. This is not the first time that one of my books has been dedicated to her in love and gratitude.

All these institutions and persons, I'm sure, have influenced my thinking in various ways, but none of them are responsible for the views expressed here. That responsibility rests with me alone.

The Soul of
Latin America

Chapter 1

Foundations of Contrast: The United States and Latin America

It has long been taken for granted that there are many and diverse routes to national modernization. During the Cold War, commentators classified countries in terms of "three worlds of development": a First World of developed, capitalist, pluralist countries centered in North America and Western Europe; a Second World of developed communist states centered in the Soviet Union and Eastern Europe; and a Third World of emerging or developing nations located mostly in Africa, Asia, Latin America, and the Middle East.[1]

Within the Third World category, furthermore, additional differentiations were drawn. Some were designated Newly Industrial Countries (NICS), others were labeled Big Emerging Markets (BEMS), still others lagged behind. If an area studies framework was used, there was an Asian or "Confucian" pattern of development, a Middle Eastern or "Islamic" model of development, as well as distinct processes at work in Africa and Latin America.[2]

But now, many of these classificatory schemes are outdated and need to be scrapped or reformulated. The collapse of the Soviet Union and the transition to democracy there and in Eastern Europe mean the Second World of developed communist countries has disappeared. Meanwhile the First World of developed capitalist countries has become somewhat testy, often unable to agree on common policy measures. The Third World category—never precise—has splintered even further, with relatively few contacts or connections between the countries and areas.

It is not just the end of the Cold War that has precipitated these changes but other, global changes as well. Francis Fukuyama has proclaimed the "end of history," meaning that the idea of democracy has triumphed definitively;[3] neither Marxism-Leninism nor authoritarianism commands widespread legitimacy any longer. Meanwhile the "world culture" (Lucian Pye's term) of rock music (including its protest lyrics), blue jeans, Coca-Cola, consumerism, and—not least—democracy and human rights has broken down earlier cultural barriers and given rise to a new, universal culture of tastes and expectations.[4] Globalization has affected all countries culturally, socially, economically, and politically. At the same time modern research has shown that many of the constants in human behavior can be explained from the imperatives of power, economics, class, the environment, genes, and the central nervous system—from the apparently universal human capacities to respond to similar wants, needs, and challenges—and not so much from the point of view of cultural differences.

And yet we all understand that cultural differences remain important. Even if democracy has become a near-universal, it is plain that American democracy diverges greatly from Continental European democracy, which in turn is very different from Asian democracy, which is quite distinct from Latin American democracy. Anyone who travels knows instinctively that the sights, sounds, smells, and political cultures of Mediterranean Europe differ from those of Scandinavia, that Asia is unlike the West, that Africa, Latin America, and the Middle East have few issues in common, and even if their power configurations, class structures, and aspirations are vaguely similar, it is still the case that the precise responses of any group or nation are mediated and filtered by ideas, habits, and unique sociopolitical institutions—that is, by culture.

The continuing importance of culture as a filtering, shaping, mediating mechanism produces four interesting effects.[5] First, owing to distinct values, ideas, and behavioral patterns, cultural responses exhibit considerable variability among peoples and nations, even within the range of the presumably universal needs they seek to meet. Second, cultural responses are learned and often deeply ingrained and therefore persist and spread beyond the time period or group that originally gave rise to them. Third, culture functions as a set of preconditions or outside parameters that shape and limit the range of human behavior and options at any given time or place. And fourth, persistent cultural patterns and behavior become imbedded in institutions that then often take on the character of independent variables in their own right. But culture is also a contested concept, it changes over time, and different groups in society may have opposing views as to what the dominant culture is or ought to be.

To me and to most readers, the continuing importance of cultural differences is so obvious as to be almost irrefutable. Culture is not just some residual category; it is crucial in understanding how societies and political systems function and how and why they differ from one another. But that is not to say that cultural factors alone explain national development. Economic, class, institutional, and dependency elements need to be factored into any explanatory paradigm. So do chance, accidents, geography, and, perhaps, sociobiology. Nevertheless culture, particularly in combination with these other factors, remains a vital explanation in understanding Latin America or any other area or country: it is a necessary but not a sufficient explanation, an important but not a monocausal explanation.

The United States and Latin America: Founding Principles

The North American colonies were largely settled by persons fleeing the feudal restraints, royal absolutism, and clerical oppression of the Old World. In Latin America, in contrast, the conquistadores sought to *re-create* in the New World the feudal society, political authoritarianism, and religious orthodoxy they had carried over from medieval Europe.[6]

The United States was, to use Louis Hartz's phrase, "born free."[7] Unlike Latin America, the North American colonies had no feudal past ("feudalism" here meaning the political, social, economic, and religious institutions of the medieval era). In contrast, Latin America, colonized and settled in the sixteenth century, a full hundred years or more before the North American colonies, was premodern and felt the full weight of medievalism in the form of an authoritarian political regime from top to bottom, a feudal landholding system and mercantilism in the economic sphere, a rigid two-class society without a large or solid middle class, an educational system based on rote memorization and deductive, unscientific reasoning, and a religious pattern of absolutism and orthodoxy that buttressed and reinforced the state concept.[8]

The United States, settled and colonized in the seventeenth and eighteenth centuries, belonged, right from the beginning, to the modern world. It was nascently capitalistic, middle class, nonconformist, supportive of representative government, religiously pluralistic, and 3 educationally and legally inductive and scientific. It had no feudal past, no feudal institutions to overcome on the path to modernity. Latin America, in contrast, was dominated from the beginning by feudal and medieval concepts and institutions. If one agrees, as the classic History of Western Civilization texts state, that the modern era begins roughly in 1500—with the Renaissance, the Protestant Reformation, the Enlightenment, the scientific and industrial revolutions, and the movement toward secular, limited, representative government—then the United States was founded on a set of principles and institutions that were basically modern (post-1500) in character, whereas Latin America was founded on principles and institutions that were still essentially feudal (pre-1500) and medieval.

The North American colonies were products of Britain and Holland, where the sway of feudalism and medieval institutions had already been broken, whereas Latin America came from the womb of Spain and Portugal, where the Counter-Reformation, the Inquisition, reaction, and the Middle Ages still held sway. Indeed, most of Latin America's five-hundred-year history since 1492 can be read as an effort to overcome or supersede its feudal past, whereas the United States, born free and equal (excepting, of course, the pre–Civil War South), had no need to overcome feudal constraints and could proceed on its course to modernity. Understanding these basic historical dissimilarities between the two Americas, their mother countries, and their respective founding institutions takes one a long way toward understanding Latin America and its differences with the United States.

The absence of feudalism in North American history means that, to become modern, the United States, unlike Latin America and other developing nations, never had to overcome the vast array of traditional institutions that the other areas did: a dominant feudal system of large, landed estates, a structure of corporate, protected, group privilege, an oligarchy or a rigid two-class social system (again, except for the South), an official state church or a theocracy, top-to-bottom authoritarianism. Of course there were elements of all these features in North American society, but they were not the dominant characteristics, as in Latin America, Hence when the thirteen colonies achieved their independence in 1776, they had few "feudal" legacies of the past to overcome and could proceed directly to modernity. In contrast, Latin America, even after achieving political independence from its mother countries, continued to be feudal and medieval in its underlying sociology, economy, and main political institutions. Its history of independence would thus always be fraught with far more violence, instability, and conflict between tradition and modernity.

Because the United States lacked a tradition of reaction and despotism on the Right, it never developed a powerful Left either. Socialism, communism, and guerrilla revolution have been remarkably absent or weak in North American history. Instead, with few exceptions, American politics have been consistently oriented toward the center, the middle of the road, the pragmatic rather than the ideological. In Latin America, because the weight of the Right and of traditional groups and institutions has long been so powerful, left-wing movements and guerrilla politics have often emerged as a challenge to them. Based on feudalism, Latin America has long lacked a middle class and the more stable, moderate, centrist politics that go with it; its politics have been much more ideological than in the United States. Lacking a truly reactionary oligarchy, the United States has never had a Robespierre or a Lenin; but in Latin America, where tradition and feudalism are so strong, it is no accident that Fidel Castro, Ché Guevara, and numerous other guerrilla movements have emerged.

In the absence of either a powerful right or a powerful left, Hartz argues, the dominant tradition of the United States is liberal. By that he means that virtually everybody in the United States—Dwight Eisenhower as well as Adlai Stevenson, Ronald Reagan as well as Bill Clinton, Trent Lott as well as Richard Gephardt—believes in representative, democratic government and the classic liberties of free speech, press, assembly, petition, and religion. There is practically no dissent from these basic liberal principles; they form part of Americans' consensus on a civic, democratic, pluralist political culture. But none of these comments apply historically in Latin America. Faced with semifeudal right-wing groups and powerful left-wing movements, liberalism there has seldom if ever been the dominant ideology. There is little consensus on either the ends or the means of political society. Instead, Latin America is what Kalman H. Silvert called a "conflict society,"[9] and what Charles W. Anderson described as a "living museum" of every political philosophy since the dawn of time, none of which is dominant and none of which is ever completely sloughed off or discarded, with the result that there is little agreement on the direction in which society should go.[10]

Hartz goes on to identify the seventeenth-century English writer John Locke as the main inspiration for the notions of liberalism, individualism, freedom, and limited, representative government at the heart of the North American tradition. Important influences also came from Montesquieu (separation of powers), Thomas Jefferson (the Bill of Rights), and James Madison (countervailing pluralism). American liberalism was then extended by Presidents Jackson, Lincoln, Roosevelt, Johnson, Clinton, and others. With Adam Smith and Ronald Reagan, greater economic freedom for both good and ill was joined with already existing political freedoms.

But if these are the fonts of North American democracy, who are the main figures in Latin America? The answer is not a simple one; as in North America there are several sources, several strains of thought. Moreover—and again like the United States—Latin America has borrowed selectively from these inspirations, and frequently these borrowings—as I shall point out in the book—have been contentious. Not everyone has agreed with them, neither at the time nor now. Nevertheless the dominant Latin American tradition—like the North American—goes back to Greece, Rome, and the Bible; but Latin America often emphasizes hierarchical, organicist, and corporatist (the organization of society by functions) concepts in these bodies of ideas that North America chose not to. Saint Augustine and Saint Thomas Aquinas are also powerful influences in providing a strong foundation of religious beliefs and institutions for Latin America, the particular form of pre-1500 Spanish and Portuguese feudalism, society, and the state carried over to Latin America. The sixteenth-century Spanish neoscholastics, the apostles of the Counter-Reformation, led by the Jesuit scholar Francisco Suárez, were immensely influential in designing the Hapsburgian model of authoritarian, corporatist, two-class society and polity that Spain and Portugal brought to Latin America. Indeed Suárez (whom we tend to ignore in our histories of political thought) should be seen as the counterpart in Latin America of Locke in the North American colonies.[11]

When Latin America (except for Cuba and Puerto Rico) became independent in the nineteenth century, it formally adopted liberalism and democracy; but its inspiration for doing so was not Jefferson or Madison but Rousseau, with his organic, centralized, corporatist, and (some would say) democratic-Caesarist or even totalitarian conceptions. It was not Adam Smith who provided the formula for Latin American economic development but Jean Baptiste Colbert, Auguste Comte, and Napoleon III, with their elitist, statist, and top-down views. Following that came the contending visions of corporatism, on the one hand, and

marxism, on the other, and, after that, of bureaucratic-authoritarianism versus democracy. Not only was there an absence of consensus and
a difference in political, social, and economic inspirations and influences from those of the United States (Suárez versus Locke, for example), but the very meaning of such key concepts as democracy deviated
as well (Jefferson and Madison versus Rousseau).

Given the historical background of the North American colonies
and the strength of the Lockean tradition, democracy, liberalism, and
pluralism may be viewed as almost natural in the United States, the
normal condition of political affairs. In Latin America, however, organicism, corporatism, and strong central authority may be viewed historically as the norm in political affairs—which may, incidentally, include democracy but commonly a top-down, organic, Rousseauian
form of democracy. Locke helps explain the North American common-
law legal tradition, the profound sense of U.S. individualism, the American sense of democracy, limited government, and checks and balances,
the emphasis on elections and the processes of democracy (as distinct
from lofty goals), indeed the whole American way of life. But in Latin
America none of these traits applied, and Locke had little influence;
Latin America had to look to other sources for its political inspiration.
And, reflecting the semifeudal nature of Latin American society itself,
many of these were not very democratic or progressive.

John Adams, the second U.S. president, frequently congratulated
his predecessors in the thirteen colonies as well as contemporaries who
wrote the Declaration of Independence and the Constitution for turning their backs on and rejecting Europe's class-ridden, corporate society, for repudiating both canon and feudal law. Americans were all of
the same estate; therefore there could be no hierarchical and class-
based system of estates as in Latin America. North America was free
and individualistic, not locked into a structure of class, place, guilds,
and corporatist, feudal, and religious rigidities and orthodoxies. Even
these introductory comments serve to indicate that it was precisely
what Adams was criticizing—a class-ridden corporate society dominated by canon and feudal law—that was in fact deeply ingrained in
Latin America. The question now is whether Latin America remains
locked into that older system or has finally made its breakthrough into
the modern, democratic world. It is not, despite the recent movement
in Latin America toward at least a formal structure of democracy, an
easy question to answer. 7

To this point I have portrayed the differences between the United States and Latin America purposely in rather stark, either-or terms—modern versus feudal, democratic versus authoritarian and corporatist, Locke versus Suárez—because such *ideal types* make the contrasts between the two parts of the Americas clear-cut and understandable; and in fact the disparities between them *are* wide. But ideal types tend to oversimplify and skate over the ambiguities and mixed patterns that exist. In North America, for example, the emphasis on Locke and the liberal tradition tends to ignore other, more reactionary influences, the conflict over liberalism as represented by the Civil War, the longtime exclusion of native Americans and African Americans from the political process, and the degree of conflict and contestation between groups that exists even within a dominant liberal tradition. After all, the South also had a feudal dream, a class- and caste-based society founded (like Latin America) on Aristotelian and reactionary principles. It is perhaps no coincidence that Comte's elitist and racist positivism made its strongest imprint there and that the South's John Calhoun, with his notion of "concurrent (geographical) majorities," was one of the few corporatist thinkers within the U.S. tradition. In Latin America, too, some qualifications of the overall thesis are required: a middle class, albeit small; some countries (Chile, Costa Rica, Uruguay) that are more democratic than others; some followers of Locke, albeit few; and a fledgling democratic tradition in all countries that was frequently snuffed out by reactionary forces or remained a minority current.

Let us acknowledge these ambiguities and mixed influences, but let us also keep in mind the main points, the admittedly oversimplified ideal types that nevertheless help us understand both areas better. The United States and Latin America were founded on very different principles. They had very different starting points, their sociologies and economics were very different, and their political systems would be fated to evolve in very different directions. The one was modern, the other feudal; the first was capitalistic, the other mercantilist and statist; the United States was more liberal and democratic even in its early stages while Latin America was top-down, corporatist, and organicist. These differences help explain the enormous gaps between the United States and Latin America even to this day. Because the founding sociologies of the two areas were so much at variance, their founding political principles—the main subject of this book—were unalike as well.

8 As the Mexican avant-garde poet, essayist, and Nobel laureate Octavio

Paz has written, "To cross the border between the [United States and
Mexico] is to change civilizations. Americans are the children of the Reformation and their origins are those of the modern world; we Mexicans
are the children of the Spanish empire, the champion of the Counter-
reformation, a movement that opposed the new modernity and failed."[12]

The question Hartz asked forty-five years ago is the same one I ask
in this book: Can a country and a people born free and equal as in the
United States ever understand peoples and countries not so blessed?
The issues raised here apply not just to Latin America, therefore, but
also to U.S. perceptions of Africa, Asia, the Middle East, and other cultures and societies not founded on U.S. principles. Can North Americans
put aside their blinders, preconceptions, sense of superiority, and rose-
colored lenses long enough to comprehend societies and whole civilizations founded on principles and sociological realities other than
their own? Can they grasp countries on their own terms, in their own
context, and nonethnocentrically—without imposing their own experiences and preferences, let alone U.S. institutions? Hartz was not optimistic, and my experience in Washington, D.C., over the past twenty
years in trying to help American policy makers see Latin America more
fully and formulate more enlightened policies for the area has often
led to similarly pessimistic conclusions.[13] Nevertheless this book is dedicated to the proposition that people can learn about, understand, and
come to appreciate cultures other than their own. And even if one
finds the task difficult, it is still well worth the effort to try.

The Approach of the Book

This book deals with the political theory and political tradition of
Latin America. It focuses on the religious tradition of Iberia and Latin
America, the political ideas generated in Spain and Portugal and trans-
ported to the New World and their evolution there, the legal and educational precepts that guided these endeavors, the political philosophies of these times, and the dominant values, beliefs, and behavioral
norms of Iberic–Latin American civilization. It is in this sense a study
of political culture, here defined as the values, beliefs, ideas, attitudes,
and behavioral patterns that shape a people's orientation to their political system. The book presents what the anthropologist Clifford
Geertz called "thick description," what Max Weber termed a *verstahen*
("understanding from within") approach.[14]

9

I choose this focus because (1) I'm interested in it; (2) it provides a convenient, useful, and manageable way to write and think about Latin America, and (3) I believe it to be important. I can't conceive that anyone would think they can understand Latin America without coming to grips fully with Catholicism and the Roman Catholic Church, the concepts of bureaucratic authoritarianism and absolutism of the Hapsburg monarchy, the legal and educational foundations (scholasticism) of medieval Spain carried over to the New World, the Iberian concepts of elites and social hierarchy, the peculiar form and institutions of Iberian and Latin American feudalism, the notions of mercantilism and statism, the social ideas of Hispanic elites about those whom they view as lower in the social (and racial) ranking than themselves, and the values and beliefs of historic Hispanic civilization as compared and contrasted with historic Anglo-Saxon civilization. All these aspects are fundamental to understanding Hispanic political culture.

By focusing on the cultural, social, and institutional components, however, I do not mean to diminish the importance of such factors as economic relations, class structure, and dependency relations.[15] In fact I see economic change (especially the transition from feudalism to capitalism—precisely the transition Latin America is presently going through) as one of, if not *the,* greatest driving forces in history; my analysis deals extensively with social structure and class relations; and I have long been persuaded of the importance of outside, or dependency, forces on internal Latin American society. What I try to do in this book, although focusing on the political culture and political tradition of Latin America, is to weave economic, cultural, class, institutional, and dependency relations into a more complex, multicausal explanation of why Latin America is the way it is. While I zero in on the political theory and tradition of Iberia–Latin America, I try to show how these ideas were shaped by the contexts of their times and how they evolved in response to real, material issues, social changes, and class configurations. I also believe the process can work the other way around, however, depending on times and circumstances. That is, the class structure, the nature of the economy, and political institutions were products of ideas and political culture just as the political culture and values are shaped by these other forces. I see ideas and political culture neither as the exact reflection of socioeconomic interests nor as autonomous from them but as interwoven in complex ways, with social, economic, political, and institutional forces shaped by these but also, in turn, influencing them.

In other words I see culture and history as important factors that must be taken into account in explaining Latin American development (or the lack thereof), but not all-important ones. Culture and history (including religion, law, philosophy, education, sociology) must be woven together with other explanations. I do not wish to give culture—broadly defined—an elevated explanatory significance it does not deserve or elevate it into the status of an all-encompassing explanation that ignores other powerful explanatory factors; on the other hand, I do not believe it can be ignored either. Hence this effort at relating ideas, values, and culture to the larger currents of economic, class, and institutional change.

Several caveats are in order. First, my approach is broad, conceptual, comparative, and interpretive. Although I fully recognize the wide (and widening) differences between the individual Latin American countries, above all as they leave behind their traditional institutions and embark on modernity, in this book the approach is to emphasize Latin America as a whole, as a civilization, as a culture area. Individual country differences are of course recognized and acknowledged, but my effort here is aimed at presenting the big picture, the sum of the parts rather than the individual pieces themselves. Both the large-canvas approach and the country-by-country approach are valid, as long as one recognizes what one is doing and duly admits the advantages and the limits of each.

Second, I need to return to the notion of ideal types. An ideal type is a model, a paradigm, an approximation of reality, not to be confused with reality itself. When I say that the formula for colonial Latin America was the Hapsburg model (explained in detail below), that is an ideal type; when I say that Latin America's understanding of democracy is Rousseauian rather than Lockean, that too is an ideal type. I do not mean either that colonial Latin America was always Hapsburgian in every way or that all Latin Americans were followers of Rousseau and not Locke. Rather, I mean these were the dominant or paradigmatic traditions. Ideal types, while extremely useful in helping one see reality more clearly, neatly, and unambiguously, are simplifications of reality. That is why they are called ideal types. They simplify reality and are useful as teaching and explanatory devices; but they are not mirrors of reality. Ideal types do not and need not apply precisely in all cases; one must always be prepared to modify them with qualifying phrases, tendency statements, or comments that they apply more or less in individual countries. Nevertheless such explanations are extremely useful in helping us understand Latin America.

The third caveat has to do with the political culture approach; it is really a series of small but essential caveats. First, in the use of political culture one needs to avoid unnecessary and misleading stereotypes (all Germans do this, all Latins are that); instead the approach must be careful, balanced, analytic and, to the extent possible, based on quantitative materials such as public opinion surveys. Second, while political culture approaches often stress continuity, one also needs to emphasize—the heart of this book—how the political culture changes over time. Third, the political culture that I emphasize here tends to be the official, dominant political culture of the elites—particularly historically, when theirs is the only recorded political culture; but one should recognize that there are folk, popular, and indigenous political cultures—often minority or submerged—as well. Fourth and related, political culture is never unanimous or universal in a society; one must recognize not only the differences but also the *conflictual* nature of political culture and realize that what emerges as the dominant political culture is often the result not just of consensus but also of power struggles, war, class conflict, and foreign intervention. Finally, that means that political culture is more fluid and ever changing—and itself a highly political concept. These complexities in the political culture approach need to be reflected in the analysis that follows.

The Plan of the Book

Chapter 2 goes way back, to the very origins of Iberic–Latin American civilization in ancient Greece, Rome, the Bible, and medieval Christianity. Spain and Portugal were profoundly influenced by Greek political philosophy, both its deductive method of reasoning and its theoretical conception of society and polity organized on corporatist and hierarchical principles. When the Iberian peninsula became part of the Roman Empire, it became more Roman than Rome itself; it also used the Roman conception of empire to govern its own empire in the Americas. When it adopted Christianity it became, as is often remarked, more Catholic than the pope: Spain itself as well as Latin America adopted a

scholastic theocratic model that intimately joined church and state.
Hence one needs to analyze the impact of these early Greek, Roman,
and Christian influences on Spain and Portugal, while also recognizing that Iberia selectively borrowed from these traditions in a form
that was quite different, eventually, from that of the north of Europe.[16]

Along with Greece, Rome, Christianity, and the Thomistic tradition, the other great formative influence on Iberia, and eventually on
Latin America, was the unique experience and institutions of Spain
and Portugal during the Middle Ages. These include both the long Moorish occupation of the peninsula and the reconquest of Iberia by Christian forces. The subject—surveyed in chapter 3—is so important that it
merits detailed treatment, yet it is almost unknown even among students of Latin America. For it was during this period, from the eleventh
through the fifteenth centuries, that the main institutions and dynamics of Iberian social and political life came together and were put
in place. And it is of course these institutions that were then conveyed
to Latin America, where they had such a profound impact: the rigidly
two-class and hierarchical nature of Spanish society, the pattern of
large, often unproductive estates, a particular kind of militaristic feudalism, the system of patrimonialism and of societywide patron-client
relations, the structure of top-down and absolutist authority reaching
from king to local landowner, and the uniquely Iberian–Latin American system of state-society relations that also formed the distinctively
Hispanic definitions of "democracy" and "constitutionalism." This
formative period was important in shaping not only Iberian society but
also, by extension, that of Latin America.[17]

That is the subject of chapter 4: the conquest of Latin America and
the practices and institutions that the mother countries Spain and Portugal carried over to the New World. Colonial rule in Latin America
lasted for more than three centuries; it indelibly stamped Latin America with the mark of Iberian civilization. In many respects Latin America is still wrestling with its Iberian heritage: some groups applaud the
Spanish-Portuguese influence, others try to discard or overcome it—
but not one is able to ignore it. In this chapter I also deal with the indigenous civilizations that the colonizers encountered in Latin America and how they were dealt with and incorporated into the Spanish
system, as well as with the importation and treatment of African
blacks into some areas. Although the Spanish colonial system was rigid
and absolutist, it began to change in the eighteenth century, opening

a schism in the Spanish and Latin American soul that persists to this day.[18]

Toward the end of the eighteenth century, as a result of the Enlightenment as well as the [North] American and French revolutions, liberal and republican ideas began to appear in Latin America for the first time. Latin American ideas of republicanism and democracy derived mainly from the romantic, idealistic Rousseau, however, not from the more prosaic Locke. These ideas resulted in independence for most of Latin America in the second and third decades of the nineteenth century and were incorporated in the laws and constitutions of the newly independent states. There they ran into the realities that Latin America's underlying institutions were mainly authoritarian and nondemocratic and that the area had no experience whatsoever in democratic self-government. The result, as described in chapter 5, was almost constant conflict, instability, and lack of progress during Latin America's first thirty years of independence.[19]

By the 1850s some of the early conflicts began to be resolved, the first generation of postindependence, authoritarian men-on-horseback had passed from the scene, a degree of stability was achieved, and Latin America began its first phase of economic development. Hence Latin American elites began to search for a political formula by which they could achieve progress while at the same time keeping aristocratic rule intact. Some continued to adhere to the older liberal or conservative philosophies, but during the last decades of the nineteenth century and up through World War I the dominant philosophy was *positivism*.[20] Under the slogan Order and Progress (still emblazoned on the Brazilian flag), Latin American elites applied positivist principles to rationalize and bureaucratize their governments and achieve considerable economic development, but without undermining elitist rule. This combination of advantages helps explain why positivism was far more popular in Latin America than it was in the United States. This is the subject of chapter 6.

Ultimately positivism produced its counterreaction in the first two decades of the twentieth century, mainly in the form of rising Latin American nationalism, although the precise forms varied considerably. In Mexico it took the form of a violent, nationalistic revolution from 1910 to 1920 that swept away an older authoritarian but developmentalist regime and its positivist advisers. In Cuba, in the writings of the great independence hero José Martí, it took the form of intense na-

14

tionalism, often directed against American imperialism, which had recently begun to flex its expansionist and interventionist muscles. In Uruguay, too, the writings of José Rodó, which became instant best-sellers throughout Latin America, emphasized the supposed culture, sophistication, idealism, and patriotism of Latin America, as contrasted with the greedy, uncultured, materialistic North Americans. The philosophy of *Hispanismo* (admiration for things Spanish—language, literature, religion, culture, roots) was another expression of rising Latin American nationalism, particularly as Hispanic culture contrasted with U.S. influence. Finally, the rise during this period of pan-Americanism and of the early mechanisms of an inter-American regional security system similarly represented Latin American efforts to achieve hemispheric solidarity especially vis-à-vis their large neighbor to the north. These themes form the subject matter of chapter 7.[21]

During these same early decades of the twentieth century, marxism made its first serious appearance in Latin America.[22] Beginning slowly among a handful of intellectuals and study groups, marxism by the 1920s and 1930s had organized a number of political parties, trade unions, and peasant associations. During the 1940s and 1950s a variety of socialist and social-democratic movements and parties were formed. The revolution of Fidel Castro in 1959 as well as a number of guerrilla groups during the Cold War era took their inspiration from marxist principles. As analyzed in chapter 8, marxism took a variety of forms and directions in Latin America; its many movements and divisions in turn served to dilute its political power, and it faced the concerted hostility of the traditional Catholic Church, the military, the oligarchy, and the United States. To offset the opposition, marxism sought to merge with nationalistic and indigenous movements. During the period after World War II marxism became one of the major alternative paradigms in the Latin American context.

The other great alternative paradigm during this period, analyzed in chapter 9, was corporatism.[23] Corporatism's rise was related on the one hand to nationalism, *Hispanismo,* and pride in things Catholic and Hispanic, and on the other to the perceived threat of marxism. It represented an effort in Latin America (as well as in Europe during the interwar period) to respond to the social question (the rise of organized labor) through Christian principles of solidarity and class harmony, in contrast to the marxian principles of class conflict. Like positivism before it, corporatism was far more popular in Latin America than it was in the United States. And whereas positivism had as its goal in the late nineteenth century the cooptation of rising business and middle-class groups into the dominant elitist structure, corporatism had as one of its goals in the 1930s and later the cooptation of growing trade union movements into the prevailing system. Corporatism presented itself as the third way, between a liberalism that did not seem to work very well in Latin America and a bolshevism as represented by the Russian Revolution that was unacceptable. Corporatism became another of the great alternative paradigms for Latin America whose presence, now in revised form (neocorporatism), is felt today.

The result of adding on all these nineteenth- and twentieth-century political philosophies, without discarding any of the older ones, is that by the 1930s Latin America had become a "conflict society," a "living museum."[24] Its history had been dominated by efforts at quick fixes, magic formulas, and easy answers that have little relation to the region's realities. Authoritarianism, liberalism, positivism, nationalism, marxism, corporatism, and indigenism, as well as Perónism, Castroism, and liberation theology have all been tried and found wanting. No one of these conceptions enjoyed majority support; not one of them ever achieved unquestioned legitimacy. Indeed in several elections of the 1960s, each major conception was able to garner 10, 15, maybe 30 percent of the vote, but almost never enough to command a majority. Moreover, because the conceptions were so far apart and literally spoke for entirely different stages of societal development—feudalism, liberalism, socialism—it proved virtually impossible to forge compromises or even working agreements between them. The result—the subject of chapter 10—was a period from the 1930s to the 1950s and beyond of intense conflict, contestation, and, in some countries, civil war between the contending ideologies that were so far apart as to be unbridgeable and that had their respective social bases in quite distinct sectors of society. The result was a virtual war of all against all, of sharply contending power contenders, of widespread violence that, except in Cuba, fell short of full-scale revolution but that seemed to be leading to societal fragmentation and collapse.[25]

In the face of the growing morbific politics and social breakdown (which began to resemble Spain in the 1930s, just before the brutal civil war that brought Generalissimo Franco to power), and particularly with the rise and challenging mobilization of lower-class elements, the Latin

16 American elites—Church, army, oligarchy—revolted, staged a counter-revolution, and sought to restore the order, discipline, and stability of the past. Not only were there new justifications for authoritarianism, but corporatism, which seemed dead and discredited after its association with defeated fascism in the 1930s and World War II, was brought back as a way of structuring and thus controlling lower-class mass movements. Where these cooptive techniques did not work, the military authoritarians in power at the time resorted to repression, torture, and widespread violations of basic human rights—or used cooptation and coercion at the same time. This system of authoritarian rule, roughly (depending on the country) from the 1960s to the 1980s, was called bureaucratic or institutionalized authoritarianism, to distinguish it from the simpler *caudillo*, or man-on-horseback, rule of the past.[26]

But turning back the clock and using increasingly totalitarian methods to do so proved no more effective in solving Latin America's long-term, deep-seated problems than had earlier simplistic, short-term formulas. Faced with widespread opposition, the military authoritarians occupying power eventually, in country after country, went back to the barracks; the great wave of "transitions to democracy" had begun. By the mid-1990s nineteen of the twenty Latin American countries (all except Cuba) were under democratic rule, at least formally. Moreover, with the disintegration of the Soviet Union and other Marxist-Leninist systems in Eastern Europe, as well as the undoubted success of the East Asian economies, democracy in the political realm was this time accompanied by liberalism (or neoliberalism)—privatization, state downsizing, lower tariffs, austerity, freer markets, export-oriented growth—in the economic sphere. Both politically and economically, Latin America seemed poised finally to shake off its past, the heavy weight of feudalism, and join the modern world.[27]

But is it? That is the question discussed in chapter 11, which surveys both the bureaucratic authoritarianism of the 1960s and 1970s and the transitions to democracy of the 1980s and 1990s. Is Latin America now solidly democratic, or is the present period just another in the long cycle of alternations between democracy and authoritarianism? Have democracy and economic liberalism really sunk in, or are these features just facades for the Americans and the international lending agencies to admire? Clearly Latin America has changed its political institutions and incorporated the formal mechanisms of democracy, but has the underlying political culture—how people treat one another, on an egalitarian rather than hierarchical basis—also become more demo-

17

cratic? And even if it is democracy that one is seeing, is it Lockean, individualistic (one person, one vote) democracy with real pluralism and genuine checks and balances, or is it still organic, corporatist, Rousseauian democracy, limited, partial, or tutelary democracy—democracy with adjectives, as it is often called?[28]

In the last chapter I assess these trends, the often mixed bags, halfway houses, and crazy-quilt patterns that emerge, to see if Latin America has overcome the powerful legacy of its past or if the heavy hand of feudalism and history still weighs powerfully on the area. On the answers to these questions hangs not only the future of Latin America but also the success of U.S. policy toward the area.

Chapter 2

Origins: Greece, Rome, the Bible, and Medieval Christianity

Iberian and Latin American culture and civilization go back a long way. The weight of a long and often oppressive history hangs heavily over the area. Hispania is, like India, China, Egypt, Persia, and others, an old civilization and culture whose origins are often shrouded in the mists of early time.[1] One does not easily or quickly overcome or supersede a long history and culture and replace it with "modernization"; neither do those who live in Iberia and Latin America always or necessarily think that is inevitable or desirable. Indeed the question of whether to try to overcome the past, glory in it, or simply adapt to it (the route of most developing nations) has long been at the heart of the debate over the future of Hispania.

Although the prerecorded history of Iberia is misty—despite the strenuous work of Spanish archaeologists and the spectacular cave paintings at Altamira—the recorded history of the peninsula is lengthy and detailed. The intellectual history—precisely my interest here—is particularly clear. Although the focus here is on the long sweep of Hispanic history, which therefore prevents our tracing every nuance and historical event, I concentrate on the main and abiding influences on Iberia: ancient Greece, ancient Rome, the Bible, and medieval Christianity. In the following chapter we look at the historical growth and development of the formative medieval institutions and political practices in Iberia itself, particularly in the time period just before the conquest of the Americas; here we look at the intellectual origins, the ideas and philosophies undergirding what came to be called Spain and Portugal and, by extension, their colonies in the New World.

Greece, Rome, and the Bible form the basis not just of Iberia but also of what we came to call Western civilization. Yet in reviewing the early texts and the influence of such founding writers and thinkers as Aristotle, Plato, Seneca, Cicero, Augustine, and Aquinas, one is struck by how the Hispanic nations borrowed or emphasized concepts different from those adopted elsewhere in the West. Aristotle, Plato, et al. are also part of the heritage of England, Holland, and North America, yet it is revealing how the north of Europe and America draws out of these classic writings concepts and ideas very different from those emphasized by the Iberian and Latin American nations. All peoples tend to be selective in their choice of ideas from history and in looking for arguments and rationalizations that reinforce conclusions, practices, culture, and institutions already arrived at. Nevertheless, the conclusion one reaches tends to support the one that scholars like Hartz, Richard Morse, and others suggested some years ago: although Iberia and Latin America are primarily Western in their ideas and orientation, they represent a fragment or branch of the Western tradition quite unlike the mainstream elsewhere in Europe.[2]

Ancient Greece

The ancient Greeks formulated the theory and practice of democracy. That discovery and North American pride and glory in democracy are part of the United States' heritage, deeply in our blood. Just recently the author of this book was at a meeting chaired by former congressman and now chairman of the board of the National Endowment for Democracy John Brademas—himself a Greek American—in which Brademas argued that twenty-five hundred years ago democracy was "invented" by the Greeks. It is clear that not only are most North Americans proud of this democratic heritage which we associate with ancient Greece but when and if we go back and read Greek or Roman political philosophy, we do so to find in it explanations and justifications for those aspects of our own political system that we deeply believe in: democracy, republicanism, and pluralism.

But many other, equally important features of Greek political thought are not particularly democratic. Westerners choose to emphasize the democratic heritage of ancient Greece because that is what suits them, but there are numerous aspects of Greek political theory worthy of attention that lead in directions other than democracy. Whereas North American political culture tends to emphasize the democratizing accomplishments of ancient Greece, Latin American political culture has tended historically to emphasize the more conservative and nondemocratic features of Greek thought.

Greek political thought did not start with a belief in equality among individuals or between men and women. Rather, the Greeks believed in hierarchy, of natural disparities between classes of persons. Aristotle accepted and championed the belief of natural inequalities among men, of slavery; there is "equality for those who are equal," he said, "and not for all." Liberalism, in contrast, begins with the idea of a classless natural equality in which, as Jefferson put it, "all men are born and created equal." But in the Iberian and Latin American worlds, acceptance of place and position still resembles the "proud tower" of medieval feudalism.[3] People are assumed to have been born unequal; equality is often proclaimed, but the practice is of hierarchy, rank, class, position. From ancient times to today, natural inequality has been widely accepted in Iberia and Latin America as a fact of life too obvious for argumentation.

Moreover, the hierarchical order is assumed to be immutable. Only rarely does Greek political thought recognize concepts of social change, dynamic modernization, or the possibilities of raising oneself in the social hierarchy. One is born into a certain station in life and one remains in that station throughout the generations. One's children and grandchildren are fated to occupy the same fixed place in the social order. Hence, seldom in Latin American folklore does one find the Ben Franklin–Horatio Alger myths of working hard, shining lots of shoes or delivering lots of newspapers, saving your pennies, and improving one's lot through initiative and diligence. "If God wishes" (Si dios quiere), fortune will shine on you, but not by dint of your own efforts. For if the social order is deemed to be unchanging, then no amount of effort on an individual's part will make more than a modicum of difference.

Acceptance of inequality among men also meant acceptance by the ancient Greeks of slavery. Slaves occupy the lowest rungs in the social hierarchy. Aristotle accepted and propagated the proposition that while some individuals are born free and privileged, others are naturally born to be slaves. That too was immutable. One part of mankind, argued Aristotle, with obvious relevance later for the native peoples of the Americas as well as the African slaves brought in by Spain and Portugal, is by nature set aside to be "slaves of masters born for a life of virtue free of manual labor." This "aristocratic ethos" would be carried over to the New World, where all Spaniards could become *caballeros,* or gentlemen. "Inferior peoples," said Aristotle, "need to be placed *for their own good* under the care of civilized and virtuous rulers, so that they too can lead a productive life and be trained in virtuous behavior."[4]

Slavery could be based on military conquest, which presumably showed the conquered peoples to be inferior, or on skin color, the darker castes occupying progressively lower rungs in the hierarchy. The Aristotelian notion of a natural slave or peasant class has transcended time and place and still exists in the minds of many persons today. Deep down, the oligarchies of Latin America do not believe that Indians and peoples of African descent are fully equal. Aristotle was cited by Spain and Portugal to justify, first, the conquest and enslavement of the native peoples of the Americas and later the importation of African slaves. Even today, although the many constitutions of the region and laws may proclaim equality, my experience in Iberia and Latin America is that middle- and upper-class persons have little conception that peasants, Indians, blacks, and mixed blends ("the other") could possibly be on the same plain as they.[5]

The acceptance of hierarchy and of natural or God-given inequalities among humans obviously makes it difficult to have democracy based on equality. In addition, it provides logical justification for top-down rule and authoritarianism. If people are by nature unequal, it makes no sense to consider each voice in society, or each vote, equally. If some are born with superior skills, talents, or intelligence, then it is only natural that they, not the masses, should rule. In Greek thought—and that is what democrats have emphasized—democracy was just one of the acceptable forms of government, so long as it did not degenerate into mob rule. Rule by an enlightened oligarchy or monarch was also acceptable, even preferable in most circumstances—and this is what Iberia and Latin America tended to emphasize. Recall in Plato that it was enlightened philosopher-kings governing presumably in the name of the public and for the public good (but not of, by, and for the people) that constituted the most desirable type of government.[6] Such concepts can readily be used to justify a top-down, oligarchic, or authoritarian regime in Iberia or Latin America, where education, land, privileges, and political power are limited to a small elite.

The Greeks believed, a legacy of the Homeric age, that people are often governed by capricious gods. To improve one's fortune, one has to gain the patronage of a deity. So not only does one's fate depend on god-given favors, as distinct from merit or achievement, but the idea of moving ahead through patronage is also introduced. This idea is not fully developed in Greek political thought, but in Roman as well as Christian medieval philosophy the concept of "the gift" and of mutual favors (patronage) will be elevated into a full-scale system of social relations.[7]

The acceptance of hierarchy and a god-given station in life is restrictive at many levels, but it implies security and certainty. Each person has a station in life and is secure and protected in that station. Such certainty applied to various classes, corporations, and functional and ethnic groups as well as to individuals: each had a secure station in life that implied both obligations and protection. The Greek polis was divided in *demes*, each of which comprised clans from distinct economic and geographic regions in Attica.[8] In the Greek political structure, individuals derived their identities as citizens from membership in a deme. One entered politics through one's membership in a group or deme. The primary political problem was not the modern one of securing individual freedom but that of ensuring each person his or her entitled place in society. The community took precedence over the individual; the good of all (later rendered by Aquinas as the common good and by Rousseau as the general will) was valued over individual well-being. Harmony became the Greek ideal and the mark of civilization, as distinct from pluralism and interest conflict. The Greek conception is, therefore, inherently corporatist or group-centered and communitarian, although it would take the Romans to fashion a fully developed system of group or functional representation. All these traits would be further elaborated in Spain and, eventually, in Latin America.[9]

If Greek society was inherently corporatist, it was also organicist. That is, political society was unified and one; all its parts had to be organically bound together. Moreover, in Aristotle and his successors, society, including political society, was viewed as both natural and good. If society is natural and good, there is no reason to have checks and balances or, in modern terms, separation of powers. Instead, under the organic conception, all parts had to be tied together into an integral, harmonious whole—another concept amenable to dictatorship. For just as in the human body all the parts must fit and function together, so in political society all the components needed to be joined harmoniously. Justice, according to the Greeks, consisted of a bond that held society together in a harmonious union and in which each person's place was determined by his or her fitness and training. The organic conception of society and politics was destined to have a long history in political theory. Organicism and corporatism (functional groups joined together harmoniously, usually under state control) were closely linked concepts, and both of them should be set against the individualism, checks and balances, and separation of powers later forged in the Anglo-American democracies. Already one can see how the organicism, corporatism, and monism of Hispanic society would stand in contrast to the pluralism of North American society.[10]

Harmony and organicism not only characterized clan relations and political society, but also constituted the ideal among the several facets of society. Once again there was no separation, no pluralism, no checks and balances. Instead, ethics, art, religion, and politics all had to be joined, to demonstrate the credentials of right reason. To the Greeks, as to the later Hispanic diaspora, it was inconceivable that morality and politics, or church and state, could be separated. The state had to have an ethical purpose and to be undergirded by moral, god-given principles. Moderns have in considerable measure separated politics and morality, but to the Greeks as well as to later, Christian Spain, Portugal, and Latin America these foundations of society had to be joined in a common purpose. Lacking a common morality, they believed, society would surely fall apart and disintegrate; for what would hold it together and preserve its unity and sense of community? In Iberia and Latin American, such unity would be achieved and preserved mainly through Roman Catholic orthodoxy and a top-down, centralized state; pure pragmatism, situational ethics, or even the separation of church and state would inevitably, they believed, lead to conflict and societal unraveling.

Although Aristotle was an empiricist, a collector of constitutions, and the first systematic student of comparative politics, and though both his logical methodology and his ideal types were often used in Thomistic-Iberic-Latin argumentation and discourse, it was Plato to whom Hispanic society was, ultimately, more indebted for its political ideals. Like Aristotle, Plato saw humans as an integral part of nature, subject to the same natural and supernatural forces. Nature, humankind, society, and polity all formed part of a continuum.[11] But more than Aristotle, Plato saw political society as part of a system, its distinct groups—military, priests, craftspeople, servants—having differential roles. The ideal state was one in which there was a division of labor and a specialization of functions, with each person in his or her place and each receiving proper due. Each functional group in turn would have its own expectations, rights, and obligations. These were to be harmonized and integrated into an organic whole; there were to be no blurred identities, no overlapping roles. Society was to be organized functionally, corporately.

Hence, even today in Latin America, society seems to be made up of almost stock types: the oligarch, the priest, the military officer, the bureaucrat, the labor leader, the student, the peasant, and so on.[12] Moreover, the pluralism that exists is limited and usually regulated, not the unfettered near-anarchy of the American interest-group conflict. Even the limited group struggle that is permitted must, by the Platonic system, take place within a moral universe (Roman Catholic in Iberia and Latin America) that shares a common idea of the common good. And the "good" is defined by a moral and ethical leadership, an oligarchy, Plato's philosopher-kings. Public opinion should not count for much in Plato's view; rather it is leadership by the philosopher-kings, who know best for their people. It is probably no accident, therefore, that whereas the United States values pragmatists in political office, Iberia and Latin America often prefer novelists, writers, and intellectuals. Only such philosopher-kings have "true knowledge," in Plato's terms, and can provide the leadership and direction for the rest of society, the uneducated masses.

The implications of all these concepts—order, authority, hierarchy, organicism, corporatism, the unity of morality and politics—imply necessarily a conservative, top-down polity run by elites. Change could take place, but only slow and controlled change. The Greeks were suspicious of democracy; Plato preferred a presumably selfless political elite to govern without popular or mass participation. But we now know such selfless politics is impossible without the kind of institutional checks and balances favored by later political philosophers like Locke and Madison. The unity and harmony that the Greeks idealized was the product of a vision imposed by the philosopher-kings, but it had its limits. It was class-biased and not so selfless as Plato supposed.[13] One can see, therefore, why Saint Thomas, the founding father of Iberic–Latin American civilization, would use Aristotle's logic and deductive reasoning but Plato's system of authoritative if not authoritarian politics. Except for Aristotle's assumption of natural inequalities among men, his politics were too empirical and malleable to suit the scholastic philosophers; they much preferred Plato and his authoritative, elitist, theocratic conception.

Two other aspects of Greek political thought and practice as they affected Iberia and Latin America are relevant. The first is the question of which Greek model had the greatest influence on Spain and Latin America: that of Athens or that of Sparta? Although Athens is for westerners the font of democracy, Sparta has as often been cherished for its attributes. The Athenian tradition, Donald C. Worcester writes in his historical studies of Latin America, implied intellectual creativity and change;[14] it stressed freedom of thought and speech and a dislike of usurping tyrants. In contrast, the more militaristic Spartan code stressed duty, responsibility, discipline, and authority. Discipline and authority were especially needed in those societies—like Latin America—that lacked infrastructure, civil society, and strong institutions. Whereas Athens stood for change and progress, Sparta represented a more stable, uncreative politics and an aristocratic government. Both of these conceptions have had their adherents throughout history; and while the Athenian tradition and model fits most closely the North American polity, it is the Spartan that took strong root in Iberia and Latin America—even though Athens remained the ideal. As we shall see, Romans like Cato and Cicero openly feared the disorderly ways and lack of discipline and authority engendered by the Athenian tradition and generally favored the orderly, static, Spartan mode. And Hispania would become, recall, the most Romanized of the Roman provinces.

The second aspect carried over to Iberia and Latin America is the Greek system of small, interpersonal city-states where everyone knows everyone else (who counts) or is interrelated. Ancient Greece was not an extended nation-state but a collection of city-states, with a primate city and a surrounding countryside. The Spanish system of regions, of giving primary loyalty to the region of one's origins rather than to the large, impersonal nation-state stems in part from this Greek model. It is friends, neighbors, and the *patria chica* (literally, "little country") that count, not the faraway, bureaucratic nation-state or its quasi-foreign central government. Those who doubt the continuing influence of this concept in Latin America should consider the fate after independence of Simón Bolívar's dream of a single pan-American political entity, the fate of Gran Colombia, which broke up into the separate nations of Ecuador, Venezuela, and Colombia, or the Central American Confederation (1821–39), which disintegrated into the small city-states that exist today, or the continuing loyalty to the patria chica even in modern times.[15]

Thus, a number of the ingredients making up present-day Iberia and Latin America are rooted in ancient Greece, including the concepts of natural inequalities among men; of hierarchy and social place; of top-down authority and even absolutism, or at least a wise and strong government; of a patrimonial society based on mutual obligation; of organicism, integralism, and corporatism; of elitism and rule by God-given authority; of militarism and discipline employed especially on the frontier and in chaotic, strife-torn societies; and of the personalistic small country as distinct from the faraway and abstract larger one. Many of these concepts and the institutions that embodied them would be taken over directly in Iberian and Latin American society and applied with only minor modifications; others would be adapted to the new and various circumstances of Hispanic society and culture. As noted, Iberia and Latin America borrowed these concepts selectively from the Greeks, often focusing on the organic and authoritarian aspects that would buttress their own system of rule while ignoring the democratic qualities. Of course, these ideas were frequently contested, and the more democratic Athenian model also had its adherents, who saw it as a goal to strive for, though usually in some far-distant future. But in the vast, empty, chaotic, war-torn, often disorganized and "uncivilized" spaces of medieval Iberia, as well as in colonial and even independent Latin America, the liberal, democratic model remained a minority strain while the bureaucratic-authoritarian, Spartan, Hapsburgian one was usually dominant.

Rome

Greek political philosophy found its way into Iberia via early Mediterranean trade patterns, through its influence on Roman political thought, which was then carried to Iberia by means of conquest, in the twelfth-century revival of Greek and Roman logic and legal concepts in the Christian scholasticism of Saint Thomas Aquinas, and in the continuing use of Greek deductive logical methods and ideals in the educational institutions of Iberia and Latin America. But whereas Northern Europe and North America tended to emphasize the democratizing precepts and arguments in Greek thought, Iberia and Latin America tended to emphasize its conservative, top-down, and Platonic-mixed-with-Spartan features.

Rome incorporated many features of Greek political philosophy but then modified and adapted them to fit new and changed conditions. Perhaps the most important change politically was the emergence of the immense Roman Empire, as distinct from the small city-states of Greece. The Roman Empire called forth ideas of governance on a scale larger than had ever been contemplated before.[16]

Most of present-day Iberia was conquered by Rome in the second century B.C. Only some small settlements in the northern provinces of Spain were able to hold out against the Roman conquest. Rome brought a unity (and a name—Hispania) to the peninsula that it had previously lacked. To this point, what we now know as Spain and Portugal had been unorganized and uncivilized and had consisted of small-scale tribal or clan units that controlled limited territory. Rome gave to Iberia a peninsula-wide system of political administration (centralized, authoritarian, imperial), a common language (Latin), a common law (the Roman codes), a uniform political culture (inherited from Greece as well as Rome), a system of society (hierarchical and class based), widespread urbanization, and eventually, a common religion (Catholicism). To help tie the peninsula together, Rome built roads, bridges, aqueducts, and public buildings—many of which are still visible in Iberia today. In all these ways Rome provided a unity and a set of institutions to Iberia heretofore nonexistent. Roman ideas and institutions gained a permanent and expanding grip over the people of the Iberian peninsula. The Roman dominion was profound, one of the two or three main historic influences on the development of Spain and Portugal.[17]

Many of the precepts brought by Rome to Iberia had their roots in the selfsame beliefs and concepts previously analyzed with regard to ancient Greece. For example, the Roman Stoics believed the world was ruled by a reasonable and just God. The state should be seen organically, as a human family, with God as the authoritarian father figure and men living as brothers. Laws should not be imposed, however, in the stoic view, but should emerge naturally, organically, from lawgivers following rules because that is the morally right thing to do. Happiness, therefore, comes not from showing initiative or from base emotions but from accepting God's will and adjusting to it—hence, the

philosophy and behavior called stoicism.[18]

Among the most important influences brought by Rome to Hispania was its concept of law. In the Roman conception, law derived deductively from divine precepts, nature, and right reason—not from everyday experience as in the more practical Anglo-American common-law tradition. Law was for the Romans above everything else a moral interpretation of life, an effort to define ethical goals for the society to strive for. Legal precepts were an expression of idealistic thinking and often divorced from the realities of life. The law represented goals for the society to strive for rather than actual operating realities. Unlike the German or Anglo-Saxon traditions, in which the law was above all practical and down to earth, an expression of folk or common traditions, and grounded in everyday realities, the Roman or code law tradition of which Iberia and Latin America were a part had little basis in reality. Law and everyday practice were separated, divorced—a situation that leads to widespread violations of the law.[19]

The emperor or king (and his representatives at regional, local, and large-estate levels) was assumed to be above the law. Because the goal of the community was to fulfill an ethical mission, the necessity arose for someone to interpret that mission and lead it: an enlightened monarch, emperor, or Plato's philosopher-kings. The ruler's powers were absolute. It was the ruler's role to be beyond the everyday struggle and serve as a symbol of unity, an interpreter of the law. At the same time the ruler had virtually unlimited authority and could mediate between contending factions. He might be an absolute monarch, but, because his duty was to fulfill the community's ethical principles, he had to rule for the common good. Hence, the ideal form of government in Spain, Portugal, and Latin America—and here the definition of "democracy" that would emerge becomes visible—would be neither a totalitarian tyrant, on the one hand, nor an inorganic democrat, on the other, but a kind of paternalistic father figure, a godfather, a democratic Caesar. It is no accident (and not just for lack of technology or developed institutions) that Iberia and Latin America never produced a full-fledged Nazi or fascist regime (some approached that level) or that inorganic democracy seldom functioned successfully there. Rather, the main tradition has been one of halfway houses: monarchy or authority that presumably governs for the common good (e.g., Franco in Spain, Antonio Salazar in Portugal, Porfirio Díaz in Mexico, Juan Perón in Argentina) or democracy that implies especially strong leadership (Alberto Fujimori in Peru, Carlos Menem in Argentina, and Hugo Chávez in Venezuela).

Cicero is well known for his contributions to the development of laws and legalism, which now took their place alongside divine providence. Cicero argued that all people are subject to the law and, therefore, are fellow citizens. Hence, all individuals deserve some measure of human dignity and respect—even a slave, who was considered a wage earner hired for life. In Cicero's conception, the state is a *res populi* (based on popular will), a commonwealth; furthermore, a good state is one in which "a number of men come together united by a common agreement (contract theory) about law and rights and by the desire to participate in mutual advantages." All these concepts—government by law, mutual respect, popular will, contract theory—are often cited as supplying the basis for equality, democracy, and representative government.

But that is not quite what Cicero meant; neither is it the complete picture. It is comparable to saying that the ancient Greeks invented democracy while ignoring the other, less attractive ideas—despotism, oligarchy, slavery, militarism, authoritarianism—that they also invented or rationalized. For when Cicero said everyone is subject to the law, he did not mean they were subject to it equally or even subject to the same law; in fact, he formulated different categories of law that applied to persons differentially—hardly an egalitarian precept. Second, when Cicero said that even slaves had rights, he did not believe they had the same level of rights as other persons in society; in fact, he accepted the Greek notion of natural inequalities among men and that some had more rights than others. Third, although Cicero indicated that authority comes from the people, he did not advocate popular participation in the modern democratic sense or the one-person-one-vote philosophy. Saying that political authority came from the people carried no democratic implications. Instead, in keeping with his hierarchy of laws and of social categories, he shared the Greek belief that government should be managed by a small nobility and that representation should be consultative and organized on the basis of corporate or group rights, not individualism. Finally, although Cicero's formulations seemed to favor popular government, what he meant by that was a type of enlightened despotism informed by the will of Roman citizens—not much different from Plato's philosopher-kings. Hence, while Anglo-American democrats have tended to emphasize the egalitarian and republican features in Cicero, it is also possible to find in his writings concepts of inegalitarianism and corporatism that are not essentially democratic.[20]

Another important ingredient in the Roman conception came from Seneca, who was Spanish (from Córdoba) by birth. Seneca was, among other things, the teacher of the notorious Roman emperor Nero. He was also a political philosopher whose notion of the gift became the philosophical basis for the Iberian and Latin American systems of clientelism and patronage. "What counts is one's attitude to wealth," he wrote in *On the Happy Life,* "which is the rich man's servant and the fool's master." It is the duty of those who have wealth, he argued, to give to those who don't. For Seneca this was a principle of practicality (one gave but also received gifts in return) as well as goodness; in the later, Christian conception, God's gift of his Son to die on the cross was often cited as the beginning of this societywide system of mutual gift giving.

Seneca, in keeping with the Greco-Roman conception of natural inequalities among men, posited three types of gifts depending on one's level in the social hierarchy: necessary gifts given to the lowest strata to ensure their survival, profitable gifts given to a higher strata to enable them to live a better life, and pleasant gifts given to the highest strata purely for their enjoyment. In return, those who received such gifts owed to those above them (the giver) both loyalty and submission. Gifts could take the form of money, land, patronage, favors, sponsorship, and the like. One can see in this the basis for a societywide system of unequal patronage and clientelism in which, once again, a small elite rules and keeps the masses content through gifts and patronage, and the masses in return owe them support and deference (now in the form of votes). In countries like Mexico, the original concept of the gift would eventually be developed into a nationwide system of patronage, clientelism, and patron-client relations. Reading between the lines, one can also see in Seneca's attitudes toward wealth ("the wise man's servant") historic Iberian and Latin American negative attitudes toward money grubbing, capitalism, and investing one's money productively.

Seneca is considered the father of stoicism. The stoic philosophers taught that happiness and the just society come from accepting one's station in life. One should not rebel against duly constituted authority or seek to upset the delicate equilibrium that reigns in society. All people have an obligation to obey those in authority over them and to adjust and accommodate peacefully to change. There is no disposition to question authority in stoic thought and no right to rebel against even unjust authority. Moreover, in later Christian thought, this obligation to obey would take on the character of divine sanction: if you rebel or seek to change the system, you risk not only the wrath of secular authority but also divine retribution in the form of eternal damnation. It is not difficult to see how stoicism and an obligation to obedience could later produce in Iberia and Latin America a passive, cowed, nonparticipatory population—a subject political culture in modern political science terms.[21] Such passivity and nonreflective acceptance of the status quo would lead to abuse, repression, and dictatorship.

Rome believed—like its "children" Portugal and Spain and its "stepchildren" in Latin America—in hierarchy and rank. The concept of hierarchy in Rome was further elaborated, and institutionalized from the earlier Greek conception, as follows: consuls (the monarchical interest); the Senate (aristocratic interests); and assemblies (popular interests). As in Greece, each rank was hereditary and locked in place. There was little social or political mobility; rather, one was born into a certain station in life and one remained in that station, as did one's children and offspring through the generations. Hierarchy of place and position was unalterable; later, in the Christian Thomistic conception, the hierarchical basis of society and politics would receive divine sanction. Note that slaves, in this inegalitarian conception, had no representation at all.

Even in pre-Christian Rome, however, the state was viewed, as it had been in Greece, as an ethical union with a moral claim on its subjects' loyalty. Rome, like Greece, viewed the world as being ruled by divine will; Roman gods were seen as being reasonable and good. A ruler must treat his subjects as a father treats his children, based on both authority and kindness, as in the concept of the gift. Man was thought to be social in nature, government was seen as being both natural and good, and political leadership should therefore be based on principles of right (authoritative but just) behavior. Just as citizens were obliged to obey the law, rulers were obliged to govern fairly.[22]

The state as well as society was viewed as depending on mutual obligations. If I as ruler do a favor for you, then you owe me loyalty and obedience in return. This is the classic patron-client relationship, one that in practice ensconces the patrons in power and the clients as supplicants before the throne of the ruler. But recall that everyone has at least some rights, and political society is founded as a moral community. Hence, although enlightened despotism—what some later Latin American republican writers called democratic caesarism—was viewed as the best form of government, it should not become outright tyranny.

Rulers were enjoined to govern authoritatively but justly; full-scale dictatorship or totalitarianism was condemned. Rulers who overstepped these bounds and violated their people's rights (as, in the modern era, the bloody dictator Rafael Trujillo did in the Dominican Republic) justified, in the much later Christian formulation, the right of rebellion against unjust authority. Thus while rulers could govern with a strong arm, they were not supposed to violate the basic rights of their citizens without inviting popular revolution.

The Roman state was not only elitist and authoritarian but also corporatist. That is, society—and representation—were organized on a functional or group basis, not on an individual one. There was precious little individualism in Roman society; rather, as in Greece, group and community interests took precedence over individual interests. Rights also tended to adhere to groups of persons, not to individuals.[23]

The Roman system comprised three types of corporate bodies: the state, at the top, viewed as a corporative collectivity; the municipalities or towns chartered as semi-independent entities, with their surrounding territories (like the Greek city-states); and private corporate or functional units, which received their charters from the state and of which there were many varieties. Private units included artisan and craft guilds, associations of priests or military men, religious associations, burial and other kinds of clubs, and *collegia* of various sorts, including a college or collectivity of medical doctors, jurists, and other professions (hence, the continuing use of the term "college of cardinals" in the Vatican).

To receive a charter enabling them to function, these entities had to be recognized by the state. Under Roman law a group could not develop a juridical personality or a political position by itself; rather, it was always chartered, recognized, and often literally created by the state. One could not as in America simply organize an interest group and then go out and lobby; one first had to get state approval. The state would establish criteria having to do with membership, leadership, purposes, and internal functioning before it would recognize the group and allow it to carry out its activities legally. Often these criteria were quite stringent, enabling the state to regulate carefully such group activity. The granting of a charter to a new group was very sparingly used. And, of course, the power to recognize or grant juridical personality to a group and give it a charter often carried with it the power to deny, delay, or withhold recognition or to impose conditions on it. For without such official recognition—very much unlike the situation in liberal-pluralist states—the group could not function, certainly not legally. Then, as in the twentieth century when corporatism as a manifest sociopolitical system was revived, particularly in Iberia and Latin America, the ability to grant recognition to a new and aspiring group gave the state enormous power to regulate and control the interest group activity that swirled around it.[24]

Representation was also on a corporatist group basis, that is, by functional groups rather than on the basis of individual representation. The groups would choose the leaders they wanted to represent them in the Roman legislative system. Frequently the state would take a strong hand in this process, too, dictating to the group which leaders it would accept as representatives. The representatives of these corporate groups were called *procuratores* (agents) or syndics (hence, the term "syndicalism," a form of government developed much later in which the corporate representatives ruled directly without an overarching state apparatus). The corporate agents were in the course of time given full powers (*plena potestas*) by their constituents to represent the interests of the corporation in the government and before the courts.[25]

Although there were differences even in Rome over the precise powers of these representatives, and though the Romans never completely developed the full system of mutual group rights and obligations of later-day corporatist states, it is striking how much the corporate-organic concepts and institutions were already present in ancient Rome. Many of these concepts were lost after the "barbarian" invasion of Rome and throughout the Dark Ages; but as Roman law was rediscovered in the twelfth century and as a modern Spanish and Portuguese state began to develop in the late Middle Ages, it was the rediscovered Roman model that Iberia employed to structure its national social and political life. Many of these same corporate, organic precepts and institutions were then carried over to Latin America in the sixteenth century. Latin American university students who have written theses on these aspects of Roman law number in the tens of thousands.

Rome bequeathed other features to Iberia and, by extension, to Latin America. Donald C. Worcester maintains that the Spanish-Portuguese and Latin American love of land and large estates came from Rome.[26] Along with the love of land, he argues, came the conviction that little honor accrued to pursuits other than large-scale agriculture. Large estates required peasants or slaves to assist with menial labor; the Roman legal codes obliged by allowing landowners to utilize the labor of those who lived on their estates. This was particularly true of conquered territories; recall, Hispania was one of those vast territories conquered by Rome. Under Roman law, all lordless land (by definition, all conquered territory) belonged to the state, which could then dole out the land as a patronage gift to those who were deserving in return for their loyalty and support.

In the case of Hispania, Rome parceled out huge territories to the soldiers of its victorious legions, who then settled in the peninsula. This was the basis of the feudal system of large estates and of rigid lord–peasant relations that would later plague Iberia and its colonies in Latin America. Although these estates were broken up and disrupted during the later Moorish conquest of the peninsula, the ideal continued to be large estates as symbols of power and prestige and large numbers of peasants doing the work on the estate, thus reinforcing the hierarchical social gaps of medieval society. In Latin America, of course, the conquistadores would find both immense territories that they could seize and hold in perpetuity as well as a ready-made "peasantry" to enslave in the form of the native Indian population. At that point the Spanish would have to go through a long and wrenching debate, based on Aristotelian ideas as well as Roman law, as to whether Indians had souls or not—that is, whether they were a natural slave class. If they had souls, then they were human (albeit of primitive rank) and qualified for at least minimum protections under Spanish law; if they did not have souls, then they were not human and did not merit even the most basic of rights—that is, they could be killed or enslaved.[27]

Another trait that Iberia may have inherited from Rome was its admiration for war, conquest, and the warrior caste. Hispania was, of course, a Roman frontier territory, and out on the frontier, as in the early American West, the niceties of law and Roman republicanism (even in its limited, corporatist forms) were not always present. Rather, this was frontier area where, to borrow a contemporary phrase, power came out of the barrel of a gun. The conqueror, the macho figure, the military man, the representative of Rome's legions were strongly admired. After all, they, like the later conquistadores in Latin America, represented civilization as against the barbarians of these distant territories. Hispania sought not, as it did later when the idea of nationalism emerged, to repel the Roman invaders but, so much as possible, to emulate the lives of the Romans.[28]

The system of government that Rome used in administering Hispania was long lasting and, in turn, carried over to Latin America. The system was absolutist and authoritarian. All decision-making power rested centrally in Rome or in the hands of the emperor; Hispania was ruled as a conquered territory. The central state could appoint and delegate its authority to a viceroy (literally, vice king) or governor-general (captain-general in Latin America) who similarly had absolute power. The next step in the hierarchy was the municipality or the landed estate, where the local official or landlord similarly had absolute, life-and-death power. All these lines of authority, at least in theory (in practice, the central government was far away and there was some limited local autonomy), reached back to the central state, which, was organic and therefore had few checks and balances. When Spain and Portugal were looking for a model of how to govern a frontier society as they reconquered their own territory from the Moors (see chapter 3), and then when they discovered and conquered another frontier territory in Latin America, they turned quite naturally to the only model they knew and were familiar with: that of imperial Rome.[29]

We have seen that although the stoic philosophy of accepting one's station in life was generally dominant, the Romans derived many of their legal and political norms deductively, from nature and reason. But after the acceptance and establishment of Christianity, the new religion elaborated the moral principles that would govern conduct in Rome's far-flung empire. The earlier ethical tenets of the philosophers and lawyers were largely related to this world, but the doctrines expounded by Christianity's fathers were otherworldly. Pagan influences were gradually purged from the law and replaced with Christian principles. Although the law's objectives now shifted from secular to spiritual concerns, the basic principles of a deductive idealistic legal system remained. The law still aimed to provide instructions in right reason and an ethical or moral basis for society. As José Moreno states, "The idealism and individualism of the Romans translated into Christian terminology gave form to the Spanish conception of law and politics."[30] That meant high-sounding ethical principles (or laws and constitutions) divorced from either local habits or reality. The fate of Iberia and Latin America was thus cast: Don Quijote tilting vainly at windmills, while the wise, pragmatic counsel of Sancho Panza was often ignored.

Rome's impact on Iberia and Latin America was profound. Roman
36 culture in all its aspects dominated Iberia for almost six centuries

(219 B.C. to A.D. 409). The Roman influence was not only long but also deep and pervasive. The Roman language and culture helped unify the peninsula and give it coherence. Roman law and the system of socio-political organization brought to Iberia had a profound effect—not just immediately but as a model well into future centuries. The acceptance of Roman law and its idealistic philosophical bases determined the direction of Spanish (and Latin American) political thought as well as social and political structure. Now, with the introduction of Christianity, a new and very powerful ingredient was added to the Iberian stew. For if, as is often said, Hispania was the most Romanized of the Roman provinces, it was also the most Christianized.

Christianity

In the first two centuries after Christ, Christianity spread slowly. Christians were often persecuted for their beliefs, and the Roman state put numerous barriers in the way of the new religion. The slowly growing religious movement lacked economic might or political structure that would have advanced the new faith, and Christians themselves were at first largely indifferent to grand concepts of social and political philosophy or organization. Christianity put forth some then novel ideas of community and solidarity, but it remained still a loose association of believers largely without organizational or political structure. However, as Christianity spread throughout the empire—and, later, after it enjoyed the status of *the* official and encouraged religion of the Roman state—it began to develop an institutional structure to go with its larger body of believers.

Our purpose in this section is not to trace the entire history of Christianity but to focus on those aspects of Christian beliefs, doctrine, and institutions that had particular impact on Spain, Portugal, and their colonies in the New World. We begin, appropriately, with the Bible.

The Bible contains numerous passages on the nature of authority, the obligations of Christians, and the ideal (Christian) structure of the state and society. Recall as we quote these passages that these are *God's* thoughts; they are immutable and unchanging, and to disobey them is to incur God's wrath and judgment, which means eternal damnation. That notion sounds old-fashioned, but we have to think of it in ancient and medieval terms, when people really believed that disobedience to God was a mortal sin subject to eternal hellfires. The society and culture in which these ideas and precepts took root and flowered (Rome, Spain, Portugal, Latin America) were not pluralist, competitive, and democratic in which one could accept, reject, or remain indifferent to the Christian imperatives. Rather, these came to be absolutist, theocratic, monolithic, inquisitorial societies in which one accepted God's word and that of religious authorities, or else! And the "or else" was not pleasant. Our message, of course, is that to understand Iberia and Latin America, one must understand them in their times and on *their* terms—unpleasant though that may sometimes be—and not through the prism and biases of our own rose-colored lenses or preferences for the area.

Let us begin with this passage from Romans 13:1–2, on the nature of authority and man's obligation to obey constituted authority: "Let every person be subject to the governing authorities. For there is no authority except from God, and those that exist have been instituted by God. Therefore he who resists the authorities resists what God has appointed, and those who resist will incur judgment."

The next two passages, the first from Romans 12:4–7, and the second from I Corinthians 12:11–27, emphasize the organic, corporatist, functional organization of society, so different from the unfettered individualism of the United States:

> For as in one body we have many members, and all the members do not have the same function; so we, though many, are one body in Christ, and individually members one of another. Having gifts that differ according to the grace given us, let us use them: if prophecy, in proportion to our faith; if service, in our serving; he who teaches, in teaching. Etcetera.

> For just as the body is one and has many members, and all the members of the body, though many, are one body, so it is with Christ. For by one Spirit we were all baptized into one body—Jews or Greeks, slaves or free—and all were made to drink of one Spirit. For the body does not consist of one member but of many. If the foot should say, "Because I am not a hand, I do not belong to the body," that would not make it any less a part of the body. And if the ear should say, "Because I am not an eye, I do not belong to the body," that would not make it any less a part of the body. If the whole body were an eye, where would be the hearing? If the whole body were an ear, where would be the sense of smell? But as it is, God arranged the organs in the body, each one of them, as he chose. If all were a single organ, where would the

body be? As it is, there are many parts, yet one body. The eye cannot say to the hand, "I have no need of you," nor again the head to the feet, "I have no need of you." On the contrary, the parts of the body which seem to be weaker are indispensable, and those parts of the body which we think less honorable we invest with the greater honor, and our unpresentable parts are treated with greater modesty, which our more presentable parts do not require. But God has so adjusted the body, giving the greater honor to the inferior part, that there may be no discord in the body, but that the members may have the same care for one another. If one member suffers, all suffer together; if one member is honored, all rejoice together. Now you are the body of Christ and individually members of it.

Here, then, is a biblical formula for an authoritarian, organic, and corporatist social and political order. Christians have a duty to obey and not to question God-given authority. God is the center of the universe; all of man's affairs are governed by His almighty hand. The method of reasoning must be deductive: one starts with God's law and, eventually, the dictates of God's Church (including the pope), and proceeds deductively from His commandments and the Church's interpretations. As in Aristotle, society and government are based on natural groupings: the family, the clan, the local community or parish. The form of society is unified, organic, integral, with all the parts tied together. Society is communitarian and organized functionally or corporatively; there is *no* sense here of individualism or individual rights. Reflecting God's universe, political authority must also be top-down, centralized, and absolutist. The role of the monarch or ruler is to maintain the Christian community and to serve the common good. All this is God's will, immutable, unchanging, and unchallengeable.

It is precisely these features that lie at the heart of the Iberian and Latin American political experience. As the Christian church grew and its institutions developed, distinctions were made between the obligations owed to outside political authority and obligations owed to God ("Render unto Caesar that which is Caesar's, and unto God that which is God's"); Christians were also encouraged to accommodate themselves to the outside (Roman) political order, a demonstration, as Sheldon Wolin puts it, of their struggle for a new life even while still entrapped within the old.[31] The obligation to obedience was a reflection of the political forces that prevented the creation of a wholly Christian state and society. Saint Augustine, in the fifth century A.D., put it in terms of the two swords: a Christian sword and a secular sword, and during the later Middle Ages the debate waxed long and acrimoniously over the papacy's right to intervene in temporal matters. Yet to believers, the Christian sword remained superior; when a conflict between the two occurred, believers owed their primary allegiance to the Christian gospel.

Christians believed the Church or religious community was superior to the secular or state community, even though they came to welcome the Roman system of justice because it provided the peace and order in which Christianity could flourish. Augustine maintained, therefore, that even a society alienated from the true God was useful as an instrument to advance Christianity; but such a secular order was only a second-best arrangement, because it relied not on Christian love but on coercion. Meanwhile, the Christian community had ceased to be only a collection of scattered and often persecuted believers and had become a larger community with a need for organization, officers, creeds, authority, hierarchy, and discipline. It had to deal with heresy, dissidents, and defections from its original dogma. It sought to enforce unity on its followers and sometimes discipline since, if unity is a good, then enforced unity (later, in Spain, the Inquisition) would presumably also be good.[32] Unity was seen as an essential element in society because it helps preserve peace and good order, which make the Christian life possible.[33]

As articulated in the Gospels of Matthew, Mark, Luke, and John, in the Epistles of Saint Paul, and then in the writings of Saint Augustine, the following ideas came to be preeminent in the Christian commonwealth.[34] Since many of the early church leaders had been trained in the classics, note how many of these ideas are derivative of earlier Greek and Roman sources.

1. *All* of life is to be undergirded by Christian principles; all human institutions must reflect the Divine law.
2. There are no sharp lines between law, politics, and religion; law and politics are to be infused with Christian principles.
3. One is obliged to render to God what is God's and to Caesar what is Caesar's. But if there is conflict between Christian and secular obligations, the Christian obligations must take priority.
4. Secular authorities must submit to Christian principles; if there is contradiction between the religious and the secular "swords," Christians owe first loyalty to the religious one.
5. The human order must follow the divine archetype. That means, in accord with the biblical passages quoted earlier, an organic

and functionalist-corporatist conception of the state and society, obedience to higher authority (especially religious authority), and the paternalistic family as a model for political authority.

6. Law and culture must be infused with moral and ethical (i.e., Christian) principles; there is no separation of society and morality.

7. Man's goal in this world is the establishment of a Christian commonwealth (Augustine); such a Christian commonwealth is not pluralistic but monist, unitary, and undivided.

8. Christianity proposed a new idea of community as distinct from individualism, a community of *believers*. Believers were to be enveloped in a unity and solidarity that called its membership to a life of participation that in turn led to a revitalization of the community.

9. The goal of the polity is to embody and promote a well-ordered Christian community among its members. It should encourage a Christian life and society and, by emphasizing unity, avoid conflicts between political and religious obligations.

10. The Christian conception of the organic unity of mankind was based on the conviction of solidarity of all classes and peoples as the beloved children of God, united in and through God's infinite charity, especially the gift of his son which serves as a divine model for all human relationships.

11. Political society (following the earlier cited biblical passages) was similarly viewed as a single and uniform whole, with an organic relationship between the divinely ordained and universal whole and its equally divinely ordained parts.

12. Every being in the universe is assigned its proper place ("the great chain of being") as well as its proper relationship to all other things; the order of being is determined by a divine hierarchy of beings with God at the pinnacle. Not only does every organism and every part thereof have its own place in the universal order of things but also its own specific order and constitution. (John of Salisbury carried this organic-corporatist conception further when he wrote that the well-ordered society rests upon the right apportionment of the various social functions to the different members of the society.)

13. The whole of mankind belongs to God's divine plan for the universe; all are unified in His sovereignty. The principle of unity was, therefore, the foundation of everything; unity is the basis of all society and social existence.

14. The destiny and preordained goal of Christendom was identical to that of mankind at large. All of mankind is but a single universal community founded and directed by God. All human

41

affairs including freedom itself were subject to God and His all-embracing Oneness.

15. Since the whole of mankind is but one single body and Christ its sole head, the proposition was advanced that upon this earth only the vicar of Christ (the pope) could be called the rightful temporal ruler of the body politic.

These are very powerful principles. Moreover, they have an internal logic and coherence. As moderns, we may no longer accept these principles; but one can see clearly that if one grants these assumptions, their logic carries one a very long way. And these were the basic principles that, whether we now appreciate them or not, strongly undergirded Iberian and Latin American civilization and political society.

Augustine was the first both to articulate this religiously centered organic-corporatist conception on a societywide basis and to synthesize systematically the dilemmas involved in church-state relations, while also succeeding in planting Christian ideals firmly in the Greco-Roman roots of Western civilization. Augustine wanted the state to promote the divine mission of the Christian religion, while still maintaining that the Church was the supreme power. But with the establishment of Christianity in Rome as the official religion, it faced the danger of losing its distinctive identity. How could Christianity support the state and be supported by it and yet avoid becoming just another civic religion? What if the state not only advanced but also sought to police religion? In Augustine's view, the spiritual and the political were distinct yet complemented each other, and both should be dedicated to the same end—a Christian commonwealth. Augustine's theory of order was a highly structured one of hierarchical and distributive law placing things in categories of high and low, good and evil. His state would also be a top-down, authoritative if not authoritarian one, dedicated to its most important tasks, the spread and deepening of Christianity.[35] One can see in these Augustinian formulations some of the most important beliefs that would eventually serve as a basis for Hispanic-Latin American sociopolitical organization.

Augustine's writings were tailored to the structure and vastness of the Roman Empire (encompassing the entire circum-Mediterranean and much of Western Europe, including Iberia); but in the fifth century A.D. this vast empire began to collapse and disintegrate, both internally of its own conflictive elements and from the outside through repeated attacks by barbaric tribes living along its borders. One of those groups was the Visigoths, a German tribe living to the north of the Roman Empire. The Visigoths streamed into present-day Italy, conquered Rome, and were instrumental in the collapse of the Empire. In the process of conquering Rome, however, they were also seduced by it and adopted Christianity as their own. From Italy the Visigoths, over time, marched to Iberia and subdued that part of the former Roman Empire as well.

Rome had dominated Iberia for six centuries, from the second century B.C. to the fifth century A.D., and left its indelible mark on the peninsula. The next two centuries belonged to the Visigoths. Although their lasting impact on Iberia was not nearly so great or deep as that of Rome, at least three major influences deserve mention. First, the Visigoths reintroduced a tribal or clan-based, decentralized, regionally organized political structure into Spain, thereby giving rise to the seemingly perpetual conflict between central government authority and regional autonomy that persists to this day. Second, the Visigoths introduced the concept of the charismatic, heroic leader, the caudillo who gallops into power and, by strength, skill, force of personality, and against all odds, saves the nation—the fictional and movie character *El Cid* is a prime example. And third, the Visigoths introduced the structure and requirement of an *official, state church.* So not only was Hispania monolithically Catholic from the Roman period, but now Catholicism became the official state religion, with Church and state even more closely unified than before, the state providing lands and resources to the Church, and all Spaniards now obliged under threat of penalty to adopt the official religion.[36]

With the fall of the Roman Empire, much of Europe entered the long period that came to be called the Dark Ages. For Spain, the Dark Ages were attenuated first by the Visigothic conquest and then by the Moorish conquest—an important theme we take up in the next chapter. Here let us only say that the so-called Dark Ages were never so dark in Iberia as they were in other parts of Europe. On the one hand, there were the Visigoths and their official state church, which though often primitive by Roman standards, kept the flame of Christianity alive and flourishing for over two centuries. Second, although Iberia was later under Moorish (North African) rule, the Moors presided over a thriving and surprisingly free and open-minded culture that made Spain dur-

ing the Middle Ages the most important European center of philosophy, art, architecture, and theology. Moreover, it was through Spain, by
way of North Africa and the eastern Mediterranean, that the classics of
Greece and Rome (Aristotle, Plato, Cicero, etc.), lost for many centuries
during the Dark Ages, were *reintroduced* into Europe, thus providing the
inspiration for a new intellectual awakening that ushered in the modern age.

The architect of the grand synthesis that combined powerful Greek
learning and methodology with the already established Christianity
into a new religious orthodoxy and sociopolitical structure for a more
modern Spain and Portugal, and also Latin America, was Saint Thomas
Aquinas. Saint Thomas is one of the most significant figures in the history of Western political thought, and certainly the most important
philosopher in the history of Christianity, particularly in those societies of Southern and Western Europe whose entire culture and society
were grounded on Thomistic principles. His contribution was to con-
struct an edifice of logic, reasoning, and truth that not only undergirded and gave new rigor to Christian beliefs but also provided a
foundation for the organization of society and the political system
that persists in much of Iberia and Latin America to this day.[37]

Thomistic philosophy had a dual influence upon medieval thought
and political development. On the one hand, there is a powerful emphasis on the creation of order through discipline, authority, and hierarchy. Saint Thomas largely accepted Augustine's emphasis on organic order, on each group and person secure in his God-ordained
station, and (going back to Aristotle) on a hierarchy of social classes.
Thomas begins with the Aristotelian notion of the world as a reflection
of an idea, that man is destined to be a copy of God's ultimate perfection. But this idealism—and the nature of the universe—is static, unchanging. Society, in Thomas's view, is a collectivity of imperfect beings for whom the afterlife is more important than worldly deeds. He
sees faith and reason as complementary in his worldview and utilizes
both; his is also a cultural and legalistic (as opposed to a socioeconomic) conception.

Thomas Aquinas is a towering figure in the history of Western
thought. He constructed an edifice of philosophy and religion that
sought to explain all of life in terms of a God-centered universe. Once
44 one grants Thomas's basic premises, an entire way of life, society, cul-

ture, philosophy, politics, and religion falls into place. He, more than any single figure, built the structure of natural-law philosophy that not only undergirded the late Middle Ages but also continued to form the basis of Catholic political thought and society into modern (at least until Vatican II) times. We know, of course, that over time, in the Protestant Reformation, in the north and west of Europe, and in modern secular thought, the Thomistic assumptions faded or were repudiated. But not in the south of Europe, particularly in Spain and Portugal, in the heart of the Counter-Reformation, and their New World colonies. There the Thomistic edifice and its assumptions of order, authority, discipline, hierarchy, inequality, and a God-centered universe lived on. Our purpose here is not to provide a lengthy treatment of Saint Thomas, even though his complex philosophy merits expanded coverage, but only to emphasize its main features and the powerful and lasting impact that Thomistic conception had on Iberia and Latin America.

Like Augustine, Thomas's conception was that of organic unity between man and the universe. Reflecting God's divine plan, he saw the universe as a hierarchy. Both society and polity were to be organized in a hierarchical way, as a reflection of the natural inequalities among men. Thomas also fashioned a hierarchy of laws to go with the hierarchy of society. There was divine law (God's explicit instructions as, for example, in the Ten Commandments); eternal law (also God-derived, such as the behavior of the stars and moon); natural law (what men, using right reason and following Christian theology, would deduce); and man-made law. Clearly with man-made law at the bottom, "mere" constitutions and this-worldly legal injunctions could often be conveniently ignored if they came in conflict with higher law.

Saint Thomas echoed Aristotle, Plato, Cicero, the Bible, and Augustine in advancing an organic and functional organization of society: "Society is an organism of different graces, and human activities form a hierarchy of functions, which differ in kind and in significance, but each of which is of value on its own level, provided that it is governed by the end which is common to all."[38] Stemming from Saint Paul's Epistles to the Romans and Corinthians (cited earlier), this organic-corporatist conception had its origins not just in natural or man-made law but in directives from God himself. As the famed German sociologist of religion R. H. Tawney would interpret it: "Each member of society has

45

his own functions. . . . Each must receive means suited to its station (just reward) and no more. . . . Within classes there must be equality, between classes there must be inequality for otherwise each class cannot perform its *function* or 'enjoy its rights.'"[39] Hence, society is held together by functional organization and a system of mutual, though varying, obligations, with rights unequally distributed according to social position.

Thomas's conception of political society was similarly derived from the notion of an all-powerful God. God's authority was unquestioned; all owed him obedience. Similarly with kings: once a community transferred the authority to rule to a king (this was the era when national kingdoms were first emerging in Europe), the king ruled by a God-given natural right. Divine-right monarchy as practiced on earth thus reflected the nature of God's heavenly authority over the entire universe. It was absolute and inviolate. Similarly in the religious realm: authority was top-down; it focused on the papacy and its divine establishment as the organ directing and governing the Christian body, and it represented and carried out the will of God.

The logic of Thomas's arguments was forceful, compelling, authoritative. God held the highest position of authority, to whom all men owed obedience. All authority figures below Him were also instituted by God and, therefore, merited the same respect, obedience, and love. In Thomas's words: "God created all things; all things are subject to his providence. He is the Sovereign, the King of the Universe. Everywhere in His Kingdom there is a certain fixed hierarchy and order, yet in all wise that all depends on Him and all tends toward Him."[40] Hence, God, pope, emperor, prince, landowner, or father represent divinely established authorities to whom all those below owe obedience. This then becomes the hierarchical social organization of the Christian commonwealth of which Augustine wrote: a society tied together by mutual obligation, working for the common good, obeying God's commands and those in authority over them. "No social life is possible," Augustine had written (and Thomas reiterated), "whether in the family, the village community, the state, the monastery, the diocese, the universal church [note again the functional or corporatist conception] unless there exists an authority to which members of society owe obedience."

A broad gamut of practical implications would follow from the
Thomistic conception of social hierarchy:

> God
> Archangels
> Angels
> Cherubim
> Seraphim
> Principalities
> Princes
> Nobility
> Artisans
> Craftsmen
> Merchants
> Soldiers
> Bureaucrats
> Peasants
> Slaves
> Lions, foxes, dolphins
> Lesser animals
> Trees, vegetables
> Inanimate objects

First, recall that this is a God-ordained hierarchy, and one does not rebel against God's will without expecting to pay the severest penalty—eternal damnation. Second, God is at the top, and it is to be emphasized that princes, nobles, and *all* others receive their positions *from God;* there is *no* conception of popular sovereignty or democratic elections here. Third, note that peasants and slaves form the lowest rungs in the *human* part of this hierarchy; after that come the more intelligent of the animals. But what happens later on when African blacks and American Indians come into the picture—where do they fit in this hierarchy? In fact, the Spanish went through intense debate over this issue. For if blacks or Indians have souls, then they are human and deserve at least some rights under Spanish law; but if they do not have souls, then they belong with the animals and can be treated accordingly. Here we are back to Aristotle's conception of a natural slave class.

The structure of political thought and sociology erected by Saint Thomas was clear, consistent, and logically powerful. Once his assumptions of a God-centered universe, an organic-corporatist conception of political society, and natural inequalities among men are granted, Thomas's logic carries the argument far. Indeed it was Thomas's thought that served as the basis for the emerging Spanish and Portuguese states in the late Middle Ages—and the extension of this system to Latin America. Thomas's *system* consisted of a hierarchical, top-down, functionally organized society dedicated to service to God. For in contrast to the secular universe of interest and conflict portrayed by such modern writers as Hobbes and Machiavelli, Thomas perpetuated a universe of order, natural law, and permanence. Yet this is the *structure* and *system* that Iberia and Latin America were blessed, or saddled, with for centuries— and which carries strong echoes even today.

But Thomas was not quite so rigid and authoritarian as he is sometimes portrayed. While on the one hand there is the emphasis on the creation of order through hierarchy, on the other he declares that it is within the rights of people to be ruled by their own choice of magistrate. The people have an obligation to obey, but rulers also have an obligation to govern justly and for the common good. There are, therefore, limits on temporal authority, a theme that comes to the fore in the next chapter in the debate in Spain between central state power and local or group autonomy. There is, further, within Thomas's writings a hint of the importance of the consent of the community, of checks and balances, through an adopted constitution or social contract. Thomas also discusses briefly the problems of a ruler who becomes corrupt or tyrannous and, as a consequence, the ability of the people to change their collective mind and find a new prince. "Princes of the earth," wrote Thomas, "are instituted by God not for their own advantage but in order that they may serve the common good." All these provisions in Thomas's thought would provide grounds for further dispute concerning the structure of Iberian and Latin American governance.[41]

Although the emphasis in Saint Thomas is on structure and order and the obligation to obedience, there is enough in his writings on decentralization, responsibility, and social compact to provide grounds for controversy. Indeed as Spain and Portugal began to emerge as distinct nation-states in the late Middle Ages, Thomas's name and writings were invoked on all sides of every controversy. For it was not inevitably fated that Spain, Portugal, and Latin America would be centralized, bureaucratic, inquisitorial, authoritarian systems. At one point, indeed, the decentralized and protoparliamentary, protodemocratic tendencies in Spain were at least as strong as those of the opposite tendency. The issue was not so much historical inevitability as it was the working

out of political conflicts and differences among groups over a long period of time. It is to these conflicts and, in the process, the emergence of a modern Spain and Portugal that the discussion now turns.

Nevertheless, the tradition of thought reflected here—authoritative, often authoritarian, organicist, functionalist, nonindividualistic, corporatist, deductive, top-down, absolutist, inquisitorial, hierarchical, based on natural inequalities, scholastic, elitist—is a powerful one. And it had a powerful impact on those countries—Spain, Portugal, Latin America, the Philippines, others—shaped by this tradition. A society that is inegalitarian is one thing, but one that is unabashedly so is quite another. Hence, it is especially difficult for Americans whose political traditions vary from these to understand, let alone empathize with, a set of societies based on frankly inquisitorial and elitist assumptions. Americans are preoccupied with horizontal pluralism, and their individual and largely secularly driven relations with one another are such that they would prefer not to have to deal with societies governed by top-down, vertical relations, by authority from the top and a God who enters history and governs all things. How quaint, old-fashioned, and downright medieval that all seems. But that is precisely the point: Iberia and Latin America have, for a long time, been feudal and medieval and governed by medieval principles. The question is, are they still?

Chapter 3

Medieval Iberia: The Distinct Tradition

Medieval Spain and Portugal had a history unlike that of any other country in western Europe. First, the Moorish invasion and occupation, beginning in 712 and lasting for more than seven centuries, gave Spain a flavor, an art and architecture, and a set of behavioral traits and institutions that cast it as different from any other Western country. Then came the Reconquest of the peninsula from the Moors, beginning in 722 and itself lasting for seven centuries, arguably an even stronger influence on later Spanish institutions than the Moorish conquest itself.

For it was out of the Reconquest that the unique character of Spanish and Portuguese feudalism emerged, quite distinct from the paradigm French case.[1] And it was similarly out of the Reconquest that the distinctive Spanish and Portuguese concepts of rights, democracy, constitutionalism, and state–society relations were developed. These institutions, fundamental in shaping the emerging Spanish and Portuguese nation-states, were ultimately carried over to the New World and are often still present there today. Spain, Portugal, and their Latin American colonies were products of a powerful feudalism and medievalism that were never present in North America—more than that, of a particular, uniquely Iberian form of feudalism and medievalism. To understand modern and emerging Iberia and Latin America, one first has to come to grips with the medieval roots from which they emerged.

Visigothic and Moorish Iberia

Even before the Roman Empire fell in A.D. 423 waves of Germanic invaders (Suevi, Alani, Vandals, Visigoths) had begun sweeping into the peninsula. The most important of these were the Visigoths. The Visi-

gothic cultural, social, and political impact on Iberia, though not
nearly so great and lasting as the Roman, nevertheless, affected some
areas. The most important of these for my purposes was the unification
of church and state and the creation of an official Roman Catholic
state church. But in other areas the Visigothic presence would also be
felt: in the introduction of certain aspects of Germanic folk law into
Iberia, in the decentralization and territorial separateness that set in
after the ouster of the Romans, in the tradition of caudillo rule, and in
the reorganization of Iberian society into smaller clan, tribal, and regional components as compared with the enforced unity and unification imposed by Rome.[2] The regionalism and localism of the Visigoths
as compared to the universalism and centralism of the Roman ideal remains a source of tension in Iberia to the present.

In 712, taking advantage of the deep divisions, lack of central authority, and ongoing civil war among the several Visigothic leaders,
Moors who dwelled on the coastal African plain north of the Atlas
Mountains began invading the peninsula. A Semitic people with roots
in present-day Syria and the Middle East, the Moors came from the Mediterranean coastal escarpment of Africa, crossing the Mediterranean
at the narrow Straits of Gibraltar, where only eighteen miles of water
separate Spain from North Africa. The Moors were carried along by
their fervent devotion to the Islamic faith, which had begun in present-
day Saudi Arabia two centuries earlier. From there Islam had spread
like wildfire throughout the Middle East, expanding east as far as India
and Indonesia and west to encompass most of the eastern Mediterranean. From this base it lapped at the breaches of west European
Christendom in the Balkans and eastern Europe and also spread along
the coastal plain of North Africa, from which the invasion of Iberia
had come.

Their religious fervor, crusading spirit, and sense of *jihad* (military-
religious crusade) impelled the Moors far into the peninsula. Within a
matter of decades they had conquered most of present-day Spain and
Portugal. Only isolated enclaves in the Cantabrian Mountains in the far
north of Spain, in the areas of Galicia, León, Andalucía, and the Basque
country, were able to hold out against the invaders. Their antecedents'
ability to resist the Moors and preserve their Christianity and culture
intact is to this day a source of pride and regional nationalism among
the people of these areas. Nevertheless, the Moors did control 90 to 95
percent of the territory, and their rule lasted, with ups and downs, for

some seven centuries. The Moors were not finally and completely expelled from the peninsula until 1492.[3]

Rome ruled and dominated Iberia for six centuries, the Visigoths
for two centuries, and the Moors for seven. One would assume, therefore, that the Moorish influence on Spain and Portugal would be at
least as great as the Roman influence. In fact, the Moorish impact on
various fields and lasting over seven centuries was important. But in
terms of the formative and truly lasting influence, the Roman impact
was considerably greater and more penetrating than the Moorish one.

The Moorish impression on today's Spain and Portugal can be seen
most visibly in the art, architecture, cooking, houses, and language.
Moorish art and architecture are present in the intricate designs of
Spanish and Portuguese gold and silver works, in porcelain and ce-
ramics, and in the delicate columns and minarets of such former Moorish centers as Toledo, Córdoba, and Granada. Moorish traces in Spanish
cooking are present in such delicacies as almonds, pomegranates, and
eggs. Those whitewashed villages glistening in the Mediterranean sun
that one sees especially in the south of Spain and Portugal are a reflection of Moorish architecture. And in the language, those words
that begin with *al* (*alma, almacén, almuerzo*) are similarly the result of
the Moorish occupation.

The Moorish influence reached deeper than this, however. Though
often forcibly kept apart, native Iberian and Moorish people intermixed
and produced children of combined ancestry. Some scholars say, in addition, that the Moorish pattern of large, extended families and quasi-
tribal politics had an enduring effect on Spain and Portugal—although
these institutions were present before the Moors arrived. The Spanish
traditions of militarism, of guerrilla warfare, of admiration for the
heroic military leader, of *caudillismo* may similarly bear in part a Moorish stamp. It is also said that Spanish *machismo* and the subordinate
place of women historically in Hispanic society stem from the Moorish
occupation.[4]

During long periods of the occupation, Moorish society practiced
considerable tolerance. The point is so stunning and so much at variance with our present attitudes toward Islamic society that it merits
brief elaboration. During much of the Moorish occupation, Moors,
Christians, and Jews lived in Iberia in mutual harmony, without overt
conflict. The Moors tolerated the Christian and Jewish faiths and engaged in no mass proselytizing campaigns. At the same time, many

Jews occupied high economic, political, and cultural/intellectual positions within the caliphate, where their contributions were valued.

Moorish Spain was also a center of cultural and intellectual life. In much of Europe during this period, the Dark Ages reigned, but in Spain intellectual life flourished. Art, culture, music, philosophy, architecture, theology—all thrived during these centuries that proved to be so dismal in other parts of the continent. Most important, in Spain Greek and Roman logic, knowledge, and political philosophy—lost for centuries in the rest of western Europe—flourished and were reintroduced into Europe via the Moors and North Africa. That is, while Greek and Roman thought had been largely snuffed out in western Europe after the fall of Rome, it survived in the East (Byzantium), was incorporated into Islamic thought, and then resurfaced in Spain thanks to the Moorish occupation. From there, Greek and Roman thought spread into the rest of Europe, stimulating the Thomistic revival of Christianity in the twelfth century and eventually helping give rise to the Renaissance and the Enlightenment. For the purposes of this book, what is especially important is the Greek and Roman impact on Thomism and the revival of Christianity for, as mentioned in the previous chapter, it was the Thomistic form of Christianity and of a theocratic state that then spread back to Spain and had such a profound impact on the formation of the early Spanish, Portuguese, and, by extension, Latin American state and society.[5]

A seldom-mentioned, wholly negative factor deriving from the Moorish conquest of Iberia was the blatant racial and ethnic prejudice directed at Spain and Portugal by the rest of Europe. Because of the long Moorish presence, Spain and Portugal were often looked down upon and thought to be tainted by North African blood. They were described as swarthy, hot-blooded, African. An old European saw reflects this prejudice: "Africa begins at the Pyrenees"—that is, not across the Mediterranean but at the border of France and Spain. Even earlier in the legends of Roland, which nearly every European schoolchild learns, the heroic knights of Charlemagne stand up against the evil Saracens, Muslim hordes, thus not only rescuing Western Christendom but also protecting its people against racial and ethnic "mongrelization."

The Roland legends and medieval literature are full of blatantly racist epitaphs directed against Spain and Spaniards because of the Moorish influence there. Racial and ethnic prejudice were also present in the so-called Black Legend, the depiction by Englishmen and others of the supposed cruelty and infamy of the Spanish conquerors of America, as compared with the supposedly benign and enlightened English colonists.[6] Such glaring slurs bred in northern Europe a sense of superiority and in Spain and Portugal a sense of inferiority and hence resentment toward the rest of Europe that persisted into modern times. And even within Spain and Portugal, racial prejudice, though never so great as that on the part of the rest of Europe directed toward Iberia, was similarly sown, chiefly by populations in the north—where the waves of German and Visigothic influence were strongest—against the "swarthier" southerners. .

Moorish rule was thus important in shaping Spain and Portugal in many particulars, but it was not so fundamental as the earlier Roman influence. Rome gave to Spain and Portugal their law, language, religion, culture, form and language of politics and society, education and intellectual paradigms, as well as unity, centralization, road system, and aqueducts. All of these were fundamental in shaping Spain's and Portugal's constant institutions and behavior and their development patterns over time. The Moorish influence was also strong in various areas but not so strong, deep, pervasive, fundamental, and self-perpetuating as the Roman impact. The Moorish conquest, by contrast, was mainly a military occupation; it never penetrated as deeply and thoroughly into the societal and cultural fabric as the Roman. That explains why even today Spain and Portugal are essentially Western, Latin, Roman, Catholic, southern *European* countries and not, like Albania and parts of Bosnia, Muslim enclaves in the heart of Europe.

The Reconquest

The Moors dominated the Iberian peninsula for over seven centuries, from the initial invasion in 712 until their final defeat and expulsion in 1492. Even before that later date, however, the Moors had been mainly confined to a smaller and smaller enclave in the south of Spain; even at their height the Moors had been unable to subjugate the rugged mountain tribes in the north of Spain. It was from these small northern enclaves that the Reconquest of the peninsula by Christendom began. The Reconquest was one of the most important events in the history of Iberia, arguably more momentous than the Muslim occupation itself and indelibly shaping the special nature of Spanish/
Portuguese feudal society and development.

The first uprising against Moorish rule, the first step in the Reconquest, had begun at Covadonga in 722. This was an era not of large-scale
professional armies and grandiose Napoleonic military strategies, but of
small, unprofessional, often guerrilla-like armed bands. There was not
a single war against the Moorish infidel but a series of often-indecisive
skirmishes that dragged on for several centuries. The tide of battle
ebbed and flowed over this long period as did the frontier between the
gradually expanding Christian kingdoms and the slowly receding Muslim enclaves. The general pattern flowed from north to south: that is,
the Christian Spanish and Portuguese armies that first rose in the
north gradually pushed the Moorish occupiers farther south—until in
1492 they were pushed out of the peninsula entirely and back across
the Straits of Gibraltar.

This centuries-long struggle profoundly influenced the shape and
development of latter-day Spain and Portugal, making Iberian feudalism very different from the paradigmatic French and European case. It
also determined the distinct character of Iberian political culture and
sociopolitical institutions. Many Spanish and Portuguese historians
argue that the Reconquest was even more important in affecting Iberian development than the Muslim conquest itself, second only to the
Roman period as one of the two or three most significant historical influences on Spanish and Portuguese national life.[7] And it was largely
the institutions that came out of the Reconquest that were carried over
to Latin America; the date of the final defeat of the Moors, 1492, was
also the date that Spain's discovery and conquest of the Americas
began. The conquest of Latin America was an extension of the earlier
wars of reconquest against the Moors.

The Reconquest influenced Spanish and Portuguese development
in myriad ways. The conflict meant that the Iberian countryside was
often torn by fighting, upheaval, war, disruption, and chaos. Of course,
the fighting did not go on uninterrupted for all those centuries, and
there were often long periods of relative peace, but there were also
long periods of conflict and centuries of upheaval. War, thievery, violence, brigandage became endemic. Because of the extended, on-again,
off-again conflict and upheaval in the countryside, Spanish and Portuguese agriculture lagged behind, never developing the agricultural
surpluses on which later industrialization could be based, and Spanish
and Portuguese feudalism was more violent and chaotic than the
French model. All these factors served to plunge Spain and Portugal

further behind the rest of Europe during the long centuries of late feudalism and early modernization, as compared with the period of enlightenment and intellectual leadership in Europe they had enjoyed under the Moors.

Second, Spanish and Portuguese feudalism was far more militaristic than the French example. Military conflict in Iberia was almost constant, and military prowess and leadership (*caudillismo*) were valued above all else. Critically important in this context of a moving, evershifting frontier was the fact that conquest gave one a right, usually ratified by the local prince, to the land that one conquered. The economic consideration served to enhance the value of military prowess even further. But the local military leader acquired a right not only to the lands he conquered, but also to the labor of those who lived on the conquered lands. In return for the military protection he offered them, the populace owed him obligations of labor and military service. Tied to conquest in these ways, Spanish and Portuguese feudalism was much more militaristic than its French counterpart. Moreover, it would be these same institutions of feudalism growing out of military conquest and the right to both land and the labor residing on it, which had its origins in Roman concepts of conquest, that would characterize Spain's and Portugal's conquest of the Americas.[8]

A third result of the Reconquest struggle was what might be called premature or preindustrial urbanization. In most countries of Europe, industrialization stimulated massive urbanization by luring peasants out of the countryside and into the urban factories. But in Spain and Portugal, the virtually constant warfare in the countryside forced peasants to take refuge within the city walls before the onset of modernization. That helps explain the Spanish and Portuguese system of walled enclave cities: cities throughout Iberia are surrounded by walls with a castle often on a hillock in the center to protect against marauding bands. From these enclaves peasants fanned out into the countryside to work the land, returning to the fortified cities for protection at night. The phenomenon of urbanization in the absence of industrialization interrupted what might be called the normal course of societal development, made Spain and Portugal urban before their time, and ultimately retarded their later efforts at modernization.[9]

The oppressive Spanish/Portuguese class and landholding systems were other results of the Reconquest. Under the Visigoths, Spain had been a quite primitive but at the same time a more-or-less egalitarian society. Land was often held communally or in small, family-sized plots. The Reconquest changed that. Leaders of the Reconquest, often military and Catholic religious orders as well as heroic individuals like El Cid, became wealthy and formed an upper-status group as a result of their military triumphs. They were granted vast tracts of land and royal titles by the emerging kingdoms of that time for ridding the countryside of the Muslim threat. Military triumphs over the Moors were rewarded usually by a grant to the conqueror to use in perpetuity (*encomienda*) the lands conquered and the labor of those living on the land—a grant that often turned de facto into a grant of the land itself and feudal rights over the local peasantry. Spain and Portugal had not had a true landed oligarchy before, but now with vast new territories opening up, thanks to conquests over the Moors, it acquired a landed elite for the first time. This landholding oligarchy—rich, pampered, reactionary—would serve to retard Spanish and Portuguese as well as later Latin American development until well into the twentieth century.[10]

The Reconquest was not just a military campaign, it was also, first and foremost, a religious crusade. The tolerance that had once characterized relations among Christian, Muslim, and Jew now gave way to intolerance and fanaticism. In this conflict no quarter was asked or given. People simply slaughtered each other. Violence became a way of life. The slogan was "Death to the infidel!"—infidels being Moors and non-Christians. As the Reconquest waxed and waned over the centuries, there were peaceful and more-or-less tolerant periods as well, but the larger pattern of mutual intolerance—of not only fighting one's foes but slaughtering them on religious grounds, torturing them, brutalizing them—had now been set. Eventually this pattern would lead to the establishment of the Inquisition, by which all heretics from the official belief systems (religious and political) were forced to recant their heretical beliefs and convert to Catholicism or else be persecuted, tortured, and driven out. All such mayhem was committed in the name of purifying Spanish blood, race, and religion of all supposedly corrosive and impure elements.[11]

The Reconquest, paradoxically, also provided Iberia with its concept of liberties, a concept that was unlike the Anglo-American one and that gave rise in modern times to continuing differences over human rights between the two areas. In Iberia, the concept of liberty (*fuero*) was forged on the frontier between the contending Christian and Muslim armies. Towns, religious orders and monasteries, the sheepherders' guild, and other groups would negotiate with the contending armies over land, over self-government, over the right to be left alone and to stay out of the fighting. Or they might ally themselves in one form or another with one of the marauding armies in return for autonomy and a charter of independence from a local or regional ruler. Such agreements often took the form of semifeudal charters: assistance in fighting the Moors in return for varying degrees of independence from whatever state or regional entity was emerging behind the frontier. This sense of "liberty" was quasi feudal in origin: an obligation in return for an obligation. Further, the notion of rights here was also feudal, involving group rights (towns, orders, guilds, eventually universities, and other groups), not individual rights as in the Anglo-American common law tradition.[12] These divergences over the meaning of the term "rights" would continue to plague understanding between the Hispanic countries (Latin America as well as Iberia) and the Anglo-American one to this day.[13]

One can also detect in this conception of group rights, building upon the earlier Roman law tradition, the origins of the Iberian–Latin American notion of corporatism. Not corporatism in some twentieth-century fascist form but in its historical form, what Ronald Newton called "natural corporatism" because it went so far back historically that it was "present at the creation" of the Iberian state, often prior to or coterminous with it.[14] The Iberian emphasis on group rights over individual rights in these early, nascent stages of nationhood led over time to the chartering of these groups as corporations with their own symbols, flags, insignia, uniforms, initiation rites, apprenticeship, and rules of self-government. Eventually, as a Spanish and Portuguese state or states began to take shape, these groups would also be represented before the crown or in the *cortes* (parliament)—but, again, as groups, not on the basis of individual representation or one-person, one-vote. And the notion of groups of interests incorporated into the state or in some contractually defined relation with it is precisely what corporatism meant.[15]

Finally, then, the Reconquest helped define the character of the Spanish state itself. The Spanish and Portuguese states—still inchoate, decentralized, organized on a regional basis, and not well institutionalized—often were militaristic, intolerant, top-down and authoritarian, organic, and corporatist. These societies were organized chiefly for war, and war against the Moorish infidel; they were states organized not in happy, prosperous, peaceful, tolerant times but in the midst of bloody conflicts, conquest, and religious oppression.[16] Confronting an immense, chaotic, and seemingly ungovernable wilderness frontier, as Spain's foremost historian Claudio Sánchez Albernoz points out, it is no wonder that these Spanish conquerors—like their successors in the vast, chaotic wilderness of Latin America in later centuries—opted for an authoritarian, top-down regime that emphasized order and discipline.[17] It is, therefore, not surprising that the later, better organized, more consolidated Spanish and Portuguese states and, by extension, those in Latin America, which faced many of the same conditions of ungovernability, should continue to exhibit many of the same authoritarian, top-down, semifeudal, organic, and corporatist traits.

The Formation of the Spanish and Portuguese States

As the frontier moved progressively from north to south and the Moors were driven out, new, Christian, political entities began to emerge in the territories liberated from Moorish rule. At first these were limited to the northern provinces of León, Galicia, Old Castile, Navarre, the Basque provinces, Aragon, and Catalonia. But as the Reconquest expanded south, it came to encompass Valencia, New Castile, Extremadura, Murcia, and eventually Andalusia (the last Moorish stronghold) as well. The territory that came eventually to be known as Portugal was liberated from north to south as well. By 1492, with the fall of Córdoba, all of the peninsula had been liberated and was under Christian rule.[18]

The first kingdoms in Iberia, during the eleventh and twelfth centuries, were thus organized on a regional basis. They were relatively small, corresponding more or less to a Greek city-state or a large American county. That is, they had a single primate city or regional capital and a surrounding countryside. Portugal (then called Lusitania) was at this time only one of a half dozen regional kingdoms beginning to emerge in the peninsula. Only later would the centralized nation-state of Spain emerge out of this collection of smaller kingdoms, while Portugal continued as a separate and much smaller kingdom. Hence, to understand politics and governance as they eventually developed in Spain, Portugal, and ultimately Latin America, one must first understand the governmental principles of these early kingdoms.

The first thing to note is that these were all Christian kingdoms. That, after all, had been the chief stated purpose of the Reconquest: to recapture Iberia for Christianity. Hence, the early Spanish kingdoms would have to be organized on those Christian principles of organic unity, adherence to the true Christian faith, and subservience to godly authority and the laws of the Bible as outlined in chapter 2. There was no room for either religious or political tolerance and pluralism, particularly because the threat of a Muslim rollback of the Christian gains continued to loom. So these kingdoms would need to be vigilant against heresy and any questioning of religious or political truth and authority. The seeds of the Inquisition would be sown in this context of constant, looming threat. At the same time, the Roman Catholic Church evolved into a temporal power alongside the state, responsible for education, censorship, morality, and charity and in effect a branch of royal, state-building central authority.[19]

Second, the new kingdoms would need to be organic, unified, hierarchical, and authoritarian. They were faced not only with a powerful external threat, the Moors, but also with internal disorder, banditry, and lawlessness. The vast plains of central Spain were under no existing governmental authority, and chaos often reigned there. To counter these external and internal threats, the state would need to be strong, forceful, and disciplined—at least in its aspirations if not always in fact. The unitarian concept of the state derived from Plato and the Roman conception and became an ideal for which Spain and its colonies would strive. No loose ends, no checks and balances, no pluralism could be tolerated. All the parts had to be integrated in a unified manner. In keeping with the medieval ideal, every being had his place in a hierarchical social arrangement in the great chain of being of Saint Thomas. Anything less than absolute unity and authoritarian rule would be to risk the kingdom's integrity and its recapture by the Moors.[20]

Third, the new kingdoms were dominated by their elites: military, economic, religious. The elites were closely interrelated, often congealing within a single family or group of families (oligarchy) or within a single person. The kingdoms, after all, were formed out of military conquest, and frequently the conqueror, who could be a military order, a religious order, or a single man on horseback, would then have a right to the land as well as to the labor of those who lived on the land. The conquests and land takeovers were in turn sanctioned by the Catholic clergy, who often came from the same elite families. Conquest and settlement were then rewarded by the bestowing of royal titles—the beginning of the Spanish hereditary aristocracy. Military, political, eco-

nomic, and religious power was thus not only concentrated but interrelated, often literally so, giving rise to the Spanish aphorism that if
one had three sons the first under primogeniture would inherit the
land, the second would join a military order or (later) go into the army,
and the third would become a bishop.

A fourth feature of the emerging Iberian states during this period
was the corporate organization of society and politics.[21] As in medieval
Europe in general, Spanish society was composed of a variety of independent corporate bodies—nobility, church, guilds, universities, military orders, and the like—that cherished their independence, sought to
increase it, and fiercely resisted efforts at encroachment. There were few
crosscutting loyalties among these various corporations; their members seldom sought support from others and only rarely would a person be a member of more than one group. In this sense Spanish society
was not only hierarchically organized on class and social lines, but also
vertically segregated into separate pillars, hermetically sealed, meeting only at the top. The members of the several corporate units were
concerned only with their own private interests, and each looked to a
wise, forceful, and Solomonic monarch for justice, unity, and the protection of their separate rights. The only institution that bridged these
highly segregated corporate groups was the extended family, which existed only at the local or regional level. Hence, at this time, once the
Moors had been disposed of, there was (more or less) stability at the local
level but instability at the national. Coalescing in this manner, Spain
experienced a transformation from the medieval to the modern world
that was both delayed and different from that of the rest of Europe.
This corporate ideal, with each person locked in place and representation based on function—the medieval answer to the question of order—
has by no means disappeared in either Iberia or Latin America.[22]

Corporatism in Iberia was aided and given legitimacy by the revival
of Roman law in Europe at this time. For it was precisely during this era
of the formation of the early Iberian nations that Roman law began to
be rediscovered and revived. Moreover, Roman law and Roman legal
precepts had by now been overlain with a particularly Christian, Thomistic philosophy and theology that not only reinforced the Roman concepts but gave them divine sanction.[23] Roman law, now with its Thomistic overlay, emphasized the hierarchical as well as the corporate or
sectoral organization of society. In contrast to the English common law
stemming (during approximately the same period) from the Magna

Carta, Roman and now Spanish Christian law emphasized group rights over individual rights. That is, one acquired rights not automatically or simply as a result of birth, but through one's membership in a group. In contrast to Jefferson's idea in the American Declaration of Independence that man is born with certain inalienable rights, in Spain such rights (*fueros,* or, in Portuguese, *foros*) had to be conferred. They were ceded from above—that is, by the emerging states or kingdoms in Iberia and the elites who controlled them. And if fueros were conferred instead of being inalienable, that meant they could also be revoked. From this point on, the corporative organization of society and politics was closely bound up with the formative foundations of Spanish and Portuguese history.[24]

The notion of corporate group rights as analyzed above implies severe limits on fundamental liberties and fits nicely with the emphasis on organic unity and authoritarianism discussed previously. If rights had to be conferred from above and then only to deserving groups, it implies a controlling and policing over these groups and the exercise of their liberties. At least three levels of policing functions were operating here, serving to limit even those frontier rights that were conferred. The first was largely self-policing; unless one was among the deserving (Catholic, a believer, non-Muslim), one could not qualify for even a minimum level of rights. That left not only Muslims but also Jews and Gypsies out of Spanish society and enjoying almost no rights whatsoever. From this time, hence, stems the notion that to be Spanish, it is absolutely essential to be Catholic.

A second policing function was performed by the corporate group itself, which oversaw its own membership and had an elaborate training, civilizing function. By a person's admission to the group and then by his rise through the ranks of apprentice, journeyman, and master craftsman, the group, guild, or corporation (the terms are often used interchangeably) controlled not only his economic or craft training but also his moral, political, and behavioral life. And third, the state also regulated, licensed, and policed the activities of the group itself. Because without being licensed or granted juridical personality by the state, the group could not function in the political process. And, lacking such recognition, the group had no standing before the law and could legitimately be repressed. Similarly, unless one was a member of a legitimately organized group, one had almost no rights at all. The

limits on such rights and on group activity served as a powerful instrument of authoritarian control.

The principal corporations during this period were military, religious, geographic, and cultural as well as economic. The military orders (Alcántara, Hospitalers, Calatrava, Santiago, Templars) often led
the fight against the Moors. As they pushed the Moors south, the orders acquired the right to the lands and to the labor of those living on
the lands that they conquered. They also received glory for their conquests and the granting of juridical recognition to them as a corporate
group by an emerging state with which the military orders were sometimes in competition. To this era dates the notion common in Iberia
and Latin America that the military is before and above the state in
time and even in legitimacy, and therefore that the American conception of strict civilian control over the military is inappropriate in the
Iberian and Latin American context.[25]

Similarly the religious orders: they often considered themselves
above and before the state, both in terms of time and according to
God's proper ordering of the universe. But if religion was above and
prior to the state, and if the state in this pre-Reformation era of Catholic orthodoxy was presumed to be infused with and governed by Christian principles, how could there ever be separation of church and state
in the American sense? Moreover, a number of these religious orders
were simultaneously fighting orders and sometimes overlapped with
the military orders. As they freed more lands from the Moors, the religious orders, too, received the right to the land and labor of the territories liberated. So the Roman Catholic Church and its various orders
also became large landowners and governors of immense provinces, a
part of an emerging feudal (but militarized feudalism) system of classes,
corporations, and estates. The Church and its various components, including monasteries, orders, and sisterhoods, emerged as one of the
major corporate bodies (really, a variety of bodies) of the realm, often
claiming authority, juridical right, and certainly moral standing above
that of the mere emerging states.[26]

As the frontier between Christian and Muslim Spain gradually
shifted from north to south over the centuries and as the territories
under Christian control expanded, new towns and regional governments came into existence in the newly liberated lands. Often it was the
towns and their peoples as well as the military and religious orders that

carried the battle against the Moors. The towns, therefore, also sought recognition from the state and a corporate charter as free towns. The awarding of such charters paralleled the grant of fiefs to the military and religious orders and to the elite families. These charters or fueros, although varying in details, usually bestowed autonomy and substantial self-government on the towns, in return for loyalty and feudal obligations to the crown and the obligation to defend the territory under their control from the Moors. So the towns took their place among the most important, self-governing entities or "corporations" in the realm. By the fifteenth century, there were upward of 1,360 villages and towns in Spain, of which 650 were free, or had charters of autonomy.[27]

Finally, there were economically oriented corporations, commonly known as guilds. The most prominent of these initially was the *mesta*, or sheepherders' guild.[28] Sheep raising and the wool that came from it were major Spanish industries in the Middle Ages. Massive seasonal migrations of sheep were involved, from the harsh, cold plains of Old Castile in the fall and winter to the more southerly grazing areas of New Castile, and then back again in the spring and summer. In the course of these treks, sheepherders crossed hundreds of miles of range and needed to protect their rights of access to and migration across these lands. So this powerful lobby also negotiated a contract with the emerging state or states that gave them access and autonomy in return for feudal obligations of loyalty and service. During the twelfth and thirteenth centuries, hundreds of other guilds organized themselves and received a charter from the state in the same or similar corporatist fashion as had the military and religious orders and the towns.[29]

At the dawn of the twelfth century, therefore, the following situation prevailed: (1) more and more territory in Iberia was being liberated from the Moors; (2) occupying this new space was an expanding number of emerging states or kingdoms organized on a regional basis; (3) within or sometimes overlapping with these emerging regional states was a growing and quite varied panoply of corporate entities— military orders, religious orders, towns and local governments, guilds, eventually universities, and other groups—usually in some kind of contractual relationship with the state; (4) a sense of rights or liberties evolved that was forged on the frontier and, as indicated, was focused on group or corporate rights over individual rights. Now the questions before us here are how did a truly national Spanish and Portuguese state emerge out of this swirl of often competing kingdoms, corporations, and regional entities? what is the nature of the Spanish and Por- tuguese state systems? and as a result, how do the Spanish and Portu- guese political systems differ from the Anglo-American ones?

The Kingdoms of Spain and Portugal

As regional kingdoms came into existence and expanded the territories under their control, they occasionally began to call meetings of corporate representatives as a way of consulting, taxing, and allowing expression of their many and often diverse interests. The first parliaments (cortes in Spanish) in the Western world were called not in England, but in Spain. The first cortes in Spain met in Aragon in 1163; the second was convoked in the Kingdom of León, where the revolt against the Moors had begun, in 1188—in both cases several decades before the calling of the first British parliament in 1215. These were followed by the cortes of Catalonia in 1218, Portugal in 1254, Aragon again in 1274, Valencia in 1283, and Navarra in 1300. The purposes of these early corteses were basically to preserve and protect the rights of the groups represented and to offer allegiance to the crown and to assist it in governing and in the struggle against the Moors.[30]

It is important to recognize in order to understand future Iberian and Latin American politics and representation that these corteses were organized on the basis of group or corporate representation, not individual (one person, one vote) representation. Moreover, the representatives were appointed from above rather than elected by popular expression. These concepts were essentially feudal rather than modern and democratic. The groups represented included the orders (military and clerical), the corporations, and professional groups. They were brought together hierarchically in terms of estates: ecclesiastics, nobles, and popular (that is, representatives of the towns). Given the economic, religious, and political power of these corporate groups, it was thought the better part of prudence on the part of the crown to consult their leaders on such issues as war, justice, administration, and taxes. Later Iberian corporatist ideologies argued that such corporate representation developed in Spain and Portugal as the counterpart to political parties in the English tradition. And, they claimed, there is no necessary reason to assume parties are more developed or modern than corporatism.[31]

Only elite groups were represented: clergy, nobility, the military orders, and the leaders of the towns, that is, the good men, not the rabble;
there was a strict, Thomistic hierarchy of classes. Common folk were
not represented and there was no popular suffrage. Instead, the leaders
of the group, usually with the approval of the crown, chose the person
whom they wanted to speak for and represent the group before the
cortes. These spokesmen were known as *procuradores*. Their job was to
represent the corporate body before the king, not to speak for the common people. While applauding the principle of representation that the
corteses inculcated, one should not operate under the delusion that
these were democratic institutions, or even that they could eventually
grow into democratic bodies: they could not and did not.

Neither did the Spanish and Portuguese corteses ever develop any
independent, rule-making, taxing, or royal power-checking authority,
unlike the British parliament. They met irregularly. They had no independent life of their own but met only when the king called them into
session at his convenience. They had no staff, no permanent home, no
institutionalized role. For a time in the thirteenth century the corteses
seemed for a short period to be increasing in independent power and
influence, but that honeymoon was short-lived. They were convened
less and less frequently; eventually the crown dispensed with their
services altogether. By the time of the Hapsburgs, a centralized, bureaucratic state had largely replaced the decentralized and corporately representative (but not necessarily democratic) state of earlier centuries.[32]

We are now in a position to begin to understand the dynamics of
the Spanish and Portuguese political systems as they emerged from the
thirteenth through the fifteenth centuries and which carried a powerful legacy for future development, both in Iberia and in Latin America.
On the one hand there was the crown or, more accurately, crowns (the
several kingdoms) seeking to enhance their legitimacy and expand
their authority over often unruly and chaotic territories, while at the
same time keeping the Moors at bay. On the other hand, there were the
myriad corporate interests—towns, guilds, military orders, religious orders, eventually universities (Salamanca, Coimbra) and other groups as
well—and their representation in the cortes, seeking to maintain their
independence from the state and protecting their positions through
corporate charters that, in return for loyalty and feudal (including war-
fighting) obligations, attempted to preserve the group's autonomy and
self-government.

The conflict between aggrandizing, centralizing royal power and a variety of autonomous corporate units gave rise to a distinctly Spanish form of contract theory—what we would call constitutionalism. This was not contract theory in the sense of the seventeenth-century English philosopher John Locke's *Second Treatise on Government* or the Mayflower Compact: individual citizens coming together and agreeing democratically to give up some rights to a very limited government in return for protection and services. Rather the Spanish sense of contract involved an already established or emerging system of absolutism but limited somewhat by God's eternal law and custom—the latter including royal respect for corporate group rights. There was no idea of limited government, popular sovereignty, or nascent democracy here— only a quasi-feudal sense of monarchy held in rein by Christian obligations and customary group rights.

This sense of contract involving royal or state authority, regional autonomous units, and corporate group rights waxed and waned in Spanish history. When royal authority dominated, it was called monarchism and eventually royal absolutism; when the regions or corporate groups had legally guaranteed autonomy, it was called democracy, representative government, constitutionalism, or the compact state. But this is a far cry from democracy in the modern, individualistic, one-person, one-vote sense, with guaranteed, inalienable human and civil rights. The tension between corporate group autonomy and encroaching state authority would long be present in Spanish and Portuguese political life, and it resurfaced in the mid-1970s following dictator Franco's death and even in the Constitution of 1977. But this Iberian concept of contract theory, while potentially more decentralized, more or less representative, and pluralistic, is very different from what is meant by constitutionalism in the Anglo-American tradition.[33]

It was an epic struggle waged over the centuries. It was often chaotic and disorganized, not quite the clear-cut struggle as portrayed here in a purposely oversimple, ideal-type model. Moreover, the struggle occurred at the same time as the crusade against the Moors was taking place. At least two major and numerous minor struggles were occurring simultaneously and often overlapping in strange ways.

For the Spanish/Portuguese struggle was not only against the Moors; often it involved conflict within and between the Christian forces themselves. For example, Portuguese independence is usually dated from 1143, but that date marks not some epic Portuguese victory over

the Moors. Instead it celebrates the emerging kingdom of Portugal re-
sisting and fending off the expansionist tendencies of León, one of the
emerging (and neighboring) *Spanish* kingdoms. León itself, in turn, was
eventually absorbed into the even larger Spanish kingdom of Castile.
Only later were the Portuguese able to turn their attention again to the
defeat of the remaining Moorish enclaves farther south, even while
simultaneously having to hold off León/Castile's virtually continuous
assaults.[34]

Even with these qualifications, however, the overall pattern of this
titanic internal political struggle remained clear. On the one side was
royal authority in the several kingdoms of Iberia seeking to consolidate, centralize, and expand its power. On the other side was the influence of the various corporations (military, religious, economic, university) and of local political power and their representatives in the
corteses, seeking to maintain the hard-earned rights, liberties, and autonomy won over decades and even centuries of struggle.

But note the terms of this classic encounter: The advocates of corporate rights and local autonomy sought to defend their positions as
standing for classic Hispanic liberties. But liberties in this context had
a particularly Hispanic and, to Anglo-American eyes, strange flavor.
There was no mention here of individual civil or human rights. Rather,
the emphasis was entirely on the medieval concept of group or corporate rights. This involved an essentially medieval political system based
on contract: service and loyalty in return for justice, protection, and
order.[35] Over the long run, it is often argued, the emphasis on group
rights might have evolved as it did in England into an emphasis on modern, individual human and civil rights; but the fact is that in Iberia it
did not. Rights (when they were discussed at all) continued to be discussed only in this medieval, premodern sense. Never, until recently,
did a modern sense of individual rights develop; and in Spain and Portugal even that sense is still circumscribed by the emphasis on group or
corporate rights. And of course, it would therefore be this medieval,
feudalistic sense of group rights that was carried over to Latin America.

This debate over corporate group liberties was conducted within and
among elites and had nothing to do with genuine democracy. One group
wanted more centralized power and the other advocated decentralization, but both groups were led and dominated by the upper classes.
Never in this debate over local fueros and group rights were the masses

or popular sectors ever consulted; they had no vote. Again, the struggle must be portrayed as premodern and intraelite. Never until modern times did the notions of popular sovereignty or democracy develop.

There are few exceptions to this last statement—and they are relatively weak ones. First, from Thomas Aquinas on (Aquinas's political philosophy, revived during this period, provided Christian justification for the hierarchical, top-down, Roman-imperium system Spain and Portugal were evolving into anyway), there was the idea that rulers had to govern justly and according to God's commands and for the common good. That meant humanely, paternalistically, and within the constructs of a Christian commonwealth. Rulers could not become tyrants; they were not supposed to run roughshod over fundamental (corporate) liberties. If they violated these injunctions and did become tyrants, then presumably their subjects had a right to resist such usurpations or to rebel against them—although this latter doctrine did not emerge until later, mainly in the writings of the sixteenth-century Jesuit Juan de Mariana. Second, there was Seneca's notion of the gift and its development in Iberia as an elaborate system of mutual, even contractual obligations (see chapter 2). Presumably that meant that if one party failed to live up to its obligations of governing justly, the other party would no longer feel an obligation to obey. But these doctrines, though occasionally cited, were seldom if ever invoked. Meanwhile, Spain and Portugal would continue on the path to absolutist, centralized, authoritarian rule.

During the thirteenth and parts of the fourteenth centuries, the epic struggle of Hispanic politics seemed to be at a standstill. Centralized royal authority expanded and consolidated its power but only very gradually. Meanwhile, corporate group life and the system of fueros seemed to be flourishing. Many new guilds and corporations were recognized and chartered by the state, and in many areas of Spain independent military and religious orders constituted almost separate sovereignties, holding out against encroaching state power. More and more towns were acquiring charters of greater independence. It was during these centuries that the corteses continued to be called and served as something of a check on royal absolutism. And in many Spanish legal documents of the time, such as the compilation of laws known as the Siete Partidas of King Alfonso X "el Sabio" (Alfonso the Wise), the group rights and autonomies emphasized earlier were incorporated into the basic law of the land and seemed to be acquiring the status of constitutional precepts. (Actually, Alfonso believed there were already too many fueros, and his efforts at codifying them both reduced their numbers and led to greater centralization.) Some authors have seen in these group charters, reciprocal rights and duties, medieval corporatism, and the idea that the king, too, was subject to the law the Spanish equivalent of English constitutionalism. The Partidas, however, assumed the basic element of society to be not individualist, Lockean, and atomistic but organic, Christian, Thomistic, societal, and corporatist.[36]

Over the course of the fourteenth and fifteenth centuries, furthermore, these historic liberties, which might have served as the foundation for later Spanish democracy, gradually gave way. Power in Spain and Portugal came to be increasingly centralized, in part because the war (crusade) against the Moors continued. More and more power was concentrated in the hands of monarchy. The corteses were called and met less frequently. The doctrine of absolute monarchy or royal absolutism was introduced and reached perhaps its fullest flowering in Spain. Gradually the rights of the heretofore autonomous towns and corporations were subsumed under the mantle of royal authority. No single battle or conflict produced this result; rather it was the product of a gradual enhancement of royal status and prerogatives and the corresponding gradual decline in the rights and independence of local and corporate groups.[37]

Two large-scale trends were occurring simultaneously. The first was the one described above: away from autonomous local units and self-governing corporations toward increasingly absolutist monarchy. But the second, perhaps equally important, involved the consolidation of the Spanish monarchies themselves. Whereas before there were upward of thirteen separate Iberian kingdoms, now these several kingdoms began to join in ever larger kingdoms. León joined with Old Castile and, as the Moors were pushed further south, with New Castile in the heartland of central Spain (including the area of present-day Madrid) and eventually with the kingdoms in the south and southwest of Spain as well. Similarly Aragon at first absorbed Navarra in the north and eventually joined the kingdoms of Catalonia and Valencia in the east as well. So in addition to the rise of royal authority over corporate and local group rights, royal authority itself was being increasingly consolidated into fewer and fewer units.

Ferdinand, Isabella, and the "Hapsburg Model"

By the middle of the fifteenth century, Iberia was divided into three major kingdoms. To the north and east was Aragon, the most cosmopolitan of the kingdoms, facing France and the Mediterranean, with a flourishing culture, trade, and civilization. In the center was Castile, the heartland of the peninsula and destined eventually to dominate it, a vast, often unruly area of wide-open spaces, immense panoramas, and frontier justice and not nearly so cosmopolitan, organized, or cultured as Aragon. To the west was Portugal or Lusitania, already emerging as a separate and consolidated nation-state, with a politics, language, and culture considerably different from those of the rest of Iberia. For centuries these kingdoms had vied and interacted not only with each other but also, as indicated, with autonomous and largely self-governing corporate units within their own borders as well as smaller, often separatist kingdoms that these larger kingdoms had uneasily absorbed.

The stage was thus set for one of the most significant dynastic marriages of all time. It brought together the scion of the Aragonese dynasty, Ferdinand, a cultured, sophisticated, and wily monarch whom the Florentine political theorist Machiavelli used as the model for his pragmatic, skillful, amoral ruler in *The Prince,* and Isabella, the provincial and devotedly Catholic queen of Castile, who was no less clever, manipulative, and skillful politically than Ferdinand. Their marriage contract provided that during their lifetimes the two kingdoms would remain separate, with Ferdinand ruling in Aragon and Isabella in Castile, but that they would live in Aragon and that upon their deaths their heirs would rule over a united kingdom combining Aragon and Castile. Later efforts would be made through dynastic intermarriage to bring Portugal into a unified kingdom, but those efforts—a fascinating story in their own right but not of central relevance to this book—ended in failure. Henceforth, then, there would be only two kingdoms in Iberia: a more or less unified Spain and a separate kingdom of Portugal.

Of the many interesting aspects of Ferdinand's and Isabella's rule, I focus mainly on their internal political strategies to achieve unity and centralization. The result of the centralizing, unifying steps was to eliminate all those corporate groups and autonomous powers analyzed earlier and thus to pave the way for Hapsburg absolutism. With this elimination also went any hopes for future Spanish or Portuguese democracy. And in its place in the next century came what I have termed the Hapsburg model of arbitrary and authoritarian political and economic organization.[38]

Because Aragon was already more cosmopolitan as well as unified, we concentrate here on Castile and on Isabella, one of the most Machiavellian rulers who has ever lived. She was a practitioner of Thomas Hobbes: the creator of Europe's first truly centralized, leviathan state. Isabella's overriding goal was to unify the kingdom of Castile, to prepare it for its eventual unification with Aragon. To that end she engaged in a series of skillfully executed political moves that are breathtaking in scope and accomplishment. For example, Isabella largely destroyed the emerging Castilian oligarchy as an autonomous political force by stripping its members of their lands and peasants, luring them out of their castles by giving them titles, and bringing them to her court, where she could keep her eye on them. Further, Isabella revoked the charters of the previously autonomous military orders, lured them to her court, where she reorganized them as a national army, and then sent them out to fight other centers of resistance to her centralizing efforts. By these means she succeeded not only in eliminating these recalcitrants but also in killing many of the orders' military leaders.[39]

Isabella's revocation of the charters of the independent towns and municipalities provoked rebellion, which she moved quickly to crush in a campaign that was not completed until 1520, after her death, when the last of the so-called *comunero* revolts was irrevocably and permanently put down. Another of Isabella's policies, the Inquisition, is usually thought of as a cruel, prejudicial attempt by Spain (and later Portugal) to rid the country of Jews, Moors, and other dissidents or to force their conversion to Catholicism. The Inquisition did have those effects; but, in addition, it centralized religious authority in Spain, thereby reducing or eliminating the independent autonomy of Spain's numerous religious brotherhoods and sisterhoods, many of which had been largely self-governing up to this point. In this sense, the Inquisition was like many other of Isabella's policies: it was meant to eliminate the power of localized authority and independent corporate groups and concentrate virtually total power in the hands of the central state. The idea of a pact or contract—and with it all possibilities for constitutionalism (albeit Spanish style) and limited representative government—gave way to absolute monarchy.[40]

When Isabella died in 1504, her work of centralization, unification, and concentrated power was still incomplete. The comunero resistance had still not been completely crushed, and there were still small centers of resistance and autonomy elsewhere in the country. And, of course, it would require time before the unification of Castile and Aragon was complete—a conflict that lives on today in the rivalry between Madrid and Barcelona and the persistent push for Catalan autonomy. It is said that in the early sixteenth century Spain was unified but not fully united.

Nevertheless, Isabella, for good or ill, had made enormous strides toward unifying the kingdom. In a sense, she created Spain—that is, as a unified nation-state, Europe's first unified nation-state. But she also completely changed the model of Spanish society and politics. Heretofore, that model had involved, alongside royal authority, a decentralized, pluralistic polity with autonomous power centers, the corporate organization of society, a representative (at least of the major groups) cortes, and at least the prospect and possibility of providing for democratic, popular rule. But now it became centralized, monolithic, absolutist, based on divine right, with no independent power centers, and all hopes for democratic, representative, popular rule wiped out. The idea of a constitutional charter, as exemplified in the concept of the fuero and as represented in the cortes, yielded to centralized absolutism. The process would be further consolidated, centralized, and institutionalized by the succeeding Hapsburg monarchy.[41]

The heir to the Castilian throne following Isabella's death was her daughter Juana, known popularly as La Loca (The crazy one). Juana was married to Philip, an Austrian Hapsburg, the first in Spanish history. Most of their children were sickly or died at an early age, frustrating their efforts to cement their dynastic relations by bringing Portugal into the kingdom. One of their sons, Charles, was healthy and vigorous. He had been born and educated in Flanders, then a part of the far-flung Hapsburg empire. His parents, the playboy Philip and the crazy Juana, had died early; hence, when Ferdinand, the adroit husband of Isabella, died in 1516, Charles inherited the thrones both of his grandmother's Castile and his grandfather's Aragon.

As the first Hapsburg ruler of a united Spain, Charles I arrived in Spain from Flanders. He spoke only Flemish; neither he nor any of his advisers spoke Spanish. Sailing for Spain across the Bay of Biscay, they were caught in a storm and got lost—in both senses of that term. They finally landed on an obscure beach on the north coast, where the local residents thought they were pirates—and in a sense they were that, too.

Because of deaths among the Austrian Hapsburgs, within two years of being crowned king of Spain, Charles was crowned as Holy Roman Emperor, responsible not just for Spain but for greater Austria, large parts of Italy, the Low Countries (Holland and Belgium) as well as most of Latin America. Thereafter, he would be known as Charles I of Spain and Charles V of the Holy Roman Empire. He and his heirs would be primarily concerned with the fate of the Hapsburg family, its larger empire, and the preservation of absolute Catholic orthodoxy throughout Europe in the face of the rising Protestant tide brought about by the Reformation. Indeed, one of the key elements in the Hapsburgs' ruination of Spain was the draining of its treasury as well as of the gold and silver of the Americas in an ultimately futile attempt to snuff out the Protestant heresy everywhere. This new religious crusade not only bankrupted Spain, but also meant the vast wealth of Latin America flowed through Spain, without creating any manufacturing or industry there, to Holland and Britain, where Spain bought its armaments and where, therefore, the industrial revolution began. But Spain benefited not at all.

The Hapsburg monarchy ruled Spain for the next two hundred years, during virtually the entire sixteenth and all of the seventeenth centuries. It is not our purpose to trace here either that period in any detail—fascinating though it is—or the long-term decline of Spain that set in that led to once-powerful Spain being described as the "sick man of Europe"—during which its once vast empire was destroyed and divided up among the powers. Rather, our purpose here is to describe the elements of the Hapsburg model that came into existence in the mother countries of Spain and Portugal over these two centuries and that was then exported to the new world.

The Hapsburg model consisted of the following five elements:

1. Politically, an absolutist, hierarchical, authoritarian, top-down, bureaucratic system based on the concept of a God-centered universe and a monarchy ruling by divine right. If and when (rarely) any representative or consultative considerations filtered into this otherwise absolutist system, they were based on the Middle Ages legacy of group or corporate rights rather than on any genuinely democratic foundation.
2. Economically, a similarly statist and top-down system based on mercantilism and aimed at exploiting and draining the considerable wealth of the colonies.
3. Socially, a rigid, hierarchical, two-class system in which elite groups presumably received their wealth, land, and cattle ac-

cording to God's just design for the universe and lower-class elements were obliged to accept their station in life for the same
otherworldly reasons. In the new world, class considerations
would be reinforced by racial criteria, with a small, white, Hispanic elite at the top and a huge Indian or African mass at the
bottom.

4. Religiously, Catholic orthodoxy and absolutism in their medieval and absolutist forms prevailed, and the Roman Catholic
Church served as an instrument and handmaiden of the political authority.

5. Culturally and intellectually, a closed, orthodox, stifling society (despite the flowering of Spain's literature in the sixteenth
century), a society whose intellectual life was based also on
Catholic orthodoxy, rote memorization of revealed truth, and a
deductive system of reasoning that stunted imagination as well
as all scientific, experimental activity.[42]

Note how closely these elements correspond to Greek, Roman, and
Thomistic conceptions. And these were the dominant institutions not
only of Spain and Portugal but also of their colonies in the New World.

Chapter 4

Spain and Portugal in America

The Colonial Heritage

The Christian Reconquest of the Iberian peninsula from the Moors brought Spain and Portugal tardily back into the orbit of prevailing west European culture and civilization. They were no longer Moorish and [North] African but Christian and, therefore, Western. But in their haste to be restored to the Western, Christian world, Spain and Portugal may have, to borrow a Freudian term, overcompensated: for in the course of the later Reconquest and under Isabella, Ferdinand, and the Hapsburgs, they resurrected and then strengthened medieval and feudal institutions that they identified with Western Christianity but that were already beginning to fade elsewhere in the West. And it is these already faded and outdated medieval institutions that the Iberian countries took to the New World, where they not only survived but received a new lease on life in the two-class and caste-ridden, rigidly hierarchical and stratified, quasi-feudal societies that grew up in Latin America.[1]

As a result of the almost constant state of warfare in Iberia for nearly seven centuries, Spain and Portugal were already lagging behind the rest of Europe in terms of institutional development. More than any other major country in western Europe, Spain and Portugal remained generally in the background of slowly advancing European civilization. Forced to catch up in the later Middle Ages, they sought to resurrect and revive what was already dying elsewhere. There was no "waning of the Middle Ages" in fourteenth- and fifteenth-century Iberia as there was elsewhere in Europe, no Renaissance and then Enlightenment; instead, medievalism was restored, updated, and fortified. As Luís

Weckman has written, "Spain was able to transmit to America, as a living product and not as a dead tradition, many of her medieval accomplishments."[2] Hence, feudalism and the Middle Ages came to Latin America not moribund but fresh and destined to live on and on.

The discovery and conquest of the Americas by Spain and Portugal was a direct continuation of the two countries' centuries-long Reconquest of the peninsula from the Moors. The coincidence of the dates is not accidental: 1492 was the year not only of the final Spanish victory over the Moors, but also only a few months later of the beginning of the conquest of America. These were not discreet events; rather, they were part and parcel of a continuous process. The energy, crusading spirit, militarism, missionary fervor, and social and political institutions that had carried Spain to victory over the Moors were now carried over into its conquest of the Americas. Even more subtle and powerful is to recall how the early kingdoms of late-medieval Spain had rewarded the conquistadores with noble titles, grants of land, and the right to the labor of the persons living on those lands. With Spain itself beginning to run short of frontier land for the taking and of peasants to work the land, these practices could now be carried over to the New World, where each conquistador (they were often the second sons of good families who could not under primogeniture inherit their family's lands) could have bestowed upon him or bestow upon himself a royal title, receive a grant of land the size of a Spanish kingdom, and possess endless "peasants" in the form of the native Indian population. These status considerations may have been as important as any other motivation in the Spanish and Portuguese conquests of vast territories in the Americas and elsewhere. In this way not only could a conquistador continue to live like a feudal lord, but the certainty, Catholicism, absolutes, and feudalism of Spain's Middle Ages could live on. Indeed, that is the way to view Latin America: as an offshoot of the West but as a particular feudal, Hispanic, medieval reflection of the West, circa 1500 and thus premodern.[3]

Latin America came into Western civilization through particularly Spanish/Portuguese forms and institutions. And these institutions were of a specific sort: premodern, feudal, medieval. Latin America was a projection of the Iberian Middle Ages; indeed, in Latin America the Middle Ages found their last expression. The Spanish and Portuguese institutions brought to America were thus not just Hispanic or a reflection of *Hispanismo* in a superficial, ephemeral sense but more fundamentally the reflection of a powerful, common, long-term, historical tradition, social structure, and even political culture that cut across all class and corporate lines.[4] The conquest of the Americas should thus be viewed as an extension of the Reconquest and of its medieval, premodern character. In its emphasis on preserving and extending hierarchy, rank, and status, the encomienda system, the power of the medieval church, a moral and ethical view of politics, and so on, the conquest was anticapitalist, anti-utilitarian, anti-individualistic, and, overall, antimodern. As the great Venezuelan historian Mariano Picón-Salas has written, "Spain remained under the kingdom of God, while elsewhere in Europe the kingdom of man had begun."[5]

Given the times and circumstances of absolutist, quasi-feudal, late-medieval Spain and Portugal, it is not surprising that they would establish their American colonies as mirror images, with variations, of the mother countries. What is surprising is that these semifeudal institutions lasted so long—through three centuries of colonial rule, through the transition in the eighteenth century from the Hapsburg to the Bourbon monarchy, on into the independence period of the nineteenth century, and in many respects into the early twentieth century, which is often referred to in Latin America as the twilight of the Middle Ages. The question is, Has Latin America remained locked in the feudal and medieval mold? or has it finally broken out of that mold and entered a new and democratic future?

Iberia on the Eve of the Discoveries

To fully understand the New World of the Americas that Columbus discovered, one must look back briefly at the Old World he left behind—and at the Old World institutions that were replicated in the New. At the close of the fifteenth century and the dawn of the sixteenth, what is perhaps most impressive is the conformity and solidarity that seemed to characterize life and spirit in Europe generally. No clear sense of national identity had emerged anywhere, although there were tendencies in those directions; the heavy shadow of a universal empire of beliefs and institutions persisted, as did the medieval dream of a reincarnation of the Holy Roman Empire. The structure of society remained essentially feudal and two-class, with a small aristocracy of nobles still standing on a vast pedestal of serfs and peasants—although in some countries cracks had begun to appear in this system and a small middle class had emerged.[6]

At least equally pronounced was the uniformity of ideological and religious beliefs. The Catholic orthodoxy of the Middle Ages still prevailed, the Protestant Reformation not having yet taken place. The spiritual leadership and superiority of the pope in Rome were still largely undisputed; no national or independent churches had as yet developed. No schismatic breaks had occurred within the established religion and little so far in the way of rival doctrines. In 1492 the spiritual unity of Europe held firm.

Much the same could be said for educational and intellectual life. All of Europe shared an acceptance of theology and philosophy as the highest forms of intellectual life. The method of reasoning was deductive rather than experimental and inductive. One began with God's revealed truth, natural law, Aristotelian truths (including the "natural" inequality of men) and logic, and the teachings of the Church fathers (Augustine, Aquinas), and one deduced everyday operating principles from these basics. Experimentation, observation, and the scientific method ushered in with Galileo, Copernicus, and Newton enjoyed no legitimacy; instead, human reason was viewed exclusively as the handmaiden of faith. The system of thought was closed, scholastic, and based on rote memorization of established, God-given truths.[7] And, of course, it was this deductive, scholastic system that was carried over to the New World, where it persisted while elsewhere newer, more scientific methodologies began to flower. As the historian Irving A. Leonard has written, "Everywhere the accepted method of seeking truth was philosophic, and it is this fundamental fact which must be emphasized in discussing the Hispanic American mind and science."[8] Leonard goes on to say, "The intellectual heritage of the middle ages passed virtually intact to Hispanic America, and it so influenced the later thought processes of that vast region that the authoritarian concept of truth and the scholastic method of demonstrating it still underlie the contemporary thinking of our southern neighbors."

Reflecting these fundamental conceptions, authoritarianism and royal absolutism prevailed in the political sphere. Under the medieval, scholastic conception all power was thought to derive from God. Kings and those in authority received their mandates from God, not from such modern and democratic conceptions as popular sovereignty or one-person, one-vote. Power, therefore, had to be hierarchical and was exercised from the top down: God, archangels, angels, monarchs, servants of the church, etc. Eventually, in the Thomistic hierarchy, one got down to men; but only certain types of men. Kings also received their authority from on high, as did landowners and other officials in positions of power. It is no accident that, even in the late twentieth century Francisco Franco was known as the Caudillo (strongman) of Spain by the grace of God, not by criteria of democratic elections or popular sovereignty.[9]

In the economic sphere the dominant concept was mercantilism. All the resources of the realm were to be used for the enrichment of the monarch. And the purpose of this wealth, under mercantilism, was not to develop the national economy but to accumulate it, put it in the national treasury, build it up but not reinvest it. Hence, the colonies had to be milked dry of their wealth and resources. Gold and silver were considered valuable in themselves, to be stored in the vaults, not invested in industry, entrepreneurship, and manufacturing. Indeed, under the prevailing Catholic conception of that time, interest, profit, and money making were equated with usury, which had been condemned by Saint Thomas as sinful, or with Jews and Protestants. Hence, gold and silver were to be accumulated because mere possession of these precious metals was defined as wealth, and land, cattle, and peasants were similarly to be accumulated as symbols of noble status, not employed productively or for profit. These are all feudal characteristics as distinct from modern ones.[10]

The sociopolitical structure of Spain and Portugal on the eve of the conquest of the Americas is central to the argument of this book. The historian Lyle N. McAlister writes that in the late fifteenth century, in addition to the monarchy, the constituent elements of Spanish society were groups and associations identifiable in terms of (1) ascribed functions or statuses largely determined by the considerations of hierarchy described earlier; (2) systems of shared values and attitudes associated with these statuses and similarly derived from Catholic teachings; and (3) distinct and unequal groups with "juridical personalities" expressed in general legal codes or special fueros, *ordenanzas,* and *reglamentos,* usually involving some degree of autonomy. McAlister goes on to emphasize that Spanish and Portuguese society continued to be conceived in organic and corporate terms, like the human body, with its several parts structurally and functionally interrelated and interdependent. The health of the body depended on the health and proper functioning of all its constituent parts, leaders as well as societal groups.[11]

The main institutions of Spanish and Portuguese society at this
time fell into two logical categories: the vestiges of the medieval estates

following Ferdinand's and Isabella's centralizing and controlling policies, and the functional corporations. In short, both class (hierarchical) and corporate (vertical) categories in society were present at the same time. The primary estates consisted of the noble, clerical, and common (towns). Note that the term "common" here does not mean its current usage of implying common, mass, and thus democratic man, but only the *homens bons* (elites) and the *organized* interests of the towns or group interests as regulated and hammered out in the system of fueros analyzed in the previous chapters. The system of estates was based on function as well as on religion and the so-called natural order. For example, as a result of the long military crusade of the Reconquest, the function of warrior was assigned a higher social value and was identified with the nobility.[12] The military was seen as both prestigious and essential because without it society would fall victim to predatory forces and social disintegration. These same attitudes concerning the special place of the military and the fear that without it anarchy and disintegration would set in were carried over to Latin America.

While the bearing of arms and military conquests were thus seen as honorable, such productive occupations as trade, agriculture, and manufacturing were seen as dishonorable. Honor and its attendant status, moreover, came to be seen as deriving not from merit but from lineage. Both the military function of the nobility and the status attendant thereto were juridically recognized in the right of noblehood, whereby the noble was exempted from paying taxes and making tributes, could not be imprisoned for debt or have his horse, arms, or residence confiscated, and could not be subject to "base punishments." Isabella had consolidated power in Castile by granting such titles to the nobility and luring its members to her courts while also stripping the elite families of much of their real power. Note also how this fuero de hidalguía also expanded the *system* of fueros to include the nobility as well as other corporate groups like the church, the military orders, the towns, the guilds, the universities, and the mesta.

Spanish and Portuguese society on the eve of the conquest, therefore, should be conceived as two parallel societal pyramids existing side by side. The one was based on hierarchy, rank, estate, and class. The other was based on corporate group rights. Both of these existed in a tenuous relationship with the crown or central authority, with the estates and corporate groups through their fueros having considerable autonomy for a time but later (just before the conquest) being subordi-

nated to centralizing royal power. Moreover, the two pyramids overlapped at various points: the nobility, church, and common were not
only functional estates but also corporations. Furthermore, *within* the
several corporations there were additional rank orderings based on
wealth, status, function, importance, and experience.[13]

The political system reflected these social structures. At the top was
the crown, now increasingly centralized and absolutist. The cortes as
well as the several corporate entities that had for long periods existed
in dynamic tensions with the crown now lost out in an epic struggle
lasting over centuries and culminating in the Catholic monarchs, Ferdinand and Isabella. In the place of these earlier representative and
consultative bodies there emerged a centralized system of royal agents
and bureaucratic councils of the realm. The royal agents were the personal agents of the crown and carried its authority into every issue and
locality in which their attention was called for. The royal councils were
bureaucratic bodies operating as the crown's agents and at its bequest.
This centralized, bureaucratic, absolutist system was just beginning to
come firmly into place, replacing the earlier and more representative
systems, at the time of the conquest. It would be further elaborated
and institutionalized by the incoming Hapsburg monarchy. And, of
course, it was this absolutist, top-down, and rigidly authoritarian political system that was copied in the New World.

Spain, Portugal, and their colonies in Latin America, in remaining
locked into medieval and feudal concepts, missed out on all the great
revolutionary transformations associated with modernization and the
modern world. These included the Protestant Reformation (which
Iberia not only missed out on but was manifestly, wholeheartedly opposed to) and the greater religious and political freedom and pluralism
to which it gave rise. The scientific revolution, too, passed them by as
they clung to an earlier scholasticism that accepted some newer empirical facts while denying their larger philosophical implications.
They went unaffected by the economic stirrings toward freer markets,
greater capitalism, and eventually the industrial revolution, while retaining an older mercantilism and feudalism. Because they refused to
change economically, Spain, Portugal, and their New World colonies
also missed out on the critical social changes that followed from economic modernization, for example, the growth of a new, self-reliant
middle class of independent farmers and entrepreneurs that might
have served as the basis for moderation and stability. And they were ill

equipped to join in the movement toward limited, democratic government begun in England and Holland; indeed, Spain and Portugal reverted during this period to greater authoritarian control and abandoned the system of mutual rights and responsibilities (fueros) as well as representation (cortes) built up in earlier centuries. Spain, Portugal, and Latin America, in short, would attempt to enter the modern world having none of the institutional or normative attributes that one associates with the modern age.[14]

The Conquest: 1492–1570

Christopher Columbus, sailing for the Spanish Catholic Monarchs Ferdinand and Isabella, is thought to have landed initially in 1492 on San Salvador, later rebaptized as Watling's Island, a small spit of land in the eastern Bahamas. But that atoll lacked gold and silver, and the indigenous population, seeking either to be helpful or, alternatively, to rid themselves quickly of Columbus and his ships, told the conquistadores that they could find the desired precious metals on the larger island farther south.

Columbus sailed around the larger island, which he promptly named Hispaniola (Little Spain) and left a small colony on the north coast. That colony, Isabella (named after the queen), was wiped out by the native population, so when Columbus returned on his second voyage the following year, he founded a new colony, Santo Domingo, on the southern coast. Hispaniola thus became the site of the first permanent European settlement in the New World. It was the initial step in what would become the Europeanization and westernization of much of the globe.

It was also on Hispaniola that Spain carried out the first social, political, and economic experiments in colonization and empire that would later be used to govern its vast empire throughout the Americas.[15] The political structure, as in Spain, was authoritarian, hierarchical, and top-down. The social structure, similarly derived from the Spanish model, was also hierarchical: the Spaniards quickly became the landed and economic elite, and the indigenous population was forced to work as slaves or a feudal peasant class. As the Indians died out—not so much from force of arms as from inhumane treatment and the diseases the Spaniards carried, for which the natives had no immunity—the Spaniards began to import a new slave class from Africa. Economically, the system was mercantilist and exploitive: the gold and silver of Hispaniola were drained away to fill the coffers of the Spanish crown; meantime, a slave-based, sugar plantation economy was put in place that was cruel and repressive and that reinforced the social–racial hierarchy. The Church blessed and lent legitimacy to the enterprise (although some individual priests like Bartolomé de Las Casas condemned the treatment of the Indians) and served as an arm of both the conquest and royal authority. As new institutions like hospitals, monasteries, and a university were established on Hispaniola, they followed the deductive, scholastic, Thomistic model of medieval Spain.

For a time early in the sixteenth century, Hispaniola and its capital, Santo Domingo, served as the administrative center of Spain's growing empire in the Americas. It was from Hispaniola that the conquests of the neighboring islands of Cuba and Puerto Rico were launched. These islands received the same imprint of Spanish institutions (authoritarianism, class/caste hierarchy, mercantilism and exploitation, enslavement of indigenous populations, and importation of African slaves, the Church as an arm of the conquest, scholastic, deductive methods) as the original colony on Hispaniola. Jamaica, the lesser Antilles, and the Spanish Main (the coast of present-day Venezuela and Colombia) were explored and claimed for the Spanish crown. Searching for the same short route to Asia that had been Columbus's quest, Spanish captains explored the coasts of Central America and Yucatan, and in 1513 Balboa crossed the Isthmus of Panama and gazed out upon the Pacific Ocean. The Atlantic coast of South America was also explored as far south as the estuary of the Río de la Plata, but at this time no permanent colony was established. Although Hispaniola had been the jumping-off point for many of these early explorations, it lacked large deposits of gold and silver, the native indigenous population was rapidly decreasing as a source of ready labor, and Spain had larger ambitions. Soon Hispaniola was on its way down; by the end of the sixteenth century, it had become a bedraggled way station in Spain's vast colonial empire.[16]

The next great conquest, launched from Cuba, was that of Mexico. In 1519 Hernán Cortés, with five hundred men and sixteen horses, landed on the Mexican mainland, which he rebaptized New Spain. Here they discovered not just a small island with small, nomadic Indian tribes but a huge mainland territory with a full-scale Indian civilization, the Aztecs, numbering some five million persons. Cortés's advantages included the horses, which the Indians had never seen before, the Indians' belief that the Spaniards represented some kind of superior gods, the ongoing civil war within the Indian community, which lent itself to divide-and-conquer tactics, Cortés's mistress and interpreter, Malinche, who helped him understand the Indians, and his own skill, courage, and Machiavellian adeptness. In one of the classic military encounters in all of history, Cortés and his men, outnumbered *fifty thousand to one,* succeeded in capturing the Aztec emperor, Montezuma, holding him for ransom, ultimately killing him, and defeating and conquering the great Aztec empire. By 1522 central Mexico had been largely subdued.

The conquest of Mexico was quantitatively and qualitatively different from the conquest of the islands. It fundamentally changed the nature of the conquest, which heretofore had been limited to the subjugation of small, relatively poor territories and sparse native populations as Spain searched for a route to the Indies. But Mexico was an immense, heavily populated territory: every Spanish conquistador could be rewarded with a title, a fief as large as an American state, and the Indian labor (encomienda) to go with it. Moreover, whereas the islands had only small quantities of gold and silver, Mexico had vast amounts, which made it of immense value to the crown as well as to Cortés and his men. And whereas the native populations in the islands were soon decimated by disease as well as maltreatment, in Mexico they proved more resilient and the source of a seemingly endless supply of cheap labor. The Spanish crown thus began to reevaluate its plans for seeking a route to Asia and instead concentrated on the large task of conquering, settling, colonizing, and exploiting the American continent. In doing so, the Spanish tactic was to capture or eliminate the leaders of the Indian kingdoms, substitute themselves and their hierarchy for the Indian rulers, subdue and pacify the Indians, and use the mass of the Indians as a vast, subjugated labor class.

Replacing Santo Domingo and Havana, Mexico now became the main focus of Spain's colonial enterprise in the Americas. Other Spanish conquerors set out from the central valley of Mexico to explore and claim for Spain the huge northern parts of Mexico, the American southwest (as far north as Colorado), and California. Meanwhile, Juan Ponce de León had explored Florida, Lucas Vásquez de Ayllon tried to establish a colony on the Carolina coast, and Hernando de Soto led his forces on a march of exploration throughout the North American southeast. To the south, Cortés sent Pedro de Alvarado to conquer Guatemala and the great Mayan kingdom, and Cristóbal de Olid to conquer Honduras. The rest of Central America was quickly subdued in a pincers movement proceeding from Mexico south and from Panama north.

Spain's imperial attention now came to focus more on South America. The conquest of Peru, launched from Panama, followed Cortés's triumph in Mexico by about a decade and was soon viewed by the Spanish crown as equally valuable. For Peru was home to another vast and fabulously wealthy empire, that of the Incas, which stretched up and down the Andes from present-day Ecuador in the north to Chile in the south. The conquerors of the Incas, the Pizarro brothers Francisco, Gonzalo, and Hernando, took their lessons from Cortés in capturing the Inca emperor, Atahualpa, demanding tribute, and then killing the emperor anyway after he had complied with the Spanish request to fill an entire room with gold. In addition, and again following the Mexican model, the conquistadores became the beneficiaries of extensive lands in the Inca territories, of the right to utilize Indian labor on those lands, and of immeasurable wealth and social status. As they had done with the Aztecs, the Spanish, after lopping off its head, left the rest of the Indian social pyramid in place, substituting themselves for the Inca emperor as overlords and nobility.

The occupation of other lands in South America followed rapidly the conquest of Peru. In 1534 Pedro de Alvarado, the conqueror of Guatemala, captured Ecuador. In 1535 Diego de Almagro, another soldier of fortune and an accomplice of the Pizarros in Peru, led an ill-fated force through the Andes to Chile. That same year Pedro de Mendoza began a settlement at the mouth of the Río de la Plata, in present-day Argentina; but that settlement was subsequently abandoned. He and his lieutenants also explored upriver, founding Asunción in present-day Paraguay and going all the way to Bolivia—then called Upper Peru. Meanwhile, other Spaniards from Peru were spilling over the Andes from the west, discovering the fabulously rich "silver mountain" at Potosí in Bolivia and subsequently establishing communities in the eastern foothills of the Andes as well as towns down along the river system into Argentina, including Buenos Aires which was *refounded* in 1580. Meanwhile, after Almagro's unsuccessful venture, Chile was reconquered in the 1540s by Pedro de Valdivia, another Pizarro lieutenant—although the fierce Araucanian Indians in the far south were not subjugated until much later.

Within fifty years of the discovery by Columbus, therefore, almost all of the Caribbean, Mexico, Central America, the North American southwest and southeast, and South America (except Brazil) had been conquered, settled, and colonized by Spain. Between 1492 and the 1540s, Spain had acquired a vast American empire many times larger than the mother country itself. These feats are all the more remarkable in that they involved relatively few Spanish forces and occurred before the advance of modern communications and transportation made such conquests easier. By contrast with the vast conquests achieved by Spain in half a century, it took the English settlers in the North American colonies fully three centuries to cross the continent. Its conquests accomplished, Spain would turn to the more difficult task of consolidating and administering its far-flung empire.

The story of Brazil is different from but parallel to the Spanish conquests.[17] Brazil was discovered by Pedro Alvares Cabral, a Portuguese captain, in 1500, and Brazil became a Portuguese colony. The line between the Portuguese territory and the Spanish lands had been set by the pope in the Treaty of Tordesillas in 1494—before either Spain or Portugal had arrived in, let alone explored and mapped, South America. The initial Portuguese colonies, called *donatarios,* were located on the tropical coastal plain of northeast Brazil, where the continent points toward Africa, and the colonies were organized on a slave plantation and patrimonialist system similar to that of the Spanish. Portugal was far more interested in its Asian than its American colonies, however, because of the rich trade in silk and spices, and for a long time its policy toward Brazil was based on colonial neglect.

Eventually Portuguese pioneers, called *bandeirantes,* or "flag carriers," began to explore the interior of the continent, gradually filling the vast empty spaces and at the same time de facto moving the Tordesillas demarcation line with the Spanish colonies farther west until it reached the farthest reaches of the Amazon basin. It was not just colonial neglect that characterized the Portuguese in Brazil, however; Portuguese colonial institutions, which, like Spain's, were authoritarian, hierarchical, mercantilist, patrimonialist, top-down, and scholastic, were nevertheless softer, more humane, and less "inquisitorial" than Spain's. Even Brazil's slave plantation system was less intense and exploitive than the Spanish system, with greater miscegenation.

The Political Theory of the Conquest and Colonization

"The old dividing line between Spanish and Hispanic-American history hardly exists," wrote the historian Charles Julian Bishko in a special issue of the *Hispanic American Historical Review* entitled "The Iberian Background of Latin American History."[18] In the past, Bishko went on to say, scholars studied either Spanish history or Latin American history, but not both together. Today investigators know that Iberian history and Latin American history are inseparable, the former flowing seamlessly into the latter. Latin America, particularly in its early phases, is really an extension of Spain and Portugal in the late Middle Ages. The year 1492 is not a breaking point but a point of continuity connecting the last episodes of the Reconquest and the first encounter with America. The two are indivisible. As the historian Donald E. Worcester has written, "Spanish American political behavior is largely a by-product of cultural traits developed in the centuries before 1492 and modified by interaction with New World native populations since that time."[19]

These comments imply that the political theory of the conquest and the Spanish empire in America would also show important continuities with the Iberian past—of course, modified in the warp and woof of new societies and new conditions found in the Americas. That theory, recall, was based on Greco-Roman-Christian-Thomistic beliefs, perceptions, and conceptions as revived and emerging in the late Middle Ages. The basic principles included a God-centered universe; subservience to God's word; the unity of faith and reason; unquestioned obedience to the precepts of the Roman Catholic Church and the Church fathers; an organic conception of the organization of the state and of society; a hierarchical as well as corporative structure of social relations with every person fixed and secure in his or her station in life; an authoritarian and top-down political system that nevertheless was conditioned by respect for law, tradition, and basic rights (fueros); a closed, mercantilist, and noncapitalist economic system; and a scholastic or deductive method of learning and knowledge. Remarkably, at a time in the sixteenth century when such medieval ideas and concepts were beginning to be challenged or to go into decline elsewhere in the West, in Spain and Portugal as well as in their colonies in Latin America they were revived and received a new lease on life, providing a continuing neoscholastic answer to the emergence of secularizing, Renaissance, and rationalizing currents found elsewhere.

The modern world in northwest Europe was ushered in with a series of events that included the Reformation of the sixteenth century, the Renaissance and the Enlightenment, the rise of capitalism and the middle class, the scientific revolution of Galileo, Copernicus, and Newton, and the movement toward limited government and individual rights that would reach fruition in England in the seventeenth century. Under the impact of the Counter-Reformation, however, Spain and Portugal rejected these modernizing currents. The Spanish and Portuguese monarchies continued to identify themselves with absolutism, medievalism, the universal (Roman Catholic) faith, and a special intolerant, Counter-Reformation interpretation of that faith. As the Mexican Nobel laureate Octavio Paz writes, the Spanish monarchy was a mixture of Theodosius the Great (theocracy) and Abd-er-Rahman III, the first Moorish caliph of Spain (absolutism).[20] Under Ferdinand and Isabella and then the Hapsburg monarchy, the Spanish state was imbued with the notion that it had a universal mission: to defend the faith against all attacks, philosophical, theological, political, and social. Paz continues, "Spain and Portugal closed their doors, locked themselves in, and rejected the modernity that was then dawning. The Counter-Reformation was the most complete, radical, and coherent expression of this rejection."[21]

In the realm of political theory, the modern Western state was ushered in with the writings of Hobbes, Machiavelli, and Locke. Hobbes was an apostle of absolutism but viewed it in purely secular terms, which would be unacceptable in Iberia. Machiavelli is often thought of as the first secular political scientist because he strictly separated religion and morality from politics, and also demonstrated—a heretical and blasphemous idea at the time—how religion could be manipulated by a prince for purely secular, nationalistic purposes. And Locke was the English apostle of limited, representative government and individual rights and is usually regarded as the main font of American pluralism and democracy. But Spain and Portugal rejected all three of these apostles of modernity. Hobbes was rejected both because of his secular views and because his "leviathan" state was unlimited even by traditional law, custom, and religious beliefs. Machiavelli was explicitly, even rabidly, repudiated by the Spanish jurists because of his separation of politics from religion and for fostering what they saw as amoral political practice; in contrast, Spain's view was that politics should continue to demonstrate the unity of religion and politics, that politics must be undergirded by morality and right reason, and that Roman Catholicism provided the unifying belief system for society.

Locke and the liberal, individualistic, pluralist tradition would, of course, be rejected as running contrary to everything that Spain and the Counter-Reformation stood for.[22]

It is often suggested in historical and social science writing that in the sixteenth century Iberia and by extension Latin America missed the boat to modernity. That is, they remained locked in a system of feudalism and medievalism at a time when other nations were beginning to break the bonds of the ancien régime and enter the modern age. Spain, Portugal, and Latin America, it is said, were dominated by tradition. It follows, then, that in order for them to modernize they too must break the bonds of tradition; they must undergo the same processes and stages of modernization as the rest of the West. In other words, in order to become developed and modern, Iberia and Latin America must abandon their traditional, neoscholastic institutions and become just like us—presumably liberal, pluralist, egalitarian, democratic, with elections every two or four years, with competitive political parties, thousands of interest groups competing in the political arena, separation of powers, a capitalistic economic system, and so forth. Such attitudes in fact have lain at the heart of U.S. foreign aid and development policy in Latin America for the past forty years.

But an alternative, more complex and interesting explanation is also possible: namely, that in the sixteenth century Spain, Portugal, and their colonies did not miss the boat but instead set sail on a different course. To continue the earlier metaphor, they took a different route and an alternative mode of transportation. The Iberian and Hispanic boat continues even today on a trajectory that differs from that of North American pluralism and democracy. And it will continue to be different.

For if one understands the word "modernity" only as the world ushered in in northwest Europe by means of the scientific revolution, capitalism, the Protestant Reformation, and Lockean-style individualism, then it is true that Iberia and Latin America missed that particular modernity boat. Or at least they missed the northwest European, Protestant, English boat. But what if one thinks of the neoscholastic model as an *alternative* to English-style modernization? what if one uses "medieval" not in a pejorative sense implying that it has to be eliminated or overcome to achieve modernization, but as a scientific term without emotive connotations? and what if one considers that this medievalism is not necessarily fated to die or disappear under the impact of Western-style influences but to revise, reform, adapt, and renovate itself? that Iberia and Latin America represent a different, distinctive, now updated form of medievalism fated not to disappear under modernization's impact but to adjust and renovate itself in order to accommodate to modernity? This latter interpretation would call for a quite different interpretation of Latin America as compared with the "inevitable Westernization" thesis.[23]

We cannot resolve all aspects of the dispute here, although we return to it at numerous points in the book and in the conclusion. Actually I believe that both forces are operating: that Iberia and Latin America are both modernizing in a Western sense (making up for having missed out earlier), and that they retain many features, now updated, of this modernized medievalism and neoscholasticism. This dispute also has far-reaching policy implications: if one believes that Iberia and Latin America must wipe their slates clean by jettisoning *all* their traditional and medieval institutions to become modern, then one set of policy prescriptions would apply. But if one believes the main dynamics of Iberian and Latin American change processes, as in Japan, China, India, Africa, and other non-Western or partially Western areas, involve the gradual adjustment, assimilation, and adaptations of traditional (medieval, neoscholastic) institutions to the imperatives of the modern age, then a different, less sweeping set of policy prescriptions is called for. We return to these complex themes later.

The foremost scholar of the ideas of neoscholasticism and the Spanish Counter-Reformation of the sixteenth century, Bernice Hamilton, has written as follows: "Spain was almost untouched by the Protestant Reformation or by the Renaissance in its Italian form; she had no Scientific Revolution to speak of, no equivalent to Hobbes or Locke, no rise of political individualism, no social contract theory, no Industrial Revolution."[24] What did Spain have instead? Definitely not a tabula rasa on which the writ of modernity could simply be later inscribed. Instead, Spain and Portugal had rich traditions and fully functioning institutions of their own. These traditions and institutions were, however, medieval rather than modern. Sixteenth-century Iberia, as the Brazilian historian Beatriz Helena Domíngues Bitarello has written, remained essentially medieval while also experiencing a great Thomistic revival, at a time when other countries were experiencing the early stirrings of modernization.[25]

The Spanish neoscholastic (mainly Dominican and Jesuit) writers of the sixteenth century (Mariana, Molina, Soto, Suárez, Victoria) tried to adapt a medieval and rigidly Catholic tradition to a time and context (Spain and Portugal of the sixteenth and seventeenth centuries) that were already being undermined and rejected in the rest of Europe. It is often said that they tried to preserve the Middle Ages, but that is not entirely accurate. Instead, they sought to adjust, accommodate, and fuse the medieval with the newer requirements of a changed and, with the discovery of the Americas, much larger world. Rather than rejecting scholasticism and medieval social and political institutions, they sought to update and reform them. They accepted innovation but without rejecting the paradigm of medieval hierarchy. In short, they modernized the medieval tradition in Spain rather than break with it. It is the classic conflict of evolution versus revolution, of adapting to modernity and modernizing tradition rather than throwing it overboard—choices which are not unheard of in present times. The Spanish neoscholastics represented the great Thomistic alternative to secularized modernity beginning in the sixteenth century, a tradition of thought and institutions that is almost entirely unknown in university courses in modern political theory.

The neoscholastics were vociferously anti-Machiavelli. By separating politics from morality, Machiavelli broke sharply with the past. The Spanish Jesuits, instead, wanted to preserve a Christian state and morality while adjusting to modernity. For example, they came to accept the Copernican findings in mathematical astronomy but then, in seeking to preserve a Christian conception of the universe, disconnected Copernicus's science from the philosophical implications of the theory. The Spanish race, the state, learning, the social and political systems, and Catholicism all had to be fused in a single, grand, Christian design. The state and its prince had to be Roman Catholic; the education system had to be Catholic; and social and political institutions had to be infused with Catholic teachings. The Spanish Jesuit writers attacked Machiavelli because they feared encroachments on the domain of Catholicism; the secular and "irrational" view of human nature found in Machiavelli would not do. Rather, they sought to preserve the divine origin of political authority and erected an incredibly complex social, political, and philosophical basis for doing so. This sixteenth-century, Thomistic, or neoscholastic philosophy would serve as the basis for Spanish, Portuguese, and Latin American political life until well into the twentieth century. From a modern, pragmatic, secular point of view, this is the chief reason the Iberian countries and Latin America continued to lag behind the rest of the West; but from the Hispanic–Latin American viewpoint this philosophy helped preserve what they considered valuable from the past.

Hamilton finds no individualism, no Locke, no democratic participation, no pragmatic, utilitarian Bentham, in the Spanish political theory of that era.[26] Rather she finds a continuous stream from the Thomism of the Middle Ages adjusted to the new realities of modernity and empire. She discovers a Christian conception of a sovereign state and people. It is scholastic, deductive, and still based on Saint Thomas's "God-given" hierarchy of laws and society, the "great chain of being." It retains the historic organic theory of natural community and the corporative organization of social and political life. Mixed forms of government were good, but the best form was monarchy supported by an orderly system of hierarchy. Church and state were to be unified in a holy partnership.

Monarchy was the preferred governmental system, yet it was, in the view of the sixteenth-century theologians, to operate under a variety of restraints. It was held in check by the Church, by God's law and natural law, by custom, and—in the fueros tradition—by the rights of various groups and social sectors. These sectors were to gravitate around the monarchy "like satellites," connected to the king by elaborate ties of mutual obligation. The independent power of the corporate groups and the cortes was to serve as a counterweight to royal authority.

There is in these jurists, thus, a sense that government operates on the basis of a contract between royal authority and the community. This is what was meant in earlier writings when Spain and Portugal were referred to as "contract states," governed in their state–society relations by a variety of organic laws, concordats, ordinations, and regulations linking central authority to a variety of societal groups (Church, military, guilds, towns, universities, regional entities, eventually business and labor) in a system of mutual, community rights and obligations.[27] These rights and obligations included the ancient idea of the gift by which those above and below in the social scale have mutual obligations to each other (see chapter 2). But note that what Spain and Portugal mean by "contract" or "the community" in this formulation is quite different from Locke's idea of contract or of constitutional government: the Lockean conception enshrines liberal individualism and

unfettered pluralism, whereas the Spanish conception emphasizes the
larger community, group or corporate rights, and limited pluralism.[28]

The foremost writer among the sixteenth-century Spanish neoscholastics was Francisco Suárez. Suárez is almost unknown in the
United States and in the history of Western thought and, when mentioned at all, is usually dismissed as a reactionary. But Suárez's voluminous writings and powerful, neo-Thomist arguments are crucial to
understanding not only the Counter-Reformation, of which he was the
foremost defender, but also the conquest of the Americas as well as the
history and political culture of Spain, Portugal, and Latin America for
the next several centuries and reaching into the present era. If Locke is
the foundation of Anglo-American individualism, liberalism, and democracy, Suárez is the font of a modern, updated neomedievalism that
lies at the heart of the Iberian and Latin American tradition. A doctoral
dissertation on Suárez is needed, or one comparing Suárez and Locke
as the founders of the two great but starkly contrasting civilizations in
the Americas, the North American and the Latin American, in terms
both of the contrasting political principles they championed and established and of the current questioning, undermining, and crises of
these principles.[29]

Suárez's system, based on the elaborate hierarchy of laws and the
great chain of being of Saint Thomas, served to legitimize and even enhance Hapsburgian authoritarianism. Suárez became the apostle of
updated, state-building, royal authority, not only internally in Spain
but in the empire as well. If Saint Thomas is the greatest Christian philosopher ever, Suárez represented a continuation, extension, and modernization of that work. He helped reprint Thomas's works in Spain,
wrote prodigiously about them, continued and strengthened scholastic studies, and was the principal architect of the neoscholastic revival
of the sixteenth century. Rather than simply accepting the past or
turning the clock back, Suárez sought to adapt Thomism to the exi-
gencies of a modern monarchy and empire.

The Suárez family was prominent, wealthy, landed, and had long
served the Spanish royal family. Through the centuries of the Reconquest, the Suárez family had fought in numerous battles against the
Moors. Its base and lands were in Castile, in the heart of the peninsula.
The family was nationalistic and strongly Catholic and saw a powerful
connection between the two. They had, like other members of the Spanish ruling class, received their estates and titles in return for their serv-

ices to the monarchy. The family had been close to and involved in the centralizing policies of Isabella and Ferdinand, and family members were in the service of the first two Hapsburgs, Charles I (1516–56) and Philip II (1556–96). Young Francisco, a brilliant student and unable because of primogeniture to inherit the family lands, found his way to the University of Salamanca, one of Europe's first and foremost universities and the center of Catholic, scholastic orthodoxy. He finished his studies in 1567, was ordained as a priest, stayed on at the university as a scholar and teacher, and, during the "Portuguese captivity" of 1580–1640, when Portugal was joined to Spain, also taught at Coimbra. So the Suárezian system was crucial not just in Spain and its colonies but in Portugal and its empire as well.

Suárez's writings helped support and legitimize the absolutist Christian system and state of Philip II and its policies. He, of course, believed in universal, Catholic principles of right and wrong. All persons had their proper place in his hierarchical schema. In *De Legibus,* his great work on law, he continues and updates the Thomistic logic that all power and authority emanate from God. Unlike Locke, Suárez allows for no private property; instead, property is subordinated to the higher ends of the state. The common good is a higher end than is private possession. The state is also a regulator of economic and property relations, thus providing legitimacy for mercantilism. Authority, wealth, and power all come from God.

Suárez set forth an organic theory of society; in book 8 of *De Legibus* he advanced a corporatist conception of state–society relations that gave modern Christian legitimacy to earlier, medieval versions. That is, while he favored a strong monarchy, he opposed tyranny and dictatorship. He preferred a more pluralist, contractual, even constitutional system in which the rights of corporate groups as well as tradition and Christian precepts served to limit monarchical authority. Although he favored a monarchical form of government, he endowed society with extensive natural rights and resolved this contradiction by having a strong king checked by the ultimate power of these societal or corporate groups. The people themselves constitute a corporate entity, he argued, as organized through society's component corporate units.

This power resting in societal or corporate groups is inalienable, but it is transferred with the consent of the people to the ruler, for the common good. The ultimate test of the juridical validity of any system, he argued, is its representative character, which must include the consent of the people and their society. Such talk of consent and contract sounds democratic, even Lockean; but by such terms as "the people" and "society" Suárez meant their organized or corporative voice, not the masses or individual voices. Furthermore, it was the state that granted juridical legitimacy to these societal groups so they could be heard. And while he believed ultimate political power rested in the community of men (including women!), "community" in Suárez again meant the elite, organized voices of society. His was what one may call a concession theory of power: while power ultimately rested with the society and was governed by contract, that power had been delegated or alienated to the monarch. There is no mention, however, of when precisely this delegation took place (actually, over the course of several hundred years in the Spanish Middle Ages) or under what precise conditions (actually by conflict and an ongoing tug-of-war).

While in Suárez this "conceded" power could be revoked under certain circumstances, in practice it vested virtually unlimited power in the monarch—unless the ruler violated all principles of morality and good government and became a tyrant. So where in Suárez did power ultimately lie: with the king or with society's corporate units? It sounds to me that it rested with the ruler, presumably in consultation with society's (by then nonexistent, having been eliminated by Isabella) corporate units, and revokable only if the ruler becomes an absolute tyrant, such as Trujillo and Fulgencio Batista and Augusto Pinochet; but what about such mixed or ambiguous cases as the elected but authoritarian Alberto Fujimori in Peru or the Mexican single-party system of the Partido Revolucionario Institucional (PRI)? The answer is: we do not entirely know but presumably it is to be worked out in the political process, as it is in Latin America to this day. So once again, as in the Spanish-Portuguese Middle Ages, the basic tension and dynamics of politics seem to be between strong central government and society's corporative units, but with the central government overwhelmingly dominant. Nevertheless note also how distinct this is from the Lockean individualistic conception. For whereas Locke stressed the inalienable legal rights (including to property) of individuals, Suárez emphasized the natural rights of the society and the collectivity. And while Locke's contract theory was between government and the individual, Suárez's involved government and corporations or society (no individuals) to protect the common good.[30]

Spanish scholasticism of the sixteenth century constitutes the main channel through which medieval, Catholic conceptions of law, state, and society were transmitted to the modern era. It was, in the words of a Suárez biographer, "an unbroken stream of ideas running across the ostensible boundary between the middle ages and modern times."[31] Suárez's thought was not wholly traditional but represented an adaptation of medievalism to modernity. In its emphasis on order, discipline, submission, rank, obedience, and God's immutable ordering of the universe, it was also profoundly conservative. It allowed for change but only guided, controlled change from above. It was not a liberal conception: rights were not conferred on individuals, but law has as its first objective the ordering of the common good. The Church was to supervise the entire legal structure of state and society, above all the relations of ruler and people, which must be in accord with Christian doctrine.

Social reality was defined in legal terms, but each community, corporation, and societal group had different laws and a different, legally defined relation to the monarch. Each community had "natural rights," but these were defined in group terms and had been delegated to the king. Suárez's was a highly legalistic conception—itself a conservative concept—and an early example of legal positivism. What Suárez did, in short, was to provide Christian legitimacy for the more centralized and absolutist system that had emerged de facto in Spain during its formative period of the late Middle Ages. He recognized group rights but those rights had already been delegated. There were theoretical checks on royal authority, but most of those limits had already been removed by Ferdinand's and Isabella's, and then the Hapsburgs', centralizing policies. Nevertheless, the first two early Hapsburg monarchs, Charles I and Philip II, were good monarchs, good administrators, and generally operated within the Suárezian guidelines for good government. The problems would come with some of the later Hapsburgs who were both incompetent and tyrannous.

And it is this Suárezian system, with both its strong central authority and its built-in tensions, that was now carried over to the Americas. Indeed, in reading Suárez's works—their legalism, their statism, their mercantilism, their organicism and corporatism, and their ambiguities and tensions of state–society relations—one can find many of the principles that dominate Iberia and Latin America until well into the twentieth century.

Spanish-Portuguese Colonial Institutions

The institutions that Spain and Portugal brought to the New World reflected and were an extension of the institutions of Iberia of 1500: of
the Roman, Moorish, and Christian traditions and influences; of the Reconquest and its militarized feudalism; of the centralizing tendencies
of Ferdinand and Isabella and the Hapsburgs; and of the neoscholastic
political theory and justifications offered by Spain's great writers of
the sixteenth century. Latin America has to be seen as a continuation
of Spanish and Portuguese history of the Middle Ages—but reshaped
and modified in the context of the New World.

The political structure was one of authoritarianism and increasing
absolutism. Ultimate authority, of course, rested with the monarchy in
Madrid, and under Charles I and Philip II in the sixteenth century that
power became increasingly centralized, bureaucratic, and imperious.
The king ruled through two royal councils: the Council of the Indies,
which decided on all policy initiatives for the colonies, and the House
of Trade, which governed all commercial transactions and whose primary responsibility was to augment the royal revenues. Over time, the
crown created four viceroyalties (literally, vice-kings) in the Americas,
in Mexico, Peru, the Río de la Plata (Argentina), and New Granada (Gran
Colombia), who served as extensions of royal authority and were responsible directly to the king. Below the viceroyalties were the captains-
general, governing smaller territories but similarly absolutist within
their areas. And below that, each landowner had unlimited authority on
his own estate. In other words, each rung in the hierarchy was absolute
within its own sphere of influence. The system conformed closely to
Saint Thomas's (and now Suárez's) great chain of being. There was no
training at any level in democratic self-government, and the local *cabildos* (town councils) established by Spain had no independent taxing
or decision-making authority.[32]

The social and economic order was similarly a reflection of the Reconquest. It was organized on an exploitive, mercantilist basis. All the
wealth of the colonies—the mines, the land, the sugar plantations, the
natural resources—belonged to the crown. The crown could alienate
and distribute lands and resources in return for loyalty and service: the
feudal contract. To the early conquistadores the crown distributed huge
tracts, called encomienda. These grants could be held in perpetuity
and, as in the Reconquest, carried with them the right to use the labor

of the Indians who lived on the land. Over time, these grants of land and labor turned into de facto private property and a slave plantation or semifeudal manorial system. Several individual friars as well as the crown sought on various occasions to modify the system and offer greater protection to the Indians, but royal authority was far away and the crown could not consistently enforce its decrees in the colonies. And it did not always want to; many of its reforms were halfhearted, particularly if they cut into the crown's revenue needs. On these grand estates (*haciendas, estancias, fazendas*) the writ of the landowner was as absolute in his domain as that of any viceroy or captain-general in his; these estates became self-contained fiefdoms in which moral, religious, political, economic, and social power were fused.[33]

The Roman Catholic Church was infused with an absolutism that rivaled and even surpassed the state concept. In the conquest and consolidation of the colonies, the Church served as an arm of royal authority—all this rationalized, of course, in the neo-Thomist writings of Suárez. The Church's missionary, Christianizing efforts among the native peoples were consciously used by the Spanish and Portuguese crowns to civilize, subdue, and pacify. As in the Reconquest, the Church itself became a large landowner and the recipient of huge tracts of territory from the crown, as well as the right to utilize the Indian labor of those who lived on the land in return for Christianizing them. A handful of priests condemned the abuses of the Spanish colonial system and the treatment of the Indians, but they were isolated voices, and, it must be said, the institutional Church itself was an instrument and beneficiary of colonialism.

Especially interesting here was the sociopolitical structure of the colonies and its theoretical basis. Society in Latin America was based on the same organic and corporatist principles that were seen so often in the formative periods of Spanish and Portuguese history. As the historian L. N. McAlister writes, "The concepts of estate and corps were integral parts of the cultural baggage which Spaniards carried with them to the Indies."[34] But in the New World the social structure established earlier in the peninsula would have to be modified. Two major forces were at work: (1) the deliberate intervention of the crown in the molding of colonial social structure, and (2) the presence of large numbers of Indians, then African slaves, and eventually mixed racial elements in colonial society.

The ethnic factor helped produce a class structure that was also based on caste. At the top were the Spaniards and Portuguese of European descent; at the bottom of the social pyramid were Indians and Africans. But, recall, the Spanish colonial system originated in military exploration and conquest; unlike the situation in North America, the conquistadores did not bring their wives and children along. Miscegenation of the three races thus occurred almost at once and was widespread. Within two or three generations, therefore, Spain and Portugal developed an elaborate vocabulary and social hierarchy to classify the various mixed types: *mestizo* (a mix of Indian and white), *mulatto* (African and white), *castizo* (white and mestizo), *morisco* (white and mulatto), and so on. This classificatory scheme was so elaborate that it reached to more than one hundred distinct categories. Not only did race or caste thus define one's place in the social hierarchy but, important for this analysis, each socioracial classification had its own rights, responsibilities, even law courts in which differential treatment was handed out, depending on one's rank. Moreover, one's place in this gradation was determined as much by cultural characteristics as by color: education, dress, speech, behavior. Class and caste reinforced each other, with whites also being the upper-class elements, blacks and Indians at the bottom, and mestizos, mulattoes, and other shades in between. In the New World, in other words, the rigid, hierarchical, Spanish/Portuguese system of classes and estates was reproduced but in new forms, with caste serving as almost the functional equivalent of the European-style medieval estates.

Because of the crown's interventions, the vertical or corporate structure of colonial society similarly diverged from the Old World model. For example, even though Spaniards and Portuguese formed the highest strata of colonial society, the crown refused to grant them seignorial jurisdiction or to give them titles of nobility. Similarly with the military: in Spain and Portugal the military orders often had special corporate rights and privileges, but in the New World the army was employed in the service of royal authority, officerships were largely honorary, and the local militias were limited to white colonials. Only in the late eighteenth century at the very end of the colonial period did the army develop as a separate unit with its own fuero.[35] A third difference had to do with the Indian communities: at one level they were thought of as the lowest of the estates (lower than "common"), but at another they were often grouped together into communities, given land (*ejidos*) to be held in common, and reconstituted as an ethnic or geographical corporation.

There was no cortes or corporately representative body in the colonies.

In other respects, colonial social structure largely reproduced the hierarchical and corporative structures of the Old World, except in America the corporate bodies were often less well organized and disciplined than in the mother countries. As the historian John Leddy Phelan has written, "The Spaniards recreated in the New World a version of the corporate society of the late middle ages."[36] The Church, of course, was part of the conquest and was both an estate and a corporation. It was further subdivided into various subcorporations: the university community, the Holy Office of the Inquisition, secular and religious orders, the cathedral chapters, and so forth. The concept of the municipal corporation also followed the conquest, but there were relatively few cities in the New World that had actually negotiated or secured a charter of self-government from the crown. Most of the artisan and craft guilds in the New World dated from the late sixteenth or early seventeenth centuries; like their Iberian counterparts, the guilds had to be recognized and chartered by the crown in order to become formally sanctioned corporations. Interestingly, while all the functional corporations were by law limited to those of European background, the reluctance of the Spanish and Portuguese upper classes to engage in manual labor meant that from the beginning mestizo elements found their way into the craft and artisan guilds—and even in the Church and the army at low levels. In general, however, class, corporate, and estate organization followed an interlocking pattern that mirrored the elite structure of the peninsula.

In such a huge frontier, primitive society as Latin America during its colonial centuries, however, the structure of the estate system and the corporations was consistently looser, less coherent, less well articulated, and less well organized than it had been in the mother countries.[37] The filling of this organizational, institutional, and corporate void is how the Iberians in the New World defined "civilization" and "progress." That is, they wanted greater articulation and organization of this corporative base rather than less. I develop this theme at length in the next chapter, but it is appropriate to raise it first in this context. For when the Spanish and Portuguese colonies moved toward independence in the early nineteenth century, the rhetoric they used was often liberal and republican; but below the surface they sought to re-create or create from scratch this organic and corporative order which was the only one they knew from their past.

To fill the organizational void not only of immense empty spaces and disorganization verging on anarchy but now also occasioned by the withdrawal of the crown, they sought to create an associational infrastructure to replace the colonial one now disappearing. They often formally abolished the older colonial system of corporations; but because cultures and behavior are harder to change quickly than institutions, they retained in most cases the habits and organic-corporatist philosophy of the past. Hence, while on the surface in the nineteenth century Latin America appeared to be going in a liberal and republican direction, below the surface it remained organicist and corporatist; indeed, in the drive to impose discipline and order on an unruly countryside it may have become more corporatist rather than less. Stemming from the late-colonial era, therefore, Latin America after independence became schizophrenic, moving in two seemingly contradictory directions—republican and corporatist—at once, or else trying to fashion ingenious compromises and overlaps between them.

The Portugal/Brazil Variant

Portugal and its colony Brazil have always been rather different from Spain and its Latin American colonies: less rigid, less absolutist, less inquisitorial, more relaxed and tolerant toward other peoples and races. Portugal's struggle against the Moors was less bloody and less a religious crusade than in Spain, and that same less intense attitude was often carried over in Portugal's colonial experiences in Brazil.

Brazil had been discovered for Portugal by Pedro Alvares Cabral in 1500, eight years after Columbus's discovery of America. Valuing its Asian colonies far more than its Brazilian colony, however, Portugal largely ignored Brazil for several decades in the sixteenth century until the threat of foreign interlopers (England, France, Spain, Holland) forced it to pay attention or else risk losing the colony. There was little immediately available gold and silver, and the native population had a reputation for cannibalism and resistance; hence, Portugal's early policy in Brazil was one of colonial indifference.

As the threat of foreign intervention loomed, Portugal was obliged to expend greater efforts in Brazil. But Portugal was much smaller, weaker, and poorer than Spain even in these early formative years and could not afford large resources spent in its colonies. Its solution to this dilemma was the *donatario,* a donation of land by the king to Portuguese settlers if they were willing to invest their own resources in the development of their land. The result was a combination of feudal, manorial estate with a kind of early capitalistic enterprise. Each donatario had sweeping political, economic, social, and religious power in his own territory, comparable to a medieval baron and rather like the power of the Spanish conquistadores on their estates. Although the Portuguese monarchy sought to centralize control under a royally appointed governor-general, the donatarios retained a large measure of autonomy. Race and social relations were hierarchical in accord with the Thomistic great chain of being but far more fluid and relaxed than in the Spanish colonies.[38]

Portugal's colonies in Brazil were initially limited to the northeast coast, but eventually Portuguese explorers spilled over the coastal escarpment (much as frontiersmen in the North American colonies, initially hemmed in by the Appalachians, soon spilled over them) into the interior. In doing so they pushed the pope's line of Tordesillas separating the Portuguese from the Spanish colonies farther and farther west, eventually reaching the foothills of the Andes and ultimately claiming most of the Amazon basin and the vast interior of South America for Portugal. These explorers were like the North American pioneers.[39]

From 1580 to 1640 Portugal was united with Spain in what has been called the "Portuguese captivity." The enforced unification of the two kingdoms implied for a time a unified colonial policy and administration. More of the rigidities and absolutisms of the Spanish system and colonial structure were now introduced into Portugal and her colonies. This was also the time when Suárez and other Spanish Jesuits taught at Portugal's Coimbra University and brought the rigor of the Counter-Reformation to Portugal. But Spain was more preoccupied with its internal affairs, and the Hapsburg royal family was already in decline, hence Spain's influence on Portugal and its colonies was less than it might have been. In 1640 Portugal regained its independence and its colonial policy again became more relaxed.

From 1624 to 1654 the Dutch occupied much of northeast Brazil, but they were ousted by the Portuguese colonists in an effort that gave rise to the first stirrings of Brazilian nationalism. Thereafter, the colony began to flourish as a manorial, slave plantation, sugar producer. The discovery of vast quantities of gold in the interior added to the colony's value. Although the social and racial system was never as rigid as in Spain, many of the same political, cultural, and intellectual underpinnings were present: top-down patrimonial authority, mercantilism, a hierarchy of class and caste, the Roman Church serving as an instrument of colonialism and state policy, organicism and corporatism, and a deductive, scholastic educational and intellectual system.[40]

Indigenous Communities

The people called Indians, of course, had arrived on the American continent long before its purported discovery by Columbus. Columbus discovered America but only for Spain and the Western world. Actually, America may be said to have been discovered thousands of years before by Asiatic peoples who crossed the Bering Straits connecting Siberia to North America and then slowly wound their way south to settle all areas of the Americas.[41]

At the time of the Spanish discovery of (really, encounter with) America, it is estimated that there were only three million Indians or indigenous peoples living on the North American continent; most of them were nomadic and organized into relatively small tribal communities. In contrast, Latin America was the home of approximately thirty million Indians, or ten times as many; moreover, many of them were organized into large-scale civilizations (Aztec, Maya, Inca) numbering five or six million persons each. The vast differences in numbers and sophistication led to radically divergent Indian policies on the part of the colonists: whereas North America dealt with its Indians either by killing them, pushing them farther west, or confining them on reservations, Spain and (to a lesser extent) Portugal had to devise more nuanced and advanced strategies for dealing with their Indian problem.[42]

The first point to note is how diverse the Indian groups in Latin America were. In the Caribbean islands where the conquistadores first landed, in Brazil around the Amazon basin, and in other interior areas of Latin America, the indigenous groups were usually small, often cannibalistic, and quite primitive. But in what is present-day Mexico, Guatemala and Central America, and Peru, Ecuador, and Bolivia, the Indians were part of large-scale civilizations perhaps as advanced as those of the ancient Egyptians and Babylonians. In between were such groups as the Chibchas in Colombia, larger and more advanced than any Indian tribe in North America but still smaller and less sophisticated than the Aztec, Maya, or Inca civilizations.[43]

The Spaniards could not simply eliminate these native civilizations, each numbering several million persons. Both the Catholic Church and the Spanish crown stood in the way of that; and in theory at least Spain's Indian policy of gradual assimilation into Western, Hispanic ways was quite enlightened by the standards of that time. In addition, the sheer logistics of eliminating thirty million Indians, had that been the policy, made that option unlikely. Spain and Portugal did not wish to eliminate the Indians because they and their labor were necessary to the success of the entire Spanish and Portuguese enterprise in the Americas. The Indians were, in fact, along with the gold and silver, the most valuable "commodity" that Spain and Portugal found in America, absolutely essential to work as miners, transporters, laborers, and peasants. The strategy was not to eliminate the Indians but rather to Christianize them, civilize them, and use them for good purposes. To that end, once the Spaniards had lopped off the apex of the Indian political hierarchy (Montezuma, Atahualpa), they kept the rest of the Indian social pyramid intact, substituting themselves for the Indian rulers and largely ruling and pacifying the Indians through the use of their own hierarchical control mechanisms.

Of immense assistance in this process—and of particular importance for the main themes of this book—was the fact that at least in the larger Indian civilizations the sociopolitical structures closely resembled and paralleled Spain's and Portugal's own. For example, the Aztecs had essentially a two-class and steeply pyramidal social system in which the ruling and priestly classes at the top enjoyed great luxury and prestige while the mass of the people were docile and obedient. Once the Spaniards had substituted themselves for the native ruling class, it was relatively easy for them to maintain control. Such docility and habits of obedience enabled a relatively few Spaniards to govern large numbers of Indians for some three centuries while facing merely a few small-scale, easily defeatable revolts. The Aztecs also had, at the top, a corporative or functional form of social organization—rulers, priests, soldiers—that similarly dovetailed with Spanish form.[44]

The Mayans, too, had hereditary ruling classes and powerful priestly groups—just like Spain. They followed an organic, communalist, and corporatist form of social organization. At the time of the conquest, the entire Mayan civilization was in a state of decline, which greatly aided Spanish subjugation. Once the Spanish had gained control of the upper reaches of Mayan civilization, it proved easy to keep control of the rest of the social pyramid.[45]

105

The Incas were perhaps the most advanced peoples in the Americas, ruling over a vast territorial empire. Inca society was strictly organized and bureaucratized under a hierarchy of hereditary officials. The Incas' greatest accomplishment was their imperial system; they had a well-developed structure of political, military, and social organization. Society was divided into three main groups organized hierarchically: a hereditary ruling class, a priestly group, and the general population. All of the land was divided among these three groups, but it was the masses that did all the work. The structure was remarkably parallel to the European, especially Spanish and Portuguese, system of estates. Moreover—and again as in Spain and Portugal—alongside and overlapping with this horizontal and class-based system was a system of corporate or functional organization: the ruling class, the priestly group, military warriors, the messengers (crucial as a means of communication in this far-flung empire), artisans and craftsmen. Applying the lessons learned from the Spanish experience in Mexico, the Pizarro brothers captured and killed the Inca leader but then continued to rule through the rest of the Inca social pyramid and, again because of the docility of the Indians, to keep them under control.[46]

Arriving in the New World and discovering these "strange" peoples whom the Europeans had never seen before, the Spaniards were perplexed. Were they men or beasts? where did they fit in Saint Thomas's great chain of being? The crown and the Church (or at least some parts of it) sought to defend the Indians' humanity; they discovered that the Indians had souls, were therefore men, and therefore qualified for basic human rights. The conquistadores, in contrast, desperately in need of Indian labor, wanted to treat them as beasts of burden that could thus be enslaved. The decision of a famous royal tribunal that held hearings from 1549 to 1551 was that Indians were indeed men and therefore deserved protection under Spanish law; but Madrid was far away, the colonists' need for labor was insatiable, the Indians were already dying out in some areas, and meantime African slave labor was being brought in—whereupon Spain had to go through the same debate again as to whether Africans had souls.[47]

Meanwhile, in the colonies the Indians were being treated as another estate, another caste or corporate group to be appended to those already in existence. As Phelan has written, "The same corporate principle that applied to society as a whole extended to the internal organization of the Indian commonwealth."[48] In addition to the already existing es-

106

tates of noble, clerical, and common, the Indians were considered a fourth estate, lower than the other three, and assigned rights and obligations accordingly. Or else they were treated in law and practice as another, separate corporate body with similarly attendant duties and rights. For example, some Indians were assigned communal (ejido) lands, often in accord with their own, pre-Columbian communal practices, in return for which—in classic feudal fashion—they owed loyalty and service to the crown. Under the control and tutelage of the Jesuits, virtually the entire present-day country of Paraguay became an Indian preserve and commune, again with certain rights to land in return for service. Elsewhere in Latin America, either on their own or under religious auspices, the Indians were treated as a similarly corporate body, enjoying juridical personality, duly recognized by the state but owing obligations in return. This was perhaps the first manifestation of new social or corporate groups being appended to the Spanish/Portuguese sociopolitical pyramid without implying any fundamental changes in the hierarchical and elite-controlled structure of the pyramid itself.[49]

Eighteenth-Century Changes

If the sixteenth century was the age of conquest and settlement in Latin America and the seventeenth century one of consolidation of empire, the eighteenth century was one of change. Not revolutionary change or change that got out of hand but change that would lead eventually to independence and to a refashioning and restructuring of the heretofore dominant model in Iberia and Latin America.

First, there was change on the ground. In Spain, the Hapsburg monarchy had declined and died out by the end of the seventeenth century, to be replaced by the French Bourbon monarchy in the eighteenth. The Bourbons, especially Charles III (1759–88) were more enlightened, more Europe-oriented, and more modern in their thinking than the Hapsburgs. Among their many reforms in Spain, the Bourbons introduced street lighting, reduced rampant criminality, drained swampy areas and turned them to productive use, introduced French styles of dress and etiquette, began reforestation projects, and established efficient, centralized systems of public administration. They brought new Renaissance ideas and even some aspects of the Enlightenment into Spain and Latin America. Similarly in Portugal, the Marques de Pombal (1750–77) rationalized public administration, centralized power, introduced reforms, and rebuilt and modernized the capital city of Lisbon after the devastating earthquake of 1755.[50]

These and other modernizing changes introduced a split into the Spanish, Portuguese, and Latin American psyche, soul, or political culture that had not been present in these monistic societies since their founding. On the one side was traditional Spain, traditional Portugal, and traditional Latin America: Catholic, conservative, orthodox, neo-scholastic, organicist, corporatist, feudal. On the other side now was a more modern society: more liberal, tolerant, open, enlightened, rationalist. This widening ideological and cultural division, first surfacing in the eighteenth century but having its origins in the seventeenth, played itself out in nineteenth-century Spain and Portugal in the form of endemic instability and disorder, the postponement of industrialization and further modernization, and on-again, off-again conflict that culminated in the bloody Spanish Civil War of the 1930s and the endemic civil war (complicated by anticolonialist struggles) in Portugal from 1950 until at least 1974.[51]

The divisions and conflicts in the Iberian peninsula from the eighteenth century on were not just ideological and cultural but also social. Conservative Spain and conservative Portugal were concentrated in the monarchy, the Church, the army, the oligarchy, and, geographically, the rural areas, including the peasantry. More liberal Spain and Portugal had their base in the urban areas, among the rising middle class who wanted to be more European, and the emerging commercial class that wished to reduce or eliminate the existing autarky so they could be free to trade with other nations. These social and class divisions, which also had a geographic base, would persist through the nineteenth and early twentieth centuries, continuing to widen until they produced class and political warfare.

In the colonies these same—and other—splits were present. First, as in Iberia, there was the division between traditional, conservative elites and those increasingly shaped by liberal and Enlightenment ideas—perhaps less pronounced, because of geography and distance, in the New World than in the Old, but present nonetheless.[52] Second, there was a widening split between what were called *criollos* (persons of Spanish descent born in the New World) and *peninsulares* (persons born in Spain who monopolized all positions in the colonial administration). One of Spain's policies as a colonial power had been to entrust positions of power only to those born in the peninsula, who would presumably remain loyal to the mother country, as distinct from those born in the New World, whose loyalties might lie elsewhere. But increasingly the monopoly on government positions which peninsulares enjoyed was resented by the criollo elites, who wanted political authority to go along with their rising social and economic power.[53]

A third factor was rising resentment in the colonies at what were perceived to be arbitrary policies emanating from Madrid and Lisbon. For one thing, the new styles of dress, manners, and comportment now practiced in the mother countries were viewed in the more conservative colonies as foreign and hostile, products of the hated French and English. Second, while one may applaud the modernizing reforms of Charles III or Pombal, one should recognize that these were carried out by an even more centralized and absolutist government than had existed under the Hapsburgs. Spain and Portugal borrowed from Louis XIV the *Intendant,* or administrative-state system of government, which employed royal agents with absolute authority to carry out the crown's decrees and which resulted in the total elimination of whatever local autonomy had remained either in the mother countries or in the colonies.

Another factor fueling resentment in the colonies was the very policies the crown was carrying out. Thus, while both Charles III and Pombal were modern, rationalist, Enlightenment thinkers—and, of course, moderns celebrate them for this—they also, as part of their rationalism, took steps to curb the power of the Catholic Church and particularly the Society of Jesus, or the Jesuits. These policies were applied indiscriminately both at home and in the colonies, but they had far greater effect in the colonies. For the Catholic Church and the Society of Jesus, which constituted symbols of order, authority, enlightenment, and civilization in the vast, empty spaces of Latin America, completely monopolized all education in the colonies, and the expulsion of the Jesuits in 1776 by Spain left the colonies entirely without an educational system. Recall also that the Catholic Church had a major role in the colonies in Christianizing and pacifying the Indians, and that immense territories in Mexico, the Andes, and present-day Paraguay had been turned over to the Church and its orders as quasi-feudal reserves. So the new restrictions on the Church and the expulsion of the Jesuits, from the perspective of the exceedingly conservative Hispanic or creole elements in the colonies, threatened to reverse all the gains of the pacification program and to unleash the Indians in ways that might prove unsettling and even revolutionary in the colonies.[54]

The rising presence of these tensions in the colonial system of the late eighteenth century helps one understand the sentiment for independence arising in the early nineteenth century. It is not my purpose to review this history in detail here but only to suggest the main factors leading to the rise of independence sentiment and to preview the changes in store as Latin America became independent. These factors include the following:

1. The growing split between creoles and peninsulares, which many scholars see as the main cause of independence
2. The rising nationalism of the colonial elites and their desire to be free of Spain's and Portugal's administrative centralism.
3. The rising desire among commercial elements in the colonies to be free to trade with such countries as England, France, and Holland and thus to break the inconveniences of the Spanish and Portuguese mercantilist monopolies.
4. The rise of that modern, liberal, Enlightenment-oriented "other" Latin America, increasingly prepared to challenge the older, traditional version.
5. The examples of the American (1776) and French (1789) progressive revolutions, which served as inspirations to like-minded republicans in Latin America.
6. The Napoleonic invasions and occupation of Portugal in 1807 and Spain in 1808, which led the Portuguese monarchy to flee to Brazil and the Latin American creoles to hold power for their deposed Spanish king. When Napoleon's troops were eventually ousted from Spain and Portugal, the creoles thought they would get their conservative monarchy back. Instead, what they received was a more liberal regime that was unacceptable to them, and that was when they moved toward immediate independence.[55]

In other words, unlike the earlier situations in the United States and France, the Latin American independence movements of the early nineteenth century were conservative. They were meant to preserve the white, conservative, Catholic, Hispanic way of life, not to change it except in various particulars, and certainly not to overthrow it. The rallying cry for these creoles was "republicanism," but this republicanism was very different from that reigning in Lockean, Jeffersonian, Madisonian North America. This was a republicanism that retained many of its organic, elitist, corporatist, top-down features. Once again, as in the sixteenth-century Counter-Reformation, the strategy would be to try to adapt traditionalism to modernity rather than jettisoning the traditional institutions.

Many U.S. commentators and policy officials have not understood this crucial factor. They believe that in the nineteenth century Latin America adopted liberalism in its laws and constitutions but that the area was continuously (to this day) frustrated in its efforts to implement liberalism. A more accurate interpretation, however, is that although Latin America elites embraced republicanism in the abstract in the nineteenth century, the form that this took was, in fact, in accord with their own conservative and Catholic traditions and very much unlike liberalism and republicanism in the United States.

Chapter 5

Liberalism and the Latin American Independence Movements

The discovery and colonization of Latin America continued and extended the Reconquest of the Iberian peninsula from the Moors. As noted in the previous chapter, the year 1492 marked not a sharp break with the past but a point of continuity. Essentially, feudal and medieval institutions, which because of the conflict and upheaval associated with the Reconquest were tardy in growing in Spain and Portugal, flowered in the Iberian late Middle Ages and now were carried over by the two mother countries to their colonies in the New World. There, protected by the powerful forces of the Counter-Reformation—the Church, censorship, the Inquisition—feudal institutions that were beginning to fade elsewhere in Europe thrived and received a new lease on life. These institutions were justified, rationalized, and legitimated by the neoscholastic philosophy that constituted orthodoxy in Spain, Portugal, and Latin America and that enjoyed a virtual monopoly of beliefs and ideology for at least three centuries of colonial rule.

In the eighteenth century, however, a split in the Spanish and Portuguese soul, or political culture, also had reverberations in the colonies. Reflecting the reformist, more rationalist, and Enlightenment ideas of the Bourbon monarch Charles III and Portugal's Pombal, a more secular, liberal, rationalist, and modern conception began to creep in. These more liberal views represented a minority strain: Thomism and neoscholasticism remained overwhelmingly dominant in the culture, the universities, the educational system, and in social and political values. Nevertheless, the alternative liberal viewpoint was now present for the first time. Liberalism never replaced or supplanted the more traditional and conservative neoscholastic view but increasingly grew up along-

side of it as a parallel but contrasting set of social and political concepts on which society might be based.

Unlike the situation in the United States, in Latin America liberalism never attained majority status or became the dominant ideology, and it never actually replaced traditionalism. Instead, it represented an alternative but still minority current, an appendage or add-on to the prevailing neoscholastic tradition that, in the absence of a definitive triumph, was forced to seek an accommodation with it. The result throughout nineteenth-century Latin American history was, as in the mother countries of Spain and Portugal, continued conflict between the conservative and liberal visions, between authority and liberty, and hence frequent breakdowns into chaos and confusion. These repeated conflicts retarded and postponed Iberian and Latin American development and produced some crazy-quilt overlaps and hodgepodge patterns of both traditional and liberalizing/modernizing patterns coexisting side by side.[1]

The question I raise here preliminarily, and then return to in later chapters, is whether U.S.-style liberalism has ever triumphed in Latin America. Even in the present context, in which nineteen of the twenty countries are called democratic, it is still not clear that liberalism has definitively emerged victorious. One of the foremost analysts of Spanish neoscholasticism has argued that liberalism is foreign to the entire political culture and political tradition of Latin America;[2] and the political scientist Glen Dealy, in a similar vein, has argued that liberalism has never become the dominant majority strain in Latin America, even to the present day.[3] I am willing to hold such strong conclusions in abeyance for now because I think there has been recently a major and perhaps permanent breakthrough to democracy in Latin America. But even today liberalism and democracy continue to mean different things in the two parts of the Americas and to imply distinct priorities. Current Latin American democracy has largely taken the form, so far, of electoral democracy but not necessarily yet of liberal democracy. Hence, while I acknowledge that a breakthrough to democracy has occurred, I am also persuaded that the continuities with the past in Latin America may be as important as the changes. Hence, one needs to know not just whether democracy has triumphed but also in what form: what kind of democracy has emerged, with what meaning. We begin with the kind of liberalism that emerged during the Latin American independence period and the struggle over liberalism in the nineteenth century.

The Precursors of Independence

In the last two decades of the eighteenth century and in the first decade of the nineteenth, the European Enlightenment arrived, belatedly, in Latin America.[4] Earlier in the eighteenth century there had been occasional proscribed books and ideas that managed to escape the censorship of the Inquisition and arrived in Latin America; but it was only in the latter decades that the writings of Montesquieu, Voltaire, and, especially, Rousseau began to be widely known among the educated elites. The examples of the American (1776) and French (1789) revolutions, the widening split between creoles and peninsulars, and the desire among the Latin American commercial classes for free trade were additional important factors in the wider dissemination of Enlightenment ideas.

Among the most important precursors of independence was the Venezuelan Francisco de Miranda (1750–1816).[5] Miranda was born in Caracas of Spanish parents. Initially buying a commission in the Spanish army, he fought with the Spanish and French against the British in the American revolutionary war. He then fought in the French Revolution, traveled widely in Europe, and became an intimate of several European royal families. Holding a vision of independence for all of Spain's Latin American colonies, Miranda tried unsuccessfully to invade his native Venezuela with a small force in 1806; in 1810 when a serious revolt broke out, Miranda joined Simón Bolívar and other Venezuelan leaders in fighting for independence.

But very much unlike the American liberal revolutionaries, Miranda was anything but a liberal democrat. When Venezuelan independence was achieved in 1811 (it proved to be short-lived), he assumed the powers of dictator. Although he defended popular sovereignty and believed abstractly in human rights, his conception of such rights was top-down and aristocratic, not democratic. Miranda remained a devout Catholic and was a strong defender of the Church. Constitutionally, he advocated a constitutional monarchy, hereditary in nature, that would be headed by, of all things, a descendant of the Incas! A conspirator more than a philosopher, he nevertheless believed in Rousseau's "general will" but saw himself as the personification of popular sovereignty. Within his system of monarchy, Miranda, rejecting Montesquieu (with whom he was familiar), would have the monarch select the members of a judicial body who would hold life tenure. There would be a fourth branch of government called the censorial power that would preserve

114

Catholicism as the one true faith and maintain strict control and even censorship over legislative enactments. These do not sound like the principles of a great liberal democrat. Indeed that is the point: Miranda wanted independence but, as an aristocrat and an authoritarian, he wanted nothing whatsoever to do with democracy and popular rule.[6]

Perhaps second only to Miranda as an important precursor of Spanish America's independence was Colombia's Antonio Nariño (1768–1823).[7] Nariño was a wealthy, aristocratic lawyer and large landholder whose private library in Bogotá numbered six thousand volumes and was among the largest in all the Americas. He also owned a small printing press that he used to print proindependence tracts that he gave to his followers. Receiving a copy of the French *Declaration of the Rights of Man and of the Citizen,* he quickly translated it into Spanish and distributed it. Although this is the act for which Nariño was most famous, he was promptly arrested by colonial authorities. His property was confiscated, and he was forced to flee to France. Eventually returning to Colombia to join the independence movement, Nariño was named vice president by Bolívar in 1822 but was prevented by his political foes from taking office. He died the following year.

Nariño's writings are sometimes referred to as the purest expression of Latin American liberty. But liberty to him and other revolutionary leaders in Latin America meant independence, not democracy. He accepted the hierarchical structuring of society and, in the Aristotelian-Thomistic tradition, believed that natural law supported that view. Nariño ardently favored separation from Spain but the last thing on his mind was to include blacks, Indians, and peasants as full participants in society and the political process. Like Miranda, he advocated a kind of aristocratic republic but not a democratic one. Power would be held by the white, creole elite, not by the popular masses. He wished to rid the colonies of the *gachopines,* as the Spanish peninsulares were derisively called, and to put the creole elite in its place. A devout believer in Rousseau but not of Locke (whom few Latin American intellectuals had ever read), Nariño was attracted to the idea of the general will, but like other independence leaders he saw himself and his fellow aristocrats as personifying the general will, without necessarily having that status decided through a popular vote. Once more the main theme is: independence, yes; democracy or liberalism, no.

A third area in which independence sentiment was strong and independence came early was in the Río de la Plata area of Buenos Aires.

Among the leaders there was Manuel Belgrano (1770–1820). Belgrano
was especially well known for his reflections on free trade and economic
liberalism,[8] but he was doubtful about political liberalism. Buenos Aires
was, after all, one of the main centers seeking to break Spain's trade monopoly with its colonies and to trade freely with other powers; Belgrano
was the chief spokesman for that position. He defended free trade and
urged the introduction of machinery into the colonies, an unheard-of
position in these agrarian, preindustrial societies. Like other precursors,
Belgrano was inspired by the principles of the French Revolution and expressed himself in favor of liberty and equality. But as chaos and anarchy spread in Argentina, he grew disillusioned with republicanism and
became in later years an advocate of monarchism and aristocratic rule.

Another leading figure, more explicitly political, in the Río de la
Plata independence movements was Mariano Moreno.[9] Born of an aristocratic criollo family in Buenos Aires, Moreno at one time determined
to study for the priesthood; he initially became prominent as the legal
spokesman for wealthy farmers. A fluent and flowery writer, Moreno
was the leader of a group of young, proindependence men who were
more radical than Belgrano and his aristocratic colleagues. The fiery
Moreno was another devout follower of Rousseau and a believer in the
theory of the social contract. Calling for the exercise of Rousseau's general will in creating true democracy, Moreno nonetheless believed that
democracy would have to be imposed from above (by himself and his
fellow revolutionaries) rather than chosen from below by grass roots
sentiments. He favored independence and liberty but, like so many
Latin American revolutionaries, was fearful of letting any real power
get out of his own hands and those of his friends and into the hands of
the "unwashed" Indian and peasant masses.

Moreno was, moreover, a very peculiar kind of democrat. First, he
harked back to the very origins of the Iberian/Latin American tradition
of political thought by grounding his philosophy in God, the Stoics, the
Roman lawyers, and the Church fathers. Second, Moreno was so in-
tensely Catholic that he excised Rousseau's anti-Catholic comments
from the *Social Contract* before translating it. Third, while Moreno believed in popular sovereignty in the abstract, he harbored misgivings
about the ignorance of the masses and, as a son of the creole aristocracy, wanted little to do with those lower and darker in the social hierarchy than he. And fourth, though he favored liberty, he feared the
prospects of postindependence anarchy and thus incorporated in the

constitution he drew up articles that preserved elite rule and countenanced authoritarian practices. Moreno is often presented as a pure,
idealistic spokesman for Latin American liberty, but once again what is
meant by that is independence, not liberalism.

In Mexico, another main center of proindependence sentiment, the
early independence movement was fanned by two priests, Father Miguel Hidalgo (1753–1811) and Father José María Morelos (1765–1815).[10]
Mexican intellectual life in the late eighteenth century had demonstrated greater independent thought than elsewhere in Latin America,
at times condemning Aristotle and his logic and praising Descartes;
and the restless Hidalgo was a product of that intellectual environment. A lowly parish priest, Hidalgo was an admirer of Rousseau and
an early apostle of independence; but unlike the other precursors Hidalgo raised the banner of social revolution by mobilizing Indians and
mestizos to the republican cause. Independence was one thing, but social revolt (especially in light of Haiti's recent bloody and destructive
slave revolt) could not be tolerated by the wealthy white, creole elite,
and Hidalgo was soon opposed by those very native-born American
upper classes that otherwise supported separation from Spain. For Hidalgo had unleashed an uncontrolled mass uprising that also carried
racial overtones, a war of revenge by the Indians directed against all
white Spaniards, and for that reason he and his movement had to be
suppressed. Hidalgo's ragtag army was defeated and suppressed and,
after a trial, the priest was shot by a firing squad. Liberalism in Mexico
quickly shrank from egalitarianism when it was confronted for the
first time by a serious Indian revolt.

The revolutionary banner was next taken up by Morelos, who similarly mobilized an Indian peasant army. Gaining control of much of
southern Mexico from which a succession of Indian-based movements
have been launched, Morelos argued à la Rousseau that sovereignty
resided with the people and that they had come together to free Mexico from Spanish rule. Note how different this social contract is from
Locke's: whereas Locke's social compact spelled out the relations between rulers and ruled, Rousseau's vision included only a society's
coming together for political action and was silent about government
institutions, except for that troublesome notion of the general will.
Going beyond the now-familiar independence agenda, however, Morelos urged that slavery, monopolies, taxation of Indians, and special
(corporate) privilege were all to be abolished. Despite promising to

support the Catholic faith and arguing that no other religion would
be permitted, Morelos's revolutionary agenda was unacceptable to
both Spanish royalists and creoles. Declared guilty of both heresy and
insurgency, Morelos was, like Hidalgo, captured and executed in 1815.
The leadership of the Mexican struggle for independence, as elsewhere in Latin America, then fell into the hands of the conservative
creole element, who would lead a conservative movement for separation from Spain but not for liberalism. Nevertheless, in Mexico at least
the spark of genuine social and racial revolution, to go along with the
more limited political changes, had been kindled, and periodically in
subsequent Mexican history racial and class-based revolution would
explode.

Surely one of the most intriguing, and perhaps most representative,
figures of the independence period in Latin American history is Simón
Bolívar.[11] Known as the George Washington of Latin America for his heroic efforts on behalf of independence, Bolívar was of an elite, wealthy,
white, creole Venezuelan family. Well educated, well traveled in Europe,
and steeped in the writings of Rousseau and the Enlightenment, Bolívar
was a man both of ideas and of action. He not only led the independence
forces in his native Venezuela but also liberated Colombia, Ecuador,
and Peru from Spanish colonial rule. In honor of his heroic exploits on
behalf of independence, the country of Bolivia is named for him.

But Bolívar was not just a romantic idealist in the manner of most
of the other leaders. He was also a practical politician, a doubter, a skep-
tic, and this endears him to us moderns. He doubted at times whether
this entire project leading to independence could ever be successful.
He greatly feared the anarchy and social revolution which the revolt
against Spain had set loose. He recognized realistically that Latin America had little institutional or associational infrastructure and no training whatsoever in self-government, and was skeptical that Latin America could govern itself. To remedy that situation, he incorporated in
the several constitutions he had a hand in drawing up a strong executive, broad emergency powers, and a unified, organic state; at various
times he thought only a king could hold Latin America together. He favored independence but wanted a strong hand at the helm in case
things went astray. That, of course, is to countenance the other fork in
the road that has long been considered a viable option in Latin America: a preference oft-expressed in theory and constitution for republi-

canism and democracy but with the option of strong government, usually held in reserve, should chaos loom.

The features that the early precursors and leaders of the independence movements had in common are striking. Almost all of them came from the white, elite, landholding, creole class. Almost all were well born and wealthy. All of them were strongly Catholic in their beliefs and grounded their political philosophy in Catholic teachings and natural law. All of them favored independence from Spain but, except in Mexico, above all else not social or racial revolution. All of them held paternalistic attitudes: they would govern for the people but not of and by the people. And all of them were grounded in the eighteenth-century French Enlightenment, especially in Rousseau, and not in the American tradition of Locke, Jefferson, and Madison.

Why was Rousseau such a central figure to these men? Because Rousseau's thought contained elements of organic unity, of top-down authority, of a corporate community, and of strong, elite leadership that was quite compatible with Latin America's past—and certainly with the background of its founders. Because Rousseau implied that a revolutionary act (expelling Spain and launching independence) could by itself create new governing institutions even in the absence of any previous training or experience in self-government. Because his concept of the general will provided justification for a strong central state and a leader who knows and personifies his people's wishes without going through the prosaic, boring, and difficult tasks of holding elections and building grass-roots institutions; Tocqueville had observed the beginning of such work in the early nineteenth-century United States, but it was almost completely lacking in Latin America. And because Rousseau's social contract implied a people coming together on the strength of a romantic, heroic idea (independence) but without any form of civil society and without spelling out any details of the relations between government and governed that were so strongly present in Locke and the American Revolution.

In other words, Rousseau presents a glorious vision of a new state forming in the absence of any training, experience, or institutions of self-government—precisely Latin America's condition in the early nineteenth century—whereas Locke and Madison present a less glorious, more mundane analysis of how to arrange institutions. But however inspiring and exciting, Rousseau's formula, as Latin Americans quickly

found out, laid the groundwork for authoritarianism and even totalitarianism. It is a dilemma that plagues Latin America (and followers of
Rousseau) to this day.

Events in Europe

The independence of Latin America was a direct result of events occurring in Europe, specifically in Spain and Portugal, in the aftermath of
the French Revolution. Moreover, the arguments over independence
were cast not in modern liberal terms but in precisely the medieval and
neoscholastic terms that had long had such a powerful impact on both
Iberia and Latin America.

The foundation for Latin American independence was laid during
the Spanish Bourbon reforms of the eighteenth century.[12] The Bourbons were reformers, centralizers, modernizers. For that reason historians have tended to laud their efforts and to paint the Bourbons as beginning to lift Spain out of the Middle Ages. But the very reforms that
we moderns tend to praise were often bitterly resented in Spain and
even more so in their strongly conservative and Catholic colonies. For
example, the expulsion of the Jesuits in 1776 was deeply resented in
Latin America for removing spiritual leaders and causing severe dam-
age to religion, education, and good morals. And the centralization
that the Bourbons sought to impose was also resented in the colonies
as eliminating their traditional autonomy and fueros. The Bourbons
sought to substitute a modern, secular state for a patrimonial and
Catholic one, but in Latin America the creoles remained faithful to
both their religion and their patrimonialism. In a famous missive sent
to the king in 1771, the colonists asked for the same rights that the
peninsulares enjoyed and emphasized their traditional (and medieval)
belief in autonomy. Presumably a government that violated their historic rights and autonomy risked breaking the social contract between
people and king that Suárez had set forth and that went back to the
Spanish Middle Ages, and could no longer expect to command the loyalty of its subjects.[13]

That is precisely what happened in 1808 after Napoleon invaded
and occupied the Iberian peninsula, removed the Spanish king Ferdinand VII, and placed his brother Joseph on the Spanish throne. The
Spanish people viewed Joseph as a usurper as well as a centralizer and
a product of the hated (and anti-Catholic) Enlightenment. They rose in

revolt, demonstrated their proclivity for guerrilla warfare, and drove the French usurpers out, actions painted by Goya in unforgettable scenes. The Portuguese people also rose in revolt and, with the aid of the British fleet, similarly forced the French to withdraw. In both countries local or municipal *juntas* were formed to hold power until the legitimate monarch could be restored. For in the Spanish medieval tradition, if the monarch was unable to exercise power, then sovereignty reverted to the people in the form of their local, corporate community.

Much the same thing happened in Latin America and was justified by the same medieval doctrines and the same idea of compact set forth by the scholastic theologians led by Suárez. To the creoles, Joseph Napoleon was viewed not just as a foreign interloper, but as a symbol of the despised Enlightenment, the French revolution, anti-Catholicism, centralization, and a violator of local rights and autonomies. Hence, as in Spain (and in accord with Spanish medieval law), local juntas were organized to hold power until the legitimate Spanish king could be restored. Except among a few extremists, there was at this time (1808–10) little sentiment in favor of a definitive break with Spain. In fact, most creoles preferred to keep their ties to Spain but to a conservative, legitimate, traditional Catholic monarch who would respect their autonomy and local ways of doing things. The holding of power by the colonial juntas, however, even if seen as only a temporary measure, marked a first step toward independence, particularly as the colonists came eventually to see that they were quite capable of governing for themselves and of handling their own affairs, that they could then trade profitably with other powers, and that they did not need the Spanish throne.

The question of loyalties in this discussion owed its origins to the medieval political thought outlined in previous chapters. First, the king was obliged to rule with justice and to act for the well-being of all; that went back to the Bible and medieval Christianity. Second, if he usurped power or became a tyrant, his subjects no longer owed him loyalty. Third, the monarch was obligated to respect the rights and grants of autonomy of corporate groups and regions, which the Bourbons and Joseph Napoleon had violated. And fourth, if the monarch was unable to occupy the throne—precisely the case at this time in Spain and Portugal—power would revert to the people organized as a community, which constituted the ultimate source of all sovereignty. One can see in these principles several legitimate reasons for the colonies to go

their separate ways. Equally striking is how medieval and scholastic—
and certainly not Lockean or Jeffersonian—the arguments all are.[14] It is
clear, therefore, that the Latin American independence movements
were not liberalizing revolutions at all but mainly echoes of events in
the peninsula.

But first, there was a respite from the independence upheavals. In
1814, with the defeat and withdrawal of the French, the legitimate Spanish king, Ferdinand VII, was restored to the throne. He interpreted his
restoration as giving renewed legitimacy to reaction and oppression.
He repudiated the liberal constitution of 1812—the first constitution
in all of Spanish history, enacted during the Napoleonic occupation—
and returned to a position of absolute despotism. He dissolved the local
juntas that had sprung up in his absence. Rather than respecting the
fueros of society's corporate groups and autonomies, he again centralized power in the manner of earlier Bourbons. His policies, rather than
being moderately conservative, which would have been widely ap-
plauded in Spain and the colonies, were instead entirely reactionary
and backward looking. These policies were too much for the growing
groups of liberals in Spain and the colonies who could have accommodated themselves to a continued monarchy as long as it was constitutional, in the Spanish sense, and respectful of traditional rights.

But then in 1820 the pendulum swung back the other way. A revolt
(the Riego revolt) in the Spanish navy against reaction forced the king
once again to accept the constitution of 1812. Liberal elements came to
power: strongly anticlerical, they battled the Church, closing convents,
renewing the decrees expelling the Jesuits, and breaking relations with
the Holy See. The government came to be dominated by Masons, who
were strongly anti-Catholic (in the United States, Masons are viewed as
similar to a social club, but in Spain at this time they were seen as a revolutionary movement). This radical (by Spanish standards) regime refused to recognize any autonomy for the Spanish colonies, insisted that
officials and bishops be appointed that were only loyal to Madrid (thus
resurrecting the old creole-peninsular conflict), and reintroduced the
centralized absolutism of the Bourbons. These steps turned the creoles
in the colonies who had been loyally "holding" power for the legitimate Spanish monarch irrevocably against the regime.

All this was too much for the colonies, especially since they had
been exercising de facto degrees of self-government for some time now.
By this point "foolish Spain," as it was called in the colonies, had suc-

ceeded during the period of reaction from 1814 to 1820 in antagoniz-
ing the liberals but in 1820 it managed to antagonize conservatives as
well. Virtually all groups were now against Spain and moving toward
independence—though the precise form of the independent states was
by no means decided. Between 1820 and 1824, which marked the final
defeat of the Spanish armies in Peru, all of Latin America became independent.

Brazil's independence from Portugal came in a way somewhat different from that of the Spanish colonies, but the issues and debate
were often similar. In 1807 invading French forces that had crossed
Spain (the next year they also seized control there) occupied Portugal.
Under British pressure and protection, the Portuguese court then
moved to Rio de Janeiro. The deposed king, João VI, enjoyed Brazil so
much that he raised it in rank to the level of a full kingdom within the
Portuguese empire and stayed in Brazil even after the Napoleonic occupation had ended. Eventually persuaded that he had to return to Lisbon
or else lose his claim to the throne, João left his son Pedro as his regent
in Brazil. Shortly thereafter, in 1822, Dom Pedro proclaimed Brazil's independence and became Brazil's first monarch. During most of the rest
of the nineteenth century (until 1889) Brazil continued as an independent monarchy, as distinct from the republics that were declared in
Spanish America.[15]

What is striking about these dramatic events is just how traditional
and conservative they all were. The debates were cast exclusively in
medieval and neoscholastic terms—holding power for the legitimate
king—not in liberal or liberalizing ones.[16] These were definitely not social revolutions—the Indian revolt had been ruthlessly crushed—but
conservative "separations" from the mother countries aimed at maintaining and enhancing the power of the creole (native-born) Spanish
elites. There was talk of liberty but this meant freedom from Spain, not
freedom for the lower classes of Latin America, of whom it was still
doubted that they possessed souls. Moreover, what passed for liberalism at this time in Latin America meant protection for corporate group
rights (fueros), not American-style individual rights.[17] Radical and more
liberal voices were heard (rather like Tom Paine's in the American Revolution) and have been picked up by historians because these were the
writers and intellectuals—but they were not the dominant elements in
independence. Rather, it was the conservative, white, Hispanic, landholding creole elite that dominated the movement to independence.

Indeed, what is striking in the analysis of Latin American independence is not how much things changed but how much they remained continuous both before and after independence.

Conservative Revolutions

Although the independence movements of 1807–25 in Latin America are often called revolutions, they were revolutions of a particular kind. Frequently, they are lumped together with the English (1689), American (1776), and French (1789) revolutions under the rubric of "the age of the democratic revolutions."[18] But can the Latin American revolutions be included in the same category as the other three? And were they truly democratic?

First, consider the class backgrounds of those who led the Latin American revolutions. Almost to a man, these leaders were white, Hispanic (creole, not peninsular), upper-class commercial and landholding elements. They believed in a paternalistic and patrimonialist state, not a liberal, democratic, and participatory one. These were not persons who contemplated a fundamental restructuring of social, economic, and political power in the colonies. Rather, these would-be revolutions were led by the "better" elements who would continue to hold power after Spain was expelled. There was almost no consideration given to bringing peasants, Indians, and Africans in as full and equal participants in the political process. The same rigid social categories of wealth, prestige, and race were present both before and after the revolutions. There is no evidence that full democracy was ever considered as a viable possibility for the postindependence republics.[19]

Second, one needs to consider who conducted the independence movements, their intentions, and who inherited power after independence was accomplished. It was again the white, Hispanic, creole elite that had grown up in America but that resented the monopoly on high-level colonial positions monopolized by the peninsulars—those born in Spain. All the evidence shows that the criollos coveted the peninsulars' positions and the prestige and salaries that went with them and wished to inherit them for themselves. The last thing they wanted to do was to upset the existing social hierarchy or to usher in any real democracy. Rather, they wanted to keep the social structure intact, inherit it for themselves, and substitute themselves in the lofty positions held by the peninsulares. They had no intention of sharing power with others or bringing the masses in as full participants in social, economic, and political life.[20]

Third, recall the neoscholastic grounds on which these so-called revolutions were fought. These were not wars of national liberation; rather, they were meant to hold power until the legitimate Spanish and Portuguese kings—temporarily unseated by the Napoleonic occupation—could be restored to the throne. The discussion and debate were almost exclusively couched in neoscholastic terms: Napoleon and his brother were viewed as usurpers of rightful authority; when that happened, under Suárez's social compact, sovereignty reverted to the people (meaning their corporate representatives or local juntas); and they would hold power until the rightful king could be restored. These are not liberal or liberating principles; instead, they have their origin in Spanish medieval law as outlined in a previous chapter, in the *Siete Partidas,* and in the scholastic writings of Suárez and the sixteenth-century Jesuits.[21]

Fourth, one needs to look at what happened to those movements that did raise the spectre of genuine social revolution. In Haiti from 1795 to 1805, the uprising of black slaves against their white masters and the widespread killing and exile of whites and the burning of their plantations served as a clear example to the whites in the Spanish colonies of what not to permit. In Peru the Indian revolt of Tupac Amaru in 1780–83, a forerunner of later indigenous uprisings, was brutally crushed; Tupac Amaru was publicly tortured and then drawn and quartered; and all the descendants of the entire Inca royal family were murdered or sent as prisoners to Spain. In Mexico, the only colony in which Indian social revolt accompanied the struggle for independence, the movements of Hidalgo and Morelos were mercilessly repressed and snuffed out so that conservative elements rallying around Agustín Iturbide could control the process and keep the Indians in their place. In all cases, any hint of genuine social and political upheaval that might change fundamentally the power structure was eliminated so that the creoles could inherit power at the top of the social pyramid without altering the base. Spanish and Latin American liberalism did not, emphatically, imply egalitarianism.[22]

Fifth, in considering the Latin American revolutions, one must always keep focused on the precipitating events in Europe. It was only when Napoleon seized and occupied the Spanish throne in 1808 that the creoles in the New World moved to hold power until the rightful king could be restored. Then when the king was restored in 1814–20, the independence movement died down temporarily—although the king's entirely stupid and reactionary policy toward the Constitution of 1812 also antagonized the Rousseauian liberals in the colonies. But it was only when the king subsequently reversed himself in 1820 and accepted liberal reforms that *conservatives* in the colonies struck for and achieved independence. Had the crown not been so thoughtless in its policies—ultrareactionary at first, ultraliberal (for Spain) later on—it might well have been able to hang on to its colonies for a longer time.[23]

Sixth, the natural law tradition of Latin America continued both before and after independence. The colonial system, of course, had been based on a system of natural law derived primarily from Thomas Aquinas and powerfully grounded on Roman Catholic religious beliefs. Independence had been justified on a similar natural law basis mainly derived from Suárez and his notions of social contract, mutual obligations, and the feudal rights of a sovereign people temporarily lacking a king. Or else, in some cases, they were based on a Rousseauian natural law concept that was secular in origins but similarly based on organic conceptions and top-down authority (the general will). But note that in every case it was a natural law tradition that provided justification for the distinct Latin American positions—not American-style pragmatism, utilitarianism, or secular, procedural pluralism. In the last analysis, it was the natural law tradition combined with stoicism, Roman legal authorities, medieval Catholicism, and Rousseau that constituted the philosophical basis for the new states of Latin America.[24]

The revolutions in Latin America for independence, thus, were never full-fledged revolutions in the proper sense. They were *separations* from Spain, not social or genuine political revolutions. They involved no fundamental class, racial, or social upheaval. They instead involved merely the substitution or rotation of one ruling elite for another: the creoles seized power from the peninsulars but left all the fundamentals of a top-down, two-class, patrimonialist social and political structure in place.[25] The wars for independence in Latin America were thus conservative revolutions rather than liberal or liberalizing ones, and they retained many features of their colonial past—authoritarianism, elitism, hierarchy, theocracy, mercantilism, patrimonialism, and so on—both before and after independence.

New Constitutions for New States

With the withdrawal of the Spanish crown, a legitimacy vacuum existed in the colonies. Sovereignty had shifted, but it was not entirely clear what that meant. New constitutions would have to be drawn up; but the precise form they would take was still open to discussion. Brazil continued as a monarchy until 1889; Bolivia as well as Central America experimented briefly with monarchy; and the realistic Bolívar, despairing over Latin America's institutional void as well as its incapacity for self-government, was not averse to monarchical rule. But for the most part, the Latin American countries after independence adopted republican forms of government.

What kind of republics would these be? A thicket of misinformation and misinterpretation surrounds answers to this question. Most foreign observers, looking superficially at the new constitutions adopted and seeing that they contained the traditional three-part separation of powers, long lists of civil and political rights, and language that is often a direct translation of the U.S. Constitution or the French Bill of Rights of Man, have concluded that what the Latin American founding fathers intended to do was to establish a liberal, democratic polity just like the American. Holding this view, these observers would be bound to consider Latin American history from 1825 on to be a failure. For if liberal democracy is the presumed goal and purpose of the constitutions, then Latin America has never quite lived up to this goal and its history is, therefore, a failure.

Moreover, if this is the goal and Latin America has not lived up to it, then presumably it is up to well-meaning, liberal, and democratic Americans to help them live up to the goals they presumably could not achieve for themselves. One can easily see in this reasoning the logic behind a whole history of American foreign policy toward Latin America, encompassing Woodrow Wilson's efforts to teach Latin America to elect "good men," Roosevelt's Good Neighbor policy, John F. Kennedy's Alliance for Progress, Jimmy Carter's human rights crusade, and recent efforts through the National Endowment for Democracy (NED) and other agencies to help bring U.S.-style elections, political parties, and democracy to Latin America.

But a closer examination of the constitutions adopted by the new states of Latin America reveals that it may not have been U.S.-style liberalism, pluralism, and democracy that Latin America contemplated then—or even now.* Nor were the Latin American founding fathers naive men who adopted unrealistic and unworkable constitutions for which they require American assistance to set them straight. Rather the creoles who wrote these new constitutions were learned and sophisticated—at least as sophisticated as the U.S. founding fathers.[26] But the conditions and realities they faced in Latin America varied widely from those in the United States, and they responded accordingly. The constitutions they wrote were, in fact, fascinating documents, compromise documents, not at all unrealistic, and well attuned to the realities of Latin America.

To begin, the Latin American founding fathers, then as now, had to respond to international fashion, to get on the bandwagon of what were considered the latest international trends. Confident, large, rich, and highly developed countries like the United States do not have to worry much about such things; but small, poor, undeveloped countries with large inferiority complexes do. They must keep up with the latest cultural and political fashions to compensate for other inadequacies. In the early nineteenth century, republican constitutionalism seemed to be the thing to do, the wave of the future, so Latin America had to do it, too. In this way they could give the appearance of being at the same level as the more advanced countries of France, England, and the United States. I do not want to overstate this argument, but undoubtedly fashion and the desire to be among the company of advanced nations had something to do with Latin America adopting the republican constitutions that it did.[27]

Second, it should be understood that, although Latin America adopted republicanism, it did not at this time—or maybe ever—adopt democracy and pluralism. There was no intention on the part of the Latin American constitution writers to share power with blacks, Indians, mestizos, and peasants as full participants in the political process. Rather, power was to be kept in the hands of the creole elites, the aristocracy, in Thomistic terms, the good men. For this reason and continuing throughout the nineteenth century, there were severe property and literacy restrictions on voting. These restrictions were more severe even than in the U.S. Constitution and, depending on the country, effectively

---

*I assume here—not unreasonably—that constitutions and fundamental laws are one expression among many others of the prevailing political culture and political theory of a country.

excluded fully 90 to 95 percent of the population from voting. Neither was the franchise gradually extended as in Great Britain and the United States during the nineteenth century. In this sense, despite the appearance of constitutions and laws, Latin America remained what it had been before independence: a regime of oligarchs and landholders, white and Hispanic, which excluded the darker mass of the population from participation and was by no means democratic. The new constitutions were written of, by, and for the same creole aristocracy that had led the independence movements; it should not be surprising that they wrote constitutions that reflected and reinforced their own interests.

Above all, third, these constitutions emphasized unity. "Unity, unity, unity," said Bolívar; unity was seen as the sine qua non of Latin America. At one level, the emphasis on unity reflected the tradition of harmony and organicism that stretched all the way back to Paul's biblical letter to the Christians at Corinth. The themes of organic unity and centralism have always been integral to the Latin American political tradition.[28] But at another level, the focus on unity reflected the influence of Rousseau, not of Locke or Madison, on the Latin American founding fathers. Rousseau had also stressed organic unity, the coming together of all elements in political society, and, in Rousseau's concept of the general will, a principle of unified leadership that would overcome all of society's pettier divisions. In the modern rationalist age, even in Catholic Latin America, political society could no longer be based exclusively on Thomistic precepts; hence, the turning to Rousseau. For Rousseau provided in secular, rationalist, and updated form a vision of the state and state–society relations that was extremely close to Latin America's hallowed, historic, Thomistic tradition.

Rousseau was popular in Latin America not just for his "glorious vision" of the social contract but because the form he advanced was so close to what the creole elites believed. For within Rousseau's social contract, private individual rights must be given up for the sake of the community because the general will incorporates a fundamental collective good; and the sovereign is the sole interpreter of this general will—an inherently authoritarian concept that is used by dictators as distinct as Pinochet and Castro to justify their arbitrary policies. This pattern of adapting old traditions to new, fashionable philosophies is repeated numerous times in Latin American history, certainly in regard to positivism and corporatism and probably in regard to nationalism, Marxism, and even democracy as well.[29]

Rousseau was attractive for other reasons as well. A single heroic act—achieving independence—could vault Latin America to the forefront of advanced nations. No interest groups, political parties, pluralism, or local infrastructure (which Latin America lacked in any case) were necessary; indeed in Rousseau's conception such features detracted from the heroic goals and violated the general will. Elections could also be dispensed with because a charismatic leader (Plato's philosopher-king, Spain's caudillo) would instinctively know the general will. Everything prosaic and boring (elections, training in self-government, civil society, civic consciousness) could be ignored in favor of the direct bonding between leaders and society. No intermediary associations between citizens and the state were necessary in Rousseau's view; instead the leaders' knowledge of the general will was all that was required: how easy, convenient, and attractive! None of the hard steps that North Americans know are necessary to build and secure democracy were needed. Instead a heroic man-on-horseback would ride out of the sunset (what Rousseau called the state of nature) to save society. He would be unfettered by Madisonian-like checks and balances or Tocquevillian associational life. In the political vacuum that was Latin America in the 1820s one can understand why Rousseau's vision would be attractive. One can also understand how, in the wrong hands, a regime without intermediary associations or institutions can, and often did, lead to dictatorship and repression.

Unity in the sense Bolívar and Rousseau meant it could be best achieved, fourth, by strong, centralized, executive authority. Virtually every Latin American constitution written in the nineteenth century (and often those written even today) vested strong authority in the executive branch. The president was given virtually unlimited powers, and in most of the constitutions of the time could rule almost as a constitutional dictator. In part, this was due to the strong tradition of centralized, top-down rule that was the main Spanish model from the late Middle Ages and was the only system for three hundred years of colonialism. In part, also, it was due to an honest assessment by Latin America's founding fathers of their realities: vast spaces, a near-empty territory, absence of institutional infrastructure at the grass roots and, indeed, at every level, and inexperience in self-government. In the face of all these problems, Latin America's constitution writers reasoned, strong executive leadership was needed to keep the political society from disintegrating. To this end the founders endowed the presidency with such strong and imperial powers that even U.S. president Richard Nixon's "imperial presidency" paled by comparison.[30] As Frank Tannenbaum once wrote of the powers of the Mexican presidency, it represented a cross between the absolutist tradition of the Spanish viceroys and the equally absolutist power of Montezuma.[31]

If the executive power was strong, fifth, other powers had to be weak. That was indeed the case. Neither the congress nor the courts in Latin America ever achieved the independent, coequal status of the American Congress and Supreme Court;[32] and it is probably a mistake for U.S. foreign aid officials to try to strengthen these institutions if the Latin Americans themselves do not want them strengthened. Similarly, local government and federalism have never been strong elements in Latin America, and it is probably a mistake for the United States to force its conception of these institutions on a society in which the traditions and practices differ from the American. For in many Latin American societies, it still requires strong executive power to keep society from disintegrating and its component societal units from spinning into separate orbits.

Latin America has never had a tradition of strong local government; its system is patterned on the French and Spanish systems of centralized control, all power, funds, and policy directions flowing from the central ministries. Second, Latin America has little infrastructure at the local level, no independent local taxing authority, no history of local self-government comparable to the New England town meeting, and hence very little policy-making authority at grass roots levels. Some of these features are now beginning to change largely because of outside (U.S.) pressure, but it is probably still a mistake to try to create in Latin America a local or regional government tradition that never existed before. It is not that the Latin American founding fathers had never heard of or read Montesquieu; in fact, they did, and even incorporated some of his precepts into their constitutions where the familiar three-part division of powers is also present. But while they divided power at one level, they strengthened executive power at others, believing, probably correctly, that in their anarchic societies lacking the Tocqueville-like grass roots infrastructure of the United States only strong executive authority could hold fractured, fissipoucious societies together.[33]

The Latin American constitutions of the new states of the 1820s provided not only for strong executive power at the expense of the courts, congress, and local government but also, sixth, for extensive emergency powers—far more than was ever contemplated in the U.S. constitution or in political practice. In situations of emergency the president could prorogue the congress, send the supreme court packing, suspend all basic rights, call out the army, and rule by decree-law. Moreover, in the often chaotic conditions of Latin America in the nineteenth and even twentieth centuries, these emergency clauses were often invoked. At times the emergency measures were abused by presidents and dictators who wanted to stay in office beyond their terms, get rid of obstreperous courts or parliaments, or deal harshly with their political foes. But when President Alberto Fujimori of Peru, for example, invoked emergency laws and sent his congress packing in 1991, it was not necessarily, as many Americans thought, an abuse of the Peruvian constitution but a series of steps authorized in the constitution. Fujimori ruled as an autocrat but an effective one, and long enjoyed widespread popular support. Such extensive and often-used emergency powers are another indicator that the Latin American political tradition is very different from the North American.[34]

Another indicator, seventh, of the nonliberal character of the early Latin American constitutions were the special and privileged positions accorded such groups as the creole elite, the Church, and the military. These provisions represented both a reflection of earlier, preindependence, and historic Iberian/Christian corporatism and also the realities of the power structure in early nineteenth-century Latin America. Entrenched corporate privilege was at this time far stronger than liberalism. As noted earlier, the very meaning of Latin American liberalism at this time involved not individual liberty but group or corporate liberties. The model was not the Lockean, individualistic constitution of the United States but the corporately based Spanish constitution of 1812. These corporations were seen as the residual holders of power and self-discipline in a state that had lost its head and was threatened by anarchy. Although in some countries there were efforts to weaken corporate privilege, in most they were strengthened; indeed, independence often meant an effort to create new corporate structures where none had existed before. The state itself became the most powerful corporation; a new hierarchy of corporate social groups was actually strengthened by independence; and the new constitutions provided for an oligarchic, corporatist, and patriarchal state. Corporatism was another of

132 those hallowed ideas, along with hierarchy, organicism, authority, and

patrimonialism, that continued before and after independence and was actually strengthened in the process. A strong, centralized state that protected the fueros of corporate groups was the great compromise reached in the constitutions of Latin America, which also provided its meaning of "democracy."[35]

In the French Chapelier Law of 1791, following closely on the outbreak of the revolution, corporate, guild, and group rights were all abolished, paving the way for individualism to triumph in the socioeconomic sphere as in the political. In one or another liberal episode in the early nineteenth century, Spain, Portugal, and most of the countries of Latin America followed the French lead in formally abolishing corporate privilege. But the reality was often quite different: (1) only some limited corporate groups and privileges (the guilds) were abolished; (2) the most important corporate units (Church, army, oligarchy) maintained or even enhanced their privileged positions after independence; (3) other groups were reconstituted as corporate bodies using new concordats or organic laws to replace the ancient feudal fueros; (4) the same corporate or group (as distinct from individual) habits and behavior often continued; (5) over time Latin America became, arguably, more corporative after independence rather than less; and (6) the same statist, authoritarian, top-down controls and requirements for recognition of new groups persisted.

I have already remarked on the literacy and property holding requirements for the suffrage, which ensured that the landed or creole elites would remain the dominant and virtually only force in the new republics. The "oligarchy" constituted the most important and powerful corporate group in the new republics. With regard to the Church, most of the new constitutions proclaimed Catholicism the official religion of the country and gave generous public assistance to Catholic schools, hospitals, and charities. Neither did these new constitutions touch the Church's extensive landholdings, which in Mexico, for instance, came to encompass some 60 percent of the national territory. The rationalist and Enlightenment principles that many of the Latin American founding fathers professed to hold at times made the establishment of an official Church and an official religion difficult or even controversial, but it is striking how many of the founders and precursors were rationalist in other areas but strongly defensive of Catholicism in the religious realm. Mexico's José María Luís Mora, for example, the most prominent liberal in the early nineteenth century, was anti-

Spanish but strongly elitist, antirevolutionary, and pro-Catholic. Recall also that when Argentina's Moreno translated Rousseau's *Social Contract* into Spanish, he omitted Rousseau's anti-Catholic sections even while strongly admiring the French philosopher's political theory. Gradually over the course of the nineteenth century, the Latin American countries did move toward the constitutional principle of formally separating church and state, but often these provisions were only partial and seldom prevented either the designation of Catholicism as a privileged religion or state aid to parochial institutions. In addition, Latin America was so thoroughly Catholic in its social and political assumptions and political culture that the mere formal separation of church and state constitutionally had little effect on the actual practice of political and social life.[36]

The armed forces constitute an especially interesting case. Already in the late colonial period, the military had been given special responsibilities and its own corporate fuero comparable to the special charters granted to the military orders in the Spanish Middle Ages.[37] Emerging from the independence struggle, in addition, it was the creole-created militias that constituted the most cohesive and often only national force in the new republics.[38] The armed forces stepped into the power vacuum created by the withdrawal of the Spanish crown to help hold these torn, fragmented, underinstitutionalized new nations together. The army was often the only instrument of order, authority, and unity. Reflecting these realities, most of the new constitutions elevated the army into virtually a fourth branch of government.[39]

This principle is very hard for Americans to understand because they have nothing comparable in their own constitution. But in most Latin American constitutions to this day the military is the subject of an entire section of articles. Usually the first of these articles proclaims the armed forces to be apolitical and nondeliberative, but then the remaining three or four articles go on to give the military special responsibilities that are themselves eminently political: to maintain domestic peace and tranquility, to defend the nation against all foes foreign and domestic, to keep out foreign-inspired political forces and ideologies, and to serve as a moderating force (the so-called fourth or moderative power) politically if the civilian political forces are paralyzed or unable otherwise to govern.[40]

These provisions often thrust the Latin American militaries into
politics and power whether they wish to be or not. And because the

military often intervenes under constitutional provisions, it should not necessarily or always be seen (as Americans tend to see it) as tyrant and usurper of the constitution (although that may also be the case) but as performing the responsibilities its constitution set forth for it. U.S.-style precepts of civil–military relations and of the strict subordination of the military to civilian authority have little relevance in this context, in which, in the absence of strong and stable civilian institutions, the armed forces are obliged to play a stronger role than U.S. citizens could countenance, and most often do so not as constitutional usurpers but because their constitutions give them the responsibility to play this role.

A particularly explicit statement of the kind of organic state and system of corporate representation as a carryover from Spanish history and the colonial period was provided by President Agustín Iturbide of Mexico in 1821 in his recommendation for the structuring of the congress of the newly independent republic.[41] Iturbide proposed that the seats in the congress be apportioned on a social or corporative basis rather than on the usual territorial basis, as follows:

Social Category	Number of Seats	Percentage
1. Public officials	24	18.5
2. Ecclesiastics	18	13.8
3. Litterateurs/Intelligentsia	18	13.8
4. Laborers	10	7.7
5. Miners	10	7.7
6. Artisans	10	7.7
7. Merchants	10	7.7
8. Army	9	6.9
9. Navy	9	6.9
10. "Rest of the People"	9	6.9
11. Nobility	3	2.3

Several features of this scheme are interesting. First, it is clear that Iturbide was continuing the tradition of strong executive authority of the Spanish monarchs because all these corporative positions were to be appointed by him. Second, although the number of seats reserved for laborers is large for this era, it is more than offset by representation from the miners and merchants guilds. Third, the army and navy combined have the same number of seats as the clergy, reflecting the traditional dominance of these strong groups. Fourth, the large number of seats reserved for public officials reflects the significance of the central bureaucracy in Iberian and Latin American political life. At the same time, fifth, the small number of seats given the nobility is not an indication of limited criollo elite influence but only of the fact that at this time there were few titled nobility in Mexico. In the final analysis Iturbide's corporatist system of representation was not adopted in Mexico, yet it is nonetheless of great significance both as a reflection of the Mexican president's thinking and of the continuing influence of organic-corporatist ideals both before and after independence.

Latin American constitutions of the early nineteenth century were thus very different in form and purpose from the American Constitution. And, underlying all these other disparities, their philosophical roots differed as well. Latin America's first statesmen all but uniformly rejected eighteenth-century political liberalism. Their ideas derived mainly from Greek, Roman, and Christian thought and, more recently, from Rousseau, not from Locke, Madison, and Bentham. They did not conceive of politics in the manner of Locke as the satisfaction of competing interests; in fact (and again following Rousseau) they were opposed to competitive interest groups. Instead, politics for them continued to be the achievement of the common good in the tradition of Saint Thomas. The common good could no longer be achieved under Spanish rule; hence, republicanism and independence—but it was still the neoscholastic concept of the common good that prevailed. Good government similarly depended not on checks and balances but on the recruitment of good men—that is, those whom God had blessed and who constituted the better people. Restraint was not procedural or institutional but, above all, moral, in keeping with Catholic religious precepts. Government and leadership were based on virtue. Opinion had to be uniform, organic. Modern democratic theory was not embraced at this time; rather, independence leaders and subsequent constitution writers were thinking still in medieval, scholastic terms. They adopted some liberal ideas but gave them very traditional meanings and put them in traditional forms. As Glen Dealy concludes, "The preponderant weight of [Latin American] political thought was derived from sources other than modern, Western constitutional philosophy."[42]

This brief review of the basic constitutional principles adopted after independence demonstrates several conclusions. First, and in keeping with a mountain of other evidence presented in this chapter, that the

Latin American independence movements did not represent as sharp a break with the past as is often thought. Second, that the independence movements in Latin America were conservative movements, not liberal ones. Third, that the Latin American founding fathers embraced republicanism and independence in the 1807–25 period but not liberalism, pluralism, or democracy. Fourth, that both before and after those dates Latin America continued to be cast in a Catholic, organicist, integral, and corporatist framework that was fundamentally different from North American liberalism and individualism. And it was not, fifth, either that the Latin American founding fathers were naive or that their countries were less developed but fated eventually to develop in U.S. paths; rather, right from the beginning Latin America opted for a political direction that was different from the U.S. one, reflecting both its own historic political tradition and its own political realities.

A word needs to be said about Latin American legal philosophies prevailing during this period and about the legal systems adopted by the new Latin American states. It should not be entirely surprising that these legal systems and philosophies were reflective of the same assumptions and traditions that undergirded the constitutions and constitutionalism; indeed, they were part and parcel of the same philosophical traditions. First, much of Latin American law derived from Roman concepts and legal precepts with their emphasis on order, unity, authority, and hierarchy. Second, it derived from the Christian and Thomistic conception of a hierarchy of laws (divine, eternal, natural, man-made—in descending order of importance) with emphasis built upon and similar to the Roman conception. Third, it stemmed from the Spanish-Portuguese medieval heritage, specifically from the Siete Partidas and the updated neoscholastic writings of the great sixteenth-century Jesuit jurists, with their emphasis on organicism, corporatism, and statism. And fourth, it came from the Spanish legal codes, themselves derived from the Napoleonic Code, and adopted almost uniformly by the Latin American countries after independence: similarly top-down, absolutist, deductive, and covering all contingencies. In short, Latin America has a powerful code law tradition, not one based on Anglo-American common law.[43]

What are the implications of these differences? Latin America's legal culture (which deserves more attention than we can devote to it here) is important in helping us understand the overall political culture and tradition. First, the codes are full and complete documents; **137** the presumption is that they encompass every possible situation. Second, the codes are promulgated from above, on the basis of Christian precepts or by an all-powerful rule-giver; they do not grow organically from below or on the basis of experience. Third, the codes are absolutist and authoritative if not authoritarian documents; they do not provide for the gradual, empirical building of precedents through cases. Fourth, the codes and legal training are based on rote memorization and deductive reasoning. In all these ways the Latin American legal systems are closely parallel to the constitutions in that they both reflect and reinforce an absolutist, closed, top-down, authoritarian political tradition and history. That is beginning to change as are many other things in Latin America, as new concepts of law (including North American concepts of individual rights, judicial review, checks and balances) come to the fore. But Americans make a mistake if they believe they can simply transfer American common-law legal precepts to the Latin American context: they simply do not fit there. They similarly are mistaken in believing they can ignore this legal system and the legal culture that goes with it in trying to understand Latin American politics.[44]

Political Realities

The discussion so far in this chapter has been at the level of political theory: the ideas of the precursors, the scholastic basis of the arguments to hold power for the ousted Spanish monarch, the conservative nature of these movements for independence, and the laws and constitutions adopted by the new Latin American states. And indeed, in the years of the independence struggles from 1807 to 1825, there was much discussion, at least among intellectuals and political leaders, of alternative political models and formulas.

It seemed possible in the early to mid-1820s that the liberal, often idealistic and even romantic point of view might triumph. In Argentina in the early 1820s; in Mexico under Hidalgo and Morelos; in the Dominican Republic under the early idealistic independence leaders Duarte, Sánchez, and Mella; in Chile, Colombia, and several other countries, the liberal (albeit in a particularly Hispanic or Rousseauian fashion) point of view actually came to power or close to it, if only temporarily.

But then reality set in. The liberals were often idealists, dreamers, naive intellectuals; they had no experience in government, in administration, in running a country. They seemed to actually believe the Rousseauian idea that the mere act of coming together into a political society and the writing of a "perfect" constitution would in themselves assure stability and prosperity. The Spanish colonial system had offered creoles no preparation in self-government. In every country, the number of trained, experienced personnel could be counted on the fingers of one hand. The situation in Latin America in the mid-1820s was similar to that in the new states of Asia, Africa, and the Middle East in the early 1960s: few experienced leaders, almost no training in self-government, and a host of insurmountable problems.[45]

Immediately after independence, crisis and disintegration set in in practically every Latin American country, with the possible exception of Brazil, which continued as a monarchy, and Chile, where the elite oligarchy moved quickly to reconsolidate power. The economies of most of the countries, in the absence of the established Spanish trade pattern, reverted to a more primitive, subsistence existence. Commerce, trade, and business—never robust—declined precipitously. Class, social, and race relations, once locked in place by the rigid Spanish-Thomistic system of caste and hierarchy, were upset, unstable, uncertain. There were only limited race or class rebellions during this period, but a strong sense of the old established order giving way. Politically, the four viceregal units of the Spanish colonial system broke up into smaller and smaller units until, as in Central America, they became the size of city-states, too small to be viable economically or as nations. Meanwhile, in the absence of strong central authority or even a viable national government, the Latin American countryside fell into anarchy and unregulated conflict.[46]

All these negative developments associated with newly won independence strengthened the arguments of conservative and reactionary elements. Liberty and even the limited liberalism allowed were portrayed as giving rise to libertinage and anarchy. The familiar conservative calls for order, discipline, authority, and stability became insistent and claimed new legitimacy because of the reigning chaos. The social order needed to be strengthened, conservatives argued, and if the old caste categories could not be restored, then at least there should be recognition of the "natural inequalities" of men and a very limited franchise that would keep the elites in power indefinitely.[47]

The anarchic conditions prevailing reinforced the argument for strong central authority that had always been present in the colonies.

The Latin American continent in the early nineteenth century was vast but underpopulated and nearly empty in interior areas. There were few serviceable roads, no railroads, no steamship lines. There was no institutional infrastructure, no network of communications or transportation grids, no webs of association to tie the continent or even its individual countries together. In the absence of solid institutions and infrastructure and in conditions of breakdown, ungovernability, and fragmentation, if not disintegration, a new principle of order and discipline was strongly called for.

Into the vacuum created by the withdrawal of the Spanish crown and postindependence chaos stepped the army. These armies, often ragtag and unprofessional, had been organized during the independence wars to battle the Spanish forces. They were the heirs of the ancient Spanish system of military fueros. During the independence period, the creole elites and the often mestizo- or mulatto-dominated armies had struggled for the same cause. In the new republics the armies left over from these wars were often the only organized, national, disciplined, coherent group. Within three or four years after independence, by the late 1820s, the army had replaced the ineffectual, liberal civilians, and in all but a handful of countries was firmly ensconced in power. Its leaders were rough-and-ready caudillos, who galloped in and out of the presidential palace with frequent regularity. The most prominent included Juan Manuel de Rosas in Argentina, Antonio López de Santa Anna in Mexico, the twin caudillos Pedro Santana and Buenaventura Báez in the Dominican Republic. For quite a number of countries the era of caudillo rule persisted intermittently throughout the nineteenth century and well into the twentieth. But for most countries the first era of caudillo rule lasted from about the mid-1820s until the mid-1850s, when a new period began.[48]

The independence armies and their often-dictatorial leaders were now in power, but they did not act alone. The military regimes were generally backed by the Church and by the creole oligarchies. Both groups saw their interests as being best protected by a military regime that reestablished discipline and order. The Church and the elites turned to and often supported the military as the last, best hope against anarchy, confusion, and disintegration. From this period stems the familiar notion that Latin American politics is dominated by a triumvirate of power consisting of the army, the Church, and the oligarchy. It is not that the oligarchy saw the often peasant and mestizo/mulatto-dominated armies as their equals in a social and racial sense. Instead, it was a marriage of convenience by which the army (along with the Church) secured order and discipline and kept the lower classes in place, and the creole elites provided the personnel to staff the cabinet and high government positions. Thus in the early republics were landed and social wealth, military power, and religious and intellectual life intimately interrelated—often literally so.

The new military authoritarians and the civilians who supported them often drew up new constitutions to replace the allegedly liberal documents adopted initially by the newly independent republics. The first constitutions in Latin America, products of the independence struggles and of the influence of Rousseau and the Enlightenment, had at least some liberal provisions. Notwithstanding the restrictions on the suffrage noted earlier, the extensive powers of the executive, the wide range of emergency powers, and the corporate privileges of the oligarchy, the army, and the Church, these earliest Latin American constitutions incorporated the principles of civil and political rights, separation of powers, and (modestly) representative government. But the new constitutions written by the military guardians of the 1820s to 1850s gave so much power to the executive as to make the president a virtual constitutional dictator, reduced the power of the congress and courts still further, expanded the list of emergency powers and made it easier to suspend human rights, and elevated corporate privilege.[49]

Henceforth, there would be two constitutional traditions in most of the Latin American countries. The first tended (within the limits already set forth) to be more liberal, democratic, civilian, pluralist, and human (or at least civil—this is pre–Jimmy Carter) rights oriented. The second tradition, while retaining republicanism, was more conservative, organic, corporatist, elitist, authoritarian, integralist, and top-down. These two constitutional traditions and the political regimes that went with them largely alternated in power for the next one hundred years and (depending on the country) more. This helps account for the large number of constitutions (thirty or more) in the history of some Latin American countries. In point of fact, most countries had two basic constitutions, with variations; but it seemed like far more because of the common practice of promulgating a new constitution every time a new regime came to power. But in actuality much of Latin America's nineteenth- and early twentieth-century history could be written in terms of the alternations between two quite distinctive basic law traditions: the one more-or-less Hispanic-liberal, Rousseauian, and democratic and the other neoscholastic and frankly and unabashedly authoritarian.

Richard M. Morse, perhaps the leading historian of Latin American political culture, has an interesting interpretation in these regards that parallels my own. He argues, as I do, that until 1820 the dominant political/philosophical tradition of Latin America was Thomistic. But with the defeat and withdrawal of the Spanish crown, Morse suggests, the "Thomistic keystone" (his term) was withdrawn. Efforts to find a substitute, a new royal family, a single unifying force were in vain, and therefore Latin America's "centrifugal separation" was for the first time unleashed. Into this chaos, Morse says, stepped the independence caudillos, unlettered followers more often of Machiavelli than of Saint Thomas. Not Machiavelli in the secular sense that separated politics from morality, for Latin America continued as a very Catholic region—but Machiavellian in the sense of the use of raw power and manipulation. In the absence of strong institutions, the experience of self-government, and a rich associational life, Latin America had to be governed by strong men, by dynamic personalities, by men-on-horseback. On top of the liberal-conservative split, therefore, Morse (and more recently Roland Ebel) sees a split between the Thomistic principles that continued (like the laws and constitutions) to be held up as ideals and the principle of raw power as personified in the caudillos. Neither of these traditions was liberal in the modern sense.[50]

The existence of these two constitutional cum political traditions, however, tells one a lot about Latin America and its change processes at this time. Heretofore, there had been only one Latin American ideological tradition: traditionalist, Catholic, Thomistic, neoscholastic, organic, integralist, Hapsburgian, and Suárezian. But after that split in the Spanish, Portuguese, and, by extension, Latin American soul in the eighteenth century, and now particularly with independence and the impact of Rousseau and the Enlightenment, a second and more liberal tradition had emerged. The liberal tradition did not replace the older, more conservative one, however; rather, the two continued to exist side-by-side throughout the nineteenth and early twentieth centuries. They constituted two rival power structures, two great and parallel pyramids of society and politics coexisting uneasily within the same countries. Each "society" had its own apostles and its own Machiavellian caudillos, each with a distinct social and often geographical base. The conservative power structure still had its base in the rural areas among landowners, peasants, the creole elite, the Church, and, now, the army. The more liberal power structure was based in the cities and included commercial elements, the middle class, intellectuals and writers (*pensadores*, "thinkers"), and mestizo and mulatto elements.[51]

Liberalism continued to grow and expand its base in the nineteenth century. In some countries, notably Mexico in 1857 and again in 1867, liberalism even came back into power and carried out significant reforms.[52] Some countries—Chile, Costa Rica, Uruguay—began to open up democratically and to evolve in a more liberal direction. That progression has led some historians, mainly liberals themselves, to portray the march of nineteenth-century liberalism in Latin America in teleological terms as showing, presumably, the inevitable march of history toward a more just, liberal, and democratic society. The enemies of liberalism—the Church, the army, and the oligarchy—would then have to be portrayed in the vilest of terms as holding back not only liberalism but also "history." History as thus presented pitted good-guy liberals against bad-guy conservatives; the end product of this moralistic, either/or struggle would be a society just like that of the United States or Western Europe.

But that view is surely too simple: (1) Liberalism in Latin America seldom if ever (and only in two or three countries) achieved a majority position. (2) The neoscholastic position all through the nineteenth century remained at least as strong if not stronger than the liberal one. (3) Liberalism never became a mass movement; it was always limited to handfuls of elite intellectuals. (4) Liberalism in Latin America (Spanish, Rousseauian) meant something quite different from North American, Lockean, pluralist liberalism. (5) Liberalism in Latin America, given its ongoing Catholic and corporatist traditions, was seldom a complete denial of the historic past but only an effort to append the new liberalism onto a neoscholastic base; the Latin American liberals of the early to mid–nineteenth century became the conservatives of the end of the century. (6) It is not at all clear, in the nineteenth century and later, if Latin America wanted North American–style liberalism and pluralism. (7) Rather than an inevitable and unilinear march toward liberalism, nineteenth-century Latin American history should be conceived as an ongoing struggle between two competing conceptions of life and society that were so far apart as to be almost unbridgeable. In many respects that struggle is still going on today.

These two power structures, the conservative and the liberal, re-mained quite distinct. They seldom touched or overlapped or blended with each other, and there was little of the leavening and moderation of views that comes with American-style pluralism with its multiple, cross-cutting memberships and loyalties. Instead, the competing power structures of Latin America formed two separate tendencies and world-views within the same nation. Representing two quite dissimilar soci-etal epochs and historical eras, the one feudal and medieval and the other more rationalist and nascently modern, these two power struc-tures remained in a state of virtual and often actual civil war through-out most of the nineteenth century and part of the twentieth. Indeed, much of Latin America's nineteenth-century history can be written in terms of the ongoing civil strife between the two paradigms and of the often desperate efforts to find a formula for bridging and reconciling the two. That search—and the solution arrived at—is the subject of the next chapter.

Chapter 6

Positivism: A Philosophy of Order and Progress

By the middle of the nineteenth century, some of the most pressing disputes associated with new nationhood in Latin America had been largely resolved. These included the issues of determining boundaries, recognition, and sovereignty for the new states; the relations between central and local or regional authority; and the church–state issue under which the Roman Catholic Church was gradually and at least formally separated from official roles. By this time, in addition, the several processes of disintegration—social, economic, political—that had set in after independence had been halted; the first generation of strong-arm men-on-horseback (Rosas, Santa Anna) had largely passed from the scene; and political power was being reconsolidated under oligarchic or military rule. The economies of the area were beginning to recover and a considerable measure of political stability had been restored in many areas.[1]

The next period, from the 1850s until approximately 1890, represents a new phase in Latin American development. This period may be termed the first stages of modernization or, in W. W. Rostow's terms, the "preconditions for take-off."[2] During this period the population of Latin America began to increase, and settlers moved into the vast empty spaces. Immigration brought more people from Europe, many of whom had commercial and entrepreneurial skills that the area lacked. New banks and financial institutions were chartered, providing economic infrastructure and reflecting the economic quickening.[3] Foreign capital, chiefly British initially but over time including American investment as well, began to come in, serving as a further stimulus to the economy. With the foreign capital, new roads, railroads, port facilities, and telephone and telegraph capabilities were built, providing additional infrastructure, knitting the Latin American countries together as real nation-states for the first time, and stimulating exports. New lands were opened up for cultivation, and the increased production of export crops brought Latin America into the world economy for the first time. During this same period the bureaucracy and the armed forces were modernized and rationalized, and political systems in many countries became more stable or at least predictable.[4]

To accommodate all these changes, to rationalize and explain them, and to bridge the gap between the older medievalism and scholasticism and the newer, updated liberalism and accompanying modernization, a new political philosophy was needed. That philosophy was positivism, a system of thought that, because of the features of Latin America discussed earlier, had far more influence in that continent than it did in the United States, where Hartzian liberalism was already ensconced as the dominant political ideology and tradition.

New Ideologies

After its first, rather unhappy and disillusioning experience with Rousseau-style liberalism in the 1820s, followed by a period of authoritarianism and caudilloism from the 1820s until the 1850s, Latin America experienced a twenty-year period from the 1850s to the 1870s of uncertainty, of questioning, and of a renewed search for first principles. Eventually positivism would fill that void, but it was not until the 1860s that positivism was first broadly introduced into Latin America and not until a decade or two later that the new philosophy was thoroughly incorporated into Latin American thought. In the meantime, a number of other, relatively minor (as it turned out) intellectual currents were introduced into the Latin American pantheon of ideas.

The Latin Americans drew mainly on European thinkers writing during the early to mid–nineteenth century, a period of immense change and conflict on the European continent. The ideas and social movements then stirring Europe included capitalism, the industrial revolution, the French Revolution and its aftershocks, the conservative reaction to the French Revolution, romanticism, liberalism, the European revolutions of 1848, Napoleon I and III, utilitarianism, socialism, Marxism, as well as positivism. Latin American political philosophy during this period, drawing inspiration from this huge variety of ideas, was largely derivative, imported from Europe, and not always adapted to Latin American realities. Further, as Miguel Jorrín and John Martz argue, "The eclectic approach of many Latin American *pensadores* prevented the development of a single, consistent, and clearly enunciated set of ideas"[5]—as happened in the United States, where the liberal-democratic ideal dominated. Latin America was still casting about for an appropriate political philosophy adapted or adaptable to its own history and circumstances. Eventually it would find that philosophy in positivism, but first there was a great deal of exploring of alternatives and experimentation.

One of the early nineteenth-century European philosophies that found its way to Latin America was utilitarianism. Utilitarianism as a set of philosophical ideas had emerged mainly in England and is closely identified with the writings of Jeremy Bentham and James Mill, father of John Stuart Mill. Utilitarianism was a practical or "utilitarian" philosophy closely related to realism and the British political economy, then undergoing industrialization and rapid social change. Utilitarianism's famous slogan was, "The greatest good for the greatest number"—a pragmatic idea in accord with emerging British realities. More concretely, this philosophy stood for the ideas of free trade, a laissez-faire economy, and a minimalist (not mercantilist!) state. But while these ideas were appropriate for England at that time, they had no grounding in Latin American realities characterized by agricultural or subsistence economies, as yet no industrialization, a powerful Catholic (not utilitarian) tradition, and a history of strong statism and mercantilism. Hence, although utilitarianism was taught at the University of Buenos Aires in the 1820s and had some influence in Mexico, it never caught on widely among Latin American intellectuals and had only a limited impact on the region.[6]

A second imported, distinctly minority philosophy during this period was utopian socialism. Utopian socialism had its origins in eighteenth-century Europe and was popular during the early stages of industrialization in the nineteenth century. Such utopian socialists as the Frenchman Henri Saint-Simon and the Englishman Robert Owen reacted against the impersonalism, impoverishment, and lack of community that characterized modern mass society as it underwent the first stages of industrialization and urbanization. Long before Marx, they urged the socialization of property; and Owen, a wealthy industrialist, was instrumental in establishing early socialized communities. Utopian socialism found some adherents in Argentina and Chile in the early nineteenth century, but again the problem was that this imported philosophy had little to do with Latin American realities and was ill adapted to them. For while some independence leaders had believed the expulsion of Spain would lead immediately and inevitably to greatly improved, often idealized social, economic, and political conditions, that, of course, did not occur. In addition, the lack of industrialization and of a genuine working class in Latin America ruled out such premature utopian schemes. Jorrín and Martz argue that it was the failure, first, of liberalism, and then of utilitarianism and utopian socialism that paved the way for the triumph of positivism later in the century.[7]

A third imported philosophy during this period was Krausism. Karl Christian Friedrich Krause (1781–1832) was a relatively obscure (not nearly so well known as his contemporaries Kant or Hegel, for instance) German philosopher who developed a system of panentheistic thought called idealism. Krause believed society was a spiritual, not a biological, organism; he was thus in line with a long tradition of Catholic thought going back to Saint Paul. Society represented the conscience of its various components (traces of Catholic corporatism here), which permitted both humans and society to progress toward the image of God. Krause hypothesized the synthesis of humans and society to produce a kind of religious humanism that also had a social conscience.[8]

Krause would have remained an obscure German philosopher with no impact on Latin America except for the fact that in 1844 the Spanish government sent a young Catholic intellectual, Julián Sanz del Río, to Germany to study. Sanz fell under the influence of Krause's ideas and, upon returning to Spain and assuming the first chair in the history of philosophy at the University of Madrid, taught that philosophy was an ideal doctrine of man's ethical life. This doctrine suggested that the individual could find freedom in the pursuit of ideals that required a social conscience. Krause's ideas, which had limited appeal in his native Germany, spread widely through Spain and had considerable impact in Latin America. They may have become popular in the Spanish–Latin American world because of their seeming compatibility with Catholicism, on the one hand, and their advancement of idealism and social justice on the other. Krausism was attractive also because it appeared to bridge the yawning, perilous gap between traditional Catholicism and conservatism *and* a modern liberalism that often tore

Latin America apart in the nineteenth century. But its popularity never extended beyond a handful of intellectuals, and it never attained the status of a full-blown ideology that would help hold the region together against the pressures of disintegration.

A fourth philosophy that gained adherents at midcentury and thereafter was spiritualism. Spiritualism was probably the dominant system of philosophy in nineteenth-century France. Indeed, it is largely viewed as a French phenomenon and is almost entirely unknown in the Anglo-American world. Identified with the French philosopher Victor Cousin, spiritualism sought a new principle for a world whose spiritual ties had been broken by the great revolution of 1789. Drawing on German idealism and literary romanticism, Cousin sought to blend idealism and materialism into a synthesis of what he called spiritualism, a term that in French and Spanish carried a double meaning involving "spirit" as well as "mind" and providing a synthesis of the two pointing to God.

To most moderns, spiritualism, as well as its predecessors idealism and Krausism, sounds like obscure gibberish, but one can understand why it enjoyed currency among intellectuals in nineteenth-century Latin America. First, it seemed to reconcile historic Catholicism with modern, rationalist philosophy. Second, it offered a way of combining materialism and idealism—then beginning to be an issue in Latin America as well. Third, it was French and therefore stylish, for by this time France had replaced Spain, England, and Germany as the country that Latin American intellectuals most admired and traveled to. And fourth, spiritualism found a following among all sectors of society: in Brazil, where spiritualism was (and is!) especially popular, a lower-class spiritualism is often combined with African beliefs while an educated, originally French, middle- and upper-class spiritualism is frequently fused with Catholicism and humanism.[9]

However, while all these philosophies had their adherents at different times, varying obviously from class to class and from country to country, none of them ever completely caught fire. None of them ever became *the* dominant philosophy for the region, comparable to liberalism in the United States. Rather, these remained minority philosophies in Latin America, often blending and fusing with the older Catholicism and scholasticism but never actually replacing them. At midcentury and beyond, Latin America still lacked a coherent political philosophy capable of holding society together and giving unity of direction.

Liberals versus Conservatives (Again)

After the initial flirtation and partial experimentation with liberalism in the 1810s and 1820s, conservatives, oligarchs, and military men-on-horseback dominated Latin America for the next thirty years. But by the 1850s, with the passing of the first wave of postindependence leaders, the conflict between liberals and conservatives flared anew. Often, depending on the country, the fights continued intermittently well into the twentieth century. But at the same time greater stability, foreign investment, and economic growth in a number of the countries began to alter the nature of the contest.

What before had largely been a clash between individual leaders or amorphous, unorganized groups now increasingly became a struggle between organized interests. During this period Latin America's first political parties were organized. Conservative forces usually organized themselves as a conservative party while liberal elements organized as a liberal party. In such countries as Colombia and Honduras, these historic conservative and liberal parties are still functioning; in other countries new ideological movements or offshoots of the original parties eventually came to the fore.

Both conservative and liberal leaders were recruited from the elites of Latin American society. At this time the suffrage remained extremely limited, slavery was still countenanced in most countries, and neither conservatives nor liberals wanted to admit the masses as full participants in the political process. The conservative party usually consisted of one coterie of elite families while the liberal party was made up of rival groups of elites: Tweedledum and Tweedledee. The two groups jockeyed for power: control of the presidential palace, from which jobs, treasure, patronage, and economic opportunities flowed. Both groups sought to mobilize regional or national caudillos to support their power bids, and both rallied the peasants who toiled in their estates and enterprises. But over time this very competition for spoils and power inexorably led to an expansion of the suffrage and, hence, at least the potentiality for greater democracy.[10]

Although the competition between conservatives and liberals was mainly a struggle for power and the benefits that accrued from controlling the government, it had ideological and policy components as well. Conservatives usually stood for a strong central state, the unity of church and state, and high tariff barriers so as to protect their local

150

production and keep out foreign competition. Liberals, on the other hand, often wanted to freely carry out their business activities unencumbered by statism, bureaucracy, and mercantilism. They stood for the classic nineteenth-century freedoms, including free trade. And they wanted an end to corporate privilege—at least in part, so they could grab the lands of the groups that held vast quantities of it, namely, the Church and the Indian communities. Neither group spoke of a meaningful democracy.

Conservatives continued to stand for all the familiar principles of the past: order, discipline, authority, hierarchy, a Catholic society in which all were secure in their station in life. Conservatives continued to cite Latin America's familiar problems as a justification for strong, even authoritarian government: the vast empty spaces, the lack of infrastructure, the absence of organizational and associational life, and the lack of experience in self-government. These are the familiar laments that authoritarians and dictators have continued to use to this day. "How can you talk of democracy in a country that lacks roads, bridges, or economic development?" questioned the longtime Paraguayan strongman Alfredo Stroessner.[11] "A country that has no highways, no literacy, no agriculture, no public buildings, no electricity, and no 'civilization' cannot possibly have democracy," said the Dominican Republic dictator Rafael Trujillo.[12]

But now conservatives also adopted a more explicit ideological stance as well. Once again the major ideas came from Europe and were derivative in nature. For in the aftermath of the French Revolution, a conservative backlash had set in in France and Spain. The chief spokesmen for the conservative cause in these years of the early to mid–nineteenth century were Joseph de Maistre in France and Donoso Cortés in Spain. Both writers were archconservatives. They wished to restore the status quo ante—an impossible task then as now—to go back to the traditional, Catholic, orderly, hierarchical society of prerevolutionary times. They rejected the Enlightenment and its concepts of rationalist inquiry, preferring the harmony and uncomplicated wisdom of revealed truth. They insisted on a restoration of order and discipline and a society based on hierarchy. They wanted the Roman Catholic Church and Catholicism restored to their earlier status as the official church and religion, with strong state support. They also urged the restoration of the society of corporate rights and mutual obligation from before the revolution, of monarchy held in check only by corporate group and customary rights, and an end to the rampant individualism, egoism, and anarchy that they saw in republicanism and liberalism.[13]

These ideas had a powerful effect on Latin American conservatives, providing intellectual and philosophical justification for what they believed and intended to do anyway. The traditional forces in Latin America adopted these ideas to strengthen their position and hang onto power. But whereas such a reactionary stance is perhaps understandable in the early nineteenth century, when society was still conservative, two-class, and nonparticipatory, it was not adequate in the latter part of the century and on into the twentieth, when new, more dynamic social forces began to appear. Then, a new, initially more progressive form of Catholic social theory began to appear: corporatism (see chapter 8).

Liberals were not exactly standing pat during this period. Their ranks continued to grow. The success and growing influence of the liberal society in the United States was one important influence on Latin American liberalism. Liberalism in Latin America also benefited from the cyclical and now (again) growing reaction against the conservatives following their tyrannous regimes of the first two or three decades of independence. As the conservative and dictatorial regimes of Rosas in Argentina and Santa Anna in Mexico, to name only two, crumbled and collapsed, a reinforced liberalism stood waiting in the wings ready to inherit power.

Only a sampling of the names and writings of the mid-nineteenth-century liberals can be offered here. What is striking about them is that they were more realistic and pragmatic than the first generation of postindependence liberals, less romantic and less influenced by Rousseau, more programmatic (even, occasionally, utilitarian) and desirous of implementing reform as opposed to simply advocating a desired ethical good. In several countries, liberalism actually came to power and even stayed there for a period of time.[14]

In Mexico, for example, the liberal writer José María Luís Mora remained a devout Catholic but rejected Rousseau, whose concept of the general will he saw as leading to despotism. Mora favored republicanism but, following Montesquieu, wanted an independent legislature and judiciary and a system of federalism so as to check and reduce concentrated central authority. In economic matters Mora valued the individualism of Adam Smith and, though a Catholic, argued that a corporation like the Catholic Church could hold property only as a civil

152

right, not as a natural right that took precedence over societal rights. Liberalism in Mora's case generally accorded with the neoscholastic, intellectual framework of Thomas Aquinas and Suárez but was modified to fit new realities.[15]

Andrés Bello (1781–1865) was born in Venezuela but spent most of his mature years in Chile. He was an economic liberal and a follower of Bentham and James Mill. A believer in natural law, Bello nevertheless rejected the particular Rousseauian version of natural law concerning the supposed presocietal natural rights of man. Instead, he based his philosophy on the classical conceptions of Roman law and on Aquinas and the sixteenth-century Spanish Thomists. Bello sought to link the republican order to Roman traditions in order to secure continuity with the past and preserve stability in the context of recent independence. Unlike some other theorists at this time, he did not reject Spain and all it stood for; rather, he saw Latin America's development as a long process of evolution that would be advanced through education. He differentiated between independence, which he believed Latin America was prepared for, and self-government, for which it had little preparation. Hence, Bello, following Bentham, had a strong belief in reform through legislation, and he generally accommodated the conservative oligarchy that would govern Chile from the 1830s until 1891, a system that promised order and stability over democracy. In his emphasis on legislation and orderly political processes, Bello was one of the few Latin American leaders who was closer to Locke than to the romantic idealism of Rousseau and the early independence leaders. He was also a firm believer in continuity and stability even within a context of republicanism.[16]

Across the Andes in Argentina, a new generation of leaders, the generation of 1837, was reacting against the continued dictatorship of Rosas. Esteban Echeverría (1805–51) was the first to argue that Argentina should not slavishly imitate Europe but should base its destiny on the climate, geography, and resources of Argentina. He further argued, correctly, that independence had not fundamentally changed the structure of Argentine society from colonial days and urged a more thoroughgoing restructuring than the one that had accompanied independence. Like Bello, Echeverría saw national salvation through education and a political liberalism in which individual freedom would be the base for progress, no longer corporate group rights or the common good.

Juan Bautista Alberdi was also a member of the generation of 1837. His political theory showed the influence of utilitarianism as well as liberalism, of laissez-faire economics as well as limited government, of Rousseau as well as Locke. His most famous work, *Bases y puntos de partida para la organización de la república Argentina* (*Bases and points of departure for the organization of the Argentine republic*), is a classic of political analysis and, as the *Federalist* papers did in the United States, served as a foundation for the democratic Argentine constitution of 1853. He favored a strong executive while also providing for a federal system, but allowing the central government to intervene under special conditions in the provinces. Like Echeverría, Alberdi wanted a political system— one over which he would eventually govern as president—that both expressed national ideals and was attuned to the realities of Argentina— that is, one that would resolve the historic conflict between the urbane, sophisticated city of Buenos Aires and the rough-and-ready countryside. Alberdi was the author of the famous phrase, "To govern is to populate," under which Argentina (and most other Latin American countries) began a vigorous campaign to entice immigrants to fill its empty spaces and, therefore, solve the historic problem of a *falta de civilización* (lack of organization) that had long plagued the area. Like other countries during this period, however, Argentina encouraged only European immigration and, therefore, the policy was fundamentally racist. Jorrín and Martz summarize his political philosophy as "liberal realism."[17]

A third member of the generation of 1837 was Domingo F. Sarmiento. Sarmiento was a fascinating figure who traveled widely, admired the United States and its accomplishments, and, like Alberdi, rose to the presidency of Argentina. He is most famous as the author of *Facundo: Civilización y barbarie* (Facundo: Civilization and barbarism), a thinly disguised fictional account of the Rosas dictatorship. The book's subtitle indicates its major theme: the contrast between the cultured, sophisticated, progressive capital city of Buenos Aires and the uncultured, barbaric, backward countryside. Through education as well as the immigration of Europeans, he argued, the countryside could be brought up to the level of the capital. Sarmiento's liberalism, therefore, implied that through the bringing of culture, broadly defined, to the countryside, the reactionary, uncivilized rural sector of the population could be progressively educated into presumably modern, universal liberal values. But the actual history of Argentina for the next hundred years did not quite work out that way.

The triumph, however short-lived, of liberalism during the 1850s was perhaps most complete in Mexico. There, following the ouster of the dictator Santa Anna, the liberals returned to power, from which they had been excluded since the 1920s. In 1858 they enacted the famed *Ley Lerdo,* which undermined the corporate basis of large, institutional property holdings. The law was aimed primarily at the Roman Catholic Church, whose holdings, under mortmain, encompassed upwards of 60 percent of the national territory. But it was also aimed at Indian communal holdings, called ejidos, which in Mexico were also immense. The freeing up of these previously corporately controlled holdings enabled Mexico's emerging bourgeoisie and private landowners to swallow up these lands, put them in production for global markets, and steadily push the Indians off these fertile lands and into the infertile hillsides—a process that was one of the major factors leading to the Mexican Revolution of 1910–20. The liberals were in power from 1855 to 1862 and then again, following a brief French occupation of Mexico during 1862–67, from 1867 to 1876.

It is plain from this brief survey of some of Latin America's main midcentury thinkers that liberalism in the 1850s was quite different from the earlier romantic liberalism of the 1820s. Liberalism now was more pragmatic, realistic, and utilitarian. Though the discourse was still largely cast in Catholic terms, it was not so rigidly Thomistic, Suárezian, and reactionary as in the earlier generation. Rousseau continued to be influential, but his ideas were now merged with those of Locke, Montesquieu, Jefferson, and even Madison. The earlier statism and mercantilism were similarly giving way in some writers to ideas of laissez-faire and a reduced state. Politically, there was greater emphasis on checks and balances, on individualism over corporate group rights, on separation of powers, and fundamental political rights. The liberals of the 1850s and 1860s were now more mature, more experienced, more willing to adjust to realities than their idealistic predecessors.

The historian Ralph Lee Woodward maintains that by the 1870s liberalism had triumphed virtually everywhere in Latin America.[18] This was nineteenth-century liberalism, however, usually limited, partial, and not very democratic. Many countries continued to alternate between conservative and liberal factions. In other countries the liberals "triumphed" but in the form of liberal caudilloism that was not very different from the authoritarian, statist, top-down variety. In yet others, the Rousseauian tradition remained powerful, or else it was combined in strange-bedfellow arrangements with more Lockean forms. In all countries the form of liberalism—still characterized by strong executive authority, strong emergency laws, corporate group rights over individual rights, frequent dictatorship and patrimonialism, a special place for the Church, and elite leadership with the masses excluded from democratic participation—looked quite a bit different from emerging liberalism in the United States.

If Latin American liberalism often seemed not very liberal, there is good reason. For precisely at the time when it seemed that liberalism was on the verge of triumphing in Latin America, it underwent a metamorphosis: it was fused with and absorbed by positivism. For the next fifty years or so, from the 1870s until World War I, it is positivism that triumphs, not liberalism. Indeed, positivism became one of the major intellectual movements in Latin American history—far more attractive there than in the United States. The seeming triumph of liberalism that Woodward emphasized was really a false triumph, for it disguised what was occurring underneath. Latin America adopted many of the trappings and appearances of liberalism (and even, as we have seen, *some* of its realities); but more fundamentally its underlying power structure had not changed all that much. And in positivism the elites found a way to maintain the existing power system even while appearing to be moving in a more liberal and even progressive direction.

The Positivist Credo

By the 1850s and 1860s, as Latin America was beginning the first stages of economic takeoff, it was abundantly clear that independence from Spanish and Portuguese colonialism and the writing of often-idealistic constitutions were, by themselves, inadequate means of securing stability and progress. Not only had the immediate postindependence political systems proved inadequate but the severing of the earlier mercantilist ties to the old mother countries had proved far more disruptive than anticipated, leading to economic stagnation and even decline. As Jorrín and Martz observe, "A kind of insularity had grown up, with backward and primitive economies staggering along on their own, no better and sometimes even worse than they had been under colonial rule."[19] In addition, politics in the region remained terribly unstable, regional men-on-horseback galloping in and out of the presidential palace with frequent regularity. The Church, the army, and the oligarchy retained reactionary views and continued to play a strong role vis-à-vis the state.

By the 1870s liberalism seemed to have triumphed as the official ideology in most if not all Latin American countries; but liberalism's triumph, if it was such, seemed to be chiefly among intellectuals. The main centers of power continued to lie elsewhere, unchanged, among the landed, clerical, and military elites. The strength of these traditional groups may, in fact, have been augmented by the foreign investment, economic quickening, and growth of infrastructure that began in the 1850s. But by this point a new commercial-mercantile-importer-exporter class was growing up alongside the traditional oligarchy. They needed somehow to be accommodated to the prevailing social and political system. Hence, Latin America was engaged in an almost desperate search for a new political formula, a formula that would solve the conservative–liberal conflict, restore stability, and open the way for economic progress.

Some intellectuals tended to believe they had found such a formula in the new, updated, more pragmatic liberalism that had emerged throughout the continent by the 1870s. But as in the 1820s, liberalism in Latin America by the 1870s took some very peculiar forms, quite different from those in the United States. Shaped and nurtured by the elite groups, Latin American liberalism now took on a positivist direction. For just as in the immediate postindependence period, liberalism in Latin America took on Rousseauian, top-down, organic, often authoritarian characteristics, so now in the 1870s it was infused with the positivist credo. The positivist orientation within Latin American liberalism remains powerful to this day; it is incumbent upon researchers, therefore, in seeking to understand both this early history and today's transitions to democracy, to understand how and why this is so and what its larger implications are.

Positivism in Latin America derived mainly from the French philosopher Auguste Comte (1798–1857), though it also borrowed from such English writers as Herbert Spencer, John Stuart Mill, and Charles Darwin. Comte was the author of two major works, *Cours de philosophie positive* (Course of positive philosophy, 1830–42) and *Système de politique positive* (System of positive politics, 1851–54). In these volumes Comte attempts the following ambitious agenda: (1) to systematize all previous knowledge, (2) to found a new and comprehensive school of philosophy, (3) to create a new science of sociology, (4) to develop a new religion, (5) to fashion blueprints for a society of the future, and (6) to found a new system of education. As Gertrud Lenzer remarks in her introduction to Comte's writing, this is a man who lacked neither ambition nor immodesty.[20]

Comte is one of those philosophers, like Saint Thomas, Rousseau, and Marx who, in Isaiah Berlin's terms, is a "hedgehog."[21] That is, he has one *BIG* idea or vision that he elevates into a principle for all of history and all of mankind. Berlin contrasts the hedgehogs with the "foxes," who have many smaller, less all-encompassing, more pragmatic ideas. In this second category Berlin places such philosophers as Machiavelli, Locke, and John Stuart Mill. In Berlin's analysis, the all-encompassing ideas of hedgehog philosophers tend to lead to absolutism if not totalitarianism. In contrast, the ideas of fox philosophers tend to lead to incremental and democratic changes. Unfortunately for Latin America, it has been dominated by hedgehogs for most of its history, seldom by foxes.

Comte's world view or grand theory (his hedgehog idea) is based on the premise of an organic natural order in the universe that encompasses and links all categories of phenomena. He divides all knowledge into five groupings: astronomical, physical, chemical, physiological, and social. He believes the social, or the study of humankind, to be the most complex of these and thus to occupy the highest plane of human knowledge. For this reason Comte is often considered the founder of modern sociology. But his was a total or wholistic system; all the parts were organically linked. If this and other Comtean themes sound familiar in Latin American history, it is not coincidental.

Comte argued that the human race's previous efforts to understand social phenomena had evolved in three stages. The three-stage analysis was attractive to Latin American followers of Comte because it seemed to fit their own history. The first of Comte's three stages was termed the supernatural, in which knowledge is seen as absolute and the universe as supernaturally created. Latin Americans identified this stage with their colonial era, in which Thomism, Catholicism, and neoscholasticism were all-dominant. The second stage Comte called the metaphysical, which is only a slight modification of the first stage because it substitutes abstract or natural law forces for the supernatural and does not change very much. Latin Americans identified this stage with their early independence period, during which such natural law philosophies as Rousseau's began to supplant the earlier Thomism. Comte's third stage is the positivist stage, in which humans abandon the search for absolute, supernatural, or metaphysical explanations and instead focus on the allegedly scientific laws that govern the behavior of the universe and all its social phenomena. Latin American intellectuals seized upon this stage as the one they were entering in the 1870s, purportedly more rationalist, modernizing, and scientific than those that had gone before.

Comte argued that there were historical and social scientific laws that governed all social phenomena, including how a society moved from one of his stages to the next. In order to understand these laws of universal sociological development, one must rely on two intellectual endeavors that apply equally to all categories of phenomena. First, one must use observation in accord with scientific methods to discover the processes that push progress along. Comte saw this as a neutral or value-free activity, although in his view people had the ability to affect the rate of progress. Second, one uses reason, in the sense of mathematical, abstract logic, to link discoveries from both the past and present, discern the laws at work, and thereby engineer practical social and political programs, such as education, industrialization, and social programs.

In Comte's analysis, the social sciences (including sociology and political science) would be governed by the same kinds of immutable scientific laws that governed the natural sciences, a highly dubious proposition. Human society cannot change these laws, Comte argued, but it can speed up the development process—a concept that lies behind a great deal of the past and present centuries' efforts at social engineering. Social and political actions formulated on the basis of these scientific laws, Comte argued, will have "real and durable results" because they are "exerted in the same direction as the force of civilization." Comte thus abandons the earlier, usually religious, search for ultimate absolute truth, suggests that his own vision of political sociology and the laws governing it be accepted as a scientific given, and argues that by following these laws humankind and all other categories of knowledge were marching inexorably toward an ultimate perfection or scientifically derived utopia. This march he calls progress or the "force of civilization." How comforting it is to know that one's own ideas are not only "scientifically correct" but historically inevitable. All teleological history (which assumes a final, inevitable endpoint to the process), whether stemming from Saint Thomas and the Church fathers, from Comte, or from Marx, employs these same inevitable and universal presumptions. **159**

Other features of Comtean positivism rendered it uniquely attuned to and attractive in Latin America:

1. Comte attacks the individualism of Locke and the United States and offers a scientific basis for the system of organic unity and corporate group rights that had long been a part of the Latin American tradition. He says the Enlightenment concepts of individual liberty and popular sovereignty represent a negative revolutionary reaction, a temporary state of "unbounded liberty" in which the "human mind was left by the decay of the theological philosophy and which must last until the social advent of positivism." Here, then, in the name of progress, civilization, and science, was a justification for limiting individual rights and imposing an authoritarian collectivity.

2. As in Saint Thomas, Suárez, and Bolívar, to say nothing of Latin American elites and oligarchs, order was the prerequisite in Comte's scheme for all progress. Order, both social and political, "was the condition of all development." At the same time, he wrote, "progress is always the object of order." Hence, the Comtean slogan of "order and progress"; hence, also, the authoritarian, conservative argument so often heard in Latin America that liberty must be limited and strict order maintained in order to achieve progress.

3. Comte emphasized the leadership role of intellectuals and elites in the process of discovering and implementing the programs that would lead to progress and the advance of civilization. This notion has always been especially attractive to those who would lead and direct Comte's plans, the intellectuals and the elites themselves. The "theoretical labors of observation," he writes, "that are necessary to obtain the special and general facts of a given country" (each country or society was at a different point of development or progress, and thus one had to know the special conditions and level of each), and the further intellectual efforts needed to ascertain or distill "the general laws of human progress in its particular historical configuration" require the respective skills of an educated scientific elite and an even higher elite of "savants" (like Plato's philosopher-kings). Such elites are capable of formulating the imperative generalized abstractions as well as practical political and social plans that can then be "implemented to guide society forward." "Human beings must then submit to the results of these theoretical labors," he wrote, "and conduct must be brought in line with the developments so established in order to avoid any oscillations that might prolong the advent of these developments." A round justification indeed of elitism and authoritarianism.

4. Comte argues that at this point in history, when the theological and metaphysical philosophies are still present—both of which are incompatible with positivism—there will be "shock and resistance" to introducing positivist plans. To minimize social disruptions, he suggests that materialism and the accumulation of wealth serve as an interim substitute, though he warns against a too uneven distribution of wealth. He also sanctions the use of force as a means to establish and maintain the order necessary for progress. Such force, he says, has two components: wealth and numbers. Although not indicating his own preference in terms of type of government, Comte notes that in most circumstances wealth and numbers should be combined. Here again an argument for the vast accumulation of wealth, for oligarchic rule, and the authoritarian, perhaps military controls to go with and maintain it.

5. Comte proposes a social order with the following key actors: the social science "knowledge leaders," who by their observation and analysis determine the plan for the social system; the "savants," who help lead and implement the changes; artists, who by "painting a picture" of the new social system encourage public acceptance of the necessary social reorganization and reforms; "industry chiefs," who are to provide the wealth and execute and operate the necessary institutions; and modern, professionalized armed forces, who maintain the order essential to the whole plan. It is no accident that it is precisely during this period that Latin America moves to expand and professionalize its military institutions.[22] And is it not convenient for Latin America's then-current leaders that Comte's social order encompasses a quite accurate portrait of Latin American society at this time: oligarchic, led by intellectual and business elites, with a strong army to maintain order.

6. Comte talked grandly of advancing through positivism the course of civilization. But it was precisely the lack of civilization (infrastructure, institutions, population, associational life) that Latin American intellectuals had been lamenting had hindered their development in the past. Another reason for positivism's attractiveness, therefore, was that it promised to fill this void, to secure the advanced civilization that Latin America had historically lacked. Even the term Comte used—"civilization"—was precisely the one Latin America had used in decrying its underdeveloped status. Positivism promised to help Latin America overcome these problems and leapfrog into the modern age.

7. Comte favored education, but it was to be a new kind of education. He sought to recast education in a positivist mold by (a)

creating elite institutions that would ensure a ready supply of managers, scientists, and savants, and (b) redirecting mass public education as a means of "directing the future of society" and preparing its members for a practical life. Comte's system of elite education, of course, fit Latin America quite nicely (Similarly, France's system of elite managerial and foreign policy schools are still based on this Comtean conception), and his idea of preparing the masses for a "practical life" fit in nicely with the prevailing perception of a two-class society in which the lower members accept their "station in life" and needed to be only minimally educated.

8. Comte had proposed that his philosophy of positivism be elevated to the status of a full-fledged religion. And in his country of origin, France, a positivist church and religion were founded. But in strongly Catholic Latin America, the religious aspect of positivism rarely caught on. Instead, positivism was grafted onto the already existing Catholicism, with its similar emphasis on order, organicism, and hierarchy, and fused with it. Only in Brazil, with its powerful spiritualist as well as Catholic currents, did the positivist religion find a strong foothold.[23]

Positivism's Reception in Latin America

Positivism's impact in Latin America was enormous. It came just at the time the region was searching desperately for a political philosophy to replace both the discredited scholasticism identified with Spain and colonialism, and the anarchic, individualistic liberalism that failed to work very well in the Latin American context. Positivism seemed to provide an answer, a political philosophy that was French and progressive, that seemed to fit Latin American history, and that offered a formula for national development at a time when Latin America was entering its first stages of modernization. Warmly received there, positivism spread quickly throughout Latin America, particularly, as would be expected, among elites and intellectuals. Virtually every regime that came to power and virtually every social or political program from, say, the 1880s until approximately World War I was infused with positivist influences. The movement was strong in every country but especially so in Mexico and Brazil.

Positivism was introduced into Mexico following the triumph of the liberal Mexican reform movement begun in the 1850s and then reconstituted by Benito Juárez in 1867 following the ouster of French forces who had briefly occupied Mexico. The driving out of the French was, according to the Mexican social and political historian Leopoldo Zea, a "mental emancipation, a kind of second independence."[24] The reformers who came to power with Juárez (known as the Abraham Lincoln of Mexico) sought to create a new, national political order; positivism was seen as offering a philosophy that could replace the older, Spanish, colonial system of underdevelopment, subordination, and backwardness.[25]

Gabino Barreda (1820–81) is credited with introducing positivism into Mexico and with adapting it to Mexican circumstances.[26] In his "civic oration," delivered in the immediate aftermath of the Liberals' triumph in 1867, Barreda took Comte's three stages of history and fit them to Mexican history. Comte's theological stage was equated with the colonial era, the metaphysical stage was seen as the war of independence against Spain, and the positivist stage was identified with the Juárez movement's victory over the French invaders. This latest stage also represented a triumph of the liberal forces over the older conservatives. Hence Mexico, by superimposing Comte's stages onto its own national history, was poised on the brink of entering the most advanced stage. As with Marxism, it is very comforting to know that one's political agenda is in accord with the "inevitable" stages of history.

For their part, the liberals supporting Juárez apparently saw positivism as progressive, in accord with the latest trends in philosophy, and as offering a platform for reform that could unite its radical and moderate factions. They also saw it as a way to substitute a modern philosophy for the reactionary beliefs they identified with Catholicism and as a means to carry out their reform agenda under the banner of a progressive, advanced, and presumably global philosophy. For Barreda's philosophy also seemed to place its faith in the emerging Mexican bourgeoisie as well as in intellectuals to hoist the banner of "liberty, order, and progress" as a counterforce to Mexico's reactionary forces.[27]

Within three months of his speech, which launched the positivist movement in Mexico, Barreda had been invited to join a commission working on a new national educational system. The educational system the commission subsequently advanced was purely secular in nature, divorced from Mexico's historic Catholicism, and heavily influenced by positivist beliefs. It provided for a complete and thoroughgoing educational restructuring from the elementary to the professional level. It was signed into law by President Juárez in December 1867. Other social and economic reforms inspired by the positivist credo were also promulgated.

The coalition supporting the Juárez government, however, was a tenuous one; it faced the strong opposition of still-powerful conservative forces, and it broke up over differing definitions of liberty. For Comtean positivists like Barreda and his now-numerous disciples, liberty consisted of unconstrained, wide-ranging freedom for the scientific and intellectual classes to identify the laws that move society forward according to the positivist philosophy. Positivism had thus become a new orthodoxy; the intellectual's role, much as in Marxism, was not to question the prevailing belief system but only to discover the supposedly immutable laws of the new faith. Nor under the positivist belief system did liberty mean laissez-faire economics or individual liberty in a Lockean sense. Instead, for Barreda and his followers, liberty was a concept compatible at all times with order and a strong state. As it was so often in the Latin American tradition, order was valued above all else, for without order, Barreda argued, there could be no liberty. In both the social and political spheres, according to the positivists, liberty meant only the freedom, within a properly-structured society, to obey what its laws indicate. Clearly this was a very narrow and conservative definition of liberty and had nothing to do with what North Americans would think of as individual civil and human rights.

In 1876 this most recent of Mexico's occasional liberal episodes came to an end, and the liberal regime was replaced. In its stead came the long-term dictatorship of Porfirio Díaz, 1876–1910. The new president presided over a period of stability and economic growth unprecedented in Mexican history, one that vaulted Mexico into a position of leadership in Latin America. He built roads and infrastructure, pacified the countryside, professionalized the army and government bureaucracy, attracted foreign investment, began industrialization, opened new lands for cultivation, and vastly expanded Mexico's exports. In the process he also squeezed the peasants and Indians off good lands, jailed and terrorized his opponents, and thereby prepared the way for the great Mexican social revolution of 1910–20. But for much of his rule, Díaz was looked on as progressive and developmentalist.

During the time Díaz was in power, positivism was at its height in Mexico. Its practitioners were no longer the liberal positivists that had supported Juárez but a larger, conservative but forward-looking group. Barreda's disciples—now known as *científicos,* or scientists, because positivism claimed to be a scientific philosophy—were instrumental in staffing and planning the Díaz reforms. The Díaz regime was more pragmatic than philosophical in advancing the positivist agenda, but clearly positivism supplied a programmatic roadmap for the regime. Significantly, "Liberty" was now dropped rom the positivist banner, leaving only "Order and Progress." The liberal constitutionalism and reform program of the *juarecistas* that the positivists had earlier supported were now ignored or repudiated on the grounds that they had given people liberties for which they were ill prepared and that produced only anarchy. The positivists argued that the earlier educational reforms had produced a new generation "capable of directing the nation along the best roads, a practical generation, positive and realistic."[28]

This was a second generation of positivists, quite different from the earlier liberals. Barreda and the positivist position had always valued order above all else. Now, in Díaz, they certainly had a regime that emphasized order—often with a vengeance and certainly at the sacrifice of individual liberty. According to Zea, this second generation of positivist intellectuals came from the rising middle class, identified with the possibilities for upward mobility under the Díaz regime, and now blended Comte with Spencer, Mill, and Darwin for the purposes of advancing their own interests, keeping the lower classes in their place, and justifying the rising power of the army, the Church, and the elites whose support the regime required. Not only was order now seen as paramount but the accumulation of wealth was viewed as an instrument of social progress that, therefore, must be protected by the state.

That wealth was increasingly unevenly distributed in Mexico was seen as confirmation of Darwin's evolutionary principles of natural selection. If Indians and peasants are deprived of their land so it can be given over to large landholders and exporters, that too was in accord with social Darwinism. When immigration and population growth were encouraged, that too, as elsewhere in Latin America, meant white, European immigration, which was justified by the positivist beliefs. Furthermore, liberty was now seen as meaningless in a country lacking economic progress. As Justo Sierra, the most prominent second-generation positivist, proclaimed, it was "natural for a people existing in the most miserable conditions in life to seek the invigorating force of a strong center." The maintenance of authoritarian rule, or a "strong center," was seen by Sierra and other positivists during the Díaz era as a "necessary sacrifice on the altar of social evolution."[29]

By the 1890s Mexico was booming, the Díaz regime was at the height of its power, and the positivist intellectuals who served it were openly linking political order with economic freedom for the rising business class. Business elites and foreign investors were viewed as the most progressive and enlightened interests in the society. Díaz was praised by these elements and the positivists as providing the required order, unity, and strong state that enabled society to develop. But the regime was becoming increasingly authoritarian and narrowly based, overbureaucratized and out of touch, and unable to see the rising discontent at lower levels. In the meantime the positivist científicos continued to assist the regime in such areas as export agriculture, military reform, financial reform, infrastructure upgrading, and foreign investment. Unfortunately, the positivist regime-servers lost touch with Mexican realities and became increasingly divorced from their own society. As the Díaz regime was discredited and eventually overthrown in 1910, the positivist philosophy so closely associated with it was discredited as well.

Positivism in Brazil, as in Mexico, became closely associated with government and regime change. But Brazilian positivism diverged from Mexican positivism in both its class base and its political impact. Furthermore, the religious aspects of Comte's positivism, never salient in Mexico, had a major following in Brazil, and a number of Temples of Humanity (as the churches in Comte's religion were called) were founded there.[30]

Positivism in Brazil began to grow in the 1850s and 1860s during the monarchy of Dom Pedro II, but it flowered in the 1870s and 1880s— about the same time as in Mexico. Positivism was introduced through some of the intellectual elites that taught at Brazil's technical and military schools. Perhaps the leading advocate of positivism was Benjamin Constant Botelho de Magalhães, the director of the military academy in Rio de Janeiro. Constant was a heterodox positivist, but he shared the general Brazilian concern about the national lack of progress, the disorder of society, the need for educational reform, and the poverty of intellectual life. His students at the military school were mainly middle-class military officers, not the white criollo elites as in Mexico.

In Brazil, positivism came to be closely identified with the fight to abolish slavery in the 1870s and 1880s, which culminated in the emancipation decree of 1888. Brazilian positivism also came to be identified with republicanism, which triumphed in 1889. Of Comte's three stages, the supernatural stage was identified with colonialism, as in the rest of Latin America, but the metaphysical stage was identified with the monarchy that continued after independence. Only by the abolition of the monarchy and the establishment of a republic, the argument was, could Brazil reach the highest or positivist stage. So the monarchy had to go, as it did relatively peacefully in 1889. And leading the charge against the monarchy were those same military and civilian elements whom Constant had trained in positivism in the military academy.[31]

For the next forty years, 1890–1930, Brazil was governed under a republican regime. But the First Republic was dominated by its elites, the suffrage was extremely limited, and national power and the presidency under a so-called gentlemen's agreement rotated between the two main Brazilian states, São Paulo and Minas Gerais. During this period Brazil enjoyed relative stability and exceptional economic progress under this regime. This was the triumph of positivism, whose slogan "Order and Progress" was now emblazoned on the flag of the new republic. It was an era not just of stability but of large-scale immigration, considerable foreign investment, infrastructure development, and economic takeoff as well.[32] For these reasons and because of the strong impact of positivism in both regimes, the Brazilian First Republic was in many ways comparable to the authoritarian Díaz regime in Mexico.

A main difference, however, may have been with regard to race. Whereas in Mexico positivism was used to justify the dominance of the white, Hispanic elite and to keep the Indians and mestizos in a subordinate position (Comte believed that the white, European race was superior to all others), in Brazil positivism was used to justify the racial democracy and miscegenation already well under way. This is not to say that Brazil had no racial prejudice or that some elites did not try to use the positivist philosophy to justify white supremacy. But in part because of the history of the Brazilian antislavery movement inspired by positivism, race relations in Brazil were generally more easygoing, fluid, and less rigid than in other countries. A particularly vivid illustration of this is one of the classics of Brazilian literature, *Os Sertões* (The badlands) by Euclydes da Cunha (1866–1909). Writing as a positivist, da Cunha admonished his countrymen not only to not ignore racial stereotypes but to glory nationalistically in the strong racial melting pot of Brazil, including Indians, blacks, and whites.[33]

Positivism had a major impact in the other countries of Latin America as well, though its influence varied from country to country.[34] In Argentina, positivism was a strong influence in the writings and presidencies of both Alberdi and Sarmiento, whose policies on population, education, and national development were in large measure based on positivist principles. But the Argentines, a better-educated and sophisticated country, were more eclectic in what they absorbed from Comte, with many accepting his scientific sociology, some accepting his three-part stages of development, and only a handful accepting the positivist religion.

The acceptance of positivism in Chile took a similar path. Chile had been governed more or less peacefully since the 1830s under an enlightened oligarchic regime that expanded educational opportunities and instituted an economic development strategy at a time when other countries were still locked in chaos, dictatorship, and confusion. The educated Chileans, like the Argentines, were selective in their borrowings from positivism, a few accepting the total Comtean scheme but most only part. For example, José Victorino Lastarría (1817–88) deemed Comte's interpretation of history and his belief in progress valid while rejecting the founder of positivism's religious and political views. Valentín Letelier (1852–1919) used Comte's analysis to further educational reforms and saw it as conferring a scientific legitimacy on social analysis, but he was not enamored of other aspects of the Comtean scheme.

Elsewhere in Latin America positivism also left a deep imprint but, again, with varying emphases. In the Spanish-speaking Caribbean (Cuba, the Dominican Republic, Puerto Rico) and in the writings of such thinkers as Enrique José Varona and Eugenio María de Hostos, positivism was often identified with nationalism and educational reform; but it also, as in Mexico, called for a strong, positive state. In Uruguay, positivism was identified with both economic development and social welfarism and formed part of the ideology of the great Uruguayan social-democrat José Batlle y Ordóñez. In Central America, positivism was similarly identified with the establishment of greater political stability after 1870, a strong, modern state under oligarchic direction, and an export-oriented and more productive economy. In the Andean countries of Peru and Bolivia, the philosophy was seen as a means to rebuild and reorder national affairs and to stimulate positive national development after their humiliating defeat by Chile in the War of the Pacific (1889–91).

With positivism its major, even official, ideology, Latin America entered a new period of growth and economic takeoff that lasted (depending on the country) from approximately the late 1880s until 1930.

This was a period of economic growth, population increase, foreign investment, infrastructure development, greater stability, and export-led growth. It was the most stable, most economically progressive era that Latin America in its independence period had experienced. Positivism helped provide the unifying cement, the justifications and rationalizations for this period of unprecedented growth.

We have so far seen two patterns of politics and growth during this period, and here we wish to suggest a third. The first of these was the order-and-progress caudillos: strong, authoritarian regimes that provided long-term stability and thus encouraged growth. The paradigm example is Díaz in Mexico with his positivist or científico advisers; but this first model also includes such authoritarian-developmentalist regimes as Juan Vicente Gómez in Venezuela and Ulises Heureaux in the Dominican Republic.

The second pattern involves consolidation and stability of oligarchic rule. These order-and-progress oligarchic regimes were also elitist and top-down, but they were based on a circulation of elites rather than on the authority of a single person. Here the paradigm cases are the big A, B, C countries, Argentina, Brazil, and Chile, all of which experienced in the late nineteenth and early twentieth centuries the consolidation of oligarchic rule coupled with unprecedented economic growth. But such countries as Peru, Paraguay, Honduras, Costa Rica, and El Salvador also saw a consolidation of oligarchic rule during this period and a period of generally unprecedented stability and prosperity.

The third pattern involves those countries of Central America and the Caribbean which remained unstable during the period when other countries were becoming more stable, and underdeveloped when the other countries were beginning to experience prosperity. The analogy is, of course, not exact (it seldom is) and obviously there are country differences that need to be taken into account. The third pattern thus involves U.S. Marine invasions and occupations beginning with the Spanish-American War of 1898 and continuing sporadically during the first three decades of the twentieth century: it thus corresponds roughly to the same periodization used in describing positivist regimes. For the Marines not only pacified the countries they occupied, but also built roads and infrastructure, installed the first telephone and telegraphy, conducted land cadastral surveys so foreign investment could come in, stripped local caudillos of their independent power, modernized the police and army, and helped initiate bureaucratic **169**

modernization—precisely the policies that the order-and-progress caudillos and oligarchs had initiated in the more advanced countries a
decade or two earlier.

The lands that the Marines occupied—Cuba, Nicaragua, Panama,
Haiti, the Dominican Republic, and Puerto Rico—were all woefully unstable or, for various reasons, lagging behind the countries that had
begun their takeoff. Not all the Marines' purposes and accomplishments were altruistic, of course (neither were those of the order-and-
progress caudillos and oligarchs), and certainly there were considerable differences between this model and the previous two as well—not
least being the intense nationalism and often anti-Americanism to
which the occupations gave rise (see chapter 7). But in many other ways
the U.S. Marines through long-term foreign occupation accomplished
a number of the same stabilizing and nation-building activities that
the authoritarians and oligarchs did, and often—albeit inadvertently—
under the same ideology of order and progress that infused positivism.

Positivism: Why So Popular?

Positivism never gained much influence in the United States, yet in
Latin America during the late nineteenth and early twentieth centuries it became the dominant ideology. In the United States the philosophy of liberalism would become during this period and subsequently
the dominant American ideology and frame of reference, while in Latin
America liberalism in the nineteenth-century sense was seldom if ever
successful and, if the historians Vincent C. Peloso and Barbara A. Tenenbaum are correct, died around the time of World War I.[35] Why these differences? Why was positivism so popular in Latin America? And why
was liberalism so unsuccessful there, even to the point of extinction?
And what does the death of liberalism in Latin America tell one about
the prospects for democracy later in the century?

First, positivism was popular because it offered a new yet similarly
wholistic belief system to replace Thomism, Catholicism, and scholasticism, which were no longer popular among Latin American intellectual elites. This belief system, at least in its founder Comte's mind,
offered an explanation for everything. In this sense it was like Catholicism, offering total and all-encompassing explanations for philosophy,
sociology, politics, education, and economics. Positivism was like a religion—indeed, in Comte's view it was a religion—although most Latin

Americans rejected its religious claims and accepted its social and political prescriptions while clinging to some version of Catholicism. Indeed, it was the very compatibility of positivism with, or its substitution for, historic Catholicism that helped make it so popular.

Second, positivism was French and à la mode. For a continent lagging
farther and farther behind, it was enormously attractive to forget the
past, leapfrog all intermediate stages, and jump into the modern world
with the most advanced nations. One should not underestimate the
power of this inferiority-complex-drive in Latin America to adopt the
latest fashions as a way of forgetting an unhappy past and being on the
cutting edge. The same or analogous phenomena are noticeable in subsequent chapters dealing with Marxism, corporatism, and perhaps even
democracy.[36]

Third, positivism seemed to fit Latin America quite closely. Certainly it fit better than the failed liberalism of the early nineteenth
century. Positivism seemed to understand and had a "scientific" paradigm for explaining Latin America's earlier backwardness and its present optimism. It held the promise of solving existing problems through
educational and social reforms. But it was gradual and evolutionary
rather than revolutionary. It emphasized institutional and infrastructure development. It seemed to be constructive rather than, like other
ideologies, purely negative and critical. It was new and redeeming and,
as Jorrín and Martz say, "although formulated in another world, it appeared suited to the needs of the New World."[37]

Fourth, positivism was optimistic, progressive, and held a hopeful
view of the future. Its three stages of history, the supernatural, metaphysical, and positivist, offered a teleological view of man's evolution,
with a clear goal and end point. In this respect, too, positivism was
much like Marxism, with its three stages (feudalism, capitalism, socialism), its historic inevitability, and its deterministic view that the "good
guys" (socialists, presumably, or in this case the positivists) won out in
the end. It is enormously satisfying, of course, to know that history is
on one's side, that one's own forces and beliefs inevitably win out in
the end. Particularly given Latin America's earlier and generally sorry
history, one can understand why the promise of positivism offered so
much hope.

Fifth, positivism offered a clear formula. It was not ambiguous
about what needed to be done. Moreover, this formula was put in terms
of historical inevitability; it offered certainty and all the ingredients of

a developmentalist model. Discipline, authority, order, social and political peace, unity, infrastructure modernization, foreign (European)
immigration and investment, industrialization—the requirements and
prerequisites were clear. Again, it is helpful to know exactly where one
was going and precisely what needed to be done.

Sixth, positivism was attractive because, while it promised change
and progress, it left many aspects unaffected. Indeed, it is instructive
to understand how many things stayed the same or could be coopted
under positivism. Positivism, after all, stood for discipline, order, authority—all conservative values in a Latin America that was itself, in
the colonial and postindependence eras, a fundamentally conservative
area.[38] Positivism required a stable government—precisely what Latin
America needed. And, most important, positivism implied continued
rule by the elites. Under either the order-and-progress caudillos or the
oligarchy or even the U.S. Marines, it would be the elites that would
continue to govern. Government would be vested in those most capable
of ruling; there would be no notion of popular sovereignty here.
Bankers, businessmen, and scientists who know and understand the
common good or the general will would rule, not the masses. And it
would be the intellectuals, the pensadores, the científicos, who would
guide the elites. How comforting it is to the elites and the intellectuals
to know that they would be leading and guiding the change process,
that it was in their hands. How convenient to find an ideology, in short,
that justified the existing power structure; moreover, one that justified one's own intellectual, social, political, and economic leadership
of the modes of reform and that was universal, progressive, and inevitable. As Jorrín and Martz remark, "Nowhere in the world did the
evolutionary, scientific thought of the European positivists become so
popular with the governing class as in Latin America."[39]

But, seventh, positivism also implied change, progress, development. The change, however, would be under elite or state auspices, it
would be controlled, disciplined, orderly, top-down. The best-educated
and wealthiest persons—and also the whitist—would be in charge. The
program was thus both classist and racist. Those who had always been
at the top in Latin America—oligarchs, intellectuals, the professional
military, high-level bureaucrats and administrators—would continue
to be at the top. Yet positivism—and here was part of its genius and
strong appeal—also offered the opportunity for new groups to be accommodated to this system, so long as they accepted its givens.

Positivism—and Latin America during this period—was not entirely stand-pat; it was experiencing not only economic growth but also the early stirrings of social change that accompany development. Foreigners who brought in investment, immigrant families (like the Vicinis in the Dominican Republic) who had entrepreneurial skills, and business and commercial elements who could stimulate the economy and increase the wealth—all these were welcomed under positivism and incorporated over a period of time into the prevailing (oligarchic, elitist) Latin American social and political systems. For example, this was the period (1890s and beyond) when the newer business and commercial elements were incorporated into the prevailing oligarchic and two-class systems of Latin America, through partnerships and intermarriage with the old landholding elite. In this way old wealth (land) was wedded (often literally) to new wealth (business, commerce, importer-exporter) without any fundamental changes in the social structure.[40]

Indeed, as discussed in later chapters, this became the prevailing formula by which other, similarly new social and political groups were incorporated into the *system* of Latin American politics without that implying more fundamental changes in the social or power structure. They had to demonstrate a sufficient power capability to be taken seriously; at that stage they would be absorbed, usually under elite or state auspices, and, as a condition, they agreed to moderate their desires for change so as not to threaten the traditional groups.[41] The business and commercial groups were incorporated in this fashion at this time, soon it would be the turn of the emerging middle class, then from the 1930s on it would be the trade unions, later other groups. But in none of these incorporations was the basic, Latin American, two-class society and power structure much altered in its fundamentals. If that is the case, however, it is worrisome in terms of the long-range prospects in Latin America for pluralism, democracy, and more thoroughgoing social change.[42]

It is a mistake to view positivism in Latin America as purely a rationalization by elites to justify their continued hold on national power. It was that but it was also other things.[43] For its Latin American adherents, positivism seemed to provide a formula for progress and change as well as stability and order. After such a long history of frustration, instability, and backwardness, positivism seemed to signify growth, development, and modernization. At the same time, it suggested social change and the integration of new social groups into the political process, but in a way that did not threaten established groups or that would bring such radical change that it got out of hand. That balance seemed attractive to many Latin Americans who had been alternating between retrogressive conservatism and chaotic liberalism for many lost decades and who had been casting about for a new national and regionwide formula. Positivism provided just such a formula. That it was hijacked and taken over by the elites and used for their own advantage should not be entirely unexpected either, given the existing power structure, the scarcity of pluralist institutions, and the imbalance in elite versus mass power in Latin America. The same co-optation would happen to other new and promising ideologies that found initial fertile ground in Latin America.

Positivism, as noted earlier, was not universally accepted in Latin America.[44] Some persons accepted all aspects of the positivist philosophy while others were more selective. There were often distinct national variations as well as several schools of thought within individual countries. Nevertheless, for a time, the 1870s to World War I, positivism swept over Latin America and was the dominant ideology, eclipsing and all but ending liberalism's popularity in the area. Examining the reasons for positivism's popularity, we saw that they were not purely ideological or philosophical but involved deep social, political, economic, and cultural orientations as well. Plagued by instability, lack of progress, and endemic conflict, Latin America was ready for a new ideology that offered progress but within existing social and political structures. Positivism furnished a model and framework for change but only change that could be controlled from above. Positivism was not the first, and it would not be the last, political formula to be embraced in Latin America for precisely these dual reasons.

Chapter 7

Nationalism

During most of the nineteenth century, the United States was generally admired in Latin America. The young North American republic was admired, first of all, for its political accomplishments in establishing and securing freedom and liberty and, second, as the nineteenth century evolved, for its economic accomplishments of wealth and industrialization. In the 1830s and 1840s, of course, the War of Texas Independence and then the Mexican-American War had been fought, and their combined effect was to deprive Mexico of approximately 40 percent of its national territory; and there were other early gleanings, even prior to the American Civil War, that the United States had its eyes on and coveted territories in Central America and the Caribbean. But despite the strong statements of U.S. interests in Latin America contained in the Monroe Doctrine (1823), the United States was for the most part inwardly oriented during most of the century, preoccupied with its own internal development and westward expansionism, and lacking the military or naval power to seek major conquests in Latin America. Hence, the general Latin American view of the United States, until approximately the 1880s, was benign and, on balance, favorable.[1]

While the United States was widely admired, the mother countries, Spain and Portugal, were often reviled—even though newly independent Latin America continued to employ many of the social, cultural, ideological, and political practices and institutions of its colonial past. Among nineteenth-century Latin American intellectuals Spain and Portugal were often rejected—accurately—as saddling the area with feudal and medieval institutions and not providing adequate preparation for independence and self-government. Hence, in nineteenth-century Latin America, Spain, Portugal, and all they stood for had to be repudiated; they were viewed as the past rather than the future. Adding to the sense of rejection by Latin America of their mother countries was the widespread realization—again an accurate reading—that Spain and Portugal were declining powers anyway, so why bother? To the emotional rejection of Spain and Portugal was thus added a quite realistic assessment of great-power realities and where the future in terms of trade, influence, and sociopolitical models lay.[2]

All this began to change in the last decades of the nineteenth century and particularly with the Spanish-American War of 1898. By then, with the United States achieving great-power military capabilities and ambitions, acquiring territories, and increasingly throwing its weight around in Latin America, the United States began to be perceived as a threat and a rival, no longer necessarily a country to be admired, or at a minimum requiring love and hate at the same time. At the same time Spain, defeated by the "upstart" United States, had reached the depths of its centuries-long fall from great-power status, not only provoking an immense amount of critical self-examination in Spain but also giving rise to a renewed sense of sympathy in Latin America for the beleaguered mother country and of pride in Spanish culture and institutions—an ideology known as Hispanismo. Meanwhile, faced with a threat from the United States as well as renewed pride in things Hispanic, Latin American nationalism—the overarching theme of this chapter—began to reach fevered levels for the first time. Nationalism intensified over the course of the twentieth century—until it began to run out of gas late in the century under the impact of worldwide democratization, the end of the Cold War, and increasing globalization. Until that time, however, as Gerhard Masur in his book on Latin American nationalism correctly says, "The ideology which has most deeply penetrated Latin American political and social thought in the twentieth century has been nationalism."[3]

Latin American Nationalism

Modern nationalism emerged first in Europe and, according to Hans Kohn, its foremost student, is "not older than the second half of the eighteenth century."[4] Of course, there had been earlier patriotism and expression of loyalty to town, region, city-state, principality, or nation; but in Kohn's analysis the distinguishing mark of modern nationalism is its identification with and inseparability from popular sovereignty, which was first conceived during and then in reaction to the French Revolution. The noted historian Carlton H. Hayes similarly defines "nationalism" as a blend of patriotism (an older and more traditional emotion) and the doctrine of popular sovereignty, a fusion that resulted in the assumption that one's ultimate loyalty belonged to the nation-state in which one lived (or wished to live).[5] Popular or mass nationalism in this sense was heir both to the medieval idea of loyalty to one universal church and religion and to the early modern notion of absolute, unquestioned obedience to a king or sovereign. Following the Enlightenment and the French Revolution, therefore, which attacked both religion and royal absolutism, nationalism became one of the—if not *the*—guiding principles of European politics and the sovereign, independent, unified nation-state the goal to which people aspired.

Nationalism in Latin America was derivative in nature, following the general European pattern. Samuel L. Baily in his excellent book argues that nationalism in Latin America may be traced to the growing self-consciousness of the creole or native-born elites, who in the seventeenth and eighteenth centuries forged an interest and an identity distinct from that of the peninsulares and of the mother countries themselves.[6] Barbarosa Lima Sobrinho argues that Brazilian nationalism began with the successful efforts of the Portuguese settlers in the mid–seventeenth century to drive Dutch interlopers out of northeast Brazil.[7] And in Argentina, it is often argued, nationalism began with the struggle in 1807 (that led eventually to independence from Spain as well) to oust British forces from the port city of Buenos Aires.

Nationalism in a modern sense in Latin America, however, began with independence from Spain and Portugal, and the efforts to fashion nation-states based on the Kohnian principle of popular sovereignty.[8] As in Europe, loyalty to the nation would now serve as a substitute for loyalty to the Spanish or Portuguese crowns. For a number of reasons, however, nationalism in Latin America was slow to develop in the nineteenth century. For one thing, it took time for sovereignty and borders to be decided in the early part of the century; for another, the processes of colonial disintegration that began in the early nineteenth century continued even after independence, as both the Confederation of Central America and the Republic of New Granada further subdivided into smaller nation-states. A third reason for the retarded growth of Latin American nationalism was that the opposite current of pan–Latin Americanism remained strong. But while pan–Latin Americanism continued as one force so, too, fourth, did extreme localism or loyalty to the *patria chica,* the "small country" of the village or region, which often commanded greater loyalty than did the larger, more impersonal nation. In addition, fifth, the often illiterate and unassimilated indigenous populations of Latin America had little comprehension of such a modern European conception as nationalism; their loyalty often went in a personalistic way to "General Peru" or "General Bolivia" but not to such an abstract and impersonal object as the nation-state. Finally, once Spain had been expelled, there was no external enemy comparable to Napoleon's invading armies to help stimulate Latin American nationalism in the early nineteenth century, as was the case in Europe during this period in the lands occupied by Napoleon's troops.

Since independence, Latin American nationalism has gone through a number of phases. The historian Arthur P. Whitaker calls the first phase "liberal nationalism," by which he means that Latin America was generally open to the outside world, open to both outside ideas (as discussed in the previous two chapters) and to foreign investment, and not at all defensive about its culture and institutions. The phase of liberal internationalism lasted through most of the nineteenth century. But this was an era in which Latin American nationalism was slow in developing and certainly not virulent.[9]

In the second phase, beginning in the 1880s, Latin American nationalism became more economic and cultural. It also became stronger and more powerful. Hence, in terms of both the time period in which it arose and of its rising strength ideologically, this second period is of greater interest here. For beginning in the 1880s, Latin America began to question, if not react against, the immense foreign investment and the accompanying influence, both British and American, that had been creeping in for several decades but was now reaching large—and sometimes controlling—dimensions. Part of this foreign influence was also cultural, intellectual, and ideological so it is of particular interest to this study.

The third phase of Latin American nationalism, arising mainly in the twentieth century, was more self-consciously political. It arose in response to repeated American military interventions, occupations, and overall heavy-handedness in the early part of the century. Once kindled, the flame of nationalism, mainly in the form of anti-Americanism, continued to burn, even though it died down somewhat during the later 1920s and 1930s as the U.S. occupation forces were withdrawn and as President Franklin Roosevelt initiated the Good Neighbor Policy. But then it flared again during the Cold War as the United States frequently returned to heavy-handedness and intervention as instruments of policy. Such political nationalism is not unique to Latin America; it is part of a more general, post–World War II phenomenon of Third World nationalism.

Latin American nationalism has thus changed, as well as ebbed and flowed over time, but it is also present in several forms. Most Americans viewing Latin America over the past several decades and thinking ideologically tend to identify Latin American nationalism with left-wing movements and anti-Americanism, as in other developing nations. But viewed over a longer period and seen in cultural terms, right-wing nationalism and anti-Americanism in Latin America may be even stronger—though seldom expressed in highly visible protests or street demonstrations—than the left-wing variety. In addition, there have been in the history of the region other forms of nationalism: fascist, racial, cultural, pan–Latin American, Hispanic, and so on. All of these nationalisms have played a part in the political theory and tradition of Latin America and form a part of the warp and woof of the fabric of the story told here.

The Inter-American System

It is indisputable that the United States has long been the dominant power in the Western Hemisphere. Beginning with the Monroe Doctrine in 1823, the United States has not only tried to exclude other powers (first, the Holy Alliance, then such individual countries as Spain, France, Great Britain, Germany, and eventually the Soviet Union) from playing a major role in the hemisphere, but also sought to be the arbiter and even policeman of relations between (and often within) the hemisphere's republics. During much of the nineteenth century the United States was preoccupied with its internal development and westward expansionism and lacked the military might to back up the moral imperatives stated loftily in Monroe's famous doctrine, but it was indisputably the leader among the American nations. When in the post–Civil War era the United States acquired both the might and the ambitions to be the hemisphere's foremost power, its dominance became even greater. The country was, in Abraham Lowenthal's terms, the "hegemon"; in Norman A. Bailey's, the "paramount."[10]

As a hegemonic and paramount nation, the United States was seldom reluctant to exercise its power in Latin America: what was frequently referred to as our backyard or our lake (the Caribbean). The litany of U.S. land grabs, interventions, and power politics in Latin America is familiar and is not the main subject of this book,[11] but the historical record does need to be briefly reviewed as a prelude to what is the main interest here: the development and various expressions of Latin American political theory and nationalistic ideology.

In the 1830s and 1840s in the War of Texas Independence and the Mexican-American War, the United States took over one-third of Mexico's national territory. During the same period, the United States began to cast its eye covetously southward toward the Caribbean and Central America with the idea of possibly annexing additional slave states and acquiring strategic outposts. In the aftermath of the Civil War, the United States sought to annex the Dominican Republic and talked openly of acquiring Cuba. Now exercising its growing power for the first time, the United States intervened against Great Britain in the Venezuela–British Guiana border controversy of 1896, during which U.S. Secretary of State Richard Olney, in an oft-cited declaration, proclaimed the United States to be "practically sovereign" in the Western Hemisphere. In the Spanish-American War of 1898, the United States acquired Puerto Rico and the Philippines and secured Cuba as a protectorate through the infamous Platt Amendment, which gave the United States virtual carte blanche to intervene in internal Cuban affairs on almost any pretext.[12]

In 1902 Teddy Roosevelt stole Panama fair and square (his words) from Colombia in order to build the Panama Canal and in 1904 proclaimed the Roosevelt Corollary to the Monroe Doctrine, which gave the United States what he called "international police power" to correct "chronic wrongdoing" or even the "impotence" of the Latin American nations to govern themselves. Roosevelt's meddling was followed by the era of "dollar diplomacy," under which U.S. capital followed the flag into Latin America, and by Woodrow Wilson's military interventions and occupations of Haiti, the Dominican Republic, Cuba, Nicaragua, and Mexico. And, during the Cold War era, there have been U.S. interventions in Guatemala, Cuba, the Dominican Republic, Chile, Grenada, El Salvador, Nicaragua, and Panama.

It is not my purpose to go into any details of this often-sorry history, to discount the often-humanitarian motives (as well as the selfish ones) on the part of the United States during many of these interventions, or even to make overly moral judgments about them. From a purely real politik point of view, such interventions are simply what a great power, a paramount, a hegemon does to protect and advance its interests. The fact is, there is a power disparity or imbalance in the Western Hemisphere, the United States being overwhelmingly dominant and not always reluctant to exercise that power. Great powers tend to beat up on or take advantage of small powers and, in the absence of very many enforceable restrictions at the international level preventing such actions, all great powers behave this way. It is, for good or ill, the law of the jungle: eat or be eaten![13]

Our main purpose here is to explore the Latin American response in theory and practice to growing U.S. hegemony. For as the United States emerged as a great power from the 1880s on and increasingly began to behave like one, Latin America began to put barriers in the way of the exercise of U.S. hegemony. Part of this response was rising Latin American nationalism, which, largely quiet or muted to this point, became a major philosophical and ideological theme and movement, to go along with the other ideologies already analyzed. And it largely emerged in response to the increasing exercise of U.S. hegemony in the hemisphere.

When faced with a dominant hegemon, small, weak countries like those in Latin America can resort to a number of strategies and tactics to try to rein the hegemon in. Here we briefly review these strategies; more detailed accounts can be found elsewhere:[14]

1. Stress international law. If the international context is anarchic, dog-eat-dog, where the strong devour the weak, then it is logical for the weak to stress international law in an effort to limit the dominance of the strong. Hence, it is no accident that around the turn of the twentieth century Latin America began increasingly to emphasize international law as a way of containing the United States, that some of the world's greatest authorities on international law emerged from Latin America, and that strenuous efforts have been made by Latin America to develop its own body of international law—such as the right of asylum and the principle of nonintervention. As the aphorism goes, the strong stress power and reasons of state, the weak emphasize international law. International law in Latin America thus became an instrument of a defensive (against the United States) foreign policy and a means of reinforcing nationalism.

2. Band together. Small, weak nations can hinder the ambitions and aggressions of larger powers by joining in common cause. As early as 1826 the Latin American states banded together in Pan-American fashion as a protection against threatened foreign interference and dominance, an effort that was repeated periodically after that initial international gathering, received new impetus in the 1880s and thereafter as a check specifically on U.S. power, and finds contemporary expression in such agencies as the Organization of American States (OAS) and the South American Common Market (MERCOSUR). Hence, the basic conflict at the heart of the OAS: the United States sees this international regional body as a way to advance its interests in Latin America, while Latin America views it as a way to check the United States.

3. Join international organizations. Latin America has been one of the chief advocates and strongest participants in the League of Nations and the United Nations. It participates in these organizations both out of a sense of commitment to them and because they give the region a stronger voice in international affairs. Unable to check the United States by itself, Latin American countries can, as vigorous members of international organizations, mobilize the support of fellow members. This is another instrument for hemming in the power of the United States and limiting its ability to act unilaterally.

4. Seek outside allies. Historically, this strategy has been difficult for Latin America's nations both because their attractiveness as a field of investment and as potential new allies has been limited and because U.S. power has been so overwhelming and directed against (the Monroe Doctrine) extrahemispheric powers. But now Latin America is vastly expanding its relations to include Germany, France, Great Britain, Spain, Japan, and China, to say nothing of such international groups as the Socialist International, the European Union, and the Ibero-American Summit. All these activities serve to enhance the power of Latin America and to apply the brakes to U.S. dominance and unilateralism.

5. Stress nationalism. Nationalism is not just an ideology that grows naturally or organically; it can also be stimulated and strengthened for quite practical political goals. Obviously, a country that is divided and torn asunder can easily be manipulated by outside powers, but one that is unified is a much stronger adversary. Nationalism was used and manipulated by Latin American elites to advance political purposes, to forge internal unity, and to keep the United States at bay.

The subjects of nationalism and the inter-American system as a Latin American defense mechanism deserve far greater attention than it is possible to give them here. Nevertheless, the main points are clear at least preliminarily: Latin American nationalism was largely dormant during most of the nineteenth century; it came alive as a major force and ideology during precisely the same period (1880s and after) that the United States was emerging as the dominant—and intervening—power in Latin America; and Latin America used every device available—international law, pan-American unity, international organizations, outside alliances, and nationalism—to try to limit U.S. hegemony. Seen in this light, nationalism can be and often is a conscious instrument of state policy and, more than likely, an instrument like others of the ideologies analyzed here by which elite groups have manipulated state policy—for example, by often stressing or exaggerating outside threats and U.S. interference as a way of diverting attention from internal systems of power and favoritism.

José Martí

José Martí is undoubtedly one of the great nationalists in the history of Latin America. Moreover, he is thought of as more or less representative of a generation of Latin American nationalists who rose to prominence in the last decades of the nineteenth century and the first decades of the twentieth, just as the United States was exercising its newfound power throughout the hemisphere.[15]

Martí was born in Cuba in 1853, which in itself makes him somewhat unrepresentative because at that time, along with Puerto Rico, Cuba was among the last of Spain's colonies to still be under the control of the mother country. At the time of his birth and as he grew to maturity, Cuba was wracked by intense nationalistic violence and civil war over its efforts to achieve independence from Spain. Moreover, he himself was born of Spanish immigrant parents, which makes him like Fidel Castro, who frequently invokes Martí's name for nationalistic purposes. That also means that Martí, again like Fidel, was from the white upper or upper-middle class in Cuba. It is striking that this son of hardworking, prospering immigrant parents should, in championing Cuban independence, turn so vociferously against the birth country of his mother and father.

After living in Cuba for the first seventeen years of his life, Martí was sent into exile for advocating an end to Spanish colonial rule. He was deported, ironically, to Spain, the land he so bitterly castigated in his fiery speeches and writings. He also traveled to France and the United States. Returning to Latin America and eventually to Cuba, Martí's nationalistic views again got him in trouble with Spanish colonial authorities. Hence, he was banished again, this time to New York, where he spent many years. From New York he wrote a variety of polemics directed against Spain and in favor of Cuban independence. From New York he also led a group of exiled Cubans aimed at ending Spanish rule in their native land. He died in Cuba in 1895 leading a renewed insurrection against Spanish colonialism—ironically on the eve of Cuba achieving independence, but under U.S. auspices. Had the heroic Martí lived, it is likely that Cuba's early independence history would have been less inglorious than it was, with incompetent governments, widespread corruption, instability, and repeated U.S. interventions justified by the Platt Amendment.

Although Martí is best known for his leadership in Cuba's wars of independence against Spain, he is also famous for his anti-Americanism. Indeed, during this period Latin American nationalism was becoming closely identified with anti-Americanism for the first time. Martí's most famous and oft-quoted statement regarding the United States is, "I know the monster. I have lived in its entrails." The statement was based on Martí's not-always-happy experience of living in New York. But he was also fearful of American foreign policy, that all his efforts to free Cuba from Spain would be in vain if Cuba were to be annexed to the United States. Consequently, Martí became increasingly critical of American political, economic, and strategic imperialism, particularly as exercised in the Caribbean.

Martí was not always so critical of the United States. After all, the United States had taken him in as an exile on two separate occasions. And prior to the 1880s he frequently expressed admiration for what had become his second home. He greatly admired such North American thinkers and leaders as Ralph Waldo Emerson and Abraham Lincoln. On the occasion of Emerson's death, Martí, a prolific essayist and polemist, wrote that Emerson "was one of those to whom the highest wisdom, the highest calm, the highest enjoyment was given."[16] One of his biographers writes that "during the early 1880s [before the United

States extended its imperial power] Martí felt thrilled at the great possibilities of the United States."[17]

Yet Martí, living at the time of the early "robber barons," became disillusioned by the growing gap between rich and poor in American society. He wrote that "the austere and admirable spirit of the *Mayflower,* which still infused the New England Transcendentalists of the previous age, was fast being choked by the demon of lucre."[18] Like José Enrique Rodó, whom we consider next, Martí believed the United States had sold its soul for the sake of greed and aggression. He said, "The North American laws have given the North a high degree of prosperity, and have also raised it to the highest degree of corruption. They have made money the chief good so as to create Prosperity. Cursed be prosperity at such a cost!"[19]

One of Martí's favorite subjects was the contrasts between the United States and Latin America. He wrote, "The North Americans put feeling after practicality. We put practicality after feeling."[20] Martí also became increasingly critical of what he perceived as positivism in the United States. His attitude is ironic because we have just spent a chapter analyzing how positivism had become the dominant philosophy in Martí's own Latin America and enjoyed little currency in the United States. The answer to this riddle is that positivism means very different things in the United States (about which Martí wrote) and Latin America. In Latin America positivism was mainly viewed as a broad, all-encompassing, academic, intellectual, political, philosophical, and sociological approach that filled an intellectual void; in the United States, in contrast, positivism was identified more narrowly with business, greed, scientific management, and making money. Hence, Martí's biographer could accurately write, "When Martí discerned the true face of positivism in all its brutality in the United States of the 1880s and 1890s, he was horrified, and in consequence turned away from that nation."[21]

Martí directed most of his barbs, however, at American foreign policy because he believed—correctly as it turned out—U.S. imperialism could become an obstacle to Cuban freedom. Eager to gain Cuban independence from Spain, Martí feared the longer Cuba waited, the greater the chance the island would be annexed by the United States. Martí was especially alarmed by the diplomacy in the early 1880s of then–Secretary of State James Blaine, who had ambitious designs on the hemisphere. Blaine not only advocated American leadership in the

Western Hemisphere but also devised plans to absorb Cuba and perhaps other islands. Martí wrote critically of the jingoist American press, especially the Hearst newspapers, which were openly stirring up passions and urging the government to take the initiative by itself, ousting Spain from Cuba and seizing control for itself. The U.S. campaign to annex Hawaii added to Martí's conviction that the United States was an imperialist nation. Martí argued that "the nation we need to know more thoroughly is the United States . . . this avaricious neighbor who admittedly has designs on us."[22]

Martí also wrote extensively about economic matters (or what moderns would call political economy). He was perceptive in warning of two things: first, that Cuba should not become overly dependent on a single crop—sugar—and, second, that it should not become overly dependent economically on a single export market—that is, the United States. Moreover, he saw the links between the two, wanting Cuba to diversify its exports and trade with a variety of partners to prevent the very dependence on the United States that would, in fact, evolve. Martí wrote that "economic union means political union. The country which buys [namely, the United States] is the one that commands. The country which sells obeys. . . . The people that wishes to die sells to a single people."[23] These comments have led some later Marxists (including Castro) to claim that Martí was a Marxist—in spirit if not ideologically. While this claim is exaggerated, it is true that the remarks cited would lead one to conclude Martí was an analyst of dependency theory long before that approach became popular as an interpretation of Latin America.

It is appropriate to conclude this discussion of Martí with his comments on Spain, since that provides a prelude to the next two sections. While as a Cuban nationalist and patriot, Martí could not be expected to be an admirer of Spain, he nevertheless asserted—contrary to almost a full century of loathing of Spain in Latin America—that Latin America had inherited some positive features from Spain. These included, in his view, an emphasis on honor, dignity, religion, and spiritual values. Bear in mind that these comments were written before the newfound sympathy for Spain in Latin America that followed Spain's ignoble defeat in the Spanish-American War of 1898. But while lauding Spain for these virtues, Martí claimed that these characteristics were not present in the United States.

José Enrique Rodó

Whereas Martí was an analyst of U.S. political, strategic, and economic imperialism, José Enrique Rodó was a staunch critic of American cultural influence in Latin America.[24] And whereas Martí's nationalism and anti-Americanism could be identified with a left position, Rodó was an apostle of right-wing nationalism and anti-Americanism. Left-wing anti-Americanism and nationalism may be more widespread and is certainly more familiar in Latin America and other developing areas; but it is the right-wing version that may be more pervasive and long-lasting.

Rodó was an Uruguayan writer who published a book entitled *Ariel* in 1900—two years after the Spanish-American War.[25] An immediate sensation, the book went through at least thirteen editions and became perhaps the best-selling work in all of Latin American history. Virtually every Latin American schoolchild grows up learning *Ariel*'s message. The book is written in a florid, exaggerated language that is off-putting to Americans brought up on Hemingwayesque short sentences, but it is enormously attractive in Latin America.

Ariel's is a story that has been told in many contexts by many authors—for example, in Shakespeare's *Tempest*. It is a story of the contest between the spiritual and the material. In Rodó's telling, Latin America represents the higher spiritual life while the United States represents the gross and the material. Rodó presents Americans as crass, materialistic, and utilitarian. In contrast, Latin America and Europe are portrayed as cultured and spiritual. It is these stark contrasts between U.S. and Latin American culture and society that give the book its nationalistic, political, anti-American tone.

But Rodó is not just anti-American. He is also against those earlier Latin American liberal lawmakers and intellectuals in the first part of the nineteenth century who tried to imitate the U.S. Constitution and political practice, and he is against liberal leaders like Sarmiento who glorified U.S. culture while criticizing so-called uncivilized Latin America. Moreover, Rodó is pro-Spain because the former mother country stands for religion, culture, and European civilization as against the unrefined, grasping, imperialistic Americans. So Rodó is opposed not only to the United States, but also to what it stands for, namely, democracy and its underlying philosophical assumptions. He is not just anti-American; if that were all, his arguments would be relatively simple. In- **187** stead, Rodó questions on sophisticated, theoretical grounds the very individualistic, egalitarian, and democratic beliefs to which Americans are committed. In addition, he presents an alternative system of thought and ideology that has particular resonance in the Latin American context, history, and value system. If Rodó's critique of U.S.-style democracy and of Latin American liberalism is as influential in the history of Latin American ideas as it appears, then it is easy to understand—among other reasons—why democracy has had such a difficult time throughout Latin American history and why today's "transitions to democracy" may still be so fragile and precarious.[26]

Rodó's story of Ariel begins in a mythical courtyard, where an aging teacher is giving his final lecture to his students. That is the literary device that Rodó uses to give his readers a long sermon. He cleverly directs his message at the youth of Latin America, flattering them with the idea that only their enthusiasm and idealism can save the region from American materialism, individualism, and pragmatism. He describes Latin American youth as "unsullied," with the power and grace to provide inspiration for the future. This theme of the saving power of idealistic Latin American youth against the barbarians of North America is emphasized throughout the book. Rodó goes on to link youth to prevailing Latin American Catholicism, in that they are both pure, exemplifying grace and inspiration. Conveying such a clear picture of idealistic youth as the salvation of Latin America, it is small wonder the book appealed to Latin American young people.

Rodó is extremely critical of the United States and U.S. culture—even though he had never visited the United States—and *Ariel* may be seen as the Latin American reaction to the growing influence of U.S. culture. But Rodó is clever in his critique: he purports to present an evenhanded picture of the United States. But his few words of praise are really meant only to legitimize his strong criticism. He writes, "With my sincere recognition of all that is luminous and great in its genius, I have won the right to complete a fair appraisal of this powerful nation."[27]

Before launching his outright attack on the United States, Rodó criticizes what he sees as the basic, underlying causes of the American "disease": democracy and its accompanying individualism. He says a democracy based supposedly on equality can lead only to mediocrity. "When democracy is not ennobled by an idealism equally as energetic as the society's material concerns," he writes, "it will inevitably lead to a favored status for mediocrity"—the lowest common denominator.[28] Universal equal rights, he argues, produce only a supremacy of numbers. Rodó asserts that egalitarianism tends inevitably toward the "utilitarian and the vulgar."[29]

In place of democracy, Rodó prefers an oligarchic regime—precisely what Latin America has been governed under during most of its history. Echoing the earliest philosophers discussed in this book, Rodó wants a government of "philosopher-kings." He offers a system of "democracy" governed by a structure of hierarchy based on intelligence and high culture. According to Rodó, there is a "natural order" (shades of Aristotle and Saint Thomas) to society that must be followed. A society based on hierarchy will allow those who are capable and intelligent to rule and establish a system of true democracy. Rodó claims that his oligarchic ruling class will be chosen on the basis of merit, which recognizes that some people are innately superior. Rodó asserts that democracy in his version needs to grant initial equality only; natural selection à la Darwin and English writer Herbert Spencer will then sort out those who are "naturally superior." "If all are granted initial equality," he writes, "subsequent inequality will be justified."[30]

This is frankly an elitist approach. It provides justification for rule by a "natural" governing class. Rodó clearly prefers a well-ordered, organic, Catholic society governed by its educated elites, a society in which everyone is sure of and secure in his/her station in life. Moreover, if one reads Rodó closely, particularly his arguments for natural selection, his message is obviously racist in that it locks blacks and native Indians into a lower-class status and prevents them from rising in the social scale. Rodó's preferences are for an earlier, quasi-medieval society in which all not only know their station but are content within it.

This very conservative position justifies rule by educated elites—not all that far from the positivists' message. Yet Rodó was critical of positivism. His critique, however, was aimed at nouveaux riches businessmen and the apostles of utilitarianism who serve them. Rodó, like the positivists, was elitist; the difference between them was that he wanted to substitute a cultural and literary elite for the pragmatic business types. But the structure of an elitist, hierarchical, organic, functionally organized society would be similar. It is thus easy to see why Latin America often elevates intellectuals to the presidency, whereas the United States does not, and why Latin American ruling coalitions often consist of combined coteries of intellectuals as well as military and economic elites: the impetus behind these formulations lies in Rodó. **189**

One can also see in them a direct linear path leading from neoscholasticism to positivism to Rodóism to corporatism (see chapter 9).*

Rodó was as critical of American education as he was of other aspects of American life. And his criticism fitted his overall philosophical approach. Rodó criticized the United States for its emphasis on mass public education. Universal education produces mediocrity, Rodó argued, and this came at the expense of excellence. Rudimentary knowledge imparted to everyone, Rodó says, means those who might excel cannot rise above the general average mediocrity. Rodó—like the French and the positivists—much preferred a cadre of specialized, high-level institutions that educate the elites and the cultured in higher knowledge. Thus, Rodó concludes that the persistent North American war against ignorance has resulted in a universal semi- or half-culture accompanied by the diminution of high culture.[31]

Rodó's criticisms of the United States are many and harsh. A number focus on the inability of Americans to appreciate high culture. Americans, he asserts, live for the present and are concerned with acquiring material possessions rather than with spiritual or cultural matters. "North American life," he says, "perfectly describes the vicious circle identified by Pascal; the fervent pursuit of well-being that has no object beyond itself. . . . as an entity this civilization creates a singular impression of insufficiency and emptiness."[32] Americans' taste in art, he says, is atrocious and sensationalist. Americans cannot appreciate subtle or exquisite art. Similarly, American literature, he claims, is of poor quality; as the United States has become more "American" and less "European," American literature and the quality of thought have

*There is a wonderful anecdote told by James W. Symington, a U.S. government official and son of a former senator, in his Foreword to the English-language edition of *Ariel* that inadvertently reveals a great deal about U.S. ignorance toward Latin America. Symington had accompanied President Lyndon Johnson to Punta del Este, Uruguay, for a meeting of the Conference of Presidents of the Americas in April 1967. In his keynote address, President Otto Arosemena of Ecuador invoked the name of Rodó and said, "May the genius of Uruguay which produced *Ariel* guide our thoughts." While every single Latin American present immediately understood that reference, *not one person* in either the American delegation or the American press corps accompanying the president had ever heard of either Rodó or *Ariel*. I happen to believe that, if you don't understand Rodó's *Ariel*, you don't understand Latin America. So it is particularly striking that not one of the Americans present had the foggiest notion what President Arosemena's reference meant. Had they known and comprehended, they might have understood what was going on in Latin America and at that meeting better than they did. Symington confesses that he immediately purchased a Spanish-language edition of *Ariel* and spent the afternoon reading it at the beach. Fortunately, one member of the American delegation could at least read
Spanish!

both deteriorated. "The bourgeois or egalitarian leveling process," he writes, "ever swifter in its devastation, is tending to erase what little character remains of their precarious intellectualism."[33]

American morality, he writes, is also becoming decrepit under the impact of utilitarianism and the love of money. America is losing its religious base, he says, and therefore its morality is in decline. Latin America, in contrast, must hang onto its moral and religious values. Reflecting the argument of the Counter-Reformation, Rodó says that Latin America must continue to value and assert its spirituality even in the face of modernization and industrialization.[34]

Rodó argues that Americans have a false sense of superiority. Americans tend to be condescending toward countries other than their own, to look down their noses at them and treat them as errant children who must mend their ways—that is, become more like the United States. But the United States is neither an Athens nor a Rome, Rodó argues, neither an intellectual nor a political leader, let alone a model to emulate, among nations. In this respect, Rodó compares unfavorably the American Statue of Liberty to Athena's likeness on the Acropolis of ancient Greece, using language typical of his florid literary style: "It is difficult to believe that when a stranger glimpses their [the Americans'] enormous symbol from the high seas—Bartholdi's Statue of Liberty, triumphantly lifting her torch high above the port of New York City—it awakens in his soul the deep and religious feeling that must have been evoked in the diaphanous nights of Attica by the sight of Athena upon the Acropolis, her bronze sword, glimpsed from afar, gleaming in the pure and serene atmosphere."[35]

In these and other passages, Rodó is intent on glorifying Latin American culture, criticizing American culture, and protecting the former from the threat of conquest by the latter. There are remarkable parallels between Rodó and Martí, except that Rodó's emphases are cultural and philosophical whereas Martí's are mainly economic and political. As a defense, Rodó says Latin America must maintain its idealism, its emphasis on art, its Catholic religion and morality, its distinctiveness, against the looming pragmatism and materialism of the North. Most important, he says, Latin America must continue to live for the future. Hence, Rodó's appeal, especially to the younger generation, to protect this superior Latin American culture against the onslaught of the American barbarians. Given this message and the required reading of Rodó in every Latin American classroom, it is probably no accident that over the decades it has primarily been Latin American university and high school students who have led the protests against American interventionism and imperialism in their countries.

It is easy to criticize Rodó. His language is too flowery and his argument full of exaggerations and falsehoods. His position is both elitist and racist. Nor is it the case that North Americans are necessarily more crass, crude, and materialistic than Latin Americans, or Latin America more cultured and moral. As for education, why not have good primary and secondary and good university education at the same time? And cannot democratic elections and accountability be combined with real expertise and specialized knowledge? Rodó's logic and argument are full of holes. Globalization is erasing many of the earlier cultural differences.

And yet, what is striking is the tremendous—and continuing—impact of Rodó and *Ariel* on Latin America. He may be the single most important influence in twentieth-century Latin American cultural history. His ability to sway generation after generation of Latin American young people is immense. The official textbooks that Latin American school systems use in their classrooms are infused with Arielism. Especially compelling to Latin Americans are his portraits of the stark disparities between the North American and Latin American cultures and his admonitions to the youth of Latin America to hang onto their culture at all costs and to resist the Americans. I don't think, given Rodó's continuing appeal, that it is mere coincidence that American officials and private sector activists often have a hard time securing cooperation from their Latin American counterparts.

Rodó is important for other reasons. He is a link between the old and new philosophies and ideologies, between the nineteenth and the twentieth centuries. His defense of order, hierarchy, authority, religion, and elite, top-down rule puts him squarely in the tradition of Saint Thomas, Suárez, and the colonial past—recently updated in the form of Comtean positivism. At the same time, his powerful nationalism and sense of an organic and corporately organized political system serve as preludes to such twentieth-century ideological developments in Latin America as Hispanismo and corporatism. So Rodó connects the past and the future. At the same time, he is probably the most important and influential writer in all the history of Latin America. I cannot conceive that one can understand Latin America without understanding

Rodó—even though one may not like all of what he says, and it may not even be very accurate. Rodó is essential—as essential, in my view, as Aristotle, Saint Thomas, Suárez, Rousseau, and Comte in the pantheon of thinkers that most strongly shaped Latin American civilization. How different this tradition is from the North American tradition!

Hispanismo

Hispanismo, quite simply, means an admiration for things Hispanic: Hispanic law, culture, politics, religion, literature, language. Hispanismo is the belief that Spain and Portugal transplanted their values and culture to Latin America, and that both Iberia and Latin America have a tradition and lifestyle that are distinct from those of the rest of the world, particularly from the "Anglo-Saxon" nations. The ideology of Hispanismo goes on to suggest that Iberia and Latin America form a separate race (raza), a distinct community and civilization, and that the connection between the two areas must be strengthened. But given the colonial history of Spain and Portugal in Latin America, that has often been a heavy—and often divisive—burden to carry.[36]

For during much of the nineteenth century, Spain (less so Portugal) was reviled rather than admired in Latin America. As the former colonial master, Spain was often blamed for all of Latin America's ills. Over time, such strong negative passions began to ease, and during the era of positivism Spain and its institutions began to be looked on in a more favorable light. The most dramatic turning point came with the Spanish-American War of 1898, when, ironically, Spain's inglorious defeat by the newly arrived Americans led to its being looked on more sympathetically in Latin America. By this time the bitterness toward Spain characteristic of the early independence years had been assuaged. In addition Latin American nationalism was on the rise, part of which was expressed in terms of admiration for things Hispanic and Latin as distinct from those crass Americans or Anglo-Saxons. And, on top of this, in the first decades of the twentieth century a Catholic revival launched by the Vatican also brought Catholic Spain and Catholic Latin America closer together. Martí's anti-American nationalism and Rodó's cultural nationalism, which included strong admiration for the religion and traditions of Spain, were also important ingredients in this rapprochement between former colonies and former mother country.

Hence, in the early twentieth century, there were considerably warmer relations and more cultural and intellectual exchanges between Spain and Latin America than in the nineteenth century. Spanish musicians, dance and theater groups, orchestras, and other artists toured frequently in Latin America. The region was now more receptive to Spanish literature, especially the writers of the Generation of '98 (Miguel de Unamuno, José Ortega y Gasset), who were themselves, like the Latin Americans, questioning the often imported (from the United States and Great Britain) liberal institutions of the recent past and seeking to discover in their own history and traditions a uniquely Hispanic political philosophy and basis for governance. Latin American university students now studied in Spain; Latin American intellectuals traveling abroad stopped at Madrid as well as at Paris and London. More Latin Americans carried dual citizenship: that of Spain and that of their birth country. During the first three decades of the twentieth century, these contacts gradually expanded and broadened. Yet Spain was still a poor country and could not afford to have a strong military, economic, or strategic presence in Latin America; in fact, its very poverty meant that the exchanges had to be largely limited to the cultural and the ideological. Frederick Pike in his important and thorough study of this period refers to these cultural exchanges orchestrated by Spain as "lyrical Hispanismo," as contrasted with the stronger political and economic programs ("practical Hispanismo") that followed.[37]

During this period leading up to and then after World War I, Hispanismo gradually took on a broader meaning. In keeping with Rodó's injunctions, Hispanismo also implied a strong, mutual, Spanish and Latin American commitment to religion, specifically Catholicism, which dovetailed with Rome's plans to revive often-declining religious sentiment in countries undergoing industrialization and secularization. Iberia and Latin America, because of the Spanish-American War and repeated U.S. military interventions, respectively, had ample reason to resent the United States, a sentiment that bound the two areas more closely. Both began to identify more with their common social and political background, which included organicism, Thomism, a strong sense of community, a corporately or functionally organized society, a guiding or directing state, and top-down authority—all this, of course, in contrast to the individualism, egalitarianism, liberalism, and democracy of the now-despised United States. And both Iberia and Latin America began a renewed search for a political formula that would reflect their history and traditions rather than simply palely imitate institutions imported from France, England, and the United States (see chapter 9).[38]

Not all Spaniards, Portuguese, and Latin Americans, of course, were in precise agreement on what exactly Hispanismo meant.[39] In Spain and Portugal—to say nothing of Latin America—the early decades of the twentieth century were years of upheaval and political disputation about the present and future. In Spain and Portugal during this period there were two main ideologies and orientations, two main political "families." The liberals, heirs to the older nineteenth-century liberals, were the "family of change." They wanted mainly a secularization of society and a reduction in the power of the Catholic Church. In historically Catholic Spain and Portugal, these ideas were often revolutionary; religion was the hinge on which much of the political debate swung. The liberals also favored the classic nineteenth-century freedoms as well as free trade.

Conservatives constituted the "family of order." They wanted to maintain not just the Catholic religion but also a religiously inspired society and polity. At this time, as the two countries were undergoing early stages of industrialization, conservatives were primarily concerned about the adverse effects of material development on Catholicism and believed in a continued, revived, strong Catholic influence over society. They were opposed to both Marxism and liberal almost with equal fervor. Yet both groups, liberals and conservatives alike, sought to transfer and expand Hispanic values in Latin America. Both were convinced that Iberia and Latin America shared certain cultural traditions and a lifestyle that was distinct from that of the rest of the world. Both liberal and conservative advocates of Hispanismo believed that the mother countries and their former colonies formed a distinct community, a special raza, a term that in Spanish carries both cultural and racial connotations.

Moreover, Spanish and Portuguese liberals as well as conservatives shared the belief of Latin American liberals and conservatives that Ibero-America, like Iberia itself, should preserve a hierarchically structured society. They may have been liberals in classic nineteenth-century terms, but they did not necessarily believe in egalitarianism. Both groups believed hierarchy would help preserve social stability in a time of change; both wanted to keep the lower (and darker) classes in their place. They were fearful of democracy as well as of materialism, sought to limit their effects, and warned Latin America against the evil effects of these influences stemming from the United States. Hispanismo was the ideology that not only brought Iberia and Latin America together but also provided at least some grounds for agreement between liberals and conservatives within the societies.

Inevitably, a movement like Hispanismo, which carried ever-stronger ideological overtones, would become politicized (as do all ideologies). That is, it would be seized upon by the dominant elites in their societies and manipulated for partisan or class advantage. That is precisely what happened to Hispanismo once Franco (1939–75) and Salazar (1928–74) seized hold of the concept. Franco especially identified his regime with the ideology of Hispanismo. In his view (which prevailed for almost forty years), Catholicism, authority, discipline, hierarchy, the obligation to obedience, an organic state, corporatism, *and his regime* were intimately bound together. In other words, Franco not only identified his regime with the ideology of Hispanismo, but went farther to identify the particular values of his regime with historic Spanish values, thus not only casting himself as the true interpreter and even personification of Spanish values but implying that the values of groups that did not share his politics were non-Spanish. Hispanismo afforded the Franco regime not only an ideology but also a way to dismiss all other points of view as being outside the realm of what a true Spaniard could believe. It was an effective if hardly democratic way to deal with his opposition.[40]

Hispanismo also became an instrument of Spanish foreign policy as Spain sought consciously to export its political and cultural influence to Latin America. Hispanismo served to strengthen Spain's influence abroad and its international position by pressing Latin America, supposedly organically joined with Spain in a common raza, to support Spanish foreign policy objectives by forming a common bloc that would help Spain, for instance, gain entrance to the North Atlantic Treaty Organization and the European Community. Hence, Spain established a special institute, the Institute for Hispanic Culture, associated with its foreign ministry, to further these goals in Latin America. It also sought vigorously to propagate the Hispanismo ideology in Latin America, to advance the conservative principles of the Franco regime, and thus to reforge the strong ties with Latin America that had been severed a century earlier following independence.

The reaction in Latin America to these overtures from Spain was mixed. On the one hand, Spain was still a comparatively poor country and often could not back up its moral and ideological injunctions with hard economic, diplomatic, or military might. At the same time, many

Latin Americans resented Spain's assays into diplomatic leadership, feeling that they could conduct their foreign policies with other countries perfectly well by themselves, thank you, without Spanish intermediation. And many liberals and democrats in Latin America did not appreciate the authoritarian values that the Franco regime was espousing or its racist overtones in their mixed-race societies.[41]

But many others—and not just conservatives—saw value in the ideas Spain was advancing. Discipline, order, authority, the family, and Catholicism were attractive values in the countries of Latin America now, like Spain, undergoing modernization and the first stages of industrialization and fearing the disruptive consequences of these changes. The ideology of Hispanismo seemed a useful way to maintain social peace and hold society together in the chaotic, disruptive circumstances of the interwar period, in the face of what was widely perceived as a serious Bolshevik threat and the specter of economic collapse occasioned by the Great Depression of the 1930s. In addition, liberalism seemed at that time a dying philosophy in Latin America; if some of the authors cited in the previous chapter are correct, liberalism in Latin America, at least in its nineteenth-century incarnation, died around the time of World War I, afflicted by a history of failure and supplanted by positivism and other philosophies.

In the early 1930s, as the Depression caused both the economies and the political systems of Latin America to collapse, sixteen of the twenty Latin American countries experienced revolutions that brought a wave of strong-arm, long-term authoritarian regimes to power. Almost all of these regimes accepted Hispanismo in one form or another, and almost all used the model of the Franco and Salazar regimes—authoritarian, corporatist—in fashioning their own governing principles. The regimes included those of Getulio Vargas in Brazil, the Argentine colonels and eventually Juan Perón, Carlos Ibáñez in Chile, Rafael Trujillo in the Dominican Republic, Jorge Ubico in Guatemala, Tiburcio Carías Andino in Honduras, Fulgencio Batista in Cuba, Laureano Gómez in Colombia, Maximiliano Hernández Martínez in El Salvador, Anastasio Somoza in Nicaragua, José María Velasco Ibarra in Ecuador, Alfredo Stroessner in Paraguay, the Mexican Partido Revolucionario Institucional (Institutional Revolutionary party). Authoritarianism in its Hispanic forms was destined to dominate most of Latin America for the next thirty years.

Almost all of these strongmen, or their agents, at one time or another found their way to Spain or Portugal to study the Franco and

Salazar regimes, to learn their methods, to understand how they did it. The "it" in this case was the dilemma almost all rapidly developing countries face: how to maintain stability, social peace, and economic progress in the face of the social tensions, divisions, and potential for instability that the modernization process sets loose. Hispanismo in its Catholic, authoritarian, and corporatist forms offered an often attractive (disciplined, organic, integral) means to solve this dilemma. Indeed, the literature of the time shows that Hispanismo was often used by dictators like Vargas, Perón, Trujillo, and others not only to justify their regimes but also to rationalize their staying in office indefinitely. Rodó, the Latin American precursor of Hispanismo, was similarly cited frequently as part of the same justification.[42]

Over time, of course, these authoritarian regimes faded or were overthrown along with the Hispanismo that helped justify their rule. The Portuguese regime fell in 1974 and Franco died in 1975: by then most of the Latin American authoritarians who had come to power in the 1930s were gone or on the way back to the barracks (see chapters 9 and 10). With the death or ouster of the earlier authoritarian regimes and the beginning in many countries of a transition to democracy, Hispanismo underwent redefinition. Democracy and human rights became the main themes, no longer authority, discipline, hierarchy, and so forth. Spain's institute for the dissemination of Hispanic culture was changed to the Institute for Hispanic Cooperation. Spain still sought to export its model to Latin America, but now that model was to be democratic rather than authoritarianism. As in the past, however, the new orientation in Hispanismo was still aimed at serving Spain's foreign policy goals and at establishing a sharp distinction from the Anglo-Saxon (read, U.S.) nations. Furthermore, Spain's attitude toward its Latin American former colonies was often condescending and patronizing ("We will lead, you follow") and, as such, continued to be resented in many circles in Latin America.[43]

Nationalism and Racism

The issue of race has come up at several points in this book but heretofore has not formed part of a self-conscious ideology. The Spanish conquistadores, for instance, going back to Aristotle for justification, devised a system of castes based on both class and race. The caste structure consigned Indians and blacks to a lower level in the social hierarchy; there was even doubt as to whether they possessed souls and, therefore, were human or not. During the colonial period the lower castes were kept in their place, and all efforts at Indian and black rebellion were brutally repressed.

Then, during the struggles for independence in the early nineteenth century, whenever the banner of social revolt accompanying the independence movements was raised, as in Mexico under Hidalgo and Morelos, it too was brutally suppressed. In some countries, in fact, black regiments were recruited to battle against the Indian uprisings, thus assuring (quite consciously so) that both groups would be effectively eliminated.

Prejudice in Latin America has long been based as much on social and cultural criteria (education, dress, family, background, comportment) as on skin color; miscegenation over the centuries has been widespread; and it is possible for dark persons to move up on the social scale. Latin American race relations are thus generally accorded to be more relaxed and malleable than they are in the United States; there are degrees and gradations of "blackness" and "whiteness." Nevertheless, race is an important criterion in Latin America—often the most important criterion for gauging a person's place on the social scale—and racism is an important ingredient. Indeed, racial criteria became more rather than less important in Latin America during the nineteenth and early twentieth centuries, and in the course of this history Latin America absorbed most of the racial theories that dominated in Europe and North America: social Darwinism, eugenics, and various theories of European racial superiority.[44]

A signal event was the Haitian slave revolt that began in 1795. The slaves threw off the yoke of slavery, burned the plantations, and cruelly killed or exiled the entire white ruling class. The dramatic events in Haiti had a profound and frightening effect on the white ruling classes throughout Latin America, who were determined at all costs not to allow the Haitian experience to be repeated elsewhere. The repression of the Indian uprisings in Mexico during independence is directly attributable to the earlier events in Haiti, as is the setting of blacks against Indians for the cynical purpose of eliminating both groups. The Dominican Republic, sharing the island of Hispaniola with Haiti, defines virtually its entire nationhood in anti-Haitian (which means anti-black and anti-African) terms. Although most Latin American countries abolished the colonial caste system following independence, most

199

continued to practice slavery until well into the nineteenth century (as did the United States); they shared the general lament about the lack of culture and civilization (often blamed on large numbers of Indians and blacks) in their countries and soon erected social, cultural, and political barriers to lower-class upward mobility that were almost as rigid as the caste system.[45]

As the nineteenth century progressed and as Latin America struggled to achieve stability and development, racially motivated public policy came more and more to the forefront. When Argentina's Alberdi issued his famous dictum, "To govern is to populate," he had in mind luring European immigration, not advocating an increase of the African and Indian populations. In Sarmiento's famous tract "Civilization or Barbarism," civilization is identified with increasing white, European influences and barbarism with black, Indian, and mestizo influences, which were to be eliminated. In Comte's enormously influential writings on positivism, the European race is accorded a position of superior importance, and a small (white) elite is to rule over the unlettered (dark) masses. Similarly, Rodó's profoundly influential *Ariel* praised the glories of white Hispanic culture, and the ideology of Hispanismo, too, was posited on a social structure that was Catholic, authoritarian, hierarchical, Hispanic, and European (that is, white).

Such values and the frankly racial criteria used are abhorrent by today's standards, but it is inappropriate to use present morality to judge past history. Moreover, one must understand these events in the context of the time. Thus, when Latin America sought to entice European immigrants in the nineteenth and early twentieth centuries, did this policy differ in any way from that of the United States during this same period, which also enacted laws and regulations to encourage Europeans and keep out all others? When Latin America sought to lighten its population and to bring civilization to the interior, did this differ from U.S. efforts to settle the West with whites, to isolate or kill the Indians, and to identify itself as a civilized, European country?

At this stage in history virtually everyone believed that white, European civilization was superior to black, Indian, or "mongrel" civilizations. Given these sentiments, the Latin American countries, with their majority black, Indian, mulatto, and mestizo populations, felt inferior to the United States and Europe. They were obliged to feel shame and inferiority for their mixed racial backgrounds. Many Latin American writers wrote scathing books about the racial miscegenation their countries had earlier experienced and how this had dragged down the national intelligence, the level of civilization, and the possibilities for modernization.[46] It is no accident that countries like Argentina, Uruguay, Chile, and Costa Rica, which did in fact have relatively few Indians and few if any slave plantations for which black slaves would have been imported, identify themselves and are often identified as "European"—with clear racial overtones; and that these countries often look down on their more racially mixed neighbors and are in turn despised by them for their airs of superiority; that these allegedly European nations still have tightly restrictive immigration laws to prevent their unwanted neighbors from flooding into their countries; that in many countries skin powders, hair straighteners, and more recently cosmetic surgery are widely used to lighten the population both to enable individuals to look whiter than they are and to make the country itself appear whiter to an international community that still makes judgments according to racial criteria. Or that countries like Brazil, Mexico, virtually all the others purposely select presidents, cabinet officers, and foreign ministry officials who look European so as to better represent the country abroad and to present a better (whiter) face to the outside world. For decades the Dominican Republic failed to elect José Francisco Peña Gómez to the presidency, not because he wasn't able and talented but because he was black, "Haitian," and this was not the image of their country they wished to convey either internally or to the outside world.[47]

While racial attitudes and prejudices are one thing, a full-fledged racial ideology is quite another. But that also began to develop in Latin America in the nineteenth century. The ingredients for such an ideology were prepared in the colonial past, in the attitudes of the creole elites, in the writings and policies of Alberdi and Sarmiento (among many others), and then in positivism, Rodó, and Hispanismo. But now these various ingredients began to crystallize in ideological form—as they did, incidentally, in Europe and the United States. For example, I have focused so far on the Comtean and sociological bases of positivism that had such a strong impact on Latin America; but an important strain of positivist thought, growing out of Charles Darwin's principles of natural selection and survival of the fittest, was that of Herbert Spencer, who actually had more influence in the United States than he did in Latin America. Spencer, more explicitly than Comte, built racial and eugenicist criteria into the positivist philosophy and social hierarchy, suggesting that in the most advanced or positivist stage of history those at the top of the social pyramid—the engineers, intellectuals, and business elites who would run things—would, on the bases of intelligence and natural selection, be white and European. The eugenics movement, which sought to correlate intelligence with racial and nationality traits, also enjoyed popularity in Latin America in the first decades of the twentieth century (as it did in Europe and the United States) as a way of justifying white, European dominance of society and the keeping of Indians and blacks at lower levels.[48]

Hispanismo was also tainted with notions of racial superiority. First, its basic premise, which involved the admiration of things Spanish, meant admiration for white, Catholic, authoritarian, European Spain—as against the several Indianist, black power, integrationist, "cosmic race," and pluralist theories that had begun to spring up. Second, the concept of la raza, also integral to Hispanismo, carried an ambiguous double meaning that was similarly exploited for racial purposes. On the one hand, la raza was used figuratively and in a cultural sense to imply identification with the Spanish language, literature, and art—all presumably nonracial matters. But on the other, la raza was also used literally to refer to the Spanish race, which was white, Catholic, European, conservative, First World, and capitalistic. As it adopted Hispanismo as part of its foreign policy ideology, Spain employed the concept of la raza in a dual way, implying on the one side the defense of a politically conservative, hierarchical, organic social order, and on the other the notion of a united Hispanic race to frustrate and contain growing U.S. influence. Hispanismo as a foreign policy instrument employed the threat of cultural influence and "contamination" emanating more broadly from the Anglo-Saxon world, meaning both northern Europe and North America.[49]

By the 1930s these ideas of the racial superiority of a white, European, Hispanicized ruling class were not only widespread, but also quite literally being put into practice by those in power. Such long-term authoritarian dictators as Trujillo. Somoza, Ubico, Batista, Perón, and others—and the intellectuals who served them—used the writings of Rodó, the positivists, the eugenicists, and Hispanismo to justify their ascendance to power, their use of authoritarian techniques, their elitist and often racist domestic and immigration policies, their identification with Franco's regime in Spain, and even their sympathies with fascism and Nazism in the first part of World War II.[50] Of course, because of U.S. influence in the Western Hemisphere, few of these regimes could outright call themselves fascist, let alone ally themselves with the Axis powers; but unmistakably that is where their sympathies lay—at least until it became obvious that the United States and its allies would win the war, whereupon most of them opportunistically came out in favor of the Allied cause.

World War II, of course, resulted in the defeat as well as the discrediting of fascism, Nazism, the Axis powers, and many of the racial themes they espoused. That meant that the several authoritarian regimes (Trujillo, Somoza, Perón, Franco, Salazar) that survived the war had to look elsewhere for their ideology, to trim their earlier ideological sails. But in other countries (Brazil, Guatemala, Costa Rica, Bolivia, Colombia, Chile) the authoritarians gave way—at least temporarily and occasionally more than that—to democratic movements that often repudiated the earlier Hispanismo. (In chapter 10 I discuss this renewed contestation at the political, power, and ideological levels.) When, however, a new wave of authoritarians came to power in Latin America in the 1960s and 1970s, the ideology of Hispanismo, the admiration for the Spanish regime, the pilgrimages by military officers and others to Madrid, and the justifications for order and discipline were all revived. In this later context, however, the manifestly racist aspects of Hispanismo were largely abandoned. It is no longer fashionable or justifiable to hold such racist views. But having interviewed many of them, I am not convinced that those rich, white Latin American aristocrats—although they cannot say so publicly—are even now entirely convinced that Indians, blacks, and lower-class persons really have souls and therefore—to go back to that ancient sixteenth-century argument—certain basic rights as persons and must be treated accordingly.

Contemporary Nationalism

More recent (since World War II) nationalism in Latin America has mainly taken a left and anti-American tone. But the earlier conservative, positivist, Arielist, Hispanist, fascist, and downright racist strands of thought are still present, seldom spoken in public anymore but so deeply ingrained in Latin American elite culture that one doubts if they will ever be fully eradicated.

While blatant and repeated U.S. interventionism is the most obvious cause of Latin American anti-Americanism and nationalism, a subtler but no less painful cause is U.S. attitudes toward Latin America. The

United States tends to treat Latin America with condescension, a patronizing attitude, and a sense of superiority. Latin America, like Rodney Dangerfield, gets no respect: the area is low on U.S. priorities, not accorded serious attention in policy circles—at least until some crisis forces action—and not paid serious attention by the public. Latin America is a subject of condescending *New Yorker* cartoons, movies (*Bananas, Butch Cassidy and the Sundance Kid*), and attitudes. The United States treats Latin Americans as little children who must, presumably, be educated by the all-knowing Americans. It does not take the area seriously—even in the present era, when for economic, demographic, trade, tourism, immigration, pollution, investment, and a host of other reasons it should be elevating Latin America in its list of priorities. Some of these prejudices and biases toward Latin America are of recent vintage, but some go back to the colonial period and the fact that Latin America was Catholic, inquisitorial, hierarchical, authoritarian, and settled by Spain and Portugal, whereas the United States was mainly Protestant, politically democratic, free and egalitarian, and settled by the English. These prejudices as between the United States and Latin America have deep historical roots and are a main cause of Latin American anti-Americanism; they will not go away soon.[51]

While U.S. interventionism has often triggered strong expressions of anti-American nationalism, U.S. inaction or indifference has often galvanized equally strong protests. Although Latin America dislikes U.S. intervention and clings to the principle of nonintervention, it equally dislikes being ignored by the United States. When Vice President Richard Nixon was booed, hissed, stoned, and rocked in his car while visiting Venezuela in 1958, it was not because of any immediate overt U.S. intervention in that country but because the U.S. had *not* done anything for Venezuela or moved against its dictator, Marcos Pérez-Jiménez. Nixon's visit helped stimulate President Dwight Eisenhower to take a new look at Latin America and pay it more attention, and it led eventually to John F. Kennedy's Alliance for Progress.[52] Similarly, the virtually daily street demonstrations in the Dominican Republic in the last half of 1961 and early 1962 were not in protest against any specific U.S. action in that country in those days but in broader frustration with the United States' long inaction in taking steps to oust the thirty-one-year dictatorship of Rafael Trujillo. In other words, the United States is often criticized by Latin America nationalists both for what it does in the hemisphere and for what it fails to do.

More complicated, the United States is often resented for what it is and stands for, and not for what it does or does not do. The United States is, by almost any measure, a successful country: democratic, having the highest living standard in the world, mainly middle class, more-or-less socially just, and ethnically a melting pot with at least the presumption (and considerable claim to success) of equality of opportunity. By contrast, Latin America is often thought of as being unsuccessful: unstable politically, plagued by degrading jokes that mock its frequent coups, underdeveloped economically, rigid and unyielding socially and racially. Latin America is, of course, aware of these unflattering portraits and bitterly resents them. It chafes under the comparison with the United States; its nationalism is thus conditioned often by a gigantic inferiority complex.

Such complexes vis-à-vis the United States have been markedly strong in a country like Argentina, which has at least the same natural resources as the United States, thinks of itself as similarly European, was once (before the Great Depression) ahead of the United States in per capita wealth, and yet in the ensuing decades fell way behind in every single measure. The Argentines—and many other Latin Americans—simply cannot stand it that the United States by all criteria is more developed than they are and that they are referred to as "developing" or "emerging." These differences and the attitudes they engender produce resentments that are deeply felt in Argentina and elsewhere to this day and that frequently produce anti-American outbursts. Usually, however, such discontent is kept bottled up by traditional Latin American politeness. Is it any wonder that Buenos Aires has more psychiatrists per capita than any other place in the world, including Manhattan?[53]

Another source of Latin American nationalism and anti-Americanism is cultural, the legacy of Rodó. Although these attitudes are changing somewhat, they are still very much present. Many Latin Americans still think of themselves as more cultured, refined, and sophisticated than Americans. They still often view the United States as crass and materialistic, an upstart nation, pushy, not devoted enough to the high arts of literature and philosophy. They still see democracy as bringing the masses to power, the lowest common denominator, implying mediocrity rather than excellence. They often see their Catholicism as more refined, sophisticated, and certainly having a longer, more glorious history than North American Protestantism. They also tend to see capitalism and moneymaking as low forms of activity, something that gentlemen should not sully their hands with, that only the utilitarian Americans should engage in, while Latin American leaders and intellectuals should concentrate on more elevated activities: poetry, high culture, the cultivation of the mind as against the moneygrubbing of the material. This form of nationalism in Latin America is more traditional, is concentrated at elite levels, and is now fading as Latin America, too, joins the mass, consumerist, democratic world culture of rock music, blue jeans, and Coca-Cola. But the legacy of this tradition is still powerful and even today finds expression in the familiar Latin American disdain for manual labor, disparagement of capitalism and moneymaking, and preference for the high, elevated life of the spirit.

The revolution in Cuba in 1959 accelerated many of Latin America's nationalistic trends. Castro, inspired by the writings of Martí, not only dramatically broke with the United States on nationalistic grounds, but also declared himself a Marxist-Leninist and closely associated himself with the United States' historic enemy, the Soviet Union. In addition, Castro sought to stoke the flames of Marxism and anti-Americanism throughout the hemisphere and aided or helped sponsor numerous guerrilla movements similarly aimed at eliminating U.S. influence. For a time Castro, Ché Guevara, and the Cuban revolution inspired the youth of Latin America, just as Rodó had done in earlier decades. Castro and the Cuban revolution also drove the United States almost crazy and distorted American policy toward the region for thirty years by bringing the Cold War to Latin America and making that virtually the sole focus of U.S. policy. But Guevara died in a frustrated effort to bring revolution to Bolivia, Castro grew old, the Cuban revolution ran out of gas and proved unsuccessful by almost all policy measures, and its chief sponsor, the Soviet Union, collapsed and cut off its essential Cuban subsidy. Soon other guerrilla movements in Latin America began drying up, suing for peace, or joining the democratic political process by reorganizing as political parties. Today, Castro-style nationalism and anti-Americanism are by no means dead in Latin America, but they have certainly faded in importance as an ideology for Latin American youth.[54]

Even more insidious for the future of Latin American nationalism is the impact of recent globalization. Globalization takes many forms: political, cultural, economic. Politically at this stage, globalization means democracy and human rights. Marxism-Leninism has collapsed, authoritarianism is no longer acceptable, and democracy enjoys worldwide legitimacy. But if democracy is the only form of government that is acceptable, what happens to the Latin American claim that it is unique, distinctive? Similarly in the cultural sphere: it is now television and modern mass communication that in large measure define the entire hemisphere's tastes in dress, food, consumption, dating, divorce, family relations, as well as politics. So how can Latin America take pride in its culture if it is being swamped by consumerism and forms of behavior emanating from the global culture, which happens to be heavily U.S.-inspired? And in the economic sphere: Latin America in this new global economy can no longer hide its traditional family-based firms and their associated inefficiencies behind protective trade barriers. The region must compete with the more advanced economies, and that means jettisoning its older, hostile attitudes toward capitalism and moneymaking. So how can one continue to be a Latin American philosophe and cultivate poetry and higher learning if those endeavors force one to be poor and miserable? All of these global, probably irreversible trends are undermining Latin America's sense of its distinctiveness and, hence, of its nationalism.

Redefining Nationhood

Nationalism has approximately a 175-year (even longer, in some cases) history in Latin America. But now nationalism and the very concepts of sovereignty and the nation-state are under attack as never before. The nation-state is still the key variable, but its status, autonomy, and independent decision-making ability are now being undermined.[55]

The first cause is, again, globalization. When political, cultural, and economic choices and decisions are increasingly the product of global, nonnational forces over which states have little control, it is clear that sovereignty and nationalism are at bay. It is global markets, global television, and the global Third Wave of democratization that are the key driving forces in the world today, and no longer so much local or indigenous cultural forces. Tastes, behavior, culture, as well as the choices of political institution and economic policy are no longer the exclusive presence of the nation-state or of a local or regional cultural background but of a set of impersonal global forces that often leave little room for local initiatives.[56]

Second and related, so many of today's problems are no longer national in character but global and regional, and therefore the solutions must be global or regional. Now that the Cold War is over, what are the front-burner issues: drugs, immigration, trade, terrorism, pollution, the environment, AIDs, global warming, weapons proliferation, refugees, hunger, and so on. Not one of these issues is purely national in scope; not one can be solved on a purely domestic or unilateral basis; all of them are international—or "intermestic," both international and domestic. But that also means international solutions—bilateral or multilateral—and international agencies like the Organization of American States, United Nations, North American Free Trade Area (NAFTA), and MERCOSUR will likely be elevated in importance as problem-solving bodies. The promotion of international tribunals, however, inevitably means a decline at certain levels and in certain areas of purely national sovereignty and decision making.

A third factor potentially undermining nationhood, nationalism, and the nation-state is the rise and greater assertiveness of the sizable indigenous communities in Latin America. Earlier, Latin America had tried to snuff out its Indian communities or isolate them or assimilate them into the national life. Such assimilation, however, was always on the terms of the dominant white elites and meant acceptance of the Spanish language, religion (Catholic), culture, social order, and political institutions. In other words, Indians, blacks, and mestizos could all rise in the social scale but only by abandoning their pasts and backgrounds and accepting Hispanic ways, behavior, and attitudes. While such Hispanization is still widespread in Latin America, another and countervailing force is being increasingly felt. And that involves the growing demand by indigenous communities in the Andean countries, Mexico, and most of Central America for greater autonomy, for protection of indigenous languages, customs, and land rights, and for greater self-government.[57]

The trouble is that some of these claims and demands cross current national boundaries: the ancient Inca empire stretched across at least five countries in the Andean group, and the Mayan empire encompassed at least five countries in Middle America. So the claim for autonomy, cultural independence, and political self-government by some of these groups involves, at a minimum, the rewriting of the constitutions of several countries, the erosion of sovereignty, even, potentially, the erasing of national boundaries. But this radical last step some groups in society, such as the military, the economic elites, and strong nationalists, are unwilling to countenance. Colombia, Bolivia, Ecuador, Peru, Guatemala, Mexico, Honduras, and Nicaragua are currently at loggerheads over this issue. But it seems clear that at least in some countries, some degree of sovereignty and, hence, of nationalism and the nation-state will ultimately be sacrificed as indigenous claims are more forcefully asserted.[58]

A fourth factor undermining nationalism in various nations is the very concept of nationhood itself. As noted, some countries—Chile, Argentina, Uruguay, Costa Rica—have long defined themselves as European. But that is a code word for white; and because it is no longer acceptable to define national characteristics in racial terms, it will no longer be possible for these countries so blatantly to describe themselves that way. Other countries in Latin America sometimes describe themselves as mestizo, Indian, black, or mulatto.[59] These racial terms, although no longer carrying the opprobrium they once did as descriptions of racially mixed countries, will likely be used less and less to refer to nations.

An especially interesting case is that of the Dominican Republic, which shares the island of Hispaniola with Haiti. Because of the black slave uprising in Haiti two centuries ago and Haiti's history after that as the first (and chaotic) black republic, coupled with the Dominican Republic's presence next door as a proud Spanish colony, the Dominican Republic has always defined itself as a nation in Hispanic terms: white, Catholic, European, Hispanic, Western. But the Dominican Republic, which is predominantly mulatto in terms of its racial makeup, often went beyond purely descriptive terms: it cast Haiti as black, "African," and therefore "barbaric" and "uncivilized," while painting itself as a bastion of "glorious" European (white) culture and civilization.[60] It is, therefore, not coincidental that the Dominicans especially, among Latin Americans, were strongly influenced by Hispanismo and the racial theories of the times. Unfortunately for the Dominicans, it is no longer fashionable or acceptable to define nationhood in racial terms. So the Dominicans as a nation are currently facing an identity crisis and casting about for a new, nonracial way of identifying their nationhood.[61]

There are other interesting cases in Latin America where national self-identity has become conflictual. Is Guatemala to be identified as a white, Hispanic, European nation or, if 60 percent of its population is indigenous, as an Indian one? Is Mexico North American and First World, Indian and Third World, or a mixture of the two, the "cosmic race" that José Vasconcelos talked about?[62] Is Brazil Portuguese and European, black and African, or a mix of all of these, a "New World in the

Tropics," to use the title of one of famed Brazilian sociologist Gilberto Freyre's books?[63] Or take the complicated case of Cuba. Before the revolution Cuba thought of itself as white and European, but after the revolution most of the middle- and upper-class whites and light mulattoes moved to Miami. Most of those left behind were darker mulatto and black, so Cuba today is considerably darker than it was in 1959. Is it conceivable that, once Castro passes from the scene and the island presumably opens up, these darker elements who are now better off in racial and social terms than they were before the revolution will welcome back with open arms those white and lighter-skinned (also richer!) Cubans from Miami who lay claims to being their liberators? Below the political rhetoric of pro- and anti-Castro Cubans, in other words, is a profoundly complicated racial divide that is likely to be enormously difficult of resolution.

All these newer forces and complications show that nationalism is either in decline or under attack on various fronts in Latin America. It remains a potent force but no longer the driving ideology of the region that it once was.

Nationalism in Latin America historically has gone through various incarnations: liberal, reactive, anti-American, cultural, economic, political. It has also taken various forms: rightist, leftist, fascist, conservative, and virtually all points in between. As nationalism became a major force and ideology in Latin America beginning around the 1880s, however, it was the right-wing variant that was most important. Positivism, Rodóism, and Hispanismo not only were anti-American in their implications, but also laid claim to being closely in accord with Latin American traditions and realities. All of these movements, moreover, were profoundly conservative in their implications, stressing discipline, order, hierarchy, authority, elitism, and eventually racism as well. What made these expressions of Latin American nationalism so powerful was that they tapped into the dominant intellectual currents of their times and at the same time reflected and rationalized the dominant elitist power structure.

After World War II, reflecting trends elsewhere in the developing world, Latin American nationalism, at least in its public expressions, took a more left-wing orientation. It is this form of nationalism that, under the impact of globalism and the other forces mentioned, is now in decline. But it is by no means certain that the more conservative position of Hispanismo and cultural nationalism has died. Currently, Latin America has undergone a transition to democracy (see chapter 11); but one would still need to be convinced that the elitist, hierarchical, top-down values championed by a long line of thinkers going back to Greece, Rome, the Bible, Saint Thomas, and Suárez and finding more recent expression in Rousseau, Comte, Rodó, Hispanismo, and ultimately corporatism have disappeared.[64]

Chapter 8

Marxism

Marxism came to Latin America late in the nineteenth century in conjunction with the first stages of industrialization and the rise of a nascent trade union movement.[1] Like so many of the ideologies surveyed here, Marxism was imported, a transplant from Europe. What appeal, strength, and influence did Marxism have? to what degree was it adapted to Latin American realities, as, to varying degrees, other imports like liberalism and positivism were in the nineteenth century? and, third, was Marxism's relative lack of success in Latin America due in part to the unwillingness or inability of its advocates to adapt the ideology sufficiently to Latin American realities to give it popular appeal? Further, if one may be permitted to speculate for a moment, are there parallels in this regard with liberal democracy, which has had similar difficulties adapting to Latin American realities and in gaining popularity? and contrasts with positivism or, later, corporatism, which *were* adapted to the realities of Latin American politics and society and did achieve widespread—and lasting—influence?

In addition to Marxism's longtime unwillingness to adapt to Latin American realities, its weaknesses in Latin America may be attributable to other factors as well. First, most Latin American countries are primarily agrarian; the industrial work force, which Marx said would lead the revolution to socialism, has seldom numbered more than 10–15 percent of the population. Second and related, capitalism and the industrial revolution arrived late in Latin America, meaning that for a long time the conditions did not exist for the launching of a successful workers' revolution. Third, until very recently, the majority of the Latin American population consisted of peasants, unintegrated Indians, and marginalized workers—all groups, Lenin recognized, that are hard to organize and mobilize. Fourth, Latin America is a predominantly Catholic area, and historically the Roman Catholic Church has served as an implacable foe of Marxism.

A fifth factor is the equally, if not surpassingly, implacable opposition of the United States. During the entire forty-five years of the Cold War, anticommunism was effectively the sole policy of the United States in Latin America, best expressed in the phrase, "No second Cubas," that is, no more socialist revolutions coming to power and allying themselves with the Soviet Union. Sixth, the several Marxist factions have often been torn by internal bickering, infighting, and even shootouts, all of which have hurt the movement. And seventh, conditions in twentieth-century Latin America are quite different from those in mid-nineteenth Europe: the stages of development have been speeded up, the timing and sequences of development are dissimilar, and globalism and international interdependence among nations and in the form of such lending-agencies-of-last-resort as the International Monetary Fund, the World Bank, and the Inter-American Development Bank are more prevalent. All these differences help explain both why Marxism has long had a difficult time making inroads, let alone establishing its dominance, in Latin America and why it is incumbent upon Marxists to adapt their strategies to the times and local conditions of the area if they wish to be successful.

The Principles of Marxism

It is not easy to summarize Marx's ideas clearly and succinctly because (1) Marx himself was not always entirely unambiguous, (2) his ideas changed and evolved over time, and (3) his many disciples have continued to revise and refine his ideas to this day.[2]

Karl Marx was born in Germany, studied philosophy and economics, was exiled to Paris for a time, and did his most serious writing while again in exile in England. He lived during the early, often excessive, robber baron phases of capitalism and the industrial revolution, which he witnessed firsthand, as did his contemporary Charles Dickens, who portrayed in fiction what Marx wrote about as a social scientist. At the heart of Marx's grand theory, formulated about the same time (mid-nineteenth century) as Comte's similarly grand and universal scheme, was a devastating critique of capitalism at that time, coupled with a strong moral commitment to social justice defined in Marx's case as socialism. Marx studied German philosophy, drew most of his political examples from French history (the Ancient Regime, the Revolution of 1789, Napoleon, the conservative restoration, upheaval in 1848, Napoleon III), and saw firsthand the industrial revolution in England. He presented his ideas, much as did Comte, as being "scientific," explaining the laws of economic change and their social and political ramifications, as having universal and inevitable applicability. So we will want to explore here not only the development of Marx's ideas but also their validity and adaptability to the Latin American context.

Marx's ideas, arrived at through his own research as well as that of his frequent collaborator Friedrich Engels, may be summarized in terms of the following seven principles:

1. Labor theory of value. Marx believed that the primary and almost exclusive value of a product was determined by the labor that went into it. Not by the marketing, research, sales, executive, managerial, or advertising costs that were also involved but solely by the labor. Anything else was "surplus value" or outright thievery in Marx's view, and by all rights belonged to the workers.

2. Historical materialism. Marx believed that whoever controlled the economic base of society, the means of production and the means of distribution, controlled all other factors; that throughout history it was the material base, or "substructure," that was all-important, not so much the political, the moral, the legal, the ideological, or the religious. In this, Marx broke sharply with such thinkers as Hegel, who elevated ideas to the forefront in history.

3. Economic determinism. Related to the above, Marx believed that economic forces, namely, classes, were the driving forces in history. Again, it was not so much kings or princes or popes or individual leaders that determined the long sweep of history but underlying economic forces. Everything noneconomic was part of the "superstructure," which was merely a mirror image of the economic base.

4. Class struggle. All of history, Marx wrote, was a history of class struggle. Again, not of ideas, religion, or great men but of classes: slaves against masters, peasants against landlords, workers against employers.

5. The dialectic. Not only was history driven by class struggle but it also proceeded dialectically, one class and one stage of development against and succeeding the other. Thus, the first stage was traditional society; it yielded through economic requirements and class struggle to slavery. Slavery's internal contradic-

tions in turn gave rise to feudalism. Within feudalism, however, a new class, the bourgeoisie or business elites, not only produced capitalism but also destroyed feudalism in the process. And within capitalism, another new class, the industrial proletariat, would emerge to both destroy capitalism and produce socialism. Each of these stages, in short—slavery, feudalism, capitalism, socialism—represented a new synthesis, but within each synthesis new contradictions would always emerge—thesis and antithesis—that would produce the next synthesis. Except that once the stage of socialism arrived, the dialectic would illogically stop—presumably because at that stage there would no longer be any more class struggle.

6. Inevitable revolution. The transition from one stage to the next, Marx thought, would always occur through violent revolution. That is because the owners of the means of production and distribution in each stage would not give up their control without a struggle; their wealth or land or capital would have to be seized from them by violent means. Hence, feudalism would follow slavery but only after a major revolution, capitalism would follow feudalism but only after a revolution (such as that in France in 1789), and socialism would succeed capitalism but only after a violent transformation (as in Russia in 1917). There is no sense in Marx—or sympathy toward—gradual, evolutionary, incremental, democratic change.

7. Dictatorship of the proletariat. In the final stage of socialism, the proletariat or workers will seize control. They will rule by themselves, as the "most advanced" class in the most advanced stage; other groups will be excluded. The workers' state will ultimately be governed by principles of mass participation and democracy, but democracy would not be extended to other groups; hence, the notion of a dictatorship of the proletariat until a stage of pure, stateless socialism could be conceived.

These basic principles of Marxism form a coherent system of thought that, like scholasticism or positivism, seems to hang together logically—if you grant its initial and very large assumptions. But it is also, again like most grand, quasi-absolutist ("hedgehog") systems of thought, quite vague and ambiguous, leaving ample room for different interpretations. Indeed, even in Marx's own lifetime, the interpretations had verged so far from the original that Marx himself could declare, "I am not a Marxist!" Hence, to understand Marx's later appeal, in Latin America and elsewhere, one needs to understand both the original ideas and the various revisions and permutations of them by his disciples and followers.[3]

One of the first splits was between orthodox Marxists and anarchists, who were inspired by Marxist ideas but advocated the immediate destruction of all coercive state institutions. Marx roundly denounced them for their lack of discipline and organization. In Britain the Fabian socialists accepted most of Marx's principles but believed in a gradual, nonrevolutionary, nonviolent, and parliamentary path to socialism. In Russia, Vladimir Lenin modified the gradualism and spontaneity of Marx's dialectic and argued that a "revolutionary vanguard" or party could lead the workers toward socialism and thus speed up the process; he also explained revolution in Russia, as distinct from the more industrialized nations of Europe, by the theory of imperialism, which made Russia "the weakest link in the imperialist chain." But in France and Germany, which were far more industrialized than Russia and had a much larger working class, some leading Marxists remained true to the original Marx while rejecting Leninism and his somewhat strained interpretations.

After the communist revolution seized power in Russia in 1917, a split developed between Joseph Stalin, who believed in securing communism in one country before attempting the worldwide workers' revolution that Marx had predicted, and Leon Trotsky, who continued to accept the idea of global upheaval. Stalin also came to use totalitarian methods while Trotsky, now exiled, favored a more humanistic approach. Two decades later Mao Zedong modified Marx to argue that communist revolution could occur in a basically feudal society in which peasants constituted the majority of the population and could lead the revolution, as distinct from its being led by workers in an already capitalist society, the basis of the original Marxian analysis. These various reformulations take Marxism a long way from its original formulation.

In Cuba, Castro and Guevara built upon the ideas of a peasant-based revolution (a misreading—perhaps deliberate—of their own multiclass revolution) and also introduced the *foco* ("nucleus") theory, by which a small, revolutionary group could supply the leadership of a broad-based revolution.[4] In Nicaragua the Sandinistas similarly advanced the idea of a broadly based antidictatorial alliance that would capitalize on widespread public aversion to the dictatorship of Somoza and then move to seize control of the revolutionary coalition after it had come to power.[5] These later permutations as applied specifically to Latin America involved not just a radical reinterpretation of original Marxism but also the elevation of political factors to a position of prominence above the economic determinants.

Two preliminary comments, in the form of hypotheses, need to be raised here. The first has to do with the reason Marxism had appeal, particularly among intellectuals and students, in Latin America. The answer is that Marxism seemed to fit, at least superficially, actual Latin American circumstances. That is, Latin America has for a long time been going through precisely the transition that Marx described, from a form of feudalism to a kind of capitalism, with its attendant robber barons, emerging bourgeoisie, and immense gaps between rich and poor. It is generally acknowledged that it is in this transition, similarly occurring in Europe at the time Marx was writing in the nineteenth century, that Marxism is insightful and relevant; it is the next transition, from capitalism presumably to socialism, that Marx got all wrong. However, as Latin America also, from the nineteenth to the twentieth centuries, transitioned from feudalism to capitalism, the Marxian categories of class change and infrastructure transformation seemed to have a considerable degree of validity that appealed to students and intellectuals.

A second preliminary comment also has to do with the reasons for Marxism's appeal—apart from its intrinsic validity—to these groups. The answer is, in part, that Marxism is in a sense like both scholasticism and positivism: it is a total, wholistic system that proceeds deductively from Marx's "truths" to individual country circumstances. It offers, as did scholasticism and positivism, a complete, closed, and absolute set of answers to all questions. Once you're a true believer in Marxism, you don't need anything else. In this way, Marxism is like a religion—just as scholasticism and positivism claimed to be. In other words, Marxism became popular in part because it was a new set of absolutist beliefs that could serve as a substitute for the monolithic Catholicism that was then in decline in Latin America, and for positivism, which had become bourgeois and capitalistic and was similarly starting to fade. But the constant of a total belief system, the one readily substitutable for the other, remained. As Octavio Paz has written, "The strangest thing is that this [scholastic] theological-political conception has reappeared in our time. Nowadays, however, it is not identified with divine revelation; it wears the mask of a so-called universal science of history and society. Revealed truth has become the 'scientific truth' of Marxism, incarnate not in a Church and a Council but in a Party and a Committee."[6]

Origins

What might be called the antecedents of Marxism appeared in Latin America in the mid–nineteenth century because of the fascination of a handful of intellectuals with the ideas of European utopian socialism. The ideas and writings of such nineteenth-century French philosophers as C. H. Saint-Simon and Pierre-Joseph Proudhon, which called for the creation of utopian socialist communities in which all work and income would be shared equally, were current in some advanced literary circles in Latin America and were occasionally discussed in articles and pamphlets. The European revolutionary movements of 1848 also attracted some attention in the area. However, as Jorrín and Martz conclude, until the end of the nineteenth century these ideas attracted only "fashionable curiosity" and registered little real impact on the area.[7]

More explicit Marxist writings and ideas began to arrive in Latin America in the 1870s and 1880—although there is occasional and brief mention of Marx's ideas as early as the 1850s. Once again, these were largely literary references, mainly and almost exclusively limited to a handful of intellectuals. After all, this was the period when positivism was at its peak and when such powerful currents as nationalism, Rodóism, and Hispanismo were either just beginning to be felt or had yet to be heard from. At this time Marxism was still very much a minority, almost invisible ideological current that had as yet no mass appeal.

All this began to change around the turn of the century with large-scale immigration from southern Europe, especially Italy and Spain and especially to the Southern Cone. It is no accident that the first serious Marxist and socialist movements and parties of any size began in Argentina, Chile, and Uruguay. These countries were among the most advanced of the Latin American nations, the most European, the most literate, and the countries of the largest European immigration. Argentina was the country of the most extensive European immigration, and quite a number of the immigrants brought with them the European ideologies then current, including Marxism. So Marxism of a more serious sort that reached beyond the scholarly and philosophical academies to encompass the working class came to Latin America largely via that great stream of immigration that began in the last two decades of the nineteenth century and continued well into the twentieth.[8]

Corresponding to the wave of European immigration were the first stirrings of Latin American industrialization. The first and largest industries were mainly oriented toward the export of Latin America's raw materials and primary products. And the first unions reflected these industries: meat-packers and stevedores in Argentina, tin miners in Bolivia, nitrate workers in Chile, sugar cane cutters in Cuba and the Dominican Republic, and banana workers in Central America. The reasons for emphasizing these developments are obvious: Marxism was meant not just as an intellectual model but as a real mass movement, a movement of workers and their organized expression in trade unions; and hence for Marxism to establish its organized mass base it required capitalism, industrialization, and factories. With the growth of Latin American industrialization beginning at the turn of the century and continuing thereafter, Marxism began to acquire the mass base that would make its future growth possible. As the historian Rollie Poppino has written, with industrialization Latin American Marxism moved out of the literary salons where it was first concentrated and into the streets and union halls in the form of an organized movement.[9]

But the kind of Marxism that emerged in Latin America also reflected the countries of origin of the immigrant workers and the ideas and movements prevailing there. In both Italy and Spain at this time, which were the primary sources of immigration to Latin America, anarchism and anarchist movements were strong.[10] The Russian anarchist Michael Bakunin (1814–76), expelled from his native country, turned his attention to western Europe, where he succeeded in organizing both rural and urban workers, particularly in Italy and Spain. Indeed, only in these two countries did Bakunin's ideas have success and attract a mass following.

The anarchist philosophy espoused the ideas that all strikes and political activities had to be approved not just by the leadership but by the rank and file as well, that such action had to be both materially and morally legitimate, that direct, even violent and revolutionary, action by the workers was the way to achieve their goals, that the anarchist organizations of workers should be decentralized as much as possible, and that agrarian reform for peasants was as important as factory reform for workers. Marx had expelled the anarchists from his First International in 1872 for holding these ideas, whereupon the anarchists formed their own international with Italian, Spanish, and Swiss members. It is significant not only that these anarchist ideas had a powerful influence on Latin American Marxism and unionism, but that many of the same reform policy agenda items that the anarchists advocated—such as agrarian reform—also carried over to Latin America.

Anarchism affected the development of the later Latin American labor movements in diverse ways. One was its emphasis on violence as an instrument of political and social change. This was often structured, controlled, and carefully orchestrated violence—usually short of revolution—to achieve quite specific policy goals.[11] Another was the belief in what Jorrín and Martz call "cure-all revolutions," the rather romantic idea that land seizures, strikes, church burnings, and direct action of all kinds would somehow generate the coming of a new millennium that would solve all problems.[12] A third lasting legacy of this early anarchism on the Latin American labor movement was the emphasis on direct political action rather than collective bargaining as the way to solve labor disputes. The general strike, the march on the national palace, the effort to topple a president or labor minister who failed to go along with labor's demands, the provocation of the police or military as a way of creating martyrs and thus evoking sympathy—all these traits of the Latin American labor movements reflect the heritage of anarchist influences. Latin American industrial and labor relations are often dominated by an anarchist-based political model of labor-management relations, and less by the relatively peaceful collective bargaining model of the United States.[13]

Like Marxism, anarchism had many branches as well as many roots. One of its branches was syndicalism. Syndicalism had its origins in France in the 1890s and, like its parent, anarchism, was carried to Latin America mainly by Spanish and Italian immigrants. The term "syndicalism" comes from the French word *syndicat,* usually translated as "trade union." Syndicalism is closely related to and grew out of Marxism; but whereas Marxism even in the socialist stage usually sought to keep control of the labor movement in the hands of a party or the state, the syndicalists wanted power to be directly inherited by the workers' syndicates themselves. The syndicates would then exercise direct management over their sphere of industry, coming together with other syndicates to provide administrative coordination but without a central state. Hence, the workers and peasants alone would control all working conditions.

In some countries the anarchists and the syndicalists for a time constituted separate movements, but in most they formed a hybrid called anarcho-syndicalism. Anarcho-syndicalism took its ideas from Bakunin and the Russian anarchists, from the French apostle of syndicalism, Ferdinand Pelloutier, and from the better-known French writer Georges Sorel. Sorel was the author of the influential *Reflections on Violence,* published in 1908, which argued that a well-organized labor movement, using controlled violence and the technique of the general strike, could paralyze a nation and bring it to its knees. And even if that failed, Sorel argued, the "myth" of the general strike's ultimate power would unify the workers and stimulate faith in the future.[14] That may have been small consolation to the thousands of workers who in the early days of the labor movement in Latin America were killed by the police and army in premature uprisings.

Argentina and Uruguay had small anarchist movements as early as the 1870s; in Chile the anarchist movement influenced the labor movement; in Peru anarchism left a deep imprint on the early Marxist writer Manuel González Prada (1848–1918); in Cuba anarchism became a part of the independence movement in the 1890s; and in Mexico the three Flores Magón brothers sought to push the Mexican Revolution of 1910–20 in an anarchist direction.

Although neither anarchism nor anarcho-syndicalism became large-scale mass movements or achieved the position of a dominant ideology in Latin America, they did strongly influence the trade union and peasant movements there—and still do to this day. The use of carefully structured violence short of full-scale revolution, the technique of the general strike, the idea of direct action, the takeovers by peasant and worker groups of private land and factories, the use of a political bargaining model over that of collective bargaining are all legacies of this anarchist and anarcho-syndicalist past. So, probably, is the attitude of writers and intellectuals who advocate anarchist strategies as a kind of emotional outburst against social injustice. And so is the almost mystical belief in a romantic, idealized "cure-all" revolution, like those of Castro in Cuba and the Sandinistas in Nicaragua.[15]

But Jorrín and Martz argue that anarchism also retarded the growth of the trade union movement in Latin America and led to a scorn for orderly political processes.[16] By its advocacy and use of violence, by its revolutionary scare tactics, and by its insistence on direct action rather than bargaining and compromise, anarchism both divided the labor movement internally and provoked such a reaction from conservative military, oligarchic, and clerical elements that it led only to repression and defeat. Nevertheless, anarchism and anarcho-syndicalism now took their place in the growing pantheon of Latin American ideologies and even served for a brief time as a kind of radical, lower-class, pan–Latin American counterpart to the dominant conservative ideologies of positivism, Rodóism, and Hispanismo. Eventually, however, around the time of World War I and the communist revolution in Russia, anarchism as a distinct ideology and movement largely disappeared (although its ideas did not), fusing back into Marxism from which it had come.

History

The history of Marxism and Marxist movements in Latin America may be traced through eight stages as follows:

1. Early Marxism, 1870–1900
2. The First Marxist Parties, 1900–17
3. The Russian Revolution and the Comintern, 1917–28
4. Stalinist Hard Line, 1928–35
5. The Popular Front and World War II, 1935–45
6. The Early Cold War, 1945–59
7. The Cuban Revolution and Its Spinoffs, 1959–90
8. The Collapse of the Soviet Union and Crisis in Marxism-Leninism, 1990–present.

Following is a thumbnail sketch of this history.[17]

Neither Marx nor Engels had ever visited Latin America and knew very little about it. What they did say or write about it was often patronizing and disparaging. Latin America was seen as primitive or backward; it had "no history," as Hegel put it, by which he meant it had no original ideas and, as of the early nineteenth century, had shown no progress. Marx shared these negative ideas about Latin America, except when he said it had no history he meant it had no capitalism, industrialization, and therefore no class struggle. In Marx's view Latin America could be equated with India, Africa, the Middle East, and Asia as lacking importance and worthy only of brief attention as outposts for investments by the colonial powers, which presumably, in the Marxian economic categories, would start the motor force of history moving. Hence, Marx wrote some journalistic articles about the French occupation of Mexico in the 1860s, but they were unsystematic. In general Marx thought Latin America, together with other developing areas, as they are called now, were not worthy of serious attention.[18]

Marxist ideas, in turn, reached Latin America late, sporadically, and with an uncertain reception.[19] Marxism in Latin America had nowhere near the same reception in the late nineteenth century that positivism did. The Brazilian thinker Tobias Barreto (1839–89), for example, noted the presence of Marxist ideas among the philosophical currents of Europe at that time but did not elevate them to any important degree. Intellectuals in Argentina, Chile, Cuba, Uruguay, Peru, and Mexico read parts of Marx or occasionally mentioned him but did not pay him very much serious attention. Martí, for instance, rejected Marx's call to revolutionary violence, but he was, as a Cuban nationalist and fighter for independence, attracted to the anarchist Bakunin. Other Latin American writers of this time (1870s–90s) mention Marx occasionally but generally see him as a remote figure, not at the same level as other great European writers like Comte, and seemingly having little relevance for Latin America. In these early years it was Bakunin, anarchism, and anarcho-syndicalism, not so much Marx or Marxism per se, that, mainly through immigration, attracted a modest following in Latin America.

That situation began to change in the last decade of the nineteenth century and in the period leading up to World War I. A central figure in this period was the Argentine Juan B. Justo (1865–1928), a medical doctor who in 1895 founded the Argentine Socialist Party in 1895. Justo not only read Marx in German but then translated him into Spanish, for the first time making Marx accessible to a wider range of Latin American readers. Trained in the natural sciences, Justo—like many other scientists, as well as humanists lacking a strong social science background—saw in Marxism a supposedly scientific basis for understanding economics, sociology, and politics that was parallel to his natural science background. Justo and his group, including Alfredo Palacios, Nicolás Repetto, and Américo Ghioldi (note the Italian immigrant names), marked a notable step beyond the earlier formative and sporadic Marxism to a more organized and disciplined kind. They were influential in helping found similarly socialist movements in neighboring Chile, Bolivia, and Uruguay; and the Argentine Socialist Party that Justo founded celebrated its one hundredth birthday several years ago. But while these were all significant steps, the Argentine Socialist Party suffered a series of schisms and, until World War I, generally occupied a minority position even on the left (which was still exceedingly weak) as compared with the anarchists, syndicalists, and anarcho-syndicalists.[20]

A key turning point among socialist parties in Latin America as elsewhere was World War I and the Bolshevik Revolution of 1917 in Russia. In the aftermath of these events, a communist party was created in Argentina in 1918, in Mexico in 1919, in Chile and Brazil in 1921, in Cuba in 1925, and in most of the other countries over the course of the following decade. The parties remained small, however: in 1928 the Argentine party had only two thousand members; the Brazilian, twelve hundred; and the Mexican, one thousand—mostly illiterate peasants. Many of the others were mini parties consisting of handfuls of intellectuals and, reflecting the limited scope of industrialization, with little mass support among urban or rural workers. The Latin American communist parties were so small that not one was invited to the First Congress of the Third International held in Moscow in 1919. In addition, the early parties were riven by ideological differences, rivalries among leaders, and numerous schisms—mainly those dividing socialists, communists, and anarcho-syndicalists as well as various subgroups. Furthermore, they had to struggle constantly against indifference, hostility, the lack of class consciousness or even literacy among a majority of workers, and the weakness and divisiveness of the trade union movement. Meanwhile, the communist parties in Latin America had to deal with the increasingly detailed orthodoxies emanating from Moscow, while recognizing that orthodox Marxism did not always fit the realities of their countries.[21]

During the late 1920s and above all from 1928 to 1935, as Russia emerged from the chaotic consequences of its revolution and Stalin consolidated his hold on power, Moscow sought through the Third International to tighten its grip on the world's communist parties. The Soviet Union used its tightening control over the Comintern to rid the organization of democratic-socialists, Trotskyites, and all those on both the left and right of the Marxian tradition who failed to conform to Moscow's definition of what Marxism meant. The result was a hardening of control by the Soviet Union over the world's various communist parties and, in Latin America, a new wave of schisms, expulsions, splits, and acrimony. The instructions emanating from the Kremlin meant that the communist parties of Latin America and elsewhere had to serve Moscow's interests first and speak to their own national issues secondarily, which again weakened the parties vis-à-vis their increasingly nationalistic constituents. Another implication of these changes was that, instead of intellectuals and students, such bureaucrats and hard-liners as Blas Roca in Cuba, Luis Carlos Prestes in Brazil, and others came to dominate the parties. Marxism was no longer just an ideological and intellectual movement but an instrument for political control at the service of Soviet foreign policy.[22]

In the mid-1930s the party line emanating from Moscow shifted back the other way. During this period, the era of the so-called popular front, Stalin began to see the looming threat of Nazi Germany and so, reversing the direction of the previous years, ordered communist parties throughout the world—including those in Latin America—to make common cause with other leftist parties to defeat fascism. Hence, in Cuba the communist party allied itself with the democratic reformers, in Argentina it cozied up to the democratic Radical Party, in Chile it came together with the Socialists, and in Peru it made common cause with the social-democratic American Popular Revolutionary Alliance (APRA). The alliances with other reformist and democratic parties increased the legitimacy of the heretofore isolated and not very popular communist parties and ushered in, from 1935 until the end of World War II, a period of marked growth—notwithstanding Stalin's flipflops in policy toward Nazi Germany. Communist parties in Latin America not only extended the hand of friendship to other parties on the left but also moderated their radical ideology, took up more nationalistic issues in the several countries, and sought with some success to move from clandestinity to legalized status—always a crucial step in the state-regulated corporatism of Latin America.[23]

The period from the end of World War II until the triumph of the Cuban revolution in 1959 was a time of difficulty, conflict, and change for the communist parties of Latin America. Although an era of "good feeling" between the United States and the Soviet Union prevailed for a year or two after the war—during which time a number of Latin American communist parties emerged from the underground and even acquired legal recognition and legitimacy—by 1947 the Cold War between the superpowers had begun, and this had an immediate impact on the communist parties in Latin America: many were now illegalized again. In the Rio Treaty of 1947 the United States sought to create a hemisphere-wide alliance against communism and Soviet expansionism. U.S. foreign policy in Latin America, which in the previous decade had often been constructive, now turned negative, based almost exclusively on anticommunism. Under the twin doctrines of containment and economy of force, the United States sought to prevent any and all communist inroads into Latin America and, because the Soviet Union was now the main and virtually only U.S. preoccupation, to do so without any serious expenditure of funds, commitment, or even attention. For a decade and a half after World War II, the United States basically ignored Latin America, turning its attention to the area—as when it intervened in Guatemala in 1954—only when the threat of communist gains seemed imminent.[24]

Other changes occurred within the socialist movement during this period. First, having often disparaged the Latin American communist parties in the past, the Soviet Union in the post–World War II period began to pay serious attention to the area for the first time. Second, the wartime alliance of popular front, left-of-center parties now broke up, the communist, socialist, and democratic-reformist parties all going their separate directions. Third, while the Latin American communist parties, illegalized and often persecuted, were in decline during this period, the socialist and democratic-left parties were ascendant. It is striking that up to World War II, the communists, dedicated, organized, and supported by the Soviets, were often the strongest party on the left; but by the 1950s it was the socialists and social democrats that were gaining strength.* And all this was occurring in a setting, during the 1950s, of increasing disillusionment with the United States because of its narrow, short-sighted anticommunism, coupled with rising discontent and even revolutionary insurgency in Latin America.

By the mid-1950s the communist movement in Latin America appeared to be well under control. Under the impact of the Cold War and U.S. pressures, the communist parties, unions, and peasant organizations had again been illegalized in most countries; communism's popularity as an ideology was in decline; and in the Guatemalan episode the United States had demonstrated that it would prevent at all costs a wobbly left-wing government from allowing communists to occupy positions

*While many of the Latin American communist parties were indeed illegalized and persecuted during this period, several right-wing dictators, such as Rafael Calderon Guardía in Costa Rica, Fulgencio Batista in Cuba, and Marcos Pérez Jiménez in Venezuela, worked out strange-bedfellow deals with the communists, allowing them a free hand in the labor movement in return for support at election time or in street demonstrations. Such alliances were often aimed at preventing the more popular democratic-left forces from challenging the dictatorship. These alliances reflect political necessity, not ideological consistency.

of power. But then came the Cuban revolution, which changed all the givens. For the next thirty years the Cuban revolution not only had a profound influence on the Latin American left but also, through the no second Cubas policy, completely dominated U.S. relations with the area.

An Indigenous Marxism?

To this point, Latin American Marxism has been portrayed as largely derivative, a reflection of events, ideas, and socioeconomic and political developments in Europe—or as a reflection of Soviet foreign policy. On the one hand, Marx had drawn almost all of his examples, his history, and his philosophy and theory from the European experience; he believed that developing areas like Latin America would simply mirror and imitate, albeit belatedly and retardedly, the European pattern. On the other hand, from at least World War I through World War II and beyond, the story of Marxism in Latin America had been largely one of dictates issuing from the Soviet Union to the communist parties there.

The questions we ask here are: first, is it possible to conceive of an indigenous Latin American Marxism? that is, a Marxism not reflecting just the earlier and quite different European experience, but adapted to the realities, history, and social conditions of Latin America? And second, could such a Marxism be divorced from great-power rivalries, specifically, in this case, from the dictates of the Soviet Union and its Cold War requirements?

The effort to fashion an indigenous Marxism in Latin America began with the Peruvian José Carlos Mariátegui (1894–1930).[25] Mariátegui was born in poverty and was largely self-educated. Afflicted by poor health, he died at the age of thirty-six. He began as a devotee of Spanish mysticism and Catholicism but later gravitated to Marxian socialism. Forced to flee Peru because of his opposition to then-dictator Augusto Leguía, Mariátegui traveled to Europe, where he was strongly impressed by the French socialist Henri Barbusse and the Italian communist Antonio Gramsci. Indeed, Mariátegui was a discoverer of Gramsci's revisionist Marxism, in which Gramsci urged a conquest of the "commanding heights," including cultural and educational institutions, long before that approach was popularized in the United States or Europe.

Mariátegui's greatest contribution was to adapt Marxism to Latin American, specifically Peruvian, history and society. He viewed Marx's teachings as being open and flexible—necessarily so if he was to apply

Marx's analysis to the situation in Latin America. At this time Latin America, and especially Peru, unlike Europe, had very little industrialization, limited capitalism, and almost no industrial proletariat or organized working class. In the Marxian scheme of things, how could you have a socialist revolution without a working class?

Mariátegui found his answer in the indigenous Indian populations of Peru, which at that time made up 80–90 percent of the population. Mariátegui was interested in the pre-Spanish collectivism and communalism of the Inca civilization and saw in them a potential for socialism. He attempted to analyze Peru's revolutionary possibilities by examining its indigenous past from a Marxian or materialistic perspective. Like the later Sendero Luminoso (Shining path) movement in Peru that drew inspiration from his ideas, Mariátegui believed that a combination of students, intellectuals, the small working class, and the great mass of indigenous elements could successfully carry out a Marxist revolution. Though a Marxist, Mariátegui was part of a long tradition in Iberia and Latin America that emphasized group or corporate rights.

In focusing on ancient collectivism and the indigenous "peasantry" as the leading forces in revolution, Mariátegui presaged Mao Zedong, whose revolution in China was based on many of the same principles. He believed the rural Indian masses could help give impetus to revolution before the bourgeoisie had succeeded in establishing capitalism. Mariátegui was also encouraged by the university student revolt that began in Córdova, Argentina, in 1918 and then spread to other countries. For like Gramsci, Mariátegui believed that students and intellectuals could play leading roles in the revolution. He concurred with Gramsci that the Marxian dialectic could be telegraphed, that capitalism could be created by socialists on their way to socialism. Mariátegui thus sought to combine socialism and Indianism through a revolution that would both destroy capitalism and restore the old Inca Indian land patterns.

Mariátegui was a strong critic of the positivist philosophy then dominant in Peru and elsewhere. Positivism, he believed, encouraged imperialism and capitalist penetration and led to increasing gaps between rich and poor. But Mariátegui had no faith in *mestizaje,* or racial mingling, either; and he was critical of José Vasconcelos's notion of a "cosmic" or mestizo "new race" in Latin America. For as a Marxist, Mariátegui believed the main problems in Latin America were social and economic, not racial.

Mariátegui was a pensador and journalist, not a trained philosopher. His writing was largely unsystematic and his understanding of Marx superficial. His historical studies of pre-Spanish Inca history and society were similarly incomplete and not always accurate. As Lenin did about the nonrevolutionary character and difficulty of organizing the Russian peasantry, Mariátegui sometimes despaired of the traditional beliefs, the lethargy, the inarticulateness, and the lack of organization among Peru's indigenous people: the same problems Sendero Luminoso faced some sixty years later. For if the revolution is to be based in large part on the Indian masses, it is essential that they support the revolution. If they oppose it, are indifferent, or, even worse, turn those who would lead the revolution over to the police or the army, then the would-be revolution is in bad trouble.

Despite these problems and limitations, Mariátegui's thought represented a breakthrough. For his was the first attempt ever in Latin America—maybe anywhere in the Third World—to adapt Marxian principles to indigenous realities. Rather than slavishly echoing Marx's precepts, Mariátegui actually built a Latin American reality—the large indigenous population of Peru—into the Marxian equation. That is the formula that other successful ideologies in Latin America, such as positivism, have employed; now it would be the turn of Marxism to try to adapt to local realities. Mariátegui's example would be an inspiration to a variety of other intellectuals and activists in the Marxian tradition.

Mariátegui was a writer, not an organizer, a voice crying in the Peruvian wilderness. But at about the same time he was formulating his ideas, another movement, APRA, was beginning in Peru, and it *would* have a powerful impact, both in that country and throughout the hemisphere. APRA became one of Latin America's first genuinely mass-based political parties and an inspiration to other left-of-center, reformist parties in other countries.[26] It eventually came together with other parties to form the League of Popular Parties, which included the Democratic Action Party of Venezuela, the National Liberation Party of Costa Rica, the Auténtico Party of Cuba, the Liberal Party of Honduras, the Intransigent Radicals in Argentina, the Febreristas in Paraguay, and the Dominican Revolutionary Party in the Dominican Republic. At one point or another—very much unlike Mariátegui's lonely voice in Peru—almost all of these parties came to power and thus had the opportunity to actually put their ideology to work.

APRA was founded by a young Peruvian intellectual and political activist, Víctor Raúl Haya de la Torre. Like many of his contemporaries (including Mariátegui), Haya was fascinated by and caught up intellectually in the great historic events of his time: the Mexican Revolution of 1910, the Russian Revolution of 1917, the Latin American student revolt of 1918, and the apparent collapse of capitalism in the worldwide depression of the 1930s. He was also strongly influenced by Einstein's theories of relativity, then gaining currency, and concocted a quasi-Marxian, quasi-Einsteinian notion of "historical time-space" that never made any sense even to his devotees. He was also, again like Mariátegui, a student of Peruvian realities: its backwardness and underdevelopment, its lack of either capitalism or democracy, its immense but inactive Indian population, and the imperialist activities of the large foreign companies. He burned with the desire to change Peru, to bring it into the modern world, to reform the social structure, and to expel the imperialist forces.

Like many young intellectuals in the 1920s and 1930s, Haya began life as a Marxist. He accepted the main Marxian categories and ideas: class struggle, historical materialism, the inevitability of socialism. The planks of the movement he began in Peru included the following:

1. Anticolonialism, anti-imperialism
2. Social justice
3. Agrarian reform
4. The incorporation of Indians, workers, and peasants into the national life
5. Hemispheric solidarity or Pan–Latin Americanism
6. The Latin Americanization of the Panama Canal
7. Democracy.

A close reading of this list reveals that, although Haya was an intellectual Marxist and anti-imperialist, he was not a Leninist or a Stalinist. Like the British Fabians earlier in the century, he believed in a parliamentary and democratic path to socialism, not a violent, revolutionary one. He remained committed to civil liberties and human rights. While his stance was anti-imperialist, his attitude toward the United States was not knee-jerk negative or violent, and he worked closely with reformist elements in the United States. In other words, while retaining his Marxism, Haya followed the path of social democracy but not communism. His approach was pragmatic, gradual, incremental, and evolutionary rather than revolutionary. And he would remain closer to the parliamentary social democracy of western Europe than to the communism and totalitarianism of the Soviet Union and eastern Europe. Haya and his movement were strongly attacked by Mariátegui and the orthodox communists.

Mariátegui had been content to articulate a Marxian intellectual critique of Peruvian society, but Haya launched a political movement to do something about it. His APRA was the continent's first mass-based political party in the European sense. It had a real program and ideology and was not just personalistic. Standing for democratic participation, agrarian reform, and programs to assist the poor, APRA emerged as Peru's largest political party. If Peru had had a fully democratic political process, it would have been in government during much of the modern period; but Peru's oligarchy joined with the army (and often with the Communist Party, which did not want its much larger rival on the left to get credit for carrying out a reform agenda) to keep the Apristas out of power. Haya was imprisoned, tortured, and sent out of the country. Peru sputtered along for many decades, alternating between military dictatorship and oligarchic civilian rule; not until the 1980s did the Apristas win an electoral victory and assume the presidency. But by then Haya was gone from the leadership ranks, the party was old and some of its members corrupt, other parties and movements had taken over and even implemented some of its reform platform planks; the party's experience in government was not altogether successful.

Several features of APRA make it of special interest here. First, it became a vigorous member of the Socialist International (SI), an organization of mainly European and Latin American socialist and social-democratic (but noncommunist) parties that believes in democratic social reform. Its affiliation with SI locates the party ideologically on the moderate left. Second, while the party was socialist and social-democratic (and gradually abandoned its Marxism over the years), its internal organization was sectoral and corporatist, with organized sections for youth, women, peasants, workers, and intellectuals. The organic, corporatist form of social and political organization on both the left and the right comes up repeatedly in the Latin American political tradition (see chapter 9 for a discussion of its modern form). Third, it is striking that APRA was more than a political party in the European sense; it was also a movement, a family, a job-training program. During a visit to party headquarters in Lima the author saw activities that as a political scientist he had never seen before in a political party: schools teaching basic literacy as well as vocational education programs in such areas as car mechanics, hair cutting and dressing, electronics, appliance repair, and so forth. Truly, this was a new kind of mass party, one quite different from the elite-dominated electoral and patronage machines long prevalent in Latin America's past.

Ironically, whereas APRA, the granddaddy of all democratic-left political parties in Latin America, took fifty years to come to power for the first time, its various spin-offs in the League of Popular Parties enjoyed considerably greater success.[27] In Venezuela with Rómulo Betancourt, Raúl Leoni, and Carlos Andrés Pérez; in Argentina with Arturo Frondizi; in Costa Rica with José Figueras; in Puerto Rico with Luís Muñoz Marín; in Honduras with Ramón Villeda Morales; in the Dominican Republic with Juan Bosch, Arturo Guzmán, and Salvador Jorge Blanco; and in other countries as well, the democratic left came to power by means of the electoral route and began carrying out its reform agenda. These individual regimes had varying degrees of success, of course, but the number of electoral victories the democratic left won and continues to win attests to the popularity of the social-democratic position. In the early 1960s, in fact, the U.S. government latched onto these parties as the best hope to avoid Castro-communism on the one hand or right wing authoritarianism on the other.[28] As they became serious electoral contenders in their separate countries and more acceptable to the United States, these parties became more mainstream, largely left their Marxism behind, and came to resemble the left wing of the U.S. Democratic Party—to the point that it became increasingly difficult to classify them as Marxist.

The Cuban revolution represented the third major (after Mariátegui and APRA) effort to devise a Marxism attuned to Latin America. In the Cuban case the contribution comes not in the form of a brilliant new philosophical breakthrough, for both Castro and Guevara were rather indifferent Marxists and viewed ideology as a complement to their activism and nationalism. Instead, their contribution lay (1) in Guevara's concept of a peasant-based revolution rather like that of China, coupled with a strong, broadly nationalist, anti-American, antidictatorial alliance of students, workers, peasants, intellectuals, and elements of the middle class and even the army that would enable socialism to triumph even in preindustrial societies;[29] and (2) in the idea of the French leftist intellectual and writer Régis Debray—who wrote a book extolling the

Cuban revolution—that a small Marxist nucleus (*foco*) within this broad-based alliance could effectively seize control and guide the revolution (as in Nicaragua) *after* the larger group had driven the dictator from power.[30]

The Varieties of Marxism

By the 1940s, 1950s, and 1960s there was a great diversity of Marxisms in Latin America. Although all stemmed from the original inspiration, the many Marxisms took a variety of directions. In most countries there would be four, five, six, or more Marxist groups. In no country did any of the Marxist groups, or even all of them together, come close to constituting an electoral majority. In many cases, vying for dominance on the left, they fought mainly among themselves, instead of against what one might assume to be their natural foes, the oligarchy and the army. The nearly constant internecine fights served to further weaken the left and hurt its chances of coming to power.

A listing of the major Marxist factions gives a sense of their variety and also a hint of why they continued mainly to fight each other:

1. *Socialist.* There are still socialist parties in Latin America, heirs to the original Socialist Party of Argentina, of which the strongest is the Chilean Socialist Party.

2. *Anarchist.* The anarchist and anarcho-syndicalist movements in Latin America have generally declined since World War I, but their influence in some Latin American trade unions is still significant.

3. *Communist.* The regular old-line orthodox communist parties of Latin America, never strong except in a handful of countries, have declined even more since the collapse of the Soviet Union. None of these parties has the possibilities of coming to power by itself.

4. *Trotskyite.* Trotskyite believers in spontaneous global revolution were influential in the 1930s in Mexico, where Trotsky had fled from Stalin, and in a few other countries; but since then, with Trotsky's death at the hands of a Stalinist assassin in 1940, the movement has declined precipitously. Trotskyism still has its strong adherents, but it never developed an appreciable mass movement in Latin America.

5. *Independent Marxist.* In all Latin American countries there are independent Marxist *pensadores*, usually university professors, who accept and think in Marxian terms but are not themselves party organizers or even activists.

6. *Apristas.* The Aprista or democratic-left parties of Latin America—those organized in the League of Popular Parties—have achieved notable electoral and political success; but in order to achieve success they have largely abandoned their earlier Marxism, adhered to a parliamentary and social-democratic position, and in most cases could no longer be considered revolutionary or even Marxist.

7. *Agrarian-socialist.* During earlier decades when the question of the unequal distribution of land seemed to be the most pressing issue in Latin America, agrarian-socialist parties and movements were launched in several countries. But as people have moved to the cities and other economic issues have become paramount, the land issue has faded somewhat and so have the parties for whom it was the major plank in their platform—although in some areas peasant seizures by direct action of privately owned land (an anarcho-syndicalist strategy) continue.

8. *Chinese Communist.* For a long time when the Soviet Union was the only communist country in the world, the Latin American countries were obliged to look to Moscow for guidance and direction. But with the emergence of communist China in the 1950s and 1960s, and especially given the basis of the Chinese revolution as a peasant- rather than worker-based revolution, many Latin American Marxists, seeing their own countries as similarly rural and peasant-based, began opting for the Chinese revolutionary position rather than the Soviet one.[31] These differences induced a severe split in Marxist ranks, led to some pitched battles between the pro-Soviet and pro-Chinese factions, and ultimately weakened the Marxist revolutionary elements.

9. *Fidelista.* The Cuban Marxist position as triumphant in the revolution of the late 1950s included nationalism, anti-Americanism (the two were synonymous), and socialism. Cuba was ideologically sympathetic to the Chinese revolutionary position, because it imagined—erroneously—its own revolution to be peasant-based; but, as the aphorism went, the pocketbook of the revolution lay in Moscow. (See below for more on the Cuban revolution.)

10. *Sandinismo.* More self-consciously than the Cubans, the Nicaraguan Sandinistas put together a broad antidictatorial, anti-Somoza coalition that included Catholics, nationalists, and social reformers of various shades, meanwhile keeping as much control of the revolution as possible in their own Marxist and Marxist-Leninist hands. This was the foco theory put into action; it succeeded for a time in Nicaragua, but not in El Salvador and other countries.

11. *Liberation theology*. Liberation theology sought to wed Marx and Jesus, an unholy alliance forged by clerics and religious persons concerned more with the social mission of the gospels than with saving souls. It gained popularity in some circles for a time in the 1970s, when religious groups were often the only voice of opposition to the then-reigning dictatorships; but as Latin America democratized in the 1980s and 1990s and as other avenues for opposition, such as political parties and civil society, reemerged, liberation theology lost a great deal of its earlier support.[32]

12. *Dependency theory*. Dependency theory grew out of 1960s Marxian analysis; its main literature suggested that the development and prosperity of the northern and western nations (mainly the United States) came at the cost of the exploitive underdevelopment of Latin America. In other words, there was an international as well as an internal division of labor that worked to advantage the United States and leave Latin America poor. Dependency theory was popular among some American academic theorists, but it was less embraced in Latin America, never catching on as a popular or mass-based movement.[33]

13. *Populist anticapitalism*. With the triumph of electoral democracy and economic neoliberalism in the 1980s and 1990s, Latin America seemed to have embarked on a new course. But there was strong opposition to the neoliberal programs, which parties like the Revolutionary Democratic Party of Cuauhtemoc Cárdenas in Mexico and the Workers Party of Luiz Inacio da Silva ("Lula") in Brazil sought to parlay into electoral power. The failed, limited, or unrealized expectations that the neoliberal agenda ignited served as fuel for these traditionally left (socialist, communist, nationalist) parties to exploit.

This list barely scratches the surface of an often bewildering (including to their followers) array of left and Marxist groups that have usually risen quickly like shooting stars in Latin America and then faded away. Often these groups were at odds with each other, frequently fighting it out for control of a labor or peasant group or the party headquarters. Usually the divisions and conflicts served to discredit and weaken overall the Marxist movements in Latin America and prevented them from building a strong popular base. But not all of these groups were consistently at odds with one another. For the list presented above not only shows the several rival factions but also proceeds more or less chronologically, with the result that some groups are successors of one another rather than competitors. Indeed, what one often finds is that over the decades the names of the groups may change while the Marxist current that they represent in each generation is continuous. There are rivalries *and* less rivalry than meets the eye.

Overall, however, these left and Marxist groups had to this point generally remained weak in Latin America. Like other groups in the region, they tend to be limited and to have little support among peasant, worker, and Indian masses. Often they consist of a handful of intellectuals—and their students—at the national university. The Marxist groups' candidates have seldom won in contending elections, have never won a majority of the vote in any country, and have seldom had great success (with a couple of notable exceptions) utilizing revolutionary or guerrilla tactics either. The only Marxist groups that have won democratic elections—the Aprista or Popular parties—have done so only after abandoning their Marxism (excluding, of course, Cuba and the Cuban revolution).

The Cuban Revolution

The story of the Cuban revolution is familiar to us and has been written about from so many different angles that we need not repeat all that material here. However, we do need to make some key points that relate the Cuban revolution to the overall themes of this book.[34] First, Cuba became the first openly socialist and Marxist-Leninist state in the Western Hemisphere. It was also the first Latin American country to ally itself with the Soviet Union and thus break out of the North American orbit.

Second, the Cuban revolution attracted enormous publicity and sympathy throughout Latin America, above all during the 1960s, when the revolution was still fresh and full of vigor. Cuba's nationalism, socialism, and defiance of the United States were enormously popular throughout Latin America. It was exceptionally attractive to Latin American nationalistic, left-wing youth, who saw in Cuba both the realization of Rousseau's idea of a popular, spontaneous revolution without the usual prerequisites that Marx's analysis required and a fulfillment of Rodó's vision of a strong, proud Latin American Ariel standing up against the barbaric Caliban as personified by the United States. But it was not just youth that admired the Cuban revolution; older Latin Americans were often sympathetic, if more restrained, as well. For many it was a David and Goliath struggle: little Cuba against the all-powerful United States; even if David did not entirely win, he at least survived. This Rodó-inspired sympathy toward Cuba had broad resonance throughout Latin America even among those older persons who would be obliged to carry out anti-Castro policies.

Third and related, the Cuban revolution inspired—and often sponsored—a variety of imitators throughout Latin America. In country after country, new guerrilla groups sprang up, trying to unseat existing authoritarian regimes and, arguing that they were too centrist or too much under the thumb of the United States, often democratic ones as well. These guerrilla groups usually sought to follow the Cuban example of a small, dedicated group of revolutionaries (the foco) launching a peasant-based revolution in the countryside aimed at toppling the existing government. But in countries like Brazil, Argentina, Chile, and Uruguay, there were arguments for an urban-based revolution as well. Guevara raised the cry of lighting a revolutionary fire up and down the Andes; and the Cubans, the Soviets, the Warsaw Pact countries of Eastern Europe, and the Chinese supplied aid and training to the revolutionary forces. For a time, it seemed that all of Latin America might explode in guerrilla revolution: as Guevara put it, "One, two, three, many Viet Nams!"[35]

The Cuban revolution, fourth, gave new impetus to Marxist thought and action in Latin America and, as noted in the previous section, opened new divisions within Marxist ranks. There was an explosion of books and articles from the Marxist left and an attempt—usually post facto—to explain the Cuban revolution in Marxist terms. For example, Guevara and many others, à la Mao, have tried to justify the revolution against Batista as a peasant-based revolution when, in fact, it derived support from practically all sectors of the Cuban population—and mainly from the middle class. All this outpouring focused continuous, hemisphere-wide attention on the Cuban revolution and made Marxism legitimate and popular once again in academic and left-wing policy circles—especially as compared with the rather tired, lethargic, old-fashioned, do-little communist party organizations of the past, which had been slowly withering away. But the success of the Cuban revolution in winning and holding power occasioned a further split in the Marxist camp between the Moscow-oriented adherents of peaceful coexistence and the new militancy and activism of the Cuban-style revolutionaries.

Another result, fifth, of the Cuban revolution is that it divided Latin America's democratic forces, enabling rightist and oligarchic elements to come back into power. For up to this point the struggle in Latin America had largely been seen as a two-part struggle: the old oligarchy (including the Church and the army) versus the popular or democratic forces. In that contest, few of us would have any doubt where our sympathies lay. But the Cuban revolution introduced a third (and troubling) force into this equation: a movement that was blatantly Marxist-Leninist, willing to employ Stalinist methods of totalitarian control, and allied with the Soviet Union against the United States. What the Cuban revolution did, therefore, was to split the popular or reform forces into pro- (Marxist-Leninist) and anti- (democratic) Castro factions. In effect, every reform, democratic, and democratic-left movement in Latin America was torn asunder by these divisions. And of course when the reform-oriented forces split, oligarchic elements and their military-authoritarian allies found it easier to defeat the genuine democrats, hang onto power, or stage a comeback—as bureaucratic-authoritarianism—from the mid-1960s on.[36]

The Cuban revolution, sixth, also skewed U.S. policy, not just toward Cuba but toward Latin America in general. Heretofore, the United States had largely ignored Latin America, given it low priority, treated it with benign neglect, and employed an "economy of force"—as in Guatemala in 1954. Benign neglect was not a bad policy—at least compared with interventionism—and made for quite good relations with Latin America, which for a long time received plaudits as the good neighbor policy. But with Marxism-Leninism implanted in Cuba, the Cuban alliance with the Soviets, and Cuba-inspired guerrilla revolutions popping up all over Latin America, the United States was forced to pay serious attention to Latin America for the first time in many decades. The strategy was determined by the larger Cold War with the Soviet Union and meant above all else "no second Cubas"—i.e., no more Marxist-Leninist regimes allied with the Soviets and allowing them to use Latin American territory for their own ominous goals. In point of fact, that often meant U.S. support of oligarchic and authoritarian regimes that supported the United States' anticommunist strategy, suspicion of and often opposition to democratic-left regimes (such as that of Juan Bosch in the Dominican Republic) for fear they might be tainted by Fidelista leanings, and a willingness to listen to and perhaps act on behalf of almost any supposedly anticommunist harangue, even if that meant

turning against the genuine democrats and allying with some pretty
nefarious characters.[37]

The policy was aptly referred to as the "lesser evil doctrine":[38] when faced with a choice between a Latin American liberal democrat who might allow freedom for communists and leftists and a right-wing authoritarian who promised to clamp down on the communists (including often the liberal democrats), the United States almost always opted to support the lesser evil of the right-wing authoritarian. For some thirty years, from 1959 to 1989, U.S. policy was skewed in these unhappy directions. Thus did the Cuban revolution not only split and weaken the Latin American democratic-left and allow the right back in power, but also warp U.S. policy toward the area.

A seventh and final point is that although the Cuban revolution enjoyed great sympathy in Latin America in the 1960s, over time its attractiveness as a model for other countries began to fade. The reasons included the failure and death of Guevara in Bolivia, the lack of success of the Cuban economy, the aging and eventual tiredness (lack of esprit) of the revolution and its leaders, the decline of the earlier successes of the revolution in education and health care, the totalitarian character and dismal human rights record of the Cuban regime, the growing success and self-confidence of the other Latin American countries who in the intervening decades had outstripped Cuba's accomplishments and no longer felt threatened by the revolution, the dying out of the Cuba-inspired guerrilla movements, eventually the collapse of Cuba's sponsor, the Soviet Union, and doubtless other factors as well. By the end of the 1980s Cuba was no longer viewed as a threat to the stability of the other Latin American countries, and by the early 1990s Cuba's attractiveness as a model of change had greatly diminished—to the vanishing point.[39] But that was a product of a larger crisis of Marxism.

The Crisis of Marxism

By the 1990s Marxism in Latin America (and elsewhere) was in steep and precarious decline. Almost everywhere democracy and free markets appeared to have triumphed while democracy's two main alternatives, authoritarianism and Marxism-Leninism, seemed to have been vanquished (see chapter 10).

To begin, most of the Marxist assumptions have not worked out; many of them we now know to be false. Some good people continue to find hope and inspiration in the Marxist message, but a close, critical look at the basic doctrines of Marxism is warranted. The labor theory of value?—other factors help create value besides labor. Historical materialism and economic determinism?—modern social science understands that most events are multicausal and not just the result of economic forces; neither are social, political, and cultural institutions the exact mirror of economic determinants. Class struggle?—of course, there is class struggle, but there are a lot of other equally important forces operating besides that. The dialectic?—again, some aspects of history proceed dialectically but not all; nor should the dialectic be elevated into a single, all-encompassing theory of history. Inevitable revolution, dictatorship of the proletariat, socialism as the highest stage of history?—none of these Marxian precepts has turned out to be particularly desirable, let alone inevitable. So the first reason Marxism is in decline, in Latin America and elsewhere, is that its basic assumptions have not worked out, are plagued by logical flaws, are not inevitable, are unattractive, and have been superseded by more complex, more realistic explanations of social and political change.

Not only are the fundamental principles of Marxism questionable, but we now know that Marxist regimes are woefully ineffective in delivering what people want. Most Marxist-Leninist regimes have terrible human rights records; their economies are not able to deliver the goods and services their people want, particularly as they enter the advanced stages of development; their political systems are insufficiently flexible to handle the social changes that modernization unleashes; they are terrible polluters because there is no accountability or responsibility; for the same reason they are corrupt and give rise to bloated bureaucracies; they stifle speech, religion, the press, all freedoms.[40] At present, given that we know far more than previously about the inner workings of these regimes, it is hard to imagine how anyone could be an apologist for Marxism-Leninism.

A third factor in the present crisis of Marxism is the collapse of the Soviet Union and its East European communist allies as organized in the Warsaw Pact. For a long time, since 1917, the Soviet Union had served as a Marxist-Leninist beacon, a model for other Marxists, and, at the practical level, an example of how central planning can presumably achieve industrialization in a very short period of time. But we now know how hollow these claims were: the Soviet Union was tremendously inefficient, corrupt, anti-Semitic, backward, unable to adjust to new contingencies, repressive, and destructive of the human spirit. The Soviet Union was more than just a model in that for many decades it materially aided and abetted a great variety of Third World guerrilla movements, terrorist groups, communist parties and labor groups, and subversive elements who sought to sow havoc throughout the world.[41] The collapse of the Soviet Union ended not only the existence of this tainted model, but also its ability and willingness to aid other Marxist-Leninist groups throughout the world, forcing many of them to curtail their activities.

A fourth reason for the decline and fall of Marxism was the nature of the regimes that called themselves Marxist-Leninist. Afghanistan, Angola, Cambodia, Cuba, Ethiopia, Mozambique, Nicaragua, North Korea, Vietnam—who would want to emulate these poor, miserable regimes or look on them as a model? Increasingly in the 1980s, Marxism-Leninism became a synonym for backwardness, inefficiency, poverty, corruption, brutality, the snuffing out of all human rights—not just in these awful Third World backwaters but in the Second World of the supposedly advanced communist countries as well, beginning with the supposed model, the Soviet Union, and including the East European countries as well.

Among the countries of the Americas, Cuba both reflected and was itself a victim of the global crisis of Marxism-Leninism as depicted here. Beginning in the 1960s as a hopeful, nationalistic, and socialist model of development, the Cuban revolution soon fell on hard times. Hindered by its woeful inefficiencies as well as by the U.S. embargo, the Cuban economy turned in a series of dismal performances, the country became even more dependent on its one-crop sugar economy than it had been before the revolution, and alone among the Latin American economies, far from showing economic gains, in fact retrogressed. The political system remained rigid, top-down, totalitarian, and dominated by a single, socialist man-on-horseback whose megalomania and personal lust for power and attention was little different from that of other caudillos in Latin America's sorry history. There was over time a crisis of ideology, a crisis of the economy, a crisis of the regime's élan and spirit after so many years of fruitless sacrifice, a crisis of generations as the old guard hung onto power beyond its time, a crisis of leadership, a crisis of values, and a crisis of change and succession. No longer in the 1990s was Cuba able financially or politically to assist like-minded guerrilla movements throughout the hemisphere; no longer was Cuba viewed as a threat by its neighbors; most important, no one—recognizing Cuba's poverty and debility—wanted to emulate the Cuban model anymore.[42] Rather than a beacon for other revolutionaries, Cuba became "just another" poor, miserable, Third World basket case.

In 1990, Nicaragua, the other socialist regime that, as Cuba's star faded, had become a model for Latin American (and North American) revolutionaries, came crashing down. The Sandinista regime, which in 1979 had overthrown the long-ruling Somoza family dictatorship, was broadly Marxist in orientation—and at leadership levels Marxist-Leninist; but with the glare of the world's spotlight on it, as well as reflecting its own internal dynamics, Nicaragua had remained more open and pluralist than the Cuban regime. That political space had enabled an opposition to coalesce and to highlight all the mistakes and corruption of the revolutionary regime, which were remarkably similar to Cuba's. In the 1990 election, opposition candidate Violeta Chamorro was able to defeat the Sandinista leader Daniel Ortega; in 1996 Ortega lost again, this time to the conservative Arnoldo Alemán. The Sandinistas remained the principal opposition and could conceivably come back to power through electoral means, but, as in Cuba, the élan, spirit, and enthusiasm have undeniably gone out of the revolution.[43]

In view of the collapse of the Soviet Union and its East European puppet regimes and the manifest failures of the Cuban and Nicaraguan revolutions, other Marxist and Marxist-Leninist groups in Latin America have lost support as well as enthusiasm for the struggle. In El Salvador and Guatemala the guerrilla groups have given up their revolutionary tactics and joined the peace process; in Venezuela and elsewhere the former guerrilla groups have reorganized as political parties and similarly joined the democratic political process; in several other countries the guerrillas have faded away or been defeated. Only in Colombia and Peru do meaningful guerrilla movements continue to operate, but in both countries they have abandoned much of their earlier Marxism-Leninism ideology in favor of kidnapping and drug trafficking.[44]

What is more, with the collapse of the Soviet Union and the failures of Cuba, Nicaragua, and the other guerrilla movements, no one wants at this stage to be a Marxist-Leninist. Public opinion surveys show that, in country after country, support for Marxist-Leninist parties and agendas is down to 2 or 3 percent of the population, the lowest it has been since the Cuban revolution first came to power as a Marxist-Leninist regime forty years ago. Reading these numbers and looking at the failures and defeats of all Marxist-Leninist regimes, globally and locally, one would have to conclude that, at least in the short term, there is little future for Marxism or Marxism-Leninism in Latin America.

The Future of the Latin American Left

In the face of these multiple crises, the Latin American Marxist left has severely declined in numbers and influence. It is currently trying to regroup and find a new formula upon which to rebuild. It has not yet, a decade after the collapse of the Soviet Union, succeeded in doing so. Yet the possibilities for a resurgent Marxism are present: democracy has been established in much of Latin America, but it is not working very well; the economies of the area are growing, but income distribution in Latin America is the worst of any region in the world; privilege, corruption, and injustice are still widespread; and more than half the population of many countries live in extreme poverty. And we are beginning to see some new thinking and new political organization on the part of the left as well.[45]

Marxism is currently in such popular disfavor in Latin America that most on the left do not even use the term anymore. Almost no one says, "I am a Marxist"—and certainly not, "I am a Marxist-Leninist." Those labels are a formula for political suicide. Instead, Marxists as well as communists have taken to calling themselves "social democrats." That is, of course, a danger to the genuine social democrats in Latin America who, as in the past, run the risk of being identified with, infiltrated by, and taken over by communists who for political reasons are trying to be something other than what they are.

Today the left in Latin America is still mainly railing against privatization, state downsizing, neoliberalism, and free trade. Those are old rallying cries for the left, but they may no longer evoke so much popular support. There is now widespread, nearly global belief that some neoliberal reforms are necessary. Moreover, the left has itself presented no viable alternative: Latin America cannot go back to import substitution industrialization (ISI), and socialism is presently out of the question. The overwhelming majority of Latin American voters do not trust the left to run the national economy—witness the repeated electoral failures of Lula in Brazil, Cárdenas in Mexico, and Ortega in Nicaragua to win the presidency—even though, as in El Salvador, they may vote for leftist leaders at the local level. In the past the left has tried to put together a combination of Marxism and populist nationalism, and it still often tries to use that formula, but this no longer seems to be a brand of leftism that offers prospects for significant success.[46]

Most of the left has by now abandoned guerrilla violence as well as the model of the Cuban revolution, which is no longer attractive anywhere in Latin America. Castro is now widely seen by the left as an aging caudillo whose revolution has failed and has made terrible mistakes: cutting itself off from U.S. markets, socializing the entire economy, relying overly on the Soviet Union, utilizing disastrous economic planning, and so forth. The revolutionary guerrilla groups that were often romanticized and captured international headlines in earlier decades are drying up, and the ones that remain show peculiar, non-Marxist features and have few possibilities of success. The Colombian guerrillas, for example, have some support among rural peasants and urban shanty dwellers, but their primary cause at present seems to be income enhancement from kidnapping and the drug trade. Peru's Sendero Luminoso has been severely weakened in recent years following the capture of its leaders and the successes achieved by President Alberto Fujimori's economic reforms. In Mexico, the Zapatistas have attracted headlines and skillfully used the Internet, but they have no chance of capturing national power and mainly use controlled and limited violence—or the threat thereof—to pry larger social programs out of the central government in Mexico City. The Sandinistas of Nicaragua and the Frente Faribundo Martí de Liberación Nacional (FMLN) of El Salvador have abandoned guerrilla struggle and hope to emerge victorious from the next presidential races in their respective countries.

If the left is to survive and thrive, a sounder strategy is needed than the old populist-nationalism or the guerrilla challenge, which has no possibilities of success. In Chile the governing coalition, which includes Socialists, Radicals, and social democrats, has attempted to improve social programs while embracing market reforms. In Brazil, the former Marxist but still social democrat Fernando Henrique Cardoso is similarly advancing market reforms and privatization while simultaneously trying to reduce the country's glaring social inequalities. In another key country, Argentina, a center-left alliance beat President Carlos Menem's Peronists in congressional elections in 1997 but only after moderating its views to support free market economic policies. In Mexico, too, Car-

denas's populist-nationalist-Marxist Revolutionary Democratic Party has shed its earlier anticapitalism in favor of a stance that is acceptable to the global economic consensus, including NAFTA.

This is a time of difficulty and self-examination for the Latin American left. Its popular support has been drying up; its international connections (mainly the Soviet Union) are gone; its guerrilla tactics have failed; it has no viable models (Cuba? Cambodia? North Vietnam? China?) anymore; and its organizational base (labor unions, peasant leagues, student groups) has shrunk drastically. All over Latin America as well as in Madrid, Paris, and the United States, Marxist leaders are meeting to talk, regroup, reassess, and find a new political formula for success. A few have even admitted their Marxism was wrong all along, but most are reluctant to abandon entirely the ideological beliefs they have held most of their lives.

If it is to be a serious contender in the future competition of ideas in Latin America, Marxism needs to be rethought and reformulated. One such attempt was recently made by the Mexican Marxist (but son of the oligarchy) intellectual Jorge Castañeda and the Brazilian philosopher Roberto Unger, who teaches at Harvard.[47] They argue that in order to succeed the left must win over the center. And that requires accepting the market as the main mechanism for allocating resources and supporting free trade and privatization. Castañeda and Unger propose to "democratize the market economy" through the use of decentralized credit institutions, to reduce dependence on foreign credit by using the pension system to generate savings, to employ consumption rather than income taxes, and to utilize frequent referendums to overcome politicians' resistance to change. But this proposal remains very short on details. It is the product of intellectuals, but it may not represent the views of entrenched Marxist union leaders, party operators, or the rank and file. One thing is certain: this and other proposals emanating from the left in Latin America are a very long way from the original ideas of Marx.

It is hard to predict if Castañeda's and Unger's proposal will be accepted by the left or if it will provide a formula to bring the left back to popularity and power. What is clear is that Latin American Marxism needs to discard the false starts and failed shibboleths of the past and, if it is to survive as a viable force, adapt itself to the realities both of Latin America and the modern world and strike out in new directions.

Chapter 9

Corporatism

The late nineteenth and early twentieth centuries were particularly fertile times for the growth of new ideologies. Marxism, anarchism, syndicalism, anarcho-syndicalism, socialism, and social democracy all have their origins in this period. So does modern liberalism, stemming from J. S. Mill and T. H. Green. To this list must now be added corporatism. Corporatism, like positivism, is one of those ideologies that is all but unknown in the United States but had an extremely powerful impact on both Europe and Latin America.[1]

The main reason for the emergence of so many new ideologies during this period is industrialization and its accompanying social and political effects. By the late nineteenth century, industrialization was taking root in all the European countries, including the less developed ones like Portugal and Spain. In Latin America large-scale industrialization came somewhat later, in the decades between World Wars I and II, which is precisely when corporatism reached its heyday. Industrialization undermined earlier feudal and medieval structures and gave rise to vast social changes, most particularly an organized, urban working class that potentially threatened the established social structure. Industrialization also gave rise to what was called the social question—how to deal with a large, potentially destabilizing urban proletariat without provoking class warfare and revolution as Marx had predicted. Corporatism was one answer to this dilemma—perhaps the major one for a time in Europe and Latin America. In addition to industrialization, the Catholic religious revival of this period was an important factor in the emergence of corporatism.[2]

Corporatism emerged first in Europe and then spread to Latin America. Yet corporatism seemed to fit Latin America quite well, better than most ideologies. In this sense, it was like positivism and unlike Marxism or liberalism, which have had trouble in adapting to Latin America. This fit helps account for the ongoing popularity of both positivism and corporatism in Latin America. For if positivism was the dominant ideology in Latin America in the last third of the nineteenth century and Arielism, nationalism, and Hispanismo in the early twentieth, corporatism became the dominant philosophy of the 1920s, 1930s, and 1940s. Although World War II led to the discrediting of the corporatist ideology, the practice and institutional organization of corporatism in Latin America continue in various forms to this day.

Origins

The idea of a corporate, organic, integralist, functionally organized, and communitarian-based society has been around for a very long time in Western political thought. It goes back to the Bible, Greece, Rome, and medieval philosophy and practice.[3] In chapter 2 I quoted Saint Paul's epistles calling for the creation of an integrated, harmonized, unified society and polity, with all its parts interrelated just as the various parts of the body are interrelated, and showed how this organic conception proved to be one of the enduring metaphors in the history of Western thought. In Greek philosophy, too, there is the notion that society should be organized in terms of its "natural" or "organic" components: families, tribes, warriors, the priesthood, workers, slaves, philosopher-kings—all content in their station and presumably working for the common good. Ancient Rome carried the Greek conception further, creating an elaborate and organized system of corporate and societal organizations—each with its own charter and group rights and with the state exercising regulatory control over them. In Catholic political theory of the Middle Ages, particularly in Thomas Aquinas and his successors, one sees the elaboration of a similarly integrated, organic, unified society, all its parts tied together, and with a king or ruler exercising presumably benevolent control over it and giving it direction.[4]

Medieval Europe was largely organized on a corporatist basis. As Europe emerged from its so-called dark period and began to develop and become better organized in the eleventh and twelfth centuries, the organizational space began to be filled by what were called corporatist groups: the military orders that had been organized to fight in the Crusades and against the Moors, the Church and its several religious orders, towns and regions struggling to maintain their self-governing autonomy against the encroaching power of the new centralizing monarchies, and the medieval artisan and craft guilds—organizations of goldsmiths, silversmiths, bakers, and the like. The guilds licensed and policed their members, regulated trade and prices within their domain, trained apprentices and journeymen to be master craftsmen, and were essentially self-governing professional associations that provided unity, progress, and social peace. It is to the guild system that later corporatist writers often looked for a model of efficient management and class harmony. In the process, they often romanticized and idealized medieval society.[5]

In the immediate aftermath of the French Revolution, the Chapelier Law of March 2, 1791, swept away the entire medieval structure of guilds and corporate privilege. Such privileged groups as the Catholic Church and the guilds lost their especially favored privileges and position. Along with the abolition of corporate privilege, the entire structure of a medieval, closed, hierarchical, orderly, top-down social and political structure came tumbling down. The abolition in France of corporate privilege and often of the corporations themselves was followed in the nineteenth century by their abolition—at least formally—in the rest of Europe, including Spain and Portugal and, to a more limited degree, in Latin America. Henceforth, it would be individual rights—liberty, equality, and fraternity—that would receive priority, at least in theory and ideology, not so much the corporate or group rights of the past. It is, of course, this very individualism and liberalism that are identified with the modern age and democracy and that Latin America attempted— most often unsuccessfully—in the early nineteenth century.

After France, Europe, and much of Latin America, often precipitously, abolished the guilds and corporations of the ancien régime, a conservative reaction set in. Many now lamented their passing. Conservatives believed that society would disintegrate without the principles of discipline, order, hierarchy, and corporate organization that they associated with the old order. They were very critical of liberalism, individualism, and the new principles of liberty for violating biblical injunctions and for sowing discord, libertinage, and potential anarchy. Most of the critics of liberalism and individualism also wanted to restore the Roman Church and Catholicism to their hallowed, prerevolutionary glory. Some of these critics, such as Josef de Maistre in France and Juan Donoso Cortés in Spain, were political reactionaries who wanted to go back to the stability, discipline, order, and authoritarianism of the pre-1789 regime.[6] Their ranks included many priests, the nobility, the landed class, and other defenders of the status quo ante. Thus was born in the early nineteenth century, alongside liberal individualism, the tradition of European reactionary conservatism that persists to this day. This form of very traditional, usually Catholic and backward-looking conservatism also found reflection in Latin America in the postindependence reaction to the chaotic liberalism that had ensued.

Until the mid-nineteenth century in Europe, the defenders of the older corporative order were largely in the reactionary camp, but in the 1850s a more realistic and even progressive form and ideology of corporatism began to emerge. Most of the early leaders of this movement were Catholic clergy and intellectuals from the historically Catholic countries (Austria, Belgium, France, Italy, and Spain), but eventually the movement included Protestant clergy and north European political leaders as well. The major figures in the corporatism school included Albert DeMun and LaTour du Pin of France, Karl von Vogelsang of Austria, Giuseppe Bosca of Italy, Bishop Wilhelm Ketteler of Germany, Kaspar Decurtins of Switzerland, Cardinal Henry Manning of England, Monsignor Antoine Pottier of Belgium, and Reverend (and future prime minister) Abraham Kuyper of the Netherlands. Although not so well known in the history of political theory, this new, revived current of corporatist thought began to serve as a major alternative to the other great currents of contemporary political ideology then emerging: liberalism on the one hand and Marxism on the other. Neither of these last two ideologies was especially popular or acceptable in conservative, strongly Catholic Iberia or Latin America, which made the corporatism option that much more popular.[7]

What the corporatism writers and activists had in common was the conviction that the liberal individualism stemming from the Enlightenment and the French Revolution, as well as the new phenomenon of laissez-faire capitalism, had left people atomized, isolated, without roots or a sense of community or the ties that had historically bound people to society and given them purpose and certainty in life. Modern individualism, liberalism, and capitalism, the early corporatists argued, were undermining religion as well as all moral values and making humans slaves of the marketplace, uprooted, urbanized but missing the

249

strong relations of family, neighborhood, and community that had tied earlier society together. This critique was, of course, an accurate one, at least in part, and did not differ much from Marx's criticisms of early capitalism. But whereas Marx saw workers' salvation in class struggle and revolution, the corporatists sought to restore the ideas of brotherhood, social peace, community, and class harmony of previous epochs. Unlike the reactionaries, they sought not to restore the status quo ante but to devise a means of reviving religious sentiment and integrating the rising middle and working classes back into a society from which they had become alienated.[8]

The corporatist writers drew on some familiar ideas: the utopian communalism of the early nineteenth century, the order-and-progress positivism of Comte, and the analysis of corporatist social and occupational groups first suggested by the German philosopher Friedrich Hegel and the French sociologist Emile Durkheim. They also borrowed from the social reformist ideas of the French theorists Saint-Simon and François LaFarrell, who elaborated a kind of guild socialism adapted to the modern age. The corporatists, like Tocqueville in America, were preoccupied with creating intermediary agencies between the atomized individual of modernity and the state so as to give protection to workers and the middle class. They sought to fashion organizations of what are now called civil society—the family, the neighborhood, the parish, various occupational, cultural, and social groups—but without that implying the unfettered and quasi-anarchic pluralism of modern liberalism.[9]

Rather than making a sharp break with the past, as in the French Revolution, the corporatist writers emphasized gradual, evolutionary adaptation to change and modernity, a synthesis that blended the benefits (stability, order, religion, family, morality) of traditional society with the newer requirements of industrial society. New corporative intermediary groups based on class collaboration would be created for newer groups (such as workers) and more traditional groups (employers, the Church). Corporatism would thus seek to ameliorate the problems (rootlessness, alienation) of modern mass man but without the class conflict of Marxism or the anarchic individualism of liberalism.

Corporatism in this newer, updated version would be flexible, accommodative, and progressive instead of reactionary. In this early version, however, corporatism was often infused with religious sentiments, emphasized order and stability as much as change, and was often closely associated with official or state power. Hence, although some variants of corporatism in the twentieth century took left and even socialist directions, in general corporatism could be seen as a more conservative (but not, generally, reactionary) alternative to both Marxism and liberalism. Rather like positivism in the nineteenth century, corporatism was appealing to Latin American elites because of these features.[10]

By the 1870s and 1880s, corporatism was moving beyond the often vague sentiments of its initial advocates and developing a full-fledged program and ideology. It also, again parallel to Marxism and modern liberalism, began to develop an organized mass movement. The adherents of corporatism were gradually growing in numbers and organization. In France, Germany, Belgium, Austria, and other countries, the first of what were called Working Men's Circles were organized. In keeping with the corporatist principle of class reconciliation and dialogue, the Working Men's Circles included both workers and employers within their ranks. Disputes in the workplace were to be solved on the basis of Christian brotherhood and reconciliation rather than class conflict and struggle. The goal of the circles was to contribute to the good of society as a whole—the common good, in Thomistic terms—and not just of one group or class within it.[11]

Modern corporatism, once again like liberalism and Marxism, was both a manifest political ideology and a growing political movement—no longer of purely historical interest. In 1881 Pope Leo XIII charged a commission of theologians and social thinkers to study this new ideology and movement in relation to Catholic teachings. They met at the German university city of Freiburg in 1884 and gave corporatism its first, semiofficial definition: "A system of social organization that has at its base the grouping of men according to the community of their natural interests and social functions, and as true and proper organs of the state they direct and coordinate labor and capital in matters of common interest." Note especially in this definition that corporatism is now a "system of social organization," that it emphasizes "community," that it groups people according to their "natural" interests and social functions, that these new corporate organizations are agencies of the state, and that their role is to "coordinate labor and capital in matters of common interest."[12]

The Freiburg meeting brought together for the first time corporatist thinkers and organizers from several nations, gave the movement international legitimacy, and stimulated the growth of new organizing activities. Soon the movement had acquired a headquarters and gained stature as an international movement at the same time as—and as an alternative to—the organization of the Marxist and anarchist *internationales*. Another international meeting held in Berlin in 1890 gave added impetus to the movement and also served as an inspiration to the Vatican. Prompted by the findings of the Berlin meeting, Pope Leo XIII in 1891 issued the encyclical *Rerum Novarum*, which became famous as the workingman's encyclical. *Rerum Novarum* afforded dignity to labor, gave the Church's blessing for the first time to the organization of trade unions, and indicated that organized labor now had to be recognized as a legitimate social movement and incorporated into the political process. For the first time, organized labor was legitimated as one of the acceptable corporate groups within society. And the preferred means and system for achieving this goal was corporatism, not liberalism or Marxism.[13]

Corporatism is often referred to as a conservative political philosophy, the conservative answer to the other great "-isms" of the modern world, liberalism and Marxism. But in its recognition of labor rights and in the context of the late nineteenth century (Bismarck's Germany, Victorian England, Restorationist Spain), it was not a wholly reactionary philosophy either and, in fact, signaled some new social and political departures. A positive conception of trade unions and the working class had replaced the earlier negative one; new concepts of social obligation and social justice came to the fore; and worker groups were now to be incorporated into the political process rather than suppressed. In addition, the older paternalistic attitudes toward labor began to give way to a recognition that workers had a right to organize unions independently and to employ collective action, including strikes. The earlier reactionary views that harked back to medievalism were replaced by a more positive view of worker rights.

All these changes were gradual, piecemeal, and within prescribed limits, however. Many of the new corporatist groups and unions remained under the control of the Catholic Church and were guided by clerics. The activities of these groups and of the Working Men's Circles were often social and educational—dances, sporting events, religious instruction—not militantly trade unionist. And although corporatism by this time had a strong social justice component, it was also quite consciously seen by its leaders and clerical advisers as comprising a coun-

terbalance to the rising Marxist, anarchist, and communist unions. In
Europe, corporatism was viewed as opening the door to trade unionism
and to social justice; but as compared with its main competitors for the
workers' loyalties, it constituted the most conservative of the emerging
labor groups.[14]

In the decades leading up to World War I, corporatism and corporatist organizations grew—but slowly. By the turn of the century a great
variety of mainly Catholic (but with some Protestant also) corporatist
workers' and social movements had sprung up. In 1895 (four years after
Rerum Novarum) the first national Catholic trade union movement was
organized in Germany to compete with the socialist unions, and in the
first fifteen years of the twentieth century similar corporatist organizations were established in other European countries. In addition to
Catholic unions, there were now Catholic youth groups, Catholic associations of businessmen, Catholic women's organizations, and Catholic
political parties beginning to compete for members and power throughout Europe. So in addition to corporatism, there was also during this
period a Catholic religious revival under way in Europe; and the two
reinforced each other. And, of course, if the Catholics were reviving
and renewing themselves, Protestant denominations had to do the
same, which partly explains the parallel rise during this period of
Protestant unionism and corporatism alongside the Catholic version
in such countries as Germany, the Netherlands, Scandinavia, and even
Great Britain.[15]

Corporatism in Power

The twenty-year period between World Wars I and II was the high point
of corporatism in Europe. The flowering of corporatism during this period was due to a number of factors. First, World War I had revealed
the fragility of both monarchal and parliamentary regimes—several of
which collapsed in the course of the war and its aftermath—and thus
enhanced the appeal of corporatism as a viable alternative. Second,
the Bolshevik Revolution of 1917 in Russia, with its anticapitalist and
antireligious orientation as well as its bloody excesses, severely frightened people throughout Europe and made corporatism seem attractive as a bulwark against Marxism's spread. Third, the world market
crash of 1929 seemed to reveal the bankruptcy of both capitalism and

liberalism and again made corporatism appear to be the only viable option.[16]

A fourth factor was the rampant antidemocratic, antiparliamentary, antiliberal writings of such pre–World War I conservative writers as Gaetano Mosca, Vilfredo Pareto, Roberto Michels, Georges Sorel, and Ludwig Gumplowicz, who heaped scorn on the democratic idea that government should be based on the vote of the people, which they saw as the lowest common denominator. A fifth factor during this period was the growth of modern state planning, social welfare, and the state's regulatory role—all of which seemed to dovetail with the corporatist ideology of social programs carried out under state auspices and of the integration of (and control over) interest groups through top-down government administration. These developments plus the requirements of a further rationalization of society, a disciplined work force weaned away from strikes and radicalism, and stable employer-employee relations thus seemed to produce circumstances that corresponded closely to what corporatist writers were offering as solutions.[17]

Two main currents that came together in the interwar years help explain corporatism's popularity in Europe and also what happened to corporatism as it went from being an ideology of intellectuals and idealists to an ideology and movement in power. The first current is the one traced here, the long history of traditional corporatism, organicism, and integralism: Catholic, somewhat conservative, largely benign, an intellectual or philosophical tradition of thought that had some impact practically in the organization of a Catholic workers' movement. This current implied an updated, somewhat modernized Catholicism inspired by the papal encyclicals that incorporated workers into the national life and that was mainly oriented toward social justice, pluralism, and what was called corporatism of society.

But alongside this benign current was another tradition that was bureaucratic, authoritarian, power hungry, wanting to use corporatism for its own partisan political purposes, and not at all benign. In power, this group stood for a strong, authoritarian, corporatism of the state as distinct from the softer societal corporatism of free associability favored by Catholic intellectuals. These two traditions—the Catholic-corporatist and the bureaucratic-authoritarian—came together eventually in the regimes of Mussolini, Franco, and Salazar. In all these instances, the more authoritarian and statist inclinations of these regimes came to dominate the softer, more pluralist Catholic orientations.

In the cases of Italy and Nazi Germany (although these two regimes differed significantly), the combination of corporatism and authoritarianism led to full-scale fascism and totalitarianism.[18] As a result, because of this association with fascism, corporatism as an ideology and movement would also come to be reviled and disgraced—with major implications for Spain, Portugal, and Latin America (see below).

The corporatist ideology and movement had been growing slowly for several decades, and now in the interwar period a variety of corporatist regimes took power. Early, brief, and partial experiments with corporatism were carried out in Portugal in 1917, in Greece from 1917 to 1920, and in Spain under Primo de Rivera in 1923–29. But the first full-fledged corporatist regime was that of Mussolini in Italy. Mussolini introduced strict corporatist controls over not only social and political groups but also the economy. Mussolini, however, corrupted corporatism by employing it as an instrument of his dictatorship, using it to secure his dominance of the national economy, and suppressing all social and political pluralism in favor of a totalitarian or fascist state. Corporatism thus served as a smokescreen for Mussolini's political ambitions and as one among many agencies of his regime's totalitarianism. He further introduced a bureaucratic and statist form of corporatism, as contrasted with the more pluralist and participatory form advanced by earlier corporatism writers. If Mussolini's regime was an example of corporatism, it was not an auspicious start for that political philosophy.[19]

Corporatism nevertheless remained popular as a way of dealing with the social, economic, and political breakdowns of the 1930s. In 1931 a new papal encyclical, *Quadragesimo Anno,* going beyond *Rerum Novarum,* published in the depths of the world economic crash, added legitimacy and impetus to the corporatist movement and ideology as the best solution for sick societies. In Portugal (1928–74), Spain (1939–75), Bulgaria and Lithuania (1926–29), Poland (1926–35), Albania (1928–39), Austria (1934–38), Yugoslavia (1929), Greece again (1936–41), Romania and Ireland (1937), and Turkey, Estonia, and Latvia (1934) corporatist regimes, some inspired by the papal encyclicals but some secular in origin, came to power. In addition, Vichy France during the years of World War II was organized in part on corporatist principles; and Nazi Germany under Adolf Hitler from 1933 to 1945 also introduced a form of corporatism into the running and organization of the economy organized on "national socialist" principles. But in the German case even more so than the Italian, corporatism was completely subordinated to the requirements of Hitler's personal dictatorship and the regime's totalitarianism and anti-Semitism. Corporatism thus seemed to be ubiquitous; virtually every country in Europe between World Wars I and II either tried corporatism or experimented with one or another of its institutions.[20]

But what were these corporatist institutions and what precisely were their functions? First, because of the global depression, the 1930s saw a tremendous increase in the economic regulatory role of the state in practically all countries—a step that the corporatist philosophy favored. Many of these new regulatory agencies incorporated functional representation (business, labor, the state) as a principle of organization. Second, as a means of heading off the potential for revolution from below that might have loomed during the 1930s, all these governments instituted new social security and welfare programs for the lower classes—another policy that corporatism supported. Third, quite a number of the regimes organized high-level, functionally representative councils of state as a way of complementing the geographic representation of their parliaments—or perhaps as a way of bypassing parliament altogether. Others instituted functional representation directly in their legislatures. Fourth, and at the heart of corporatism, almost all European governments of this period devised means to bring both organized labor and capital into the counsels of government, either directly by placing their representatives on various regulatory and planning boards or indirectly by incorporating both business and labor under the control of the national ministries. These methods involved both cooptation and control: cooptation in the form of new social programs bestowed on the workers, and control by means of governmental oversight and regulation of their activities.

Through these means, in a time of crises, a number of precarious governments could head off the possibility for instability (or even for Marxist revolution) by bringing their now-sizable and potentially threatening labor movements into the realm of official activities, where they could keep an eye on them, shower them with benefits to head off radicalism, and at the same time keep them under control. All of these devices to coopt and control organized labor through corporatist incorporation were ingeniously clever politically and bureaucratically, but they represented a long step from the idealism and notions of brotherhood of many of the early corporatist writers of the nineteenth century.

There are distinct meanings and definitions of "corporatism," I have found it useful in my own writings to distinguish among four forms of corporatism.[21] These four forms are distinguishable not only as distinct types but also in terms of chronological development. The first has been termed "natural corporatism."[22] By this term I have in mind countries and areas whose particular histories, sociologies, and cultures have given rise to early kinds—the family, the clan, the region or neighborhood, the parish, the Church, the military orders, the guild, the shepherds—of corporatist organizations, whose corporatism is so ancient that it is almost "natural." Medieval Spain and Portugal as well as colonial Latin America, with their organic, communitarian, integralistic, Thomistic, neoscholastic sociopolitical organizations, fall into this historic, ancient, natural type.

The second form is ideological corporatism, which emerged in nineteenth-century Europe and whose history was just described. The third form is manifest corporatism or corporatism in power (also described above), which turned out to be quite different—more bureaucratic, more statist, more authoritarian—from the ideological conception. And the fourth form is modern neocorporatism, which emerged in Europe in the post–World War II period and is just beginning to emerge in Latin America. Given its long history of corporatism in all its other forms, however, one might expect Latin America to be peculiarly receptive to this newest form of corporatism as well—a theme to which I return in chapter 10.

The case is quite clear as to the importance of some form of natural or medieval corporatism in Spain and Portugal of the Middle Ages. Indeed, corporatism was so ubiquitous in the organization of early Spanish and Portuguese national life that, rather like Catholicism, to which it was intimately related, it seemed to be an integral part of being Spanish or Portuguese.

Although corporatism was weaker in the colonies than in the mother countries, the case for a corporatist structure of society and politics during the colonial era is also powerful. Those who doubt the corporatist structure of Spanish and Portuguese colonial institutions should go back and read the classics: Sergio Bagú, Américo Castro, John Lynch, L. N. McAlister, Donald Worcester, Magali Sarfatti, Charles Gibson, C. H. **257**

Haring, and others.[23] To the extent the colonies were organized at all, they were organized with the Thomistic, Suárezian, neoscholastic principles in mind. Again, that included a medieval corporatist structure as one of the central organizing principles. Recall also that in the colonies the structure and system of castes served as a functional equivalent to the estate system of the mother countries.

The case is harder to make after independence and through part of the nineteenth century. Most of the Latin American countries, following the French, Spanish, and Portuguese examples, formally abolished the guilds and corporate privilege after independence; and there is no doubt that corporatism diminished in the nineteenth century. For from independence on (and even reaching back into the eighteenth century) there were now two pillars of power and politics in Latin America: the one conservative (including corporatism) and the other liberal. These two rival power centers competed for power all through the nineteenth century and beyond. Corporatism no longer had the field to itself; it had to jockey, fight, and maneuver for power. And the presence of a rival, more liberal power structure meant corporatism no longer had monopolistic legitimacy in the new republics.

But corporatism was by no means dead. First, the legal abandonment of corporatism in Latin America after independence was always incomplete, partial, and not carried out at all in some countries (see chapter 5). Second, some of the most powerful corporate groups—including the Church and the oligarchy—retained their power *after* independence. Third, after independence, some new, vitally important, and very powerful corporations—primarily the army—were created and took their place alongside the other corporate groups. And fourth, therefore, although corporatism was in some countries formally repudiated, its practice continued largely unabated, in the form of the functional organization of society and a continuation of top-down, elitist, integralist rule. Indeed, one can make the case that some Latin American countries were more neoscholastic and corporatist after independence than before.[24]

Corporatism is, moreover, not just a set of dry, mechanical institutions; it is a way of thinking. It is a part of the political culture, a weltanschauung, a set of assumptions that are Thomistic, scholastic, and a part of the Iberic–Latin political tradition as outlined here. In this, I am at one with Octavio Paz.[25] Paz argues that the Spanish and Portuguese monarchies identified themselves with a universal faith—Roman Catholicism—and a unique interpretation of that faith. The unique interpretation involved the taking on of a universal mission, the defense and expansion of the Christian faith and of Western (Hispanic) civilization, to the point of elevating that into official state ideology. The ideology involved was Thomism, neoscholasticism, revealed truth, top-down authority, and deductive reasoning.

Paz argues that the philosophical foundation of the absolute Catholic monarchy in Spain and Portugal was the neoscholasticism of Suárez and his Jesuit disciples and followers. These theologians, he goes on to say, were geniuses who rebuilt Thomism and made it into a philosophical fortress. Along with the historian Richard Morse,[26] Paz emphasizes that Iberian and Latin American Thomism had a double function: on the one hand, it constituted the ideological foundation on which the imposing juridical, political, sociological, and economic structure of the Spanish and Portuguese empires rested. On the other, it was the training ground and philosophical methodology—the political culture—in which the habits and thought processes of the Latin American political and intellectual class were molded. In this sense, Paz argues, as a mental attitude and general philosophy if not always a set of concrete institutional relations, the influence of neoscholasticism and the communalist/corporatist features it enshrines lives on among Latin American intellectuals and political elites.

And not just among the elites, for the philosophy and institutions of the dominant political culture were transferred to and inculcated in the lower classes as well. In this way, Paz concludes, although medieval and scholastic philosophy and institutions began to come under challenge in the eighteenth century and to go into partial and temporary eclipse in the nineteenth, "the attitudes and habits that were its [neoscholasticism's] sum and substance have lived on to our time." Paz goes on to say, "Our intellectuals have embraced liberalism, positivism, and Marxism-Leninism. Yet in almost every case, regardless of philosophical outlook, the psychological and moral attitudes of the former champions of neoscholasticism are only too obvious, out of sight but still alive. The paradox of modernity: today's ideas, yesterday's attitudes."[27]

While the historic neoscholasticism and corporatism of which Paz writes were challenged by new ideas and ideologies as never before in the nineteenth century and had to compete with liberalism and eventually other ideologies as well, there are enough continuities in the Latin American tradition, both before and after independence, to see this ideology as an unbroken chain stretching from the natural and medieval corporatism of the colonial period to the twentieth century's version of ideological and manifest corporatism. Challenged, yes, but broken, no. Illegalized in certain particulars, but strengthened in others. The case of Mexico illustrates these themes.

When news of Napoleon's invasion of the Iberian peninsula reached Mexico in 1808 and the earliest stirrings of independence began, the first reaction of the *ayuntamiento* (city council) in Mexico was neoscholastic and corporatist, not liberal. In the absence of the Spanish king, the ayuntamiento proclaimed, "Sovereignty reverts to the whole kingdom and the *functional groups* that make it up" [emphasis added]. The arguments of the ayuntamiento were not those of liberals in either a Lockean or a Rousseauian sense; rather, it was thinking in traditional neoscholastic terms of a society made up of corporations and classes.[28] When a junta was formed to hold power until the legitimate king could be restored, its organization was also corporatist: the audiencia, the archbishop, representatives from lesser tribunals, municipal corporations, ecclesiastical and secular *cuerpos* ("bodies"), the nobility, leading citizens, and the military estate. Neither "the people" nor individuals were represented under this concept: only corporate groups. The concept was a direct continuation of Suárez's and Luís Molina's arguments in the sixteenth century that there were only two legitimate authorities: the sovereign (now absent) and the corporations.[29]

When the Spanish liberal constitution of 1812, written under the influence of a French occupation army, was proclaimed, Mexico reacted strongly against it and began to move preliminarily toward independence. Subsequently, when the Spanish king Fernando VII was restored to power in 1814 and repudiated the constitution, Mexico calmed down. But the constitution of 1812 was restored in Spain's liberal revolt of 1820, whereupon Mexico and the other Spanish-American countries, rather than accept the new liberal order, severed the relationship with the mother country. Such influential corporate groups as the army, the creole elite, and the Church took the lead in moving toward independence. The liberalizing, even revolutionary (in the form of an indigenous insurrection) tendencies that had been present in Mexico in the immediately preceding years were snuffed out; corporatism quickly reestablished itself. The basic conflicts between liberalism and corporatism, however, and the role and position of such vital corporate groups as the Church, the army, and the creole landed elite were unresolved and would prove contentious for the next hundred years and beyond.

After Mexico declared its independence in 1821 and Agustín de Iturbide became president, a new constitution was drawn up. The new constitution made Iturbide the equivalent of a monarch; the legislature was to function as a rubber stamp. One plan called for a bicameral legislature in which the upper chamber would be called a chamber of corporations; Iturbide's proposal was for a unicameral house that would be exclusively based on corporatist (classes as well as guilds) representation. The compromise that was fashioned involved a mixed chamber, partly corporatist and partly based on the more familiar territorial basis of representation, but with the popular constituency held as much at arm's length as possible. Once again the theme is as much continuity, in constitutional and sociopolitical organization, as change in Mexico's passage from colony to independence.[30]

By 1823, however, Iturbide was out of power, and a new, more liberal constitution modeled on the controversial Spanish constitution of 1812 was soon promulgated. Though supposedly liberal, this constitution proclaimed Roman Catholicism the official religion of the Mexican state, left intact the oligarchic landholding system, and allowed the military and the Church to retain their corporatist fueros. This new constitution would represent the liberal pole in Mexican history that would continue to alternate with the conservative or corporatist pole, as exemplified by Iturbide's "royalist constitution," for much of the next one hundred years. But there was not much difference between these constitutions in their retention of corporatist features.

From 1821 to 1824, mainly under Iturbide, the conservatives were in power; during the next few years the liberals made a short-lived comeback. For most of the next three decades until the 1850s, however, Mexican political history was dominated by man-on-horseback Antonio López de Santa Anna, who restored a more conservative corporatist order. In 1857, once again, a new constitution restored a liberal and more individualistic society; legislation promulgated by the reform movement of this time—interrupted by the French occupation of 1861–65—went further by stripping the Church of its lands and special privileges. But in 1876 and for thirty-four years after that, Porfirio Díaz dominated Mexico, restored a more conservative order, and ruled through his positivist, científico advisers. If his regime was not fully corporatist institutionally, it was organic and integralist in the sense that Paz referred to as a "mental attitude." Indeed, in speaking of the two poles between which Mexican history had alternated for the preceding century, Paz calls the conservative one the "Catholics of Peter the Hermit" and the liberal one the "Jacobins of the Third Era."[31] In divided Mexico, neither of the two poles could offer long-term stability or effective rule; yet the poles were so far apart that compromise between them seemed all but impossible.

In 1910 Díaz was overthrown, and in the following years Mexico exploded in violent social revolution. The revolution was chaotic and generally devoid of ideology. A new, highly liberal constitution enacted in 1917 stripped the traditional wielders of power of their privileges but at the same time continued in the corporatist tradition by elevating peasant, Indian, and worker groups to positions of special rights within the system. And in the early 1920s some elements in Mexico appeared to be going in a radical Marxist direction. By the late 1920s, however, fearing continued instability and wishing to preserve his influence in the face of the constitutional prohibition against reelection, President Plutarco Calles created an ingeniously organized political party to help preserve continuity while remaining true to the revolutionary tradition and at the same time institutionalizing a new form of corporatism. The Mexican Party of Revolutionary Institutions (PRI—originally the National Revolutionary Party, or PRN) was sectorally or corporately organized, with sections for peasants, workers, the popular sector, and the military—later, the military sector was dropped from the official apparatus. The PRI was one of the first parties (and perhaps the most successful for a long period of time) to bridge the historic gap between liberalism and corporatism in Latin American history and between traditional and modern corporatism; and it did so in ways that benefited Mexico's development and realistically reflected the country's history, tradition, and divided society.[32]

While the PRI consolidated a top-down, monolithic, corporatist, unitary, monopolistic, and even authoritarian sociopolitical structure—in keeping with certain aspects of Mexico's long, historic political tradition—it also incorporated liberal, pluralist, participatory, social justice, and even revolutionary ingredients from Mexico's other, emerging tradition. The structure was corporatist; but importantly some historic groups, including the Church, the oligarchy, and the army, were left out of the arrangement, while other corporately organized groups, among them peasants, workers, and indigenous elements, were especially favored. And although President Calles had intended for the party to be a stable, quite conservative political machine and patronage body to preserve continuity as well as his own power, under President Lázaro Cárdenas in the 1930s, the PRI swung in a radical direction that verged on syndicalism—only to swing back again to the conservative, probusiness side after 1940. These points are emphasized to suggest that corporatism, though often associated with the right and conservative forces, is sufficiently flexible to take centrist, left, populist, and radical directions as well.

The Mexican PRI combined elements that went back to Roman law, Thomas Aquinas, the neoscholastics, Rousseau, and positivism, as well as liberal, radical, anarcho-syndicalist, and revolutionary themes from Mexico's more recent history. This was a party that for the first time brought together Mexico's natural and historic corporatist tradition with its newer, more urgent needs, reform and modernization. No other party or movement in Latin American history has ever so successfully or for so long bridged these two traditions. For the PRI not only ended (for a time) the chaotic violence and fragmentation that had often torn Mexico apart—and that plagued the other Latin American countries as well—but also, in presiding over the country for the past sixty years and more, helped bring about conditions eventuating in a long period of political stability and economic progress that has lifted the country out of the ranks of the Third World and positioned it on the verge of entering the First World of modern, industrialized nations. It was precisely this kind of formula—one that combined Latin America's historic (including corporatist) traditions with the requirements of change and modernization, even while avoiding the alternatives of liberalism or Marxism-Leninism—that other Latin American countries sought to fashion in the 1930s and 1940s.[33]

Corporatism in Power in Latin America

Although corporatism in its modern, ideological form was born in Europe and enjoyed considerable popularity there, it also found an enormously receptive audience in Latin America—and for many of the same reasons. First, corporatism offered an alternative to the despised liberalism and North American–style individualism that had never worked very well or established a strong base in Latin America. Second, with its Catholic origins and history, corporatism seemed to be adaptable to

Latin America better than other secular ideologies. Third, in a period of rising nationalism, corporatism appeared to offer Latin America a way of avoiding solutions favored by the United States (see chapter 6). Fourth, in an era of threatening Marxism and growing communist parties, corporatism offered an alternative to unacceptable socialism or Bolshevism. Fifth, in the midst of the depression, corporatism provided a means for Latin American states both to secure greater regulatory power over the economy and to prevent the possibility of disruptive, possibly destabilizing labor activity. Sixth and perhaps most important, corporatism was in keeping with a long tradition of Iberian and Latin American thought and seemed to fit the area quite comfortably.[34]

In Latin America, corporatism's heyday, intellectually and institutionally, stretched from the 1880s through World War II and even beyond, into the modern era. It thus overlapped with positivism, with which it had close affinities at the beginning, and with democracy in more recent times. Corporatism spoke to and assimilated other prevailing ideologies and social movements of that time, including positivism, arielismo, Hispanismo, nationalism, indigenismo, Catholic social action, and antiparliamentarism. It reinforced both the Latin American elites' disillusionment with liberalism and the military's demand for order, discipline, and stability and thus moved both leadership groups toward corporatist systems in rhetoric and law. Frederick Pike maintains that during this same period Latin American elites came in contact with U.S.-style economic liberalism for the first time and that what they saw, in the form of crass materialism and a robber-baron mentality, they did not like, thus further reinforcing the appeals of the corporatism alternative.[35]

There are other reasons for corporatism's widespread receptivity in Latin America. Corporatism was both integralist and unitary and hence close to a number of other historic, Catholic, and traditional Latin American ideological traditions. It was also elitist and top-down and thus (like positivism in the previous century), while appearing to place the continent at the forefront of advanced political change, provided a rationalization for the perpetuation of Latin America's existing social and political institutions. In addition, and as in Europe, corporatism furnished a formula for coopting the emerging labor movements of the area and for placing them under state control. It was a way to appear progressive while at the same time retaining historic social structures and political authoritarianism. For all these reasons, corporatism seemed to correspond to Latin American thinking and realities particularly well, both because it was in accord with historic Latin American ways of doing things (elitist, top-down, organic, unitary) and because it offered an acceptable formula to the hated alternatives of liberalism and Marxism.

In August 1941, just before Pearl Harbor and the American entry into World War II, a quite remarkable letter was printed in the *New York Times* explaining Latin America's affinity for corporatism.[36] The letter was sent by Marie R. Madden, a distinguished professor at Fordham University and author of a well-known book on medieval political theory,[37] in response to a series of articles on Latin America by a *Times* correspondent, articles that had reported that Latin American Catholics were very suspicious of an American foreign policy that had gone from being antifascist to being anticorporatist as well, specifically with regard to Salazar's corporatist regime in Portugal. The *Times* had reported that priests, laymen, and Catholics in general in Latin America regarded the Salazar regime as an "almost ideal state," but that this did not correspond to U.S. views of the most desirable form of government. Madden's letter set out to try to explain why corporatism was so popular at that time in Latin America and to distinguish Catholic corporatism from Nazi fascism.

Madden argued that "what is not in the American tradition but is very deeply imbued in the Portuguese and South American tradition is the corporate organization of society—that is a functional organization of institutions." She went on to say that corporatism and the conception of rights in Catholic societies emanated from Saint Paul's doctrines that all authority comes from God, and "there is no bond and free but all are free because of their common origin and common destiny." She further elucidated that "it is from the great Catholic thinkers, Saint Augustine, Saint Thomas Aquinas, Saint Bellarmine, Suárez that these ideas have been elaborated and applied to the practical realities of government." Though this Catholic and corporatist tradition, "under the impulse of secularist theories and the Manchester School of Economics," had been weakened in all the Latin American countries in the nineteenth century, it had survived and was now coming back to life again in a new form. It was coming to life not just in Spain and Portugal, she said, but in Brazil and "all the Latin American countries," where it is "much discussed among South American leaders." Madden concluded by contrasting corporatism in Iberia and Latin America with liberalism and the New Deal in the United States and by suggesting that "the functional order—that is, a corporate order of society"—is not incompatible with American interests and foreign policy but merely "not familiar to our people in general."

From the list of reasons discussed above as well as from Madden's letter, which probably captured the spirit of Iberia and Latin America *at that time* better than any other single source, one can easily understand why corporatism received such a warm reception in Latin America. Its first appeal was to intellectuals, especially Catholic intellectuals, who had long been looking for a Catholic answer to modern problems, who favored a Catholic approach to social issues but did not want to return to the reactionary politics of the previous century. During the 1920s, a large number of Catholic intellectuals in Latin America were attracted to the corporatist writings of their European counterparts. They liked the traditional emphasis on order and stability in corporatism while also admiring its progressive outlook toward worker organizations. They found in corporatism strong echoes of the arguments of Aquinas and Suárez that government had to be based on the consent of the governed, of the community, that it needed to respect the corporate group rights of political society, over which first absolute monarchy and then Latin American authoritarians had run roughshod. Corporatism in their view restored the proper balance, lost for centuries, between the legitimate authority of the central state and the autonomy and self-government held by society's functional groups. In this way, the corporatist ideology of the twentieth century was connected with the corporatism of the Middle Ages, both in its religious base and in its vision of the proper ordering of political society. Note how close this conception is once again to the similarly scholastic roots of the Latin American independence movements.[38]

It is difficult to convey to Americans, who in the dominantly liberal tradition have had little contact with corporatism, just how popular the corporatist ideology was in Latin America, and how much the alternative conceptions of liberalism and Marxism were despised. Americans tend to assume that, given a choice, all peoples everywhere would naturally choose a liberal, democratic, pluralist political system. But they forget that in Catholic political theory Marxism and liberalism (equated with disorder and libertinage) are roundly condemned by Rome. And not just in the political sphere but in the economic as well: Catholic thought has historically condemned both socialism *and* capitalism. Given the unacceptability in Catholic thought (and hence in the Catholic countries) of liberalism and Marxism, corporatism provided the "third way" that preserved the Catholic tradition of serving the common good while also reflecting the "majesty of facts": the reality of changed circumstances and of a new social group (organized labor) that had to be accommodated.[39]

Virtually every regime that came to power in Latin America in the 1930s and 1940s was infused, in one way or another, with this corporatist ideology and program. These include the regimes of Getulio Vargas in Brazil, Juan Perón in Argentina, Carlos Ibáñez in Chile, Oscar Benavides in Peru, Laureano Gómez in Colombia, Rafael Trujillo in the Dominican Republic, Arnulfo Arias in Panama, José María Velasco Ibarra in Ecuador, Marcos Pérez Jiménez in Venezuela, Anastasio Somoza in Nicaragua, Alfredo Stroessner in Paraguay, Maximiliano Hernández in El Salvador, Jorge Ubico in Guatemala, Rafael Calderón Guardía in Costa Rica, the PRI in Mexico, the Bolivian National Revolutionary Movement (MNR), as well as the Peruvian social-democratic party APRA. It is impossible to understand Latin America during this period or subsequently without coming to grips with the phenomenon of corporatism.[40]

In this list of names and the regimes over which they presided, a number of points stand out. First, the list contains left-wing, populist regimes (the MNR, the PRI under Lázaro Cárdenas in the 1930s, APRA, Arias, Velasco Ibarra) as well as right-wing, conservative, authoritarian regimes—but with the latter predominating. So corporatism is not just a right-wing and conservative ideology, although its emphasis on order, stability, and controlled change seems to make it particularly attractive to that side of the political spectrum. Second, it is striking that almost every country in Latin America is represented, showing how ubiquitous the corporatist philosophy was during this period. Third, few regimes in Latin America became completely corporatist; instead, they tended to build some new institutions grounded on corporatism while retaining many features (legislatures based on geographic representation, for instance) from their republican and democratic pasts. And fourth, corporatism was attractive to both civilian and military regimes, indeed, providing some common ground between them and serving in part as a way to bridge this historic dividing line and source of instability in Latin America's past as well.

A few examples will show the pervasiveness of the corporatist philosophy and the new institutions that ideology affected. In Vargas's

Brazil, for example, both the Constitution of 1938 and the system of labor laws that Vargas's regime enacted were heavily infused with corporatist principles.[41] Perón's philosophy of "justicialism" was also heavily infused with corporatism, as was his incorporation of trade unions into the political structure of his regime.[42] In Paraguay a high-level, corporately representative Council of State was created to incorporate the main functional groups in society and to serve as an advisory body to the president. Ecuador's Velasco proposed a two-house legislature, one of which would be geographically representative and the other functionally representative. Mexico's PRI, Bolivia's MNR, and the Peruvian APRA are all political parties that, under corporatist influence, are sectorally or functionally organized: peasants, workers, youth, business, women. In addition, practically every labor law enacted in Latin America during this period was derived either from the Spanish or the Portuguese corporatist labor codes, which were themselves adapted from Mussolini's *Carta del Lavoro*.[43] Similarly, almost all the social security and welfare programs enacted during this period as a way of buying off the labor movement and incorporating it into a system of government benefits and controls were inspired by corporatist principles of group rights and eligibility and not the American liberal presumption of individual rights.[44]

My study of a number of these corporatist regimes in Iberia and Latin America—the Trujillo regime, the Mexican PRI, the Vargas regime, Perón, the Stroessner regime, Franco and Salazar, the Peruvian revolutionary regime of 1968–75[45]—has brought to the fore several conclusions:

1. How pervasive the corporatist ideology and entire way of thinking were in Iberia and Latin America in the 1930s and thereafter. These were societies thoroughly infused with Catholic teachings and, indeed, way of life. When Franco, Salazar, Stroessner, Trujillo, et al. gave speeches or had their intellectuals write justifications for their regimes, emphasizing the need for order, discipline, authority, hierarchy, and the corporatist organization of society, they often came straight out of the Catholic social theory of *Rerum Novarum* and *Quadragesimo Anno*.[46] Corporatism in this sense is not just a set of ephemeral political institutions that come and go with each regime change; it is, following Octavio Paz, a complete conception of society, philosophy, politics, and economics. Just as North Americans almost automatically think in liberal and pluralist terms, just as auto-

matically Latin America thinks in corporatist and integralist
terms.

2. Although the Catholic influence was pervasive, perhaps equally important in Iberia and Latin America were the bureaucratic and authoritarian forms of corporatism stemming from Mussolini's Italy and other not-very-pleasant regimes. It was not just idealists and well-meaning Catholic ideologues who shaped these Iberic-Latin systems but also hard-nosed dictators who used the Catholic philosophy to justify authoritarianism. Increasingly as the 1930s wore on, the ideological corporatist idealists often influential in the early days of these regimes yielded, or were forced to give way, to the tougher practitioners of full-fledged state corporatism and authoritarianism.

3. Corporatism was not just a way of thinking during this period but also a profound determinant of institutional arrangements, leading to the creation of corporately organized councils of state, economic regulatory agencies, systems of labor relations, social welfare laws and ministries, and even legislatures. In the Latin American context, however, these corporatist institutions almost always overlapped with or coexisted alongside liberal and republican institutions stemming from the nineteenth century.

4. Corporatism influenced virtually every regime in Latin America in one way or another during this period, but the form that these manifestations took varied considerably. Look again at the list of regimes above shaped or influenced by corporatism: there are civilian regimes as well as military ones, dictatorships as well as democracies, left-wing regimes as well as right-wing ones. Corporatism is not only pervasive, it also seems to be infinitely flexible.

5. While corporatism is largely identified with the interwar period in Europe and Latin America and was discredited because of its association in the popular mind with fascism during World War II, it nevertheless continued to survive after the war—even though its practitioners now generally avoided using the term "corporatism." Corporatism even thrived in some countries—until it was reborn and rediscovered once again, this time in neocorporatist forms (see the following section below).

In going from a set of intellectual and ideological constructs to a set of governing precepts, corporatism in Latin America took much the same path it had taken in Europe. First, the governments of the area used corporatism as a way to coopt and control the emerging labor movement rather than bringing it in as a full partner. Second, in numerous regimes the emphasis on order, discipline, authority, and stability found in corporatism was used to justify strong-arm tactics and a variety of authoritarian regimes. Third, corporatism's strong emphasis on regulation became a way to centralize economic decision making, to control all economic groups (business as well as labor), and to reinforce the statist, quasi-mercantilist economies that persist to this day. Fourth, corporatism was used by elite groups to justify the existing social structure and as a means to control the admission of new groups (in this period, labor) into the political process. Fifth, the ideologues and intellectuals who were attracted to corporatism in the 1920s and 1930s were now often incorporated into the regimes as speechwriters, law drafters, sycophants, and rationalizers but were seldom given any real power—that usually remained in the hands of the authoritarians who came to power during this period and who, along with the elites, used corporatism for their own political purposes.[47]

In short, a top-down, authoritarian, corporatism-of-the-state came in Latin America, as in Europe, to supplant the earlier, ideological, often idealistic corporatism of free associability ("societal corporatism") as advanced by intellectuals. The models for Latin America during this period were mainly Franco's Spain and Salazar's Portugal—but not the full-fledged fascism of the Italian or, especially, the German regimes. That is, to use a familiar distinction advanced by Juan Linz, the Latin American corporatist regimes were authoritarian but not often totalitarian.[48] Moreover, in Latin America in these various regimes, the ideology of corporatism often came together with the similarly conservative ideologies of Hispanismo (also derived from Spain), arielismo, and nationalism. To be Latin American, it was argued, it was necessary and perhaps even required to also be Catholic, corporatist, and a believer in strong government. In other words, both corporatism and the Hispanic and nationalist traditions of Latin America were manipulated for the private political purposes of those in power. And, again as in Europe, corporatism would be discredited because of this association.

Post–World War II and Neocorporatism

During the 1930s and on into the 1940s, essentially every government in Europe and Latin America practiced some kind of corporatism to one degree or another. Corporatism was seen as the wave of the future, a third way between what then, because of the world depression, seemed to be a failed capitalism and an unacceptable Marxism-Leninism. As the corporatist intellectual Mihail Manoilesco confidently predicted in 1936, the twentieth century would be the century of corporatism just as the nineteenth had been the century of liberalism.[49]

But during the war, corporatism, because of its identification with fascism, was widely discredited. Both Mussolini and Hitler claimed to have put in place corporatist practices and institutions—although in neither case did the corporatist institutions function as the corporatist planners and ideologues had thought or expected. There is considerable evidence that Mussolini and Hitler intended it that way: that they wished to appropriate the popularity that corporatism then enjoyed for their political purposes, but that they had no intention of fully implementing genuine societal corporatism and used the ideology and movement as a smokescreen to disguise the totalitarianism and dictatorial practices of their regimes. In addition, workers and writers on the left argued that the supposed coequality of business and labor under corporatism was a sham: that corporatism had resulted in significant benefits to big business but meant only repression directed against workers. They denounced corporatism as a fraud.[50] Because of these associations, and because the fascist regimes had been defeated in the war, the corporatism that was identified with them was discredited as well.

In Europe, despite corporatism's discrediting at the ideological level, quite a number of governments continued to practice corporatism after the war—in their labor relations, social welfare programs, and government regulatory agencies.[51] The term "corporatism" was seldom used anymore even by Catholic writers,[52] but meanwhile a disguised form of corporatism continued to be practiced de facto. Eventually, these practices would be rediscovered, and a new body of literature, focused on what was called neocorporatism, sprang up to explain it.[53]

The situation in Latin America regarding corporatism and its postwar legacy was different from that in Europe. Latin America fought no war on its soil over fascism, and no full-fledged fascism ever came to power in Latin America. Even Perón's regime—perhaps the closest of all to European-style fascism—was never fully fascist. In Latin America, hence, the discrediting association between fascism and corporatism never fully developed, as it did in Europe. As a result, there was no sharp break—except in a few countries like Brazil, where Vargas stepped down in 1945 even while his corporatist labor laws continued—between the pre- and postwar periods. Corporatism, which had grown up in Latin

America in the 1930s, often continued unabated. Obviously, there was some, but limited, pressure from the outcome of the war for Latin America to abandon corporatism; and as a sop to the United States, who after all had just completed a war against fascism, as well as to liberal pressures within their own societies, the term "corporatism" was no longer used to describe regime ideology. However, in basically every Latin American country the practice of corporatism not only continued but was often considerably expanded.[54]

During World War II virtually every country in Latin America was under authoritarian, if not dictatorial, control. But with the victory of the Allies over fascism, and then in the brief era of good feeling (1945–47) after the war but before the onset of the Cold War, prodemocracy sentiment ran strong. The war was over; the United Nations was founded; there would hopefully be no more war; and democracy would presumably blossom. Under these pressures, quite a number of Latin America's authoritarian regimes allowed opposition political parties to form, briefly legalized their communist parties, and allowed somewhat greater press and other freedoms. Some of these regimes—Vargas in Brazil, but also Ubico in Guatemala, and Batista (his first period in power) in Cuba—were obliged to leave office. With the beginning of the Cold War in 1947, however, the existing authoritarian regimes were able to clamp down again, illegalize their communist parties, snuff out the earlier freedoms, and restore full authoritarian rule. And in the three countries mentioned above as having had temporary democratic breakthroughs, Vargas came back into power in 1950, Batista staged a coup and seized power again in 1952, and, with the aid of the United States, Guatemala's revolutionary government was toppled in 1954 and a military-authoritarian regime returned to power. Meanwhile, new corporatist regimes—for example, Perón's in Argentina—were inaugurated.

The restoration of full-fledged authoritarianism in the late 1940s and on through the 1950s also enabled corporatism to survive and even thrive. In essence every country in Latin America enacted new labor charters during this period, which had the familiar corporatist features of outlawed strikes and lockouts, obligatory and often enforced bargaining between labor and capital, government-regulated and -approved trade union movements, strict controls against dissident unions, and strong state control over all aspects of labor activities. There were new and nonliberal so-called organic laws for just about every group in society: the armed forces, the press, students and the university, even the

Church—in the form of new concordats signed with the Vatican. In every country the government vastly expanded its oversight and regulatory role over the economy and over socioeconomic groups, including business, commerce, industry, the professions, as well as labor. The new social security and social welfare laws enacted during this period also had a corporate or sectoral character. All of these features are corporative in essence, not liberal and certainly not pluralist. The outward forms were, of course, republican but the basis of society remained corporatist.[55]

The reasons for corporatism's popularity during this period were the same as they had been before the war. First and most obvious, corporatism was in accord with a long tradition of Latin American political thought, and its leaders knew and felt quite comfortable operating within that framework. But more than that, it continued to provide the elite with a means by which they could control and regulate lower-class groups who were increasingly challenging them from below. Corporatism also offered a means to control and regulate the economy without going in the direction of either unacceptable socialism or the still-despised system of free-market capitalism. Corporatism provided, in addition, a means to allow gradual, evolutionary, controlled change without the risk that it would degenerate into chaos, liberalism, or systemic breakdowns. For under corporatism, new and clamoring groups could get a share of the expanding economic pie (assuming they accepted the corporatist rules of the game; if they did not, they could be repressed) without depriving traditional wielders of power of any of their share. Corporatism thus appealed to all groups in the society, but it was especially attractive to the traditional power holders, the elites, who in controlling the state apparatus controlled, regulated, and set the conditions for the entire process by which new groups were admitted to the system.[56]

Beginning in the mid-1950s and continuing into the early 1960s, there was another brief democratic interlude that gave renewed hope to liberals and democrats both in Latin America and in the United States. Perón was overthrown, Vargas left office, the dictator Pérez Jiménez was ousted in Venezuela, Batista was overthrown by revolution, the dictator Trujillo was assassinated. These democratic openings corresponded with and were in part the product of the changed policy winds that blew through the Eisenhower administration in its last two years and then of John F. Kennedy's Alliance for Progress. While these often represented hopeful breakthroughs to democracy, what is equally striking is how seldom they affected the underlying sociopolitical base, which remained not wholly but predominantly corporatist. Even under democracy, the old corporatist labor laws remained in effect, the social security laws were still group-based, the organic laws remained largely unchanged, the regulatory role of the state continued (not just over wages and prices but often over political parties and interest groups as well), and, if anything, with the creation of new planning agencies and a host of new government offices under the alliance, the state's control over the economy and business was expanded. In the changes from dictatorship to democracy in these countries, there was often much greater continuity—including that of corporatist institutions and practices—than would at first glance meet the eye. The Kennedy administration, at least initially, gave a boost to liberals and democrats throughout the hemisphere; but because so many underlying institutions—labor laws, the state system, the military, and so on—remained corporatist, the changes not only were incomplete but also gave elites a variety of institutionalized mechanisms whereby to continue controlling the change process and, eventually, to revert to statist controls and authoritarianism.[57]

Meanwhile, changes were taking place in another most important corporative institution, the Church—that is, the Vatican and the Roman Catholic Church universal, if not yet the Church in Latin America—that would also have powerful long-range effects. For in the post–World War II period a variety of new currents began to appear in the Church, at first in Europe and eventually in Latin America. These included the more liberal Catholic philosophy of Jacques Maritain and others, the worker-priest movements of Belgium and France, and the modernized Christian Democracy of Germany, Austria, and others with their reformist trade union, farmer, and youth branches. In addition, with Vatican II and then liberation theology, the edifice of medieval Thomism and natural law that had undergirded the Catholic Church for some eight hundred years began to give way to newer, updated concepts. In the form of the Christian-Democratic parties and movements of Chile, Venezuela, and other countries, these new reformist, sometimes even revolutionary currents began in the 1960s to make strong inroads into Latin America as well. But first, and in part stimulated by the reformist changes these new currents within the Church had set loose, Latin America had to go through at least one more cycle of renewed authoritarianism and corporatism.[58]

In the early 1960s and continuing through the 1970s, a new wave of authoritarianism swept over Latin America. In one country after another the fledgling democracies born only a few years earlier were overthrown. Starting in Argentina in 1962, then in Ecuador, Honduras, and the Dominican Republic in 1963, next Brazil in 1964, military regimes brushed aside elected governments and installed themselves in power. In subsequent years, even in such usually more democratic countries as Chile and Uruguay, the army came into power—often with a vengeance. In the 1960s in Guatemala, El Salvador, and Nicaragua—countries that were already under military control—easy-going and centrist regimes gave way in the 1970s to brutal repression. By the mid-1970s fourteen of the twenty Latin American countries were under military/authoritarian rule; in three others the military was so close to the surface of power—the power behind the throne—that the distinction between civilian and military rule was meaningless. The new wave of dictatorial governments was often referred to as bureaucratic-authoritarianism to emphasize that they were run by the military as a corporate or bureaucratic entity and not just by one man (caudilloism) and because they included civilian officials as well as military.[59]

The causes of this new wave of authoritarianism were several, including economic downturn as well as Cold War pressures. But one of the causes—if not the major cause—might be termed the crisis of corporatism or, better, the decline thereof. For with the democratizing currents of the earlier years, plus the pressures of the Alliance for Progress, the Peace Corps, and other groups intended to organize workers, peasants, Indians, and the lower classes generally on a liberal basis of free (not corporate) associability, the fabric of Latin American society seemed to be unraveling. Society seemed to be fragmenting, pulling apart, becoming, in Ortega y Gasset's term, "invertebrate"—just as it had in Spain in the 1930s, and there it had lead to collapse, disintegration, and civil war.[60] Among often unsophisticated militaries, these changes were often seen as leading to what they regarded as "communism." Among more sophisticated clerics, oligarchs, and conservative intellectuals, the new changes seemed to imply that society was pulling apart, becoming atomized, and, with its various groups going into separate orbits, that the organic unity that everyone in the Catholic tradition from Saint Paul on had said was necessary to the good society was being irrevocably lost. To a Catholic corporatist, and even to many Latin Americans who had no ideology, this was impermissible; the armed forces had an obligation to intervene to set society back on its proper course.[61]

Many interesting features of the authoritarian regimes of the 1960s and 1970s distinguish them from the earlier authoritarian regimes in Latin America—not least their widespread human rights abuses. But the focus here is on the political theory of Latin America and specifically in this chapter on corporatism, and in these areas too several interesting developments occurred. First, these regimes moved, often quite self-consciously and on a variety of fronts, to restore unity, cohesion, order, and discipline to society. In these regards they were most often operating within their own historic "integralist" tradition, even if that was not in accord with North American liberal and pluralist conceptions—but it is also clear that in their violations of human rights they often went beyond the pale, beyond what the Thomistic-Suárezian tradition of central authority limited by group and customary rights would permit.

Second, there was in some of these regimes a revival not just of corporatist institutional forms but of the manifest corporatist ideology that had not been heard since the early 1940s. Several of these regimes practiced not just a disguised form of corporatism but a quite open and blatant ideological corporatism that harked back to the nineteenth century, the papal encyclicals, and the voluminous corporatist writings of the 1930s. In this sense, corporatism had now, again, come out of the closet in which it had been locked since World War II. But some further distinctions need to be made. In some of the not-very-sophisticated military regimes of Central America, the soldiers, even the officers, usually had no idea of the philosophical ideas and traditions traced here—although they did usually have strong ideas about societal order and discipline, which were part of corporatism's body of beliefs. Behind these officers, however, stood better-educated religious leaders, Catholic intellectuals, and businessmen who did know the Catholic social tradition and often supplied the articulated programs and ideological justifications that the military lacked. In Argentina, Brazil, Chile, Uruguay, and Peru, where the officers corps were more sophisticated, the officers themselves, as well as their civilian supporters, often articulated a manifest corporatist ideology.[62]

A third manifestation of the corporatist resurgence during this period was the growth of the selfsame Christian-democratic political parties, trade unions, peasant associations, businessmen's groups, and study and educational groups mentioned earlier. In Europe, the Christian democrats had enjoyed great electoral success after World War II in such countries as Germany, Austria, and Italy; they were viewed as an extension of the earlier Catholic social tradition but now democratic and shorn of its previous fascistic tendencies. In Latin America, given its Catholic background, the third way of Christian-democratic corporatism had similarly seemed to offer great possibilities; but given the weak parties coupled with frequent and long authoritarianism and deep splits between conservative and reformist Catholics, Christian democracy had never made such strong showings as in Europe. But now in the 1960s and on into the seventies, eighties, and nineties, Christian democracy seemed poised to make a stronger impact; indeed, in some countries—Chile, Costa Rica, El Salvador, the Dominican Republic, Venezuela—Christian democracy appeared to be one of the few (and in some cases the only) alternatives to military authoritarianism. But some of the practitioners of Christian democracy in these countries—Rafael Caldera in Venezuela and Joaquín Balaguer in the Dominican Republic—were so old that they had been socialized in the 1930s version of corporatism and not its more updated forms. In addition, the military regimes themselves had their own authoritarian and traditionalist interpretations of Christian democracy, which seemed in some cases to imply a reversion to 1930-style fascism. Nonetheless, Christian democracy in its many manifestations seemed to have new and strong possibilities in Latin America, either as an alternative to military authoritarianism or as a successor regime and as one of the few ways of peacefully reconciling the earlier tradition of conservative, Catholic corporatism with the newer demands of social justice.[63]

A fourth aspect of the new 1970s corporatism was its extension to new social groups that had never before been organized. Recall that the original impetus to corporatism's rebirth as an ideology and political movement in the nineteenth century had been "the social question," the need to bring organized labor into the political system on a more-or-less coequal basis but still under some degree of state control. That remained one of the aims of 1970s corporatism: to coopt and control the trade unions. But by the seventies it was not just urban workers who demanded participation; peasants, indigenous peoples, women, and other groups were also clamoring for a place at the table and were sometimes employing force—land seizures, violence, sabotage, guerrilla activity—to gain it. Hence, the corporatist regimes of the 1960s and 1970s—in the same time-honored way they had earlier handled business groups, the rising middle class, and the unions—extended, selectively, the corporatist labor laws and social welfare legislation to these newer groups as well. The formula was the classic corporatist trade-off: benefits in return for government regulation and oversight, cooptation as well as control. The groups that refused to go along with this bargain, that were not recognized and lacked juridical personality, were usually suppressed, often brutally. In other words, the Latin American state now added a number of new corporate pillars to its still-vertical, pyramidal structure. But the structure usually remained corporatist and top-down, not pluralist and democratic.[64]

The fifth feature of the new corporatist regimes involves their economic policies. As a general rule, when corporatism comes to power, the regulatory role of the state in the economy increases. The corporatist state exercises a strong hand not only in controlling sociopolitical groups as above, but economic activity as well, in the form of wage and price controls, state-led industrialization, increased regulation, and so forth. For the most part, that occurred in Latin America as well, both during the first wave of corporatism in the 1930s and in the more recent wave in the 1970s. During the seventies, the mercantilist state extended its reach in all countries; in some, the banking sector was nationalized; in most, state industries and enterprises came to generate upward of 40, 50, and 60 percent of total GNP. That put the Latin American mercantilist or corporatist state almost at the level of some of the socialist countries in percentage of GNP generated through the public sector.[65]

The main exception, however—and it is a big one—was Chile. There the regime of Augusto Pinochet, after it had spent the first two years consolidating its political hold on the country (partly through the use of widespread human rights abuses and political murder), began in 1975 to implement a neoliberal economic agenda, reduce state size, and withdraw from a strong state economic role. Under the urging of the so-called Chicago boys, a topflight group of Chilean economists who had gotten their Ph.D.s in the conservative economics department of the University of Chicago, Chile began to free up its economy, move away from corporatist economics, and lean toward a free-market or liberalized economic system. Pinochet's may be the only authoritarian-corporatist regime in history that actually reduced state size and moved toward full-blown, unencumbered, liberal capitalism. For the whole history of corporatism so far had involved increased state regulation, over both the economy and associational life; the two were viewed as being intimately related. But then the obvious question must be raised: if you commit to freedom in the marketplace, how long will it be—since the two go together—before you are forced to also open up the political system to freedom? And that, of course, means democracy, not corporatism or authoritarianism. It was a question Pinochet would have to face sooner or later.[66]

Finally, sixth, the new corporatism in Latin America during the 1960s and 1970s was military corporatism, not, as in the 1930s, civilian corporatism. Of course, these military governments had civilian advisers, but what was new about the corporatist regimes of more recent vintage was that it was the officers themselves who had often been steeped in corporatist thinking. The new military corporatism reflected both rising Latin American nationalism, particularly strong in the officer corps, and rising Catholic social-action and Christian-democratic movements aimed at reestablishing unity and purpose in society. But perhaps above all, the new military corporatism reflected the failure of civilian elites to carry out modernization in Latin America without raising the specter of social breakdown. Hence, the military often felt compelled to step into the void.[67]

Two questions remain: first, if corporatism deals with change by repeatedly expanding the number of corporate pillars on which the regime rests, what does the end product of that process look like? The answer is clear: It begins to look like Argentina in the 1960s and 1970s. In that country virtually all groups had by now taken their place in the corporate scheme of things, not just the socioeconomic groups mentioned so far but also journalists, actors, doctors, lawyers, moviemakers, business people, farmers, bureaucrats, the military, professionals of all kinds, women, domestics, religious bodies, *everyone*. Nearly everyone in the entire population was on the public payroll, enjoyed a state-sponsored entitlement, received a *verba* ("grant") from the state, or was a member of a corporate group tied into the state apparatus. The Argentine lawyer and scholar Jorge Bustamante, in his pathbreaking book on this phenomenon entitled *La República Corporativa* (The corporative republic),[68] contrasts such a polity with a liberal or pluralist one. Bustamante, who has worked at numerous levels of the Argentine government, not only documents the incorporation of all these groups into **279** the regime, the benefits they receive, and their cooptation by it, but also shows the sheer paralysis, gridlock, fragmentation, corruption, and ultimately breakdown that result. Mexico, Venezuela, and other corporatist regimes have followed this route. The final product of this tradition seems to be not a happy, functioning, efficient corporatist government but a deeply divided, inefficient, unhappy, and chaotic one. In this sense corporatism has a parallel with pluralism: when both these modern systems have too many groups involved, all crying for control and special privileges, the system becomes saturated, ungovernable, and unable to function. Only a sharp break with the past, a throwing off of all these corporatist barnacles from the past, seems capable of restoring efficient government dedicated genuinely to the public good and not just to myriad private interests.[69]

The second question involves neocorporatism. Neocorporatism is the term given to post–World War II European corporatism to describe the softer, more pluralist, more democratic and participatory "corporatism of association" or "societal corporatism" that replaced the earlier, fascistic "corporatism of the state." Will the same thing now occur in Latin America? That is, will a softer democratic corporatism now begin to replace the harder, authoritarian corporatism of the past? Three issues immediately come to mind. First, it is not known whether Latin America even now has the level of associational life and pluralist interest groups to support a genuinely democratic, European-like neocorporatism. Second, since corporatism in Latin America is so closely associated with earlier dictatorships and is now widely discredited, it remains to be seen if it can regain sufficient legitimacy and popularity to serve as the basis for a new type of regime. Third, an as-yet new form of pluralist, democratic, electoral, societal, and grass-roots corporatism must be devised that is nonetheless compatible with the long, powerful history of top-down, integralist and organic, and state-dominated corporatism as traced in this book. These unknowns are at the heart of the current debate and discussion about the transitions to democracy in Latin America.

Chapter 10

The Conflict Society, 1930s–1980s

To this point—that is, until roughly the 1930s—Latin American history and the Latin American political and ideological tradition had shown some remarkable continuities. Born of feudal, medieval, Thomistic, and neoscholastic Spain and Portugal, Latin America was a creature of and echoed the political culture and institutions of the two mother countries. Indeed, because of the added influence of the indigenous institutions and practices that were remarkably parallel to those of Iberia—corporatist, authoritarian, integral, hierarchical, theocratic—it could be said that Latin America was even more feudal and its medievalism more deeply entrenched than in Spain and Portugal themselves. The Spanish-Portuguese systems—here termed the Hapsburg Model—not only survived for three hundred years of colonial history but also continued virtually intact into the independence period.

The first cracks in this monolithic occurred in the eighteenth century when, under the impact of the Bourbon reforms and the Enlightenment, a split developed in the Latin American soul (or political culture) between the older scholastic and more modernist thinking. Then in the early nineteenth century a major disruption occurred under the impact of both independence and the importation of republican and liberal ideas; in the early to mid twentieth century another—though arguably lesser—disruption occurred as Marxism and its accompanying mass movements had their impact.

But through all these changes—and it attests to the remarkable durability of traditional institutions—the older structures and ways of behaving not only survived but thrived. Sometimes they simply suppressed the newer forces and ideas; at other times—usually simultaneously—the traditional groups and political process coopted the newer, rising groups into the political system. The traditional neoscholastic ideology exhibited a genius for continuously reinventing itself in the form of postindependence conservatism, positivism, arielismo, Hispanismo, and, most recently, corporatism; or else, as in the case of Rousseauian-style liberalism, it redefined itself to change superficially the outside appearances and surface aspects while keeping largely intact the persistent authoritarianism, elitism, or corporatism underneath. One may not like the resultant policies and the consistent lack of genuine democracy and egalitarianism; but as students of politics one has to admire the improvisations, flexibility, adaptability, remarkable survivability, and sheer genius that Latin American elites have shown in protecting their power structure, enabling it to survive and thrive well into the twentieth century.[1]

But in the 1930s—earlier in a few countries, later in a few others— all this began to break down. The world depression of 1929–30 was one major factor, undermining the economies of the area and, with them, their political systems as well. Between 1930 and 1934, fourteen of the twenty Latin American countries experienced revolution—not just the usual, comic-opera coups but fundamental changeovers.[2] By this time also the class structure was changing drastically, there were new and challenging ideologies and political movements out there that were not subject to the usual cooptation methods, and the legitimacy basis of the old order was increasingly undermined. Latin American elites tried to adapt in the usual fashion by adopting the ideology of corporatism, which promised a way of incorporating the rising working class; but those efforts were only partially successful, and the ostensibly corporatist regimes in Latin America of the 1930s and 1940s were never completely corporatist but consistently had to make compromises with liberal, democratic, and other forces.

Joseph Maier and Alfred Weatherhead refer accurately to the interwar period as the "Twilight of the Middle Ages" in Latin America.[3] What they mean is that feudalism and medievalism ended in Latin America not with the onset of independence and the expulsion of Spain and Portugal, but a full hundred years and more later with the mammoth economic, social, and political changes of the 1920s and 1930s. What followed medievalism was not a smooth transition to democracy and pluralism, however, but, to use Kalman H. Silvert's term, the emergence of a "conflict society" torn apart by tension and division.[4] The conflict society phenomenon lasted for the next fifty years in most countries—

beginning to change only in the 1980s and 1990s as more and more countries, finally, began the transition to democracy and more open markets.

The Living Museum

One element of the undermining of Latin America was the sheer proliferation of competing ideologies. By the 1930s and in the decades following, there were so many ideologies present in Latin America that they were almost unmanageable. No one of them had complete legitimacy any more; it was doubtful if in most countries any one of them could command a majority of support. Not only were there many ideologies, but they were so far apart that the gaps between them were all but unbridgeable. Hence, the use of the term "the conflict society" as the title of this chapter.

Closely related to this idea of a conflict society was the "living museum" concept. It was the University of Wisconsin political scientist Charles W. Anderson who in the 1960s coined this term.[5] According to Anderson, Latin America was a living museum of every political ideology that had ever been invented since the dawn of time. Moreover, all these ideologies, he argued, were still alive and well in one form or another in Latin America. In contrast to other countries and geographic/culture areas, which, as social and economic change occurred and societies went from feudalism to modernity, had discarded or sloughed off old and discredited ideologies, Latin America had adopted every ideology but never cast off any of them. That was because few countries in Latin America had ever experienced full-scale social and political revolutions like the British, French, and Russian revolutions that discarded one social class and its attendant ideologies and replaced them with another. In Latin America, through the tenacity of the neoscholastic tradition and the absence of revolutionary change, such discarding and replacement never occurred. Instead, each ideology managed to hang on with some degree of popular support, usually attenuated but never completely abandoned. Only in Mexico so far, in 1910–20, had there been full-scale social revolution that destroyed the old order and established a new one, but even there the older system gradually reasserted itself after the revolution.[6] The result was that Latin America remained a nonrevolutionary society in the sense of never experiencing full-scale social revolution, and it remained the home of every ideology conceivable going back to Greece, Rome, and the Bible.

283

Let us list all these ideologies here to convey an idea of their numbers, range, and approximate sequence:

The Ideologies of Latin America

Platonism
Aristotelianism
Christianity
Augustinianism
Thomism
Scholasticism
Theocracy
Neoscholasticism
Feudalism
Pantheism
Hapsburgism
Traditionalism
Republicanism
Conservatism
Liberalism
Idealism
Utilitarianism
Krausism
Positivism
Capitalism
Spiritualism
Arielism
Nationalism
Hispanismo
Marxism
Anarchism
Syndicalism
Anarcho-syndicalism
Socialism
Communism
    Russian
    Chinese
Social Democracy
Corporatism
Fascism
Christian Democracy
Fidelismo
Liberation Theology
Democracy
Pluralism
Neoliberalism
Neocorporatism

Forty-some ideologies! Plus there were numerous factions, subfactions, and variations of these main movements. They stretch back to the very beginning of recorded history. They include both the ideologies of the long course of Western history and the indigenous belief system native to Latin America, with which they are merged. Moreover, it is certain that some ideologies and movements have inadvertently been left off the list; other students will doubtless come up with other "-isms" not included here. Now, obviously some of these ideologies enjoyed more popularity and lasted longer than others. But the sheer number of ideologies present in Latin America over the course of history is remarkable.

It was not just the numbers of ideologies that added to the phenomenon of the conflict society, however, but the wide gaps between them as well. Look again at the list: here are scholasticism and medievalism, liberalism and republicanism, and Marxism and socialism. These are not just widely separated ideologies but they also pertain to distinct historical epochs: feudalism, capitalism, and socialism or social democracy. In much of the West these historical epochs largely followed or superseded each other or both. But in Latin America, again in the absence of a genuinely revolutionary tradition that would undermine and destroy one epoch and then move on to the next, these various historical epochs continued to coexist, side by side, the one never entirely replacing or supplanting the other. Feudalism, capitalism, and more recently socialism and social democracy continued to coexist as parallel pillars of society, but one never fully replaced the other. That remains true to this day: the most modern cities and societies continue to live cheek by jowl with the most traditional and backward institutions. Unable historically ever to slough off its past completely, Latin America remains a living museum not just of all Western and some non-Western ideologies but also of sociopolitical forms pertaining to distinct epochs that have never quite disappeared either.

The Latin American Political Process

Some writers have doubted that there is a Latin American political system or political process. Their argument is that Latin American politics are so chaotic, disorganized, and coup-prone that they defy all system or organized process.

Others respond, however, that even coups, revolutions, and violence often have a systemic character to them; that these are not wholly ran-

dom events but occur regularly, even predictably, within a political process; that the political process is clearly more violent and chaotic than
is the case of politics in the United States, but even chaos can have a pattern to it; and violence, we now more clearly understand, is not always
just mindless and random but is often used rationally by various groups
to put pressure on the system and get from it what they want. Just because a political process and system are violent and chaotic does not
mean there are no regularities, no *system,* in them. Indeed, as Silvert re-
minded us, violence and revolution may be among the most predictable, regular, and systemic aspects of the Latin American political process.[7] It may not be the preferred system of the United States, but of its
systemic, regular patterns and processes there can be no doubt.

Building on Silvert's arguments, Anderson has posited probably the
most elaborate model of the Latin American political process and system.[8] He begins with a number of observable, empirical facts, among
them the following:

1. Latin American politics is more informal and less well institutionalized than in the United States.
2. Violence, coups, and revolutions are an integral part of that political process.
3. The armed forces, not necessarily always subordinate to civilian
   authority, are also part and parcel of that political process.
4. The political system operates in general within a political culture that is, or was, strongly shaped by such Catholic political
   assumptions as the supremacy of God and his authority, the organic and integral nature of society, mutual obligation and rec-
   iprocity, and the necessity of pursuing the public good.
5. Society consists of a variety of what Anderson calls "power
   contenders," or what I have here called corporate groups: the
   Church, the military, the oligarchy, trade unions, peasants, students and intellectuals, professional associations, autarchies,
   the bureaucracy.
6. These groups revolve around and try to capture the central
   state, from which jobs, favors, patronage, and benefits all flow.
7. These efforts often involve elaborate competition between and
   coalition building among the several groups involved; and the
   efforts to control or capture the state may involve elections but
   may also include other means (coups, revolutions) of gaining
   power.
8. Patronage at all levels is the "grease" that makes the system
   work.

These facts depict a very informal, sometimes violent, often disrupted political process in which alliances of political groups seek to capture the seats of wealth and power through a variety of means. As Anderson elaborates, elections are not the only legitimate route to power in these systems, for regimes that come to power through non-democratic means can also acquire legitimacy through the public policies they carry out—that is, by governing for and in the name of the public good (again, a Thomistic and then Rousseauian conception). In keeping with the medieval tradition analyzed earlier, a regime that respects the corporate group rights of its subjects may also be said to be democratic—in that distinctive Iberian and Latin American sense of the term—even if it is not necessarily democratically elected. It is in this sense that Mexico has always claimed its political system is democratic because, even though there was only one party and it never lost the manipulated elections that Mexico had, that party was corporately organized and, therefore, representative of the main groups in society and democratic in the Thomistic-Suárezian sense.

Originally, in the nineteenth century, only three main groups were part of the Latin American political process: the Church, the army, and the oligarchy. But as the economy grew and society changed, new groups began to clamor to become a part of the political system: business and commercial elements, the middle class, trade unions, peasants, eventually women, domestics, and indigenous people. Anderson indicates that two conditions had to be fulfilled before a group could be admitted to the political system. First, it had to demonstrate a "power capability" sufficient to be taken seriously as a potential threat to the system by other groups in it. That meant, for example, that in their early years of existence, such weak organizations as labor, peasants, and the indigenous could be and often were suppressed; only when they achieved sufficient numbers and organizational strength to be taken seriously as a potential threat would mechanisms (a new labor ministry, social welfare ministry, or indigenous rights ministry) be put in place to absorb or coopt these groups into the system. And second, as a condition of being granted recognition (that all-important "juridical personality") and admitted into the regime's benefits, the group had to give up any wishes it might have had of destroying the more traditional groups and capturing the entire system for itself. That helps explain, for example, why in the 1930s and 1940s compliant and cooperative labor groups

were granted recognition and given benefits while more radical Marxist and Communist groups continued to be suppressed. To be accepted
into the system, in other words, the new group had to give up any ex-
tremist or revolutionary pretensions and accept the rules of the game
as given.[9]

Anderson goes on to describe this as a virtually continuous fusion–
absorption process. At first, in the late nineteenth and early twentieth
centuries, using the legitimacy given to them by the positivist philosophy of order, progress, and industry, the new business, commercial,
industrial, and importer-exporter groups were admitted to the system,
tying together older landed and oligarchic wealth with the new-rich
business wealth. Then in the teens and 1920s, in advanced countries
like Argentina and Chile, it became the turn of the middle class to be
absorbed in this way. In these two countries the agency of this absorption was recognition by the elite power structure of the newly created
Radical parties that served as the avenue for upward middle-class mobility. In other, less-developed, less-institutionalized, and not very democratic countries like the Dominican Republic and Nicaragua it was
often the national guard or the army that served as the upward trans-
mission belt for aspiring, ambitious middle-class (and usually mestizo
or mulatto) elements.[10]

By the 1930s, 1940s, and into the post–World War II period, it had
become the turn of the working class. This was a more difficult process
than had been the admission of the previous groups because (1) there
were larger numbers of people involved—mass politics—and, hence, the
issue was complicated, and (2) the labor groups were often organized
on a Marxist, anarcho-syndicalist, or communist basis that implied total
change, total revolution, and thus violated the rules of the game described earlier. That is, in the last analysis, what the ideology of corporatism was meant to do. For corporatism promised a system of class harmony rather than the dreaded Marxian class conflict and a way of
dealing with the social question in a peaceful, orderly, nonrevolutionary way. It offered a convenient way to defuse the supposed Bolshevik
threat by bringing organized labor into the political system but not
thereby implying revolutionary change. Hence, the writing during this
period of elaborate labor codes and new social welfare programs designed to give benefits to organized workers in return for labor's giving
up its revolutionary pretensions. Hence, also, the creation of official,
government-controlled trade unions in many countries to serve this

purpose or else the cooptation of more conservative, less-militant labor groups into the system. Meantime, the more radical, Marxist unions continued to be suppressed.

By the 1960s had come the time for peasants and peasant associations to be coopted in this way; hence, the initiation of agrarian reform and other programs for farmers, not so much to actually redistribute land but, in the traditional way, to absorb peasants into the system and give them limited recognition and benefits as a way of defusing potential rural-based revolution.* For the Latin American elites managing these increasingly complex systems, Cuba and its peasant-based revolution became an example to avoid; thus the plans to coopt peasant movements by, once again, bringing in and buying off the more compliant peasant leagues and isolating and repressing the others. Beginning in the 1970s and continuing to the present, it became the turn of women, domestics, and indigenous groups to be absorbed, coopted, and often bought off in this way (themes discussed in chapter 11).

These comments imply that, within the limits mentioned, the Latin American political systems have been more flexible, adaptable, and accommodating than they are often given credit for. Rather than standing against all change, they have in fact bent to change, absorbed new groups into the prevailing system, and initiated a variety of new reform programs. But these have been changes within a corporatist framework, not always or necessarily a liberal or pluralist one. The groups that have been absorbed or coopted have consistently been the most compliant ones, or else the regime has created its own official labor unions and peasant associations, meanwhile repressing more radical and threatening groups. This is limited, controlled, or official pluralism, not the unfettered, free-wheeling, chaotic, almost anarchic pluralism of U.S.-style democracy.[11]

In addition, while some limited, controlled change has gone forward under this system, much has remained the same:[12]

1. The system is still top-down, hierarchical, and often authoritarian.
2. The system is still controlled in its essentials by the elites, who have usually been smart enough to recognize that if things and

*Conveniently, enacting an agrarian reform program also enabled Latin American countries to qualify for U.S. Alliance for Progress assistance. Hence, the Latin American countries adopted agrarian reform programs, got the assistance money, used these to defuse the peasant threat, but seldom redistributed much land.

the system they control are to remain the same, then some modest changes are necessary.

3. It is still a bureaucratic and state-centered system in which the state, controlled by the elites, regulates and licenses the admission of acceptable new groups into the system, while excluding others.

4. The system remains corporatist rather than genuinely liberal and pluralist; there are often still severe restrictions and limits on activity by political party and interest group and on spontaneous movements of any kind.

5. The system remains pyramidal. The pyramid has been broadened somewhat to include the newly created corporate sectors; it is "representative," "participatory," and "democratic" only in this quite restrictive sense. The mass of the population is still largely excluded from full, genuine democratic participation, except perhaps at election time.

6. Patronage rather than merit or genuine democracy remains the lubricant of the entire system.

It is striking how closely this system—and it is a system—resembles and is a continuation of the historic systems discussed in earlier chapters. The system is still based on the notion of government serving the common good, from Thomas Aquinas and the Christian tradition. It is still authoritarian, hierarchical, and top-down but also usually limited by custom and corporate group rights as in the Hispanic and Suárezian tradition. It is statist, centralized, pyramidal, and bureaucratic—from the Hapsburg model. It incorporates a more republican and liberal orientation but from the centralist and organic tradition and Rousseau, not Locke, and a progressive, modernizing, and developmentalist spirit from Comte and positivism. It absorbs all the elements from corporatism and borrows strongly from Arielism and Hispanism. But it has almost nothing—until recently—from Madison, Jefferson, or John Stuart Mill. It is based on patronage, mutual obligation, the tradition of "the gift" rather than on impersonal democracy.

This Andersonian/cooptive/corporatist model worked tolerably well for a long time. As long as there were only three, four, or five (Church, army, oligarchy, business class, middle class) groups involved, the system could function more or less effectively and at the same time absorb new elements into itself. But when it came the turn of the trade unions, in which the numbers were far larger and the groups often organized on a Marxian and revolutionary basis considered illegitimate by the rest of the society, trouble for the system began to grow, as evidenced by the tremendous instability of the 1930s. Trouble again brewed in the 1960s (and for the same reasons) when the peasants grew restive and the winds of revolution were in the air, and when in the less-developed countries of Latin America the labor movement emerged tardily onto the scene. In some of these countries—the Dominican Republic, El Salvador, Guatemala, Bolivia, Peru, eventually Nicaragua—restive trade unions and peasant leagues, instead of emerging in sequence—which the system could probably have handled—exploded onto the political scene at the same time, provoking crises and sometimes national breakdowns into violence, repression, conflict, and endemic civil war.[13]

A further problem with this system—and at the heart of the theme of this chapter—was the sheer numbers of groups involved. When the number that needed to be satisfied swelled to ten or more—including now groups based on widely disparate assumptions and beliefs—the system started to get out of hand, fragmented, unmanageable. And when as in Argentina—the most advanced country—or perhaps Venezuela, virtually everyone was a member of one resource-sucking entitlement group or another—what Bustamante called "the corporative republic"[14]—the system began to break down altogether. It became an "invertebrate society,"[15] one in which every group is out for its own advantage, the common good is subordinated, and ungovernability sets in. The end product of a corporatist polity, therefore, is not ordinarily a happy system based on class and group harmony and collaboration but conflict, guerrilla terrorism, right-wing counterviolence, and societal collapse. As the most developed country in Latin America, Argentina provided probably the model of what the rest of the continent would come to look like; but if Argentine history from the 1930s to the 1980s, with its frequent breakdowns, near-fascism, morbific politics, and quasi–civil war, represented the wave of the future, it was not a very attractive picture at all.[16]

One other feature of this Latin American system is how dependent it is on perpetual economic growth. For in order continuously to absorb and in effect buy off ever more groups in the system and keep them contented with patronage, programs, and spoils, a constantly expanding economic pie is needed. There always have to be more and more pieces of the pie to hand out to more and more groups, more and more benefits to keep all the players content. For in this type of system, with its weak institutions whose legitimacy is precarious, with its few political or economic reserves, and with little in the way of social safety nets, even the slightest economic downturn can turn the political process into a zero-sum game and wreak havoc on the entire system. So if the economy becomes stagnant or, worse, begins to contract, then the political system will be quickly in trouble as well. That is precisely what happened in the 1930s depression, in the 1960s crisis of import substitution industrialization (ISI), and in the 1980s debt crisis. In each of these periods, economic downturns led quickly not just to political instability (although that, too) but often to wholesale systemic breakdowns. And when economic crisis was combined with a group-saturated, gridlocked, and hence ungovernable political system (as in Argentina, Chile, Uruguay, Brazil, Peru, Venezuela, and eventually Mexico, to say nothing of the smaller, less-developed countries), it was a formula for bad trouble indeed.

Crisis of "the System"

Other crises began to afflict the system. (Again, the focus here is the large sweep of history, from the 1930s on into the postwar period.) First was the decline of religion and religious sentiment in Latin America and—the opposite side of that coin—increasing indifference and secularism. As urbanization and industrialization proceeded, religion—as in other countries—became less important. Latin America remained nominally Catholic, but figures indicated that only 10 to 15 percent of Catholics actively practiced their religion. In addition, the numbers for Catholic orders, vocations, charity, education, hospitals, social services, and so forth were all down. There was a severe shortage of priests and nuns; foreign-born clergy came to outnumber native-born by ratios of four or five to one. The Church was facing an institutional crisis of major dimensions.[17]

The downturn in religious observance had a profound effect on the social and political systems of Latin America, which had for so long been grounded on Catholic and Christian principles. With the decline of religious sentiment, the whole basis of political society began to erode—including the support for corporatist and Christian-democratic solutions. Indeed, one could say that the entire Catholic and corporatist revival of the 1920s and 1930s was a sign not of a strong Church, but of a weak Church trying desperately to hang onto its communicants and to bring lapsed believers back into the fold. In any case, the rise of secularism and eventually Protestantism and other beliefs in twentieth-century Latin America had the long-range effect of gradually un-dermining the influence of the Catholic beliefs and theology that had long undergirded the society and polity. By the 1960s, in response to the crisis, the Church itself began to change, abandoning the Thomis-tic hierarchy and injunctions and moving in reformist directions—this turn only added to Latin America's legitimacy crisis.

Second and related were broad-scale, political-cultural changes. The old idea of a God-given hierarchy among persons, of natural human in-equalities , became less and less acceptable. Some of the old fatalism re-mained, of course, but increasingly in a more secular society the case cannot be justified that poverty is good for the soul or that children should be malnourished, diseased, or with bloated bellies because God or Saint Thomas had willed it that way. Increasingly, ideas of democ-racy, egalitarianism, social justice, and individual rights (as distinct from corporate group rights) began to infuse Latin America. The no-tions that one had to accept one's station in life and that the social order was immutable were no longer acceptable. The rise of evangeli-cal Protestantism also played a major role in changing the older fatal-istic ethos to one in which men and women increasingly took charge of their own lives. As these ideas and political-cultural changes spread, so ultimately would the social and political system that rested upon them have to change.[18]

A third change was ushered in with modern transportation and communications. New highway systems, new farm-to-market roads, radio, television, the Peace Corps, political party and other prosely-tizers (including new Protestant missionaries), vcr's, satellites, cell phones, electronic money transfers—all combined to break down tra-ditional attitudes and isolation and the traditional loyalty to the patria chica and to instill a new consciousness of the larger, better, brighter, outside world. It is almost impossible to go anywhere in Latin America today without coming across satellite television. And the shows being watched—*Dallas, Melrose Place, Beverly Hills 90210, Friends*—are both enor-mously popular and enormously subversive of a traditional lifestyle. In-creasingly, it is blue jeans, Coca-Cola, rock music, consumerism, and the values that go with them—not least democracy and human rights—that form the core values of society, and no longer the austere, very con-servative, Augustinian and Thomistic values of medieval Catholicism. In addition, the Peace Corps teaches grassroots involvement and pres-sure-group tactics, the Maryknoll Order instills New England–style, town-meeting government, and liberation theology brings Marxism into the national cathedral; and all these values and ideas are tremendously subversive of the old order.

A fourth area of change was economic. Between 1960 and 1990 the per capita income of many Latin American countries quadrupled. There was still immense poverty, to be sure, but more and more people were making a comfortable living wage. There remained vast socioeconomic gaps and inequality, but the middle class was growing, and some of the new wealth even trickled down. A portion of the wealth came through foreign aid; some was generated domestically; some came from the remittances of Latin Americans living abroad; some came from foreign investment. There was a general economic quickening, greater affluence, major construction projects that put people to work, and greater dynamism and *movimiento* (movement) in the economy. Even in the debt crisis of the 1980s (the lost decade), economic growth continued in many countries and then accelerated again in the 1990s. All these economic changes not only altered profoundly the face of Latin America but also integrated the region more closely into the world economy.[19]

A fifth area of massive change, stimulated by economic growth, occurred in the social order. An older two-class system began to give way to a multiclass and even semipluralist one. Of course, these changes had been occurring gradually before, but now, driven by economic growth and massive urbanization, they accelerated. A static, pyramidal, and closed society began to be replaced by an open, more dynamic one. A "sleepy" and largely illiterate rural society became a lively, mobilized, literate, and urban one. New classes—urban labor, organized peasants, the middle class, business, women, indigenous elements—emerged and began to demand their rights.

At the same time there were increased divisions in the older, traditional wielders of power: the Church, the military, and the elites. Younger military officers were often more reformist and nationalistic than their senior officers, and the officer corps split along other factional lines as well. Similarly in the Church: clerics came no longer from the upper but the middle class, and many were foreign born; the old alliance between the Church and the oligarchy was no longer assured. The elites were also divided: agricultural versus business interests; criollos versus foreign-born ethnic communities (Italian, Spanish, German, Arab, Jewish, American); younger, better-educated elements versus the older standpat paternalists. Meanwhile, among the newer so- cial groups, laborers, peasants, and others were genuinely liberal, socialist, and independent and not just corporately organized under state control.

The corporatist ideology and political system described earlier was largely designed for—and was the product of—an earlier, slower, more traditional, rural, Catholic, and more static, pre-1930s society.[20] Corporatism in its more traditional, statist, and authoritarian forms might have worked in this context. But by the 1990s Latin America was 70 percent urban compared to 70 percent rural only four decades earlier. It was 70 percent literate compared to 70 percent illiterate in the 1950s. Economically, Latin America was much more developed and dynamic by the 1990s than it had been in the 1950s; socially, with new escalators of upward mobility, it was also far more pluralistic than in earlier decades; and in the political realm there were new, dynamic political parties, labor movements, technocratic elites, and so forth. In other words, the type of corporatist, closed, top-down political system that had served Latin America not entirely inappropriately in earlier centuries was no longer appropriate in the changed, more dynamic circumstances of the modern age. Either corporatism would need to be scrapped and a new political system put in its place, or else corporatism itself would need to be radically transformed (perhaps in neo-corporatist fashion)[21] to bring it into accord with the changed circumstances.*

A new society was emerging in Latin America and at the same time the pillars of the old were crumbling: not only the main institutions of the old society—Church, army, oligarchy—but its values and political culture as well. The older values of strict hierarchy, rank, order, and discipline would no longer serve in the changed circumstances of modernity. Peasants and others are no longer willing to accept their miserable station in life. Patronage may still oil the machinery of government but by itself it is no longer adequate in a context in which people want real programs, such as jobs, health care, education, water supplies, electrification—or else, the "or else" meaning popular with-

---

*It may be there are parallels here with Marxism-Leninism; perhaps it is no accident that both of these overly rigid, bureaucratic, and unresponsive systems—authoritarianism-corporatism on the one hand and Marxism-Leninism on the other—collapsed at about the same time.

drawal of support for a regime that fails to provide such programs. In other words, the old "subject" and "parochial" political cultures that Gabriel Almond and Sidney Verba found in Latin America four decades ago are now giving way to a more participatory, even nascently democratic political culture.[22] So, is Latin America still more authoritarian, more hierarchical, more inherently corporatist than Western Europe and the United States? It probably is—but certainly the differences are less clear-cut and the lines between them more blurred than in previous decades.

Finally, there were changes in the international order. No longer could Latin America live in isolation from neighboring countries and the outside world, as it had for the previous 450 years. The small, closed, withdrawn world of the patria chica was breaking down; at the same time, the Cold War, the World Bank, the International Monetary Fund (IMF), radio and television, the Peace Corps, U.S. embassy programs, world market forces, the OAS and the United Nations, the Soviets and their Cuban "advance troops," the European countries, and others were all having their impact on Latin America. So did globalization. All these forces helped bring Latin America into the modern, interdependent world really for the first time. And with all these new international influences operating, the stature and legitimacy of the old values and institutions were being continuously subverted.

And yet, none of these changes was ever complete. As in other developing nations,[23] traditional institutions remained strong. It was not, contrary to both the Marxian and Weberian paradigms, that modernity definitively replaced or supplanted traditionalism. Rather, the two existed side by side, as two parallel power structures, seldom fully merging but always interacting, with the relations between them constantly being renegotiated and with new ad hoc coalitions constantly coming into existence. But isn't that precisely how Anderson described the traditional or criollo ("native" or "home grown") Latin American political process, with new groups constantly being appended but old ones seldom being sloughed off? Only in Mexico and Cuba and to a lesser extent Bolivia and Nicaragua have there by now been full-scale social revolutions in Latin America that resulted in discarding of the old society and the old power contenders—and in at least three of these the older society has since staged a major comeback. So maybe the Andersonian or corporatist model is not obsolete after all.

Paralysis, Gridlock, Breakdown

By the late 1950s and early 1960s, Latin America's traditional society
and the political model that went with it were clearly in decline. "Decline," however, not full disintegration or breakdown. At the same time,
the newer forces associated with a more liberal, pluralist, democratic,
and socially just society were emerging but were not yet fully institutionalized or consolidated. In some ways Latin America has the worst
of all possible situations: a traditional society fading and being increasingly challenged, while the new one is still inchoate, still insufficiently strong to take its place. The result in most countries was conflict, paralysis, accelerating tension and violence, and often gridlock
and national breakdown into chaos and even civil war. Latin America in
the 1960s with its invertebrate, polarized, and conflict society was like
Spain in the 1930s just before it too broke down into full-scale civil war.

The Dominican Republic is one paradigm case. There, a bloody, authoritarian dictator, Rafael Trujillo, had been in power for thirty-one
years, 1930–61. Trujillo helped develop his country and its economy,
but he also used dictatorial controls and a corporatist state to control
all groups in society.[24] Following his assassination, a democratic opening occurred in the early 1960s. A reformist, left-of-center government
under Juan Bosch was democratically elected in 1962. Bosch attempted
to bring the Dominican Republic's traditionally forgotten elements—
peasants, workers, the poor—into politics for the first time. But that
earned him the unmitigated hostility of the traditional groups, the
Church, the armed forces, and the business elite, who ganged up to oust
Bosch in a coup d'etat after only seven months in office.

A repressive military regime and then a repressive civilian one succeeded Bosch during 1963–65. As the Bosch forces plotted a comeback
and launched a military-civilian rebellion to restore constitutionalism,
the forces of reaction also mobilized and the country broke down into
chaos, violence, and civil war. The United States militarily intervened
and occupied the country, leaving only after the conservative Trujillo
puppet Joaquín Balaquer was installed in the National Palace. Meanwhile, the polarization, conflict, and sporadic violence continued.[25]
The Dominican pattern, though not quite so dramatically, was repeated
in Honduras with the overthrow of the democratically elected Ramón
Villeda Morales and his replacement by a military-authoritarian regime. **297**

In Brazil the picture was similar—but on a much larger canvas. After the Vargas dictatorship, Brazil in the late 1940s and 1950s had embarked on a more democratic course while retaining many corporatist forms and institutions. But in the early 1960s under, first, Janio Quadros and then João Goulart, Brazil's democracy looked shakier and less stable. Labor strikes were threatening to disable the economy and perhaps bring down the political system, rural peasants were seizing private land apparently with government acquiescence, and the last straw was the government's apparent encouragement of younger military men to rebel against their senior officers. Faced with rising violence, conflict, and endemic civil war, the Brazilian armed forces intervened in 1964 determined to set Brazil on a new and reformed track that included discipline, order, and authoritarianism. Military rule proved little or no better than civilian, and eventually the armed forces were obliged to return to the barracks but not before occupying power for twenty years and compiling a deplorable human rights record.[26]

In the three so-called crisis countries of Central America—El Salvador, Guatemala, and Nicaragua—parallel developments occurred. In El Salvador a centrist, moderate, and nationalist military regime under Julio Rivera in the 1960s actually carried out some positive reforms but gave way in the early 1970s to a brutal, repressive military regime whose numerous human rights abuses paved the way for the guerrilla uprising and full-scale civil war of the later 1970s and 1980s. In Guatemala in the 1960s, more or less centrist military and civilian regimes were similarly replaced in the early 1970s by a brutal, extreme right-wing government that terrorized the people and polarized the country. And in Nicaragua, the moderate successors in the 1960s of the old dictator Anastasio Somoza, the puppet René Schick and Somoza's first son, Luís, yielded to the brutal second son, Anastasio Jr., whose repressive, corrupt tactics in the 1970s paved the way for the Sandinista revolution. The parallels in the three cases are remarkable: a moderate regime gives way to an extreme right-wing one whose policies polarize the country, provoke immense conflict and even civil war, and eventually draw the United States into the conflict.[27]

In the Andean countries the dynamics involved appear to be quite varied, but in fact there are some fascinating parallel causes and outcomes. In Colombia the level of violence and political conflict in the 1950s became so intense that the two major parties signed a corporatist-like pact agreeing to alternate in power and to share the spoils and patronage of the system—an interesting variation on the theme of organic unity and integralism but one that did not prevent Colombia from degenerating still further into violence, narco-trafficking, and national paralysis and conflict.[28] Venezuela also continued as a two-party and generally democratic system during the 1960s and 1970s, but there the main corporate groups were absorbed as sectoral organizations into the parties, monopolizing whole ministries and programs, siphoning off funds, accelerating corruption, and helping produce the crisis that is Venezuelan politics today.[29] In Peru a succession of ineffectual civilian and military governments gave way in 1968 to a reformist and nationalist military regime that was self-consciously corporatist, determined to root out the older "criollo politics" but, after a vigorous and hopeful start, failed to solve any of Peru's massive, endemic problems any more effectively than had its predecessors.[30] Ecuador under the five presidencies of José María Velasco Ibarra experimented on and off with a kind of corporatist populism, but neither that nor any other type regime prevented the country from sliding into repeated instability and becoming one of the most corrupt governments in the world.

Two countries, Bolivia and Mexico, attempted to solve the problems of a conflicted, disintegrated polity by creating all-inclusive, corporately organized, single-party regimes. In Bolivia, following decades of violence culminating in the revolution of 1952, the MNR came to power. The MNR revolution destroyed the old landowning, mining (tin), and aristocratic class and substituted a dominant, single-party regime that was itself organized along corporate lines but included left-wing groups rather than right-wing ones: organized labor (especially the miners), peasants, and students. This solution to solving Bolivia's long-term problems of poverty, violence, and fragmentation worked no better than others: the MNR soon split, it proved corrupt, the military came back into power, narco-trafficking became all-pervasive, and the country continued to fragment.

The Mexican case is at least as interesting. As noted earlier, in 1928, following the Mexican Revolution, President Calles attempted to stabilize the country by creating a single-party system. Originally called the National Revolutionary Party (PRN) and later rebaptized as the Institutional Revolutionary Party (PRI), the party contained corporate sectors for all the major, postrevolutionary groups: the military (later dropped from the party's organizational structure), the trade unions, peasants, and the popular (a catchall category) sector. For several decades the PRI

provided political stability and a climate in which the Mexican economy could flourish. But in the 1960s, as in the other Latin American
countries, the system began to pull apart, and cracks appeared in the
once-monolithic arrangement. The massacre of students by the military in Tlatelolco Square, the violent swinging of the political pendulum between left and right, economic and debt crises (it was Mexico's
announcement that it could not pay its debts that triggered the great
Third World debt crisis of the 1980s), the emergence of new political
parties on the left and right that broke the PRI's monopoly on political
office, and widespread corruption and drug trafficking were all signs
of Mexico's spiraling crisis.[31]

The key tests, however, were in the Southern Cone because these
were thought to be the most developed and modern of the Latin American countries. Seemingly paradoxically, they were also the countries
that came closest to a system of fragmentation, paralysis, and breakdown. The paradox is resolved if one recognizes that development in
the Latin American tradition of thought and of the historic model of
continuously adding new corporate groups and power contenders tends
not to happy, peaceful pluralism and democracy but instead to invertebrate societies, crises, gridlock, and civil conflict.

First, Uruguay. For a long time Uruguay had a reputation as the most
democratic and socially just country in Latin America. Under the able
and charismatic leadership of José Batlle y Ordoñez early in the twentieth century, Uruguay moved toward not only what appeared to be a
stable, democratic, two-party system but also such advanced social welfare programs that it was called "the Switzerland of Latin America."[32]
But then cracks began to appear in this happy picture: the two main
parties subdivided into various factions that effectively made Uruguay
a multiparty system; political sclerosis set in; declining prices for Uruguay's exports caused the bottom to drop out of the economy; the country's elaborate social welfare program could not be paid for anymore;
discontent spread, and an urban guerrilla movement (the Tupamaros)
was launched; and the democratic, civilian political system began to
wobble. Between 1969 and 1973 a "creeping coup" gradually stripped
the elected president of his authority, and in 1973 the military, which
had little history of political involvement in Uruguayan politics but
was always a major corporate actor, seized power, instigated a regime
of repression, and stayed in power for the next twelve years.[33]

In Chile, another of the most developed and sophisticated of the Latin American countries, the divisions, fragmentation, and class conflict leading to paralysis and crisis were again present, this time in extreme forms. Chile had had a strong democratic tradition for many years, but it also had an organic and corporatist one that is often obscured by democratic appearances and is seldom acknowledged by outside scholars or the Chileans themselves. By the 1960s Chile had developed a European-like multiparty system that consisted of two parties on the right (Liberals and Conservatives joined as the National Party), two in the center (Radicals and Christian Democrats), and two on the left (Socialists and Communists). The right, center, and left blocs each were able to control, with obvious fluctuations between elections, approximately one-third of the popular vote. Not only were the party divisions deep but each of these divisions represented wholly different visions of society and even of distinct historical epochs: the right symbolized feudalism and an older aristocratic and corporatist society; the center represented the middle class and an early twentieth-century liberal society; the left stood for socialism in its two main forms.[34]

The divisions between these groups and the eras they represented were so deep as to be all but uncompromisable. And with each bloc able to garner only 30–35 percent of the vote in each election, the result was weak, minority presidents, absence of majoritarian legitimacy, and spreading paralysis. The culmination of these trends was the election of 1970, in which the Socialist-Communist candidate, Salvador Allende, won the presidency with only 36 percent of the popular vote. The United States tried unsuccessfully to prevent Allende from taking office; nevertheless, as a minority president he had a limited political base and the hostility of both the right and center. Faced with mounting turmoil, violence, chaos, and gridlock, the Chilean armed forces led by Augusto Pinochet intervened in 1973 to overthrow Allende. Given the corporatist (albeit often disguised) background of the Chilean right and the military, the military coup is not surprising; what was shocking was the behavior of the armed forces after the coup: the killing of fifteen to twenty thousand persons, and gross violations of human rights.[35]

Argentina, the most modern of the Latin American countries, is also for that very reason the most paradigmatic in terms of the argument made here. Here is a very wealthy, highly sophisticated, highly literate, highly differentiated society with a large number of interest associations. Yet, for precisely those reasons, Argentina is the most prone to fragmentation and crisis. The process began, reflecting Argentina's developed status, earlier than in the other Latin American countries, in the 1930s, after the breakdown of the older aristocratic society in the 1929–30 world market crash. There followed in the 1930s and early 1940s a succession of military, unstable civilian, even quasi-fascist regimes. Next came Juan Perón, 1946–55, representing a combination of corporatist, authoritarian, and populist tendencies. Perón was overthrown by the military in 1955, but his legacy lived on: whenever the mass-based Peronista Party showed signs of an electoral revival, as in 1962 and 1966, the elections were canceled and the civilian government that administered the election was immediately overthrown. A modern, advanced country like Argentina cannot continue to exist on the basis of excluding 50 percent of the population—the Peronistas—from having a role in the political process. In 1973 as a way out of this predicament Perón himself was allowed to return to power as elected president, but he died shortly thereafter and an incompetent vice president, Isabel Perón (Juan's wife), was unable to hold the country together, precipitating another military coup in 1976 that ushered in Argentina's "dirty war" against the left and all opposition.[36]

In the meantime, what Jorge Bustamente calls the "corporatization" of Argentine sociopolitical life was going forward.[37] By this he means no longer the corporatism of the 1930s but the tremendous proliferation of corporative interest groups and their latching on like bloodsuckers to the Argentine political process, leeching its funds and policy programs for their private purposes. Virtually every social group in Argentina was now organized and incorporated into the government system of entitlements, benefits, and patronage. These included not just the usual corporative business and labor groups but also journalists, filmmakers, the Church, the armed forces, government workers, the middle class, ranchers, professional associations, everyone. Every group had an entitlement or special access of one sort or another—often several.

The system was so drained of resources that almost nothing was left for development, reinvestment, or actual public programs. Corruption, featherbedding, and patronage (including whole public programs and even ministries) had gone beyond the pale. Moreover, each political party had a set of corporatized core groups associated with it—one for every sector of society—thus adding further to the fragmentation. There was little attachment to a central core of values or to the nation itself; rather, all groups were spinning off in their own separate orbits. Argentina was disintegrating as a society. It was the classic case, explored theoretically by Mancur Olson, of a society so saturated with private-regarding interest groups that the nation was both bankrupt financially and stalemated politically.[38] It was Argentina that Silvert had in mind when he coined the title of his famous book, *The Conflict Society*.

As the most developed, most modern country in Latin America, Argentina is automatically thought of as leading the way, as pointing toward the future for the other countries. To rephrase the student chant of the 1960s, when Ché Guevara launched his ill-fated guerrilla campaign there, the future lies not in Bolivia but in Argentina. But that "future" seemed to imply a fragmented, invertebrate, corporatized, corrupt, bankrupt, disintegrated regime prone to conflict and on the verge of civil war like Spain (1931–36) and Portugal (1974–76).

In the Argentine case—and presumably for all of Latin America, including neighboring Mexico, which is just now transitioning away from its long-standing corporatized polity—development and modernization pointed not toward pluralism, liberalism, and social justice but toward chaos, conflict, mutual hatred, and social and political breakdown. If that is the future of Latin America, if that is the end product of the long, assimilative process and tradition we have been describing in this book, then Latin America is in even worse shape than it seems. And so is U.S. foreign policy, which has long been based on the liberal American assumption that development leads to democracy, pluralism, and social justice, not to breakdown and civil war. Yet from the vantage point of the 1960s and early 1970s, it was precisely this latter scenario that Latin America—with Argentina, Chile, and Uruguay leading the way—was pointing toward.[39] Whatever of the now-familiar metaphors is used—the "conflict society," "morbific politics," "sclerosis," "invertebrate society," "gridlock"—Latin America seemed to be in very deep trouble during this period and with no way out. Democracy and genuine liberalism seemed unattainable, Marxism-Leninism was unacceptable, and the older corporatist paradigm had either already failed or pointed to a dead end of conflict and ungovernability.

The Collapse into Authoritarianism

During the 1960s and early 1970s a wave of authoritarianism swept over Latin America. In country after country military dictatorships seized power from elected civilian governments. This was, of course, the forerunner and setting for the reverse "third wave" of democratization that would occur in the 1980s and is analyzed in Samuel P. Huntington's book by that title.[40] By the mid-1970s fourteen of the twenty republics were under direct military rule. In three others—Cuba, Mexico, and the Dominican Republic—civilians were in power, but it would be hard to characterize any of these three regimes as democratic; in fact, the military constituted part of the backbone of each. Of the remaining three—Colombia, Costa Rica, and Venezuela—two (Colombia and Venezuela) were civilian-led but still quasi-corporatist regimes, and all three could be considered elite-directed and subject regimes, not necessarily fully pluralist and participatory ones.[41]

The military-authoritarian and civilian-authoritarian regimes alike were major human rights violators. The human rights records of the Argentine, Brazilian, Chilean, Uruguayan, and numerous other regimes were especially atrocious. They killed thousands of people; many thousands more were jailed, tortured, and exiled. The abuses were not directed just against individuals, however, but against whole classes of persons: trade unions, peasant associations, journalists, students, reformist political parties, indigenous organizations. Whereas an older inclusive corporatism had sought to bring many of these groups into the political process, the newer forms of bureaucratic-authoritarianism sought to exclude people on a group basis. Inclusionary corporatism gave way to exclusionary corporatism.[42]

Bureaucratic-authoritarianism was an attempt, after the earlier wave of democratic openings in the late 1950s/early 1960s, to turn the clock back to an earlier, sleepier, prerevolutionary era. It was an effort to re-exclude those groups that now seemed to be threatening the very stability of the Latin American political system as previously described. Bureaucratic-authoritarianism had very little to do (and even that was peripheral) with the supposed "crisis of import substitution industrialization (ISI)" economic strategy, as alleged by Guillermo O'Donnell in various writings.[43] Rather it had to do mainly with the class and political crises of the 1960s, crises that had indigenous roots but had been accelerated by U.S. policy under the Alliance for Progress. That policy had, ironically, been initiated by President Kennedy in the hope that it would enhance democratic stability and preserve anticommunism by advancing social and economic development in Latin America. Instead the policy produced the opposite effect.

For by encouraging the mobilization and organization of peasant, labor, Indian, and lower-class elements, the Alliance for Progress frightened the traditional wielders of power: the military, the Church, and the economic elites. In Brazil under Goulart, to these other woes had been added the factor of enlisted men revolting against their officers. And in quite a number of countries the presence of guerrilla movements, general unrest, peasant land takeovers, and urban violence were added reasons for the armed forces to intervene. Hence, in country after country the military, aided by the economic elite, the middle class, and usually the Church, intervened to prevent these newer groups from acquiring power, taking the country in a reformist direction and—not least—destroying the base of the traditional groups' hold on power.[44] It was these political and class factors, not economic ones per se, that served as the primary cause of the wave of military takeovers in the 1960s and 1970s—although to the extent the economies of the area declined, the cooptive mechanisms described earlier could not be used and the coercive option was relied on instead.

In every country in which the bureaucratic-authoritarians took control, political parties—especially those on the left—were illegalized, trade unions were broken up, peasant movements were dissolved, indigenous groups suffered repression, and the guerrilla groups were pursued, often ruthlessly. Many countries restored or reinvigorated the labor codes enacted during the earlier era of corporatism as a way of keeping labor and farmer groups in check and under state control. Many of these regimes wrote new and more conservative constitutions that reverted to nineteenth-century forms; others created new official political parties (in Brazil, both an official state party and an official, loyal opposition) to replace the outlawed parties; these same regimes likewise often created official peasant and labor branches to replace the more independent interest groups that had grown up in the earlier, more liberal decades.

The bureaucratic-authoritarian regimes of the 1960s and 1970s represented an effort to restore the status quo ante, to go back to the more traditional, Catholic, pre-1930s, conservative society. It was an attempt, obviously in updated, twentieth-century form, to restore the Hapsburg model, the neoscholasticism of Saint Thomas and Suárez, the ordered and orderly society of the Middle Ages, a Franco-like regime. It sought to snuff out the liberal current that had been present since the eighteenth century and the socialist, Marxist, and social-democratic currents that had emerged in the twentieth. Recall the earlier comments about the two Spains and the two Latin Americas that had coexisted as two parallel power structures since the nineteenth century; well, this was an attempt by the more traditional power structure to either wipe out the newer liberal and socialist one or to return to the earlier 1930s corporative model that had enabled the traditional groups to carefully regulate and control the admission of new groups to the system.

Some further distinctions are necessary because not all the bureaucratic-authoritarian regimes followed the exact same strategy. Some of the military regimes in Central America (Guatemala, Honduras, Nicaragua, El Salvador) and South America (Paraguay, Bolivia) were simply brutish dictatorships often devoid of ideology except the power principle and without a sophisticated knowledge or understanding of the political theories and currents traced here. In Panama and especially Peru, a corporatist military regime sought to take the country in leftist, populist, and nationalist directions as a way of heading off rebellion from below as well as preserving the military's place in that system. As one Peruvian colonel perceptively put it: "The bulls [the people] are starting to stampede. When the bulls start to stampede you have three choices. The first is to kneel and pray; we have not found that the most useful strategy. The second is to turn and run, and that is no better than the first strategy. The third is for us the armed forces to lead the bulls onto higher ground."[45]

In the larger, more sophisticated countries—Argentina, Brazil, Chile, Uruguay—some more refined strategies were used. First, a conscious effort was made to resurrect a number of the corporative agencies and mechanisms of the 1930s, for example, price and regulatory agencies, official trade unions and peasant associations, councils of state that had a corporative or functional representative character. Second, new efforts were made to find models that were successful modernizers but that had not been "corrupted" by liberal, let alone socialist, tendencies. Franco's Spain achieved special prominence in this quest, and during the 1960s and early 1970s a steady parade of Latin American strongmen and their advisers made their way to Spain. For Franco appeared to have achieved what the Latin American countries wanted: miracle economic growth rates now reaching 8–9 percent per year but seemingly without the usual social and political concomitants of modernization, including democracy, liberalism, unfettered pluralism and social change, and radical challenges to the status quo.[46] Whereas in the 1930s version of corporatism, it had often been the Salazar regime in Portugal that was widely admired in Latin America, by the 1960s Portugal was facing severe economic and political problems and, hence, it was the allegedly successful Spanish model that received all those admiring Latin American representatives of the bureaucratic-authoritarian regimes.[47]*

The political orientation of these regimes was reinforced by a growing body of academic literature that portrayed authoritarianism, corporatism, and organic-statism as likely permanent features of the Iberian and Latin American systems.[48] This body of literature often had its origins in studies of Spain and Portugal and the regimes, respectively, of Franco and Salazar; from Iberia these interpretations spread to Latin America. Some of them derived from studies of Iberian–Latin American political culture; others, from political-institutional forms; still others, from political sociology; some more, from economics. But they all pointed in similar directions and toward similar conclusions: first, that modern, corporatist, bureaucratic-authoritarianism was likely to be not just a temporary but perhaps a lasting feature of these systems; and, second, that authoritarian-corporatism, along with liberalism-pluralism on the one hand and Marxism-Leninism on the other, was one of the three great, modern systems of sociopolitical organization by which distinct national societies sought to cope with and harness the great engines of change, modernization and industrialization.

Investigators now know that such a formulation was too simple. For one thing, Marxism-Leninism has collapsed. For another, it is now understood more clearly than it was then that social, cultural, political as well as, obviously, economic change can and does go forward even within authoritarian systems. And that these sweeping changes ultimately affect the nature of the political system itself—even in those counties, Portugal and Spain, that were once thought of as models of stable, Catholic, yet modernizing regimes. Portugal and Spain were, in fact, for some time examples of stable, corporatist, authoritarian modernization, but in the mid-1970s both of these regimes—one by revolution and

---

*Actually, had they examined it more closely, the Latin Americans would have seen that Spain was also undergoing vast social and cultural changes even while Franco was still alive that would lead to vast political change and democratization in the 1970s and 1980s; but in the late 1960s, early 1970s, this was not immediately apparent.

the other by evolution—gave way to democratization.[49] Indeed, Portugal and Spain, along with Greece, were the forerunners of the great transformation to democracy that began in the mid-1970s and spread to the rest of the world, Huntington's third wave.

Bureaucratic-authoritarianism was a way to solve the impasse, the fragmentation and paralysis. It was a way of reinventing the cooptive, accommodative model of the political process à la Anderson that in the charged circumstances of the 1960s seemed to be getting out of hand. That older model in its cooptive aspects had not been entirely unresponsive or even undemocratic in its populist forms, but the mass mobilizations of peasants and workers and the guerrilla-leftist challenges of the 1960s put unprecedented pressures on it that the model could not handle. Hence, the period of reaction ushered in with the wave of military-authoritarian coups of the 1960s that seemed, to the elite groups, to offer a tougher alternative to what the military leader of Peru's corporatist revolution accurately called criollo politics.

But the bureaucratic-authoritarian regimes of this period offered only a one-sided alternative. It was an attempt to turn the clock back to an earlier, more conservative, ordered, and hierarchical society. But while that current was still strong in Latin America—supported perhaps by one-third of the population—it was no longer the only one. By this time both the liberal and the socialist or social-democratic currents were also strong. For the conservative conception now to reestablish itself as the dominant or only one would (and did) require massive repression and, as in Pinochet's Chile, virtual totalitarianism. But that was no longer acceptable either, not just on liberal grounds but because it violated the ancient Thomistic-Suárezian requirements of ruling justly. The region had by this time sufficiently changed that it could no longer regress to an earlier conception that was itself declining and that would require such stringent policies (turning up the lights in Buenos Aires nightclubs, for instance) that they were ridiculous and unacceptable at the same time.

What was required was a new model that incorporated and brought together all of the three main societal conceptions, that sought to accommodate them in some way without the use of unacceptable repression and totalitarianism. The bureaucratic-authoritarian model was not that formula. On the other hand, I am not sure that the present, increasingly wobbly democratic regimes of Latin America are either.

Chapter 11

Transitions to Democracy— or Something Less Than That?

Over the past two decades, Latin America has become an area of celebration instead of the usual derision. It is said that Latin America has finally gotten its act together, both politically and economically. An area that used to be the subject of cruel *New Yorker* cartoons for its supposed comic-opera politics, that U.S. politicians would regularly and ignorantly demean, and that the *New York Times,* on its maps, found confusing—once mixing up Brazil and Bolivia—is now being praised because nineteen of its twenty republics are "democratic." Not only is Latin America, according to the popular wisdom, becoming democratic but it has also supposedly begun to follow the U.S. lead to free trade and open markets. Democracy, open markets, and free trade have even been elevated into what is usually referred to as "the Washington consensus," an agreement, at least in the United States, after decades of conflict, on what should constitute American policy toward the area.[1] The questions are whether *Latin America* is in accord with this consensus and, if so, to what degree? and does it understand by "democracy, liberalism, and open markets" the same thing Washington does?

Certainly, the analysis presented in this book provides ample reason for skepticism on these questions. After 500 years of history during which most countries have experienced only 10 or 20 years of democracy, is it realistic to expect that full-blown democracy will sprout and, overnight, reach full maturity in Latin America? Is it possible that countries which have had 490 years of mercantilism and statism in the economic sphere and authoritarianism in the political will suddenly flower into market-driven economies and pluralist, liberal politics? Can countries based so solidly in history on patrimonialism, *personalismo,* family favoritism, and patronage politics so quickly become lean and mean and able to compete without high tariffs in a competitive, no-holds-barred, global marketplace with the Japans, Taiwans, South Koreas, Germanys, and United States of this world? Posed this way, the questions suggest why some skepticism is still needed as one assesses Latin America's democratic, open market, and free trade transitions.

The Collapse of the Bureaucratic-Authoritarian Regimes

There have been hundreds of studies of the military intervening in politics but few of its withdrawal from politics.[2] Here the focus is on four main factors in the military's retreat to the barracks in Latin America in the late 1970s and 1980s: factors relating to the military institution itself, the reassertion of civil society (political parties, interest groups) during this period, contextual factors, and external forces.

The armed forces have a long history of intervention in political affairs in Latin America. As the heir to the historic Spanish corporate concept of the military fuero, to the notion that the army is historically before and perhaps even above civilian authority, to constitutional provisions that make it almost a fourth branch of government, exercising the traditional "moderative power" once reserved for the crown, and operating within a context of underdeveloped economies and weak institutions, the Latin American armed forces function at a political level that would not be condoned in American constitutional law.[3] In addition, the armed forces had come into power in the 1960s with fresh new development ideas gleaned from their military academies and war colleges. It was not Napoleonic tactics that these officers were learning but modern public administration, development theory, modern management, finance, international trade, international relations—all subjects that equipped them to effectively run their countries, perhaps run them better than the civilians whom they replaced.[4]

What the Latin American militaries meant by "professionalism," therefore, was quite different from what Americans meant, but it was very much in keeping with the long tradition of the military fuero and the corporate-organic conception of society, including monitoring the political process and taking over civilian authority in times of crisis. The threats posed by guerrilla insurgencies, the mass mobilization of peasant and labor elements, and the frequent incompetence of civilian leaders in facing these challenges seemed to pose just such a crisis, thereby justifying military intervention. Frequently, the military was

310

also goaded into action by the worried upper and middle classes and conservative clerics. At least initially, most of these military regimes were greeted not as pariahs but as saviors of the nation—or at least met with apathy—by populations for whom liberalism and democracy had meant chiefly conflict, chaos, and national fragmentation.[5]

But once in power the military over time often proved as corrupt, venal, and—surprisingly—inefficient as the civilian governments whom they had replaced. The military regimes proved no more able to deal with Latin America's pressing social and economic problems than the earlier democrats had. The residue of good will or at least indifference that had ushered in the military coups now evaporated. As they turned to greater repression to keep themselves in power and to quell the rising opposition, the armed forces were even more discredited. To these other problems of the military institution was added, in the Argentine case, inglorious defeat in the Falklands/Malvinas War. Internal dissent within the military itself replaced the unified front of earlier years.[6]

In the end it was chiefly political combined with professional considerations that determined the military's withdrawal from power. The military *withdrew*: nowhere in Latin America was it forced from power by armed force or uprising. Rather, the armed forces had been discredited as managers and governors, the institution of the military came under strong political attack, and the military's political coalition (including civilian supporters) began to break up until in virtually all cases it was left with only a handful of diehard supporters. The bureaucratic-authoritarian regimes had lost almost all legitimacy. Faced with such widespread opposition that it threatened not only continued military rule but also the integrity of the military profession and its institutional place in society, the armed forces prudently began extracting itself from power—hopefully in a way that would leave the institution intact. It was not military defeat or the triumph of the democratic forces that obliged the army to leave power; instead, it was the corporate, institutional self-interest of the officer corps that was at stake and that would, from their point of view, be best served by a voluntary retreat from power before that could turn into a rout and further discrediting.[7]

As military rule proved weak and even vulnerable, civilian institutions that had been either snuffed out or held in abeyance for many years began to make a comeback. The resurgence of these civil society groups was fueled by the general discontent with the military. People were simply fed up with military bumbling, corruption, cruelty, and ar-

rogance. As popular apathy gave way to popular mobilization, the political parties, trade unions, and other groups that had been quiescent,
illegalized, suppressed, pushed underground, or rendered inactive for
many years began again to play a role. In addition, there were now new,
activist religious groups fueled by a reformed Catholic Church, community organizations, nongovernmental organizations (NGOs), and new
social movements (of women, the indigenous, others) that sprang to life.
Eventually, these new mass organizations would be mainly absorbed
into the major political parties and larger movements and their importance would decline as democracy was institutionalized, but while
the militaries were still in power and there remained restrictions on interest group activities, these informal groups played a notable role.
Moreover, the two main forces at play—the military and civil society—
played upon each other: as military rule became more and more discredited, the civilian groups became more emboldened; and as civil society became resurgent, the military came under stronger attack.[8]

But then something potentially very significant happened for the
future of Latin American democracy. At first, the NGOs and other informal groups operated in a largely unregulated, unfettered context.
But as democracy was consolidated, local as well as national officials
began requiring that these groups register with and be recognized by
the state, reveal their membership lists, show their sources of funds,
and obtain juridical personality. Such regulation and official oversight
of interest group activity, as distinct from laissez-faire pluralism, are
precisely what lie at the heart of corporatism. So even as democracy
reemerged, corporatism remained in new forms; indeed, one could say
that for many NGOs and interest groups a new layer had been added: at
the local level as distinct from the national level, where corporative
controls have usually been concentrated in the past. In Mexico, such
control mechanisms were used to keep track of the NGOs operating in
the country, especially foreign ones, whose sympathies for the Zapa-
tista guerrillas in Chiapas served as a pretext to expel a number of the
NGOs from the country.*

---

* The U.S. Agency for International Development (AID) has been quietly collecting data on
these new local-level forms of corporatist controls, but it has been reluctant to release
this information for fear that it will weaken the argument (and thus AID's own funding)
that Latin America is becoming progressively more democratic rather than corporative.
Based on the author's review of the AID data and on interviews with AID officials.

We need also to ask the fundamental question of who led these movements away from military rule and toward democracy? As usual in Latin America, it was chiefly the elites, not so much the masses, who led the movement for change. A major paper entitled "Why Power Contenders Choose Liberalization" by Columbia University's Douglas A. Chalmers and Craig H. Robinson has not received the attention it deserves.[9] The answer from their Latin American cases is that opting for democracy was purely a pragmatic action on the part of the elites and did not derive from great love of democracy or any firm commitment to it. Rather, the elites saw which way the wind was blowing: that military rule was discredited; that the U.S. government and its human rights campaign insisted on democracy; that credits, aid, loans, and investments came from that same source as well as the international lending agencies whose policies would also be dependent on progress toward democracy; and that no other alternative—certainly not Castroism or Sandinismo and no longer authoritarianism—was acceptable. Hence, the elite business, commercial, governmental, and industrial groups of Latin America opted for democracy as the least objectionable option and as one that, in classic criollo ways, they could control. But if their motives were thoroughly practical and not necessarily driven by any firm or lasting commitment to democracy, then at some future point they might equally pragmatically choose to abandon democracy in favor of something else.

The third main set of factors helping to explain the resurgence of democracy in Latin America in the late 1970s to early 1980s may be termed contextual. First, the revolution in Portugal in 1974 and the death of Franco in 1975 and the successful transitions to democracy in those two countries demonstrated that even in the Iberian mother countries, where it was often assumed that authoritarian corporatism might be a permanent feature of the political system, democracy was not only possible but desirable. Second, from its initial base in southern Europe (including Greece as well as Spain and Portugal) the third wave of democratic transitions began to spread, now encompassing Latin America as well.[10] Third, Jimmy Carter's human rights campaign, though strongly criticized at the time for emphasizing soft issues like human rights over "hard" issues like the national interest, had a major impact on Latin America, encouraging those with democratic aspirations and, over time, delegitimizing and shaming the military and their supporters into acquiescence on the need for democracy. And fourth, there was a demonstration effect among the Latin American nations themselves: if Argentina chose democracy, then Brazil would have to do the same; so, too, would Uruguay and Chile; Peru, Ecuador, Bolivia, and even Paraguay would eventually follow. In other words, democracy became the thing to do, the military was out of date and out of touch and would have to go; elections and democracy seemed the wave of the future. Once this massive shift in popular consciousness had taken place in Latin America, there seemed no longer any question of what had to occur. It had to be democracy.[11]

The fourth set of factors helping to explain the resurgence of democracy at this time involves pressures from the external world. This factor has often been ignored in the literature on transitions to democracy because the Latin American scholars involved and many of their U.S. academic collaborators would prefer to give credit only to the Latin American forces at work and not the international ones.[12] But, in fact, outside pressure was critical—maybe *the* deciding factor in many cases—in Latin American democratization. President Carter's human rights campaign and its effects have already been mentioned; during this same period, West European countries began to pressure Latin America to democratize and improve its human rights situation. The two major oil price hikes of the 1970s and the global recession that set in afterward also served to undermine the credibility as efficient managers of the Latin American militaries then in power and increase the demand for major political change.

On top of these pressures came the Cold War and the conflicts in the 1980s in Central America. Faced with the unhappy choice between rapacious, corrupt military regimes and the triumph of Castro-like guerrilla movements—plus the fact that the U.S. public was not supporting its policy—the Reagan administration began to push for democratic elections as a way to overcome the domestic political impasse as well as to provide a third and more acceptable alternative in Central America. First in El Salvador and then in Honduras, Guatemala, Nicaragua, and eventually other countries as well (Russia, Haiti, the Philippines, Eastern Europe, Bosnia; what began in Central America was elevated into a global campaign), the United States pressed hard for democratic elections.[13] Not only did this give the policy greater legitimacy and enable it to gain public, media, and congressional support, it also worked to solve the immediate political problem in Central

314

America, namely, that neither of the other choices—military and guerrilla—was acceptable. (Later in this chapter we will weigh just how
strongly democracy could be institutionalized in this area if the motives involved were mainly U.S. domestic politics and the [now defunct]
Cold War.)

All of these outside as well as inside forces propelled Latin America
toward democracy. But nothing has been said so far about the quality
of that democracy, how deeply democracy has set in, what precisely
Latin America means by democracy, whether it will last, and the implications of democracy being—in some cases—imposed from the outside rather than emerging naturally from within. All these questions
will have to be answered before the Latin American transitions to democracy can be deemed successful.

Democratic Successes

In 2000, nineteen of the twenty Latin American countries were considered more or less democratic. If one includes the smaller countries of
the Caribbean, thirty-four out of thirty-five may lay claim to being
democratic. Within the hemisphere only Cuba remains outside the
democratic tent, and there is hope that even in that island a democratic
transition may take place. Beyond mere formal democracy and elections, however, no one doubts that the human rights situation in Latin
America has improved considerably over the past twenty years and that
the overall political climate is better: freer, more open, more pluralistic. The question is not whether Latin America has democratized, but
to what degree? and to what kind of democracy? and what does Latin
America have in mind by that term? Is it genuinely Lockean, liberal, pluralist democracy as the United States knows it and prefers? or something else and, if so, what? And does this new democracy represent a
sharp break with the past or are there still important continuities with
the historical tradition traced in this book?

To provide further context to the discussion, we here present a brief
overview of the transitions to democracy in all the Latin American
countries. Such a brief treatment cannot do justice to the complexities
of the forces and political dynamics involved, which are, in any case,
treated in other studies;[14] but it can at least provide the dates, main actors, and a little of the context. We proceed alphabetically.

Argentina, a relatively developed but long fragmented and troubled nation, returned to democracy in 1983 when the military stepped aside and Radical Party leader Raúl Alfonsín defeated his Peronist rival for the presidency. Bolivia—unstable, poor, and often chaotic—returned to democracy in 1982, after eighteen years of military government. Brazil restored democracy in 1985 after twenty-one years of military rule but in a context of weak institutions and, initially, fragile, uncertain leadership. Chile restored democracy later than these, beginning in 1988 with a plebiscite on continuing the Augusto Pinochet regime (which registered a resounding "no") and then with elections in 1989 won by the Christian-Democrat Patricio Aylwin. Colombia and Costa Rica continued as democracies all through the period when other countries had bureaucratic-authoritarian regimes, although both were referred to as elite-directed democracies.

The Dominican Republic in 1978 experienced one of the first democratic transitions in Latin America, although it was not from military authoritarianism to democracy but—aided by pressure from the Carter administration—from civilian authoritarianism under longtime leader Joaquín Balaguer to a more democratic government under Antonio Guzmán.[15] Ecuador was also an early democratizer in 1979 after seven years of military government, although its democratic institutions remained weak and shaky. El Salvador was one of the Central American crisis countries referred to earlier; it held elections for a constituent assembly in 1982 and for the presidency in 1984, the winner of the latter being José Napoleón Duarte, whose election began the process of returning the country to the center. Guatemala, another country torn apart by conflict, civil war, and U.S. intervention, began a reform program in 1982 that led to constituent assembly elections in 1984, national assembly elections in 1985, and a democratically elected president, Mario Vinicio Cerezo, in 1986.

In Haiti, the extended dictatorship of the Duvalier family came to an end in 1986, when Jean-Claude Duvalier, ushered onto a U.S. military transport aircraft, was sent into exile. But Haiti's democratic opening proved short-lived because the military overthrew the elected president, Jean-Bertrand Aristide, who was restored to power only after a destructive U.S. economic embargo and, eventually, full-scale military intervention and occupation; Haiti's democratic institutions remain extremely tenuous. In likewise underinstitutionalized Honduras, the

military had been in power for eighteen years when a constituent assembly was convoked in 1980 and presidential elections were held in 1981. Mexico is a special case: a one-party corporatist-authoritarian regime that had been in power for seventy years and that is now—perhaps—moving in evolutionary pattern toward a more liberal, pluralist, and competitive system.[16]

In Nicaragua, the dictatorship of Anastasio Somoza, Jr., was overthrown in 1979, but the succeeding Marxist Sandinista government did not agree to genuinely democratic elections until 1990, which the Sandinista leader Daniel Ortega lost to Violeta Chamorro. In Panama the military was in power from 1968 to 1983, when democratic government was restored; but that government was overthrown by Gen. Manuel Noriega, who was in turn ousted and arrested by invading U.S. military forces in 1989; a kind of elite-directed democracy was restored. In Paraguay the long-lived authoritarian-corporatist dictatorship of Gen. Alfredo Stroessner was in power during 1954–89, but it gave way eventually to a wobbly democracy inaugurated in 1993. Peru had a military coup in 1968 that took the country in a nationalist and reformist-corporatist direction for a time, only to be replaced in 1975 by a less-reformist military regime which, in turn, yielded to democracy in 1980. Uruguay had full-fledged military government from 1973 to 1985 but then reestablished democratic rule while also seeking to define what its new normalcy would be. Finally, Venezuela, like Colombia and Costa Rica, continued as a democracy during this period, even while corporatism was working its way into the political parties and the government system.[17]

In sum, fourteen countries (Argentina, Bolivia, Brazil, Chile, Ecuador, El Salvador, Guatemala, Haiti, Honduras, Nicaragua, Panama, Paraguay, Peru, Uruguay) have in the past twenty years made transitions from military dictatorships to democratic rule. Two (the Dominican Republic, Mexico) had authoritarian but civilian regimes that became more democratic. And three countries (Colombia, Costa Rica, Venezuela) remained democratic all through this period rather than going in a bureaucratic-authoritarian direction. That leaves only Cuba with a nonelected, nondemocratic government.

While these transitions to democracy are certainly impressive in their breadth and numbers, and while the political and human rights situation in Latin America today is certainly improved over the 1970s, many difficulties remain. Even in the brief summaries above there are numerous hints of problems ahead: weakly institutionalized democracies, partial democracies, limited democracies, regimes that are both democratic and organic-corporatist in keeping with an older tradition.

Democratic Disquietudes

Everyone recognizes that Latin American democracy is uncertain and tenuous; that it is not working very well in most countries; that it is still wobbly and fragile; that it could still be reversed; that there are many problems.

Moreover, there is general agreement on what the main problems are. The list includes a weak, not very effective, and often corrupt judiciary; weak institutions and infrastructure: congress, political parties, interest associations, government bureaucracy; widespread corruption, patronage, and patrimonialism. The list includes such problems as not very efficient or dynamic economies that have not yet successfully made the transition to globalism, neoliberalism, and competitiveness; it also includes societies with immense social and racial gaps and the worst pattern of distribution of income of any area in the world. Public opinion surveys have revealed that the Latin American political cultures contain values like apathy, indifference, tolerance for authoritarianism, and so on that are not particularly conducive to democracy.

Faced with these problems, countries can respond in two ways. The first and by far the most common is to accept the goals—democracy, free markets—as givens and to go on and fix the problems. That is a very [North] American, can-do, problem-solving solution. It is also the stated position of the U.S. government and of those establishment think tanks like the Inter-American Dialogue that have been particularly close to U.S. policy making on Latin America. If the Latin American judiciary needs fixing, then surely American lawyers with the assistance of the U.S. Agency for International Development (AID) and the Ford Foundation can fix it—even if Latin America's code law legal systems are fundamentally different from U.S. common law systems. If Latin American political parties are weak, then U.S. organizers and like-minded Latin Americans will strengthen them; if Latin American democracy needs further institutionalization and consolidation, then U.S. scholars will undertake academic studies hopefully to institutionalize and consolidate them.

The United States will also strengthen their congresses as independent bodies—despite Latin America's five-hundred-year experience

of concentrated executive dominance; strengthen local government—
despite a Napoleonic tradition that gives practically all decision-making power to the central ministries; strengthen NGOs and civil society—despite mounting evidence that many foreign-supported NGOs are deeply resented in Latin America and that Latin American civil society looks increasingly less pluralist and more corporatist. And Americans will presumably eliminate corruption in Latin America—without ever defining precisely what that means, distinguishing between low-level and probably indispensable patronage and truly objectionable bribery, or recognizing that the wholesale elimination of "corruption" in Latin America will doubtless bring every government in the region—still dominated by patrimonialism—to a complete halt.[18] Meanwhile, they push neoliberalism and free markets on a society whose traditions have always been mercantilist and statist. At the same time they ignore entirely those political-cultural variables that cast doubt on whether Latin America wants democracy, or wants it all that much, or wants it in precisely U.S. terms.

The second response to the problems of democracy in Latin America—one that this book seems to support—is to suggest that maybe the goals Americans have set—democracy U.S.-style and neoliberalism—are wrong or inappropriate or unrealistic given Latin America's history and level of development. This argument suggests that the bar—a pure, unfettered democracy patterned after U.S. democracy and representing an idealized vision even of U.S. democracy—has been set too high. Given the region's weak institutions, weak economies, divided societies, often disorganized politics, and a historical and political cultural tradition very different from that of the United States, the U.S.-style model set for Latin American democracy is impossible of realization. What is needed is a model that suggests various halfway houses, crazy-quilt patterns, and mixed systems on the way to democracy. One that reflects the very mixed nature of the Latin American countries themselves, which are often a jumble of traditional and modern features, of democratic and not-so-democratic characteristics, at the same time. The issue, it is argued, is no longer the dichotomous, either-or one of authoritarianism versus democracy but of finding a formula that combines various aspects of the mixed and by now quite complex Latin American tradition into a workable amalgam and that also points toward greater democracy in the future. For if *all* the Latin American countries are showing problems in their democracies, then one has to—however reluctantly— **319**

reach the conclusion that maybe it is not so much the countries that
are at fault but the very democratic model and criteria against which
they are being judged.

The situation is analogous to that which surrounded the idea of development in the 1960s. Early in that decade a theoretical notion of
political development was advanced (largely by scholars who had not
spent extensive time in the Third World) that suggested that, to be modern, Third World countries required an interest group structure, a political party system, and a legislative and executive branch that looked
just like those of the United States. If they lacked these features, countries were pronounced "underdeveloped" or "dysfunctional." By the late
1960s enough students had written doctoral dissertations and books on
these countries that a whole generation of scholars had concluded it
was not so much the developing nations who were at fault for lacking
the features the theory required but the developmentalist model itself
for not being based on the realities of the countries. It is out of this re-
examination of developmentalism that a variety of alternative theoretical approaches emerged in the 1970s: corporatism, dependency theory, organic-statism, indigenous models, and so forth.[19] The same now
applies to democratization theory: if no country in Latin America can
possibly live up to the pristine democratic model the United States has
set forth for the area, then there comes a time when the model needs
to be reexamined rather than continuing to blame the countries for not
having the institutions the model unrealistically posits for them (see
chapter 12).

Why is Latin American democracy in so much trouble? The reasons
go beyond the mere institutional tinkering and reform agenda advanced in the first response above, to the deeper, more philosophical
issue of why Latin American democracy is not working well. If the issue
were only institutional and other reforms, the problems would be relatively easy to fix, for institutions can be changed almost literally
overnight. But the problems are much deeper and more fundamental
than that. They require basic, core changes in how the institutions
function, in the values and political culture of Latin America, and
those are much harder to effect. Such changes require two or three generations, perhaps fifty to seventy-five years. Observers now accept the
idea that changing Russia and the countries of the former Soviet Union
into functioning, pluralist democracies and open-market systems will
require two to three generations, perhaps longer; it is difficult to see

how Latin America, which like Russia is on the periphery of the developed world, has a similarly long authoritarian tradition, and is also a less-developed fragment of the main Western tradition, could be expected to accomplish such massive transformations as democratization and liberalization in any less time.

In the following pages we move away from the relatively easy institutional changes—reforming the judiciary, etc.—that are required for democratization in Latin America to examine the more fundamental issues that go to the heart of the argument of this book.

Electoral versus Liberal Democracy

Since the 1970s, the countries of Latin America have unequivocally made successful transitions from authoritarianism to electoral democracy. By now every country in Latin America except Cuba has had at least one fair and competitive election since the end of authoritarianism; many have had several such elections. Moreover, several have passed what is thought to be the acid test of successful transitions to democracy: at least two democratic elections in which power has passed peacefully from one party or ruling group to another.[20]

But while Latin America has been for the most part successful in institutionalizing electoral democracy, it has not yet in most countries institutionalized liberal democracy. This important distinction has been made most recently in a classic article by Larry Diamond, who is himself a member of the reformist camp but is now becoming more pessimistic about democracy's further expansion.[21] Diamond lauds Latin America for its accomplishments in holding democratic elections, but he argues that the mere holding of elections should not be equated with the development of fully liberal democracies. Liberal democracy requires not just institutional changes—elections—but changes in the class structure, social relations, and the political culture sufficient to lead to genuine egalitarianism, full participation, civil liberties, pluralism, and a civic and genuinely democratic political culture. Although Diamond finds improvements in many of these areas in Latin America, he concludes that most of Latin America is not yet at the level of a genuinely liberal-democratic polity. Moreover, given the weaknesses and, according to some of our sources (see chapter 5), virtually nonexistent character of Latin American liberalism after the triumph of positivism in the late nineteenth century, one has to wonder if such a genuinely liberal form of democracy can ever come into existence.

"Para Inglés Ver"

How genuine is Latin American democracy? Does Latin America really want democracy and, if so, how badly? Have Latin American elites and masses really committed themselves to democracy? Or is this some gigantic confidence game—a smokescreen—by which Latin American elites, who are very skilled and have pulled these tricks often in the past, have provided the appearance of democracy but not much of its substance. "Obedezco pero no cumplo" (I obey but do not implement)—is a phrase that has a long history in Latin America.

Another expression used in both Iberia and Latin America is "Para inglés ver" (For the English to see). Elites have long used it to describe an action they have taken that they would ordinarily be reluctant to take. But they take it anyway because, as small and weak countries, they know it is what their bigger, more powerful masters on whom they are dependent for protection, aid, and largesse want them to do. The phrase originated in the nineteenth century when the English were the most powerful outside force and investor in these countries; now we need to substitute the word "Americans" for "English" in the phrase. Thus, if the English wanted a parliament, a loyal opposition, a two-party system in Iberia or Latin America—or even if these countries thought that's what the English wanted—they would institute it. It was not that Iberia or Latin America necessarily desired such institutions or intended to give them any real power. Rather, they were for the English (now substitute Americans) to see, admire, applaud, and, most important, financially support.[22]

The suspicion is strong that a similar sentiment is now at least partly in play vis-à-vis democracy; that is, Latin America does not really want democracy or want it all that much but has opted for democracy because it knows that the Americans want them to do so. "Democracy," it is feared, is like "agrarian reform" and "community development" and "family planning" in the past—all programs that the United States wanted and that Latin America went along with, not because it was committed to them but because it knew the Americans were committed to them and that financial aid, loans, and investments were made dependent on their adopting such programs. The region was not, however, strongly wedded to these programs and usually allowed them to die on the vine as soon as the American commitment to them had waned. So the question has to be asked: Will that also be the fate of Latin

American democracy? That once U.S. enthusiasm and commitment for democracy and for grandiose projects and foreign entanglements fade, this program, too, will wither and be allowed to die? For after all, no Latin American government can now qualify for loans, aid, or investment without having democracy as a prior condition.

I do not think such conditionality is the sole reason for Latin American democracy, but the issue is worrisome and deserving of study. The reason I think Latin American democracy is not purely "para inglés ver" is that many Latin Americans are themselves genuinely committed to the democracy agenda. The poll and survey data cited below are clear: Latin America wants democracy. Democracy is not just a foreign implant, a strange institution imposed from the outside. But there is enough evidence on the other side to cause worry. First, this is traditional and habitual Latin American elite behavior: say one thing, do another, and get the Americans to pay. Second, one needs to look at outcomes; and the fact is that Latin American democracy is not working very well in a large number of countries—perhaps purposely so. And third, my extensive interviews of elites as well as considerable anecdotal evidence suggest that, although democracy may be mainly a result of widespread Latin American desires for democracy, the notion that democracy is principally for the Americans (and the IMF, the World Bank, and so on) to admire, applaud, and financially reward is sufficiently present that it needs to be considered seriously.[23]

Transitions versus Consolidation

A related issue involves the distinction between transitions to democracy and the consolidation or institutionalization of democracy. Most scholars are convinced that by now Latin America has successfully completed and weathered its transitions to democracy. But the full consolidation and institutionalization of democracy, especially liberal democracy, will obviously require a much longer time; again, two or three generations seem a reasonable estimate.

In terms of the institutionalization and consolidation of democracy, various major problems are involved. To begin, political parties, considered by most essential to the interest articulation and aggregation functions of democracy, are weak, fragmented, personalistic, and oriented as much toward patronage as toward the proper functioning of parties in a democracy.[24] Second, Latin America is more pluralistic than before, but the organized expression of that pluralism—interest groups—tends similarly to be weak, disorganized, personalistic, unbalanced in favor of elite groups, and often ineffective; Latin America practices pluralism of sorts but it is still a system of limited pluralism and, as indicated, with extensive corporatist-like controls.[25] In addition, despite the presence of new NGOs and social movements, Latin American associational life remains weak and often nonexistent; by no means has the institutional void that has long plagued Latin America been filled; in no way is Latin America a Tocquevillian society with the vast web of crosscutting associations characteristic of North American democracy. Indeed, on all levels—local government, congress, the justice system, the executive branch, cabinet ministries, planning agencies, the presidency—Latin America remains woefully underinstitutionalized and its democracies, therefore, unconsolidated. And, of course, to the degree institutions are weak and associability undeveloped, the area might still be subject to coups and violent takeovers in which a small but concentrated group (militaries, oligarchs, guerrillas) can march in and take over precisely because other institutions are so weak.

In many respects Latin America remains true to its monistic, organic, and legalistic past.[26] Its conception of democracy does not, for the most part, countenance unfettered pluralism, but rather still a controlled, regulated pluralism. For one thing, much of Latin America's private sector, rather than exercising real independence or pressuring the state in the style of American interest group pluralism, continues to defer to the state. It remains dependent on the state for goods, programs, contracts, and favorable treatment and is usually unwilling to challenge the state, lobby it, least of all take it on. A second indicator of limited, controlled pluralism is the minimal grass-roots participation in decision making. The state remains a godfather, patrimonialist, a dispenser of favors (gifts) and patronage, a paternalistic figure; it does not take kindly to grass-roots participation in this process, let alone to American-style pressure.[27]

A third aspect is state attitudes toward the plethora of NGOs that have sprung up in the past twenty years, working on behalf of democracy, elections, and other issues. From the point of view of most Latin American states, the proper, duly recognized (with juridical personality) agents of democracy and elections are political parties, electoral juntas, and the like—usually approved and formally accredited with some reluctance and after some difficulty. States, therefore, resent it when NGOs or interest groups jump into this act, a perfectly normal step in the American political process but inappropriate in Latin America's legalistic culture, in which a group may be recognized for one specific purpose but not multiple, laissez-faire purposes. Many NGOs are being forced to register with the host governments, to have their juridical personality or right to participate in the political process recognized, and to submit to government oversight and direction—all distinctly corporatist features and certainly not very democratic ones. Recently, several countries have taken to expelling or limiting the activity of NGOs that go beyond their specific mandates. All of these factors show how limited the concept of pluralism in Latin America still is.[28]

Economic Versus Political Logic

With the collapse of the Marxist economic model and the near-simultaneous discrediting of the statist-mercantilist one, Latin America has turned to the model of neoliberalism. Pressures to liberalize their economies have also come from the United States and the international lending agencies; the looming prospect and reality of globalization are forcing the Latin American economies toward state downsizing, privatization, and greater effectiveness as a way of remaining competitive.

Elaborate statistics are available from the U.S. government, the World Bank and IMF, and the Latin American countries on these reductions in state size, the number of privatizations, the downsizing and belt-tightening. Of course, all these entities have a vested interest in presenting inflated figures on these trends. And there have been real privatizations in Latin America, real trends toward neoliberalism. But at some levels the books are "cooked." They are false or inflated—again, "para inglés ver." For example, five state-owned enterprises may be consolidated into one large enterprise; or a state-owned enterprise may be "sold" to an ostensibly private organization that (as in Mexico) turns out to be the official, government-sponsored, trade union organization; or a state-owned enterprise is unloaded at a low price to insider groups who have advance knowledge of government transactions. The result of such shell games is that few of the statistics on privatization can be accepted at face value: the diet of widespread privatizations that observers have been fed in recent years needs to be taken with several large grains of salt.

The death knell for neoliberalism in Latin America appeared to have been sounded at the time of the Mexican peso crisis of 1993. That cri- **325**

sis led to a devastation of the Mexican middle class, a sharp jump in unemployment, skyrocketing price rises, a severe bank crisis, loss of investment, and at least a 25 percent drop in the standard of living. Since
then Mexico has begun to recover; but as a result of the Mexican crisis,
it became clear to politicians throughout Latin America—the so-called
tequila effect—that the political costs to be paid for neoliberalism were
just too high. No politician—particularly in the newly emerging democracies of Latin America—could absorb such severe losses and hope to
survive electorally. Indeed, in some countries the neoliberal agenda, if
pushed too hard, would threaten democracy itself and not just a particular regime-of-the-moment. Neoliberalism will continue as a work in
progress, but no one in Latin America can risk embracing it too rapidly
or too thoroughly.[29]

The problem with neoliberalism is that two diametrically opposed
logics come into play. The first is economic; it receives the most attention from analysts and is most evident. Almost everyone acknowledges
that to become competitive globally Latin America must downsize, privatize, streamline—although this economic orthodoxy has never been
fully accepted in Latin America, and the advocates of protectionism and
a statist-mercantilist approach are still powerful and could well stage a
comeback. This last fear was stoked by the Mexican peso crisis, which
in fact has slowed the pace of privatization to a crawl. Nevertheless, the
economic logic is clear: to become a dynamic, growth-oriented economy
in the modern, global era, you have to downsize, privatize, cut tariffs,
and free up markets to competitive forces.

The other logic is political, and it is equally important. To the extent
state size is reduced or state-owned companies privatized, so the opportunities for patronage, government jobs, contracts, corruption, special access, insider knowledge, and opportunities for self-enrichment
are forfeited. No politician in Latin America or elsewhere can favor policies that undermine the jobs and patronage base of his political support. That is political suicide: if U.S. congressmen can barely mention
reforming social security because to do so carries suicidal political costs,
why should one expect Latin American politicians to embrace a neoliberal agenda that will hurt their constituents and cost them their positions? Advocating neoliberalism in Latin America is like signing your
own political death warrant; one should not realistically expect such
profiles in courage. In short, economic logic calls for neoliberalism, but

political logic insists on terminating all such proposals. So far it looks like a standoff.

Motives

The question of what motivated Latin America to opt for democracy in the 1970s and 1980s is an especially interesting one. Was it genuine affection for and commitment to democratic values and practices? The evidence seems not to support this view. Or was it more pragmatic considerations, reasons of expedience and opportunity? The evidence does point in this direction. But if the motives were pragmatic and conditional, doesn't that mean that democracy may also be only tenuously established? And if the conditions that led to democracy in certain particular circumstances change, is not loyalty to democracy also likely to be undermined? Democracy, in other words, was not the result of some grand, universal process or inevitable third wave;[30] rather it was a calculated response by Latin American elites to changed circumstances and particular conditions that could well change again.

Take the military elites. All the evidence indicates that the military withdrew from power in the 1970s and 1980s not because they experienced an epiphany and suddenly saw the democratic light. Rather, they recognized that the military institution itself was being discredited and its professionalism destroyed by the bumbling incompetence and widespread popular criticism of the armed forces. International criticism was also strong. So the military saw that the best way to deflect such criticism and salvage its professional, corporate, and institutional prestige, identity, unity, and respect was to withdraw from politics. It is striking, as noted earlier, that nowhere were the armed forces driven from power.[31]

How about civilian elites? Here again the motives are clear, even if they do not augur well for democracy. The elites saw that the U.S. government under Presidents Carter and Reagan, human rights groups, religious bodies, and that amorphous presence called "international public opinion" favored democracy. They also perceived that their own military regimes had been discredited, that authoritarianism was no longer acceptable, and that Marxist guerrillas too were unacceptable; by process of elimination, that left only democracy as a viable option. Plus, public opinion in their own countries, NGOs, the newly resurrected civil society, religious groups, social movements, and political parties, were all clamoring for democracy. So the elites went along, like

327

the military, not out of any great love of democracy, but because it was the pragmatic thing to do at that moment and there were no other options. The situation was analogous to that pictured by the Peruvian colonel quoted earlier: the bulls (democratic sentiment) are starting to stampede and, rather than totally oppose this push and risk being stampeded or stand by helplessly, it is up to us, the elites, to lead and direct the bulls into the new democratic territory. But not to give the bulls much real power after arriving there.[32]

It is similarly on this pragmatic basis that democracy has been sustained. I am not convinced that either the Latin military elites or civilian elites are necessarily fully convinced of democracy's efficacy. But the Americans want it, the Europeans insist on it, world public opinion is in favor, and, most important, none of the international lending agencies will provide loans or sanction investment if democracy is upset. That all-important private capital that has been so critical to Latin America's economic recovery and takeoff in the 1990s could be immediately cut off if democracy were to be overthrown. Interviews that I and others have conducted with Latin American military officers, for example, show clearly that, while many of these officers have only a limited and often quite primitive conception of democracy and human rights, they do understand the notion that their "water" (aid, investment, hardware) will be cut off if they try to overthrow democracy. The threat of international ostracism is a real one and not to be taken lightly, but it may not be the strongest foundation on which to build a long-term democracy.

If these are the attitudes of the elites, what of the masses? The answer is complex, as we see in the next two sections; preliminarily, one can say that, although the masses enthusiastically supported democracy early in the transition phase, now their attitudes have become more questioning and skeptical. Democracy has not delivered on its promises of social and economic reform or brought the instant improvements the masses had expected; widespread disillusionment is setting in. In addition, public understanding of what democracy is or stands for is remarkably uninformed in Latin America.

The Meaning(s) of Democracy

Public opinion surveys reveal that Latin Americans often hold to diverse meanings of "democracy," not all of which are in accord with Lockean, North American, or acceptable, political science definitions of the term. For example, in Uruguay—not surprisingly, given that country's early history of advanced social welfare—democracy is often defined as "welfarism" or "the government taking care of you." In Brazil—again not an unexpected response given the powerful impact of patronage on Brazilian society—democracy is frequently equated with patronage, U.S.-style logrolling, a favor for a favor. Throughout Latin America surveys show that a democratic government is often seen as one in which government respects the rights of the people, doesn't beat you up, leaves you alone, and respects local customs. But that definition differs hardly at all from the definition of constitutionalism and of "rights" of historic Hispanic political theory going back to the Middle Ages.[33]

Of special import to the discussion here is the oft-quoted definition in Latin America that democracy means strong government. That is, while 65 to 70 percent of the population, according to various opinion surveys, prefer democracy, when asked what they mean by that term, a large number, 40 to 45 percent or higher, say strong government. By that they imply a strong, authoritative, nationalistic government, one that, in populist or patrimonialist fashion, takes care of their needs. But those are precisely the two forks in the Latin American road since independence—democracy or authoritarianism. The implication may be that, if democracy fails, authoritarianism or strong government is still available as a perhaps regrettable but acceptable alternative. Or perhaps what Latin America is looking for is a regime that combines all these traits: formal democracy, strong government, nationalism, and populism. But such a government sounds suspiciously like that of Perón in Argentina or of Vargas in Brazil or of others (Fujimori in Peru or Chávez in Venezuela), which one would be hard-pressed to call democratic. Or maybe this is a realistic reflection by Latin America that, although it prefers democracy, it yet recognizes that in these fractured, invertebrate (Ortega y Gasset), disorganized, and weakly institutionalized societies, a little strong government or autocracy may not be all bad, or at least something to hold in reserve, particularly as democracy or the economy or social stability falters.[34]

In addition to the preference for strong, authoritative but fair and paternalistic government, it is striking in these surveys how often the preference for an organic, corporatist, and Rousseauian-style democracy comes out. Latin Americans clearly want an effective congress and judiciary, but they also want a strong president who integrates the several parts of the system and serves as the core or hub for the various

329

spokes in the system. In addition, when Latin Americans speak and act on behalf of their rights, they still as often as not mean corporate group rights as well as individual rights. And in Rousseauian fashion, they prefer an organic, unified polity, one that comes together as a community even in the absence of strong institutions, and in which the leader knows and personifies the general will—preferably as reflected through elections but perhaps just as importantly through his leadership capabilities as well.

In an intriguing article that has not received the attention it deserves, Tina Rosenberg has called this form of democracy "magical liberalism."[35] Just as Latin American fiction writers have become known for a style of literature called magical realism, so in the political sphere does Latin America have magical liberalism. Magical liberalism she describes as a highly fanciful semblance of the kind of spare, elegant, pragmatic democracy that Locke and Madison had in mind. But, she argues, "the French Revolution and French thinkers—most notably Rousseau—had a far more decisive effect on Latin American liberalism than did Anglo-American ideas and experience." Rosenberg explains that "from Rousseau and the French model, Latin American liberals inherited a strong statist orientation, both political and economic." She says, "While Locke and the Anglo-American tradition emphasized tolerance, civil society, individual rights, and limits on central power, Rousseau (particularly as interpreted by Latin American intellectuals) tended to emphasize the subordination of all social interests to central authority and even, if necessary, to a powerful, visionary leader. Accompanying this centralizing, authoritarian tendency was an equally powerful corporatist influence."[36]

Rosenberg goes on to say that "curiously—one might even say magically—the liberal ideal in Latin America seems to endure precisely because of its lack of substance." And certainly that notion is borne out by the survey data regarding democratic institutions. For while popular support for Latin American democracy in the abstract may be in most countries in the range of two-thirds of the population, support for what U.S. citizens would consider democracy's requisite pluralist and supporting institutions is exceedingly weak. For example, support for political parties—any party—in Latin America is only in the 25 to 30 percent range; support for trade unions—any union—is even lower, in the 15 to 20 percent range. Support for congress and for politicians is even

lower than it is in the United States.[37] Here is a disconnect and a potential source of major problems. For if Latin America's expressions of support for democracy are quite high, why is the support for democracy's putatively essential underlying pluralist institutions—parties, trade unions, legislatures—so low? The answer is that Latin America, though it may be democratic in the Rousseauian organic and integrated sense, is not necessarily or fully democratic in the pluralist, liberal, Lockean sense. But can one really have democracy without liberalism, without pluralist structures, the vast webs of underlying associational life that Tocqueville talked of? Most persons who are true democrats doubt it. But then, observers need to question precisely how democratic Latin America is without such pluralism and whether democracy can survive without it.

Degrees of Support

When Latin America first opened up to democracy in the late 1970s and 1980s, the degree of support for democracy was overwhelming, virtually unanimous. In public opinion surveys carried out during the 1980s, in country after country upward of 80, 85, or even 90 percent of the respondents said they favored a democratic regime.[38] Such high figures lent democracy as a system of government overwhelming legitimacy. The figures for Latin America, in fact, were as high during this period as those measuring democratic legitimacy in Western Europe or North America. In part, however, the high figures were more volatile and even temporary than they appeared, a reflection most likely of the total discrediting of the earlier bureaucratic-authoritarian regimes and of the newness and even euphoria that surrounded the recent openings to democracy.

In the early to mid-1990s these figures began to slide. The euphoria accompanying the earlier transitions had begun to fade. In addition, the democratic regimes then in power had often proved disappointing, failing to deliver on their promises and not living up to the earlier—probably unrealistic—expectations. In nearly every country, support for democracy began to slip, from 80, 85, or 90 percent down to 65, 70, or 75 percent; levels of voter abstention from elections began to rise, showing continuing erosion of confidence in elected rule. Obviously, some countries ranked higher than others on these scales: as usual, support for democracy in Chile, Costa Rica, and Uruguay remained high, one suspects because these were real, effective, functioning democracies able to deliver on their economic promises. But in the poorer and weakly institutionalized countries of Central America, in Ecuador, in Bolivia and Paraguay, support for democracy frequently dipped to 50 percent or lower. In these countries, democracy was in bad trouble.[39]

A critical country is Venezuela, which had a democratic breakthrough in the mid-1940s, then, after the ten-year dictatorship of Pérez Jiménez, a second transition to democracy in the late 1950s; it remained a stable, well-institutionalized democracy for more than forty years. But corruption, economic downturn, and ineffective governments had slowly sapped Venezuela's support for democracy. The figures went from 80 percent support in the 1980s to only 60 percent in the mid-1990s. Even more worrisome was the simultaneous rise in Venezuela in support for an authoritarian, nationalist, populist solution or "out." In 1992 there had been two military coup attempts in Venezuela, one of which came within a whisker of succeeding. And, as the democratic political system proved incapable of dealing satisfactorily with the country's mounting crises, support for an authoritarian solution—or at least for considering authoritarianism as a possible solution—crept up to 40, even 45 percent.

In other words, public support for possible authoritarianism in Venezuela rose perilously close to support for democracy itself. And this is stable, wealthy, well-institutionalized, solidly democratic Venezuela, not some poor "banana republic."[40] In 1998 Venezuela elected Hugo Chávez, the man who had led the coup attempt of 1992, who reflected all the ingredients (authoritarianism, populism, nationalism) that the earlier polls had shown were rising in Venezuela, who was highly disparaging of Venezuela's long-established democratic institutions, and who, ominously, was a self-proclaimed "Rousseauian democrat." The fear is strong that such antidemocratic or Rousseau-style populist sentiments may become increasingly widespread throughout Latin America.

Recently, support for democracy throughout Latin America has crept up once again but only marginally. A seventeen-country opinion poll coordinated by Latinobarómetro of Chile (December 1997) showed that around two-thirds of the respondents hemisphere-wide see democracy as the best form of government. That is lower by 15–20 percent than support for democracy a decade ago but marginally up from the situation in 1995–96. The averages conceal a wide range of country differences: Chile, Costa Rica, and Uruguay remain solidly democratic, but uncertainties abound in other countries. In big, important Brazil, with its population of roughly 170 million people, support for democ-

racy hovers at only 50 percent, a dangerous level in terms of democ- Transitions to
racy's survivability. But in Paraguay the figure is down to 44 percent (as Democracy
opposed to 59 percent in 1996), and in Ecuador it is down to 41 percent
from 1996, when the figure was 52 percent. Democracy is also precarious in Bolivia, Colombia, Central America (outside of Costa Rica), and
the Dominican Republic.[41]

In Paraguay—the reverse side of the prodemocracy coin—support
for authoritarianism is increasing, and that country as well as others
may elect military men to the presidency. Bolivia in 1997 elected the
ex-dictator Hugo Banzer to the presidency. Meanwhile, in virtually all
the Latin American countries, less than 40 percent of the population
were satisfied with the workings of their democracies. But in Central
America the degree of satisfaction with democracy was actually up, at
49 percent, and in Mexico—reflecting that country's recent democratic
openings—satisfaction had risen to 45 percent from the previous dismal 11 percent. The only country in which people showed less satisfaction with the workings of democracy was Peru, down from 28 to 21 percent. But support for President Alberto Fujimori was up, showing that,
while democracy was precarious, people recognized Fujimori's effectiveness as a quasi-authoritarian leader in dealing with the guerrillas,
the economy, and other problems.

Will it last? The slight upswing in support for democracy at the
end of 1997 probably owes a great deal to the upturn in the economy
that also occurred that year. As long as the economy is doing well, democracy is probably safe in most countries. As long as there are more
pieces of the economic pie to hand out to new and old political groups,
as in the Andersonian model, then stability can be maintained and democracy will survive. But doesn't this suggest once again that Latin
American democracy is very precarious? It depends on the continued
flourishing of the economy; its democrats may be termed success or
fair-weather democrats. As long as there is successful economic growth,
Latin America's people will support democracy. But what if the economy turns sour or takes a nosedive—because of a faltering European,
Asian, or Russian economy or of a host of other causes? Then will its
people support democracy? The truth is, no one knows. And just ask-
ing the question this way and the uncertainty of the answer show just
how precarious Latin American democracy is. Surely with public support for democracy declining and support for strong government or
even authoritarianism rising to the point it comes perilously close to

the support for democracy, it seems likely that even a modest economic decline or just stagnation could in some countries tip the balance toward the "evil option" of strong government.[42]

Democracy with Adjectives?

When democracy was reestablished in Latin America in the late 1970s and 1980s, there was a great deal of talk that a definitive breakthrough had occurred; that genuine democracy had been established; that it would now, finally, be possible to have "democracy without adjectives."

But now, a decade and more later, the adjectives are coming back. The literature on Latin America is full of references to "limited democracy," "elite democracy," "controlled democracy," "tutelary democracy,"[43] or "top-down democracy." O'Donnell has been using the term "delegative democracy" to refer to the fact that voters in Latin America may practice democracy every four, five, or six years when they elect a president; but between elections they delegate essentially all power to the executive to run things as he sees fit without much democratic participation by the public.[44] Both Diamond and Fareed Zakaria[45] have employed the term "illiberal democracy" to suggest that, although Latin America has had democratic elections, it has not yet developed the practices and political culture of a truly liberal society. And Robert Kaplan in his excessively pessimistic way lumps Haiti and other less-developed Latin American countries together with certain African and Central Asian countries to show that authoritarian leaders have learned how to manipulate the democracy agenda by allowing just enough democracy and free elections to qualify for U.S. and other international aid, but not enough to allow the opposition to win or democracy to reach full flower.[46]

I have used the adjectives "Rousseauian" and "corporatist" to describe and qualify Latin American democracy.[47] By those terms I mean that Latin American democracy remains often top-down, organic, elitist, centralized, statist, nonparticipatory, patrimonialist, executive-centered, and group- rather than individual-oriented. And to the extent it remains all these other things, it is not fully democratic. Others are using even stronger terms: "democratic dictatorship" or "democratic Caesarism."

The use of these adjectives by a great variety of scholars to qualify democracy in Latin America carries major implications. It means that democracy is yet incomplete, unfinished, only part way there, a work in progress. It means the glass of Latin American democracy is only half full—which implies the glass is half empty as well. But what does the half-empty part contain? Will it continue to be the evil option of strong government verging on, if not actually practicing, authoritarianism? Can the glass be filled with more, better, or consolidated democracy, or with what President Clinton at the Santiago Summit in 1998 called a "second generation" of democratic changes to include broader social, economic, and political reforms? Will the democratic half of the glass continue to increase? which is to say, will the empty half be filled with greater or renewed democracy? Or will the part that is still incomplete, traditional, or authoritarian continue to expand, perhaps at democracy's expense? Or, most likely, will the half-full and half-empty parts continue to coexist in a dynamic, changing, always precarious relationship? On the answers to these questions hangs not only the future of Latin America but also, heavily committed to the democracy agenda, U.S. policy in the region.

Democracy: Permanent or Cyclical?

Undoubtedly, a major breakthrough to democracy occurred in Latin America in the late 1970s and 1980s. The question is whether this new democracy is permanent. Or will Latin America go through another of its cycles, in which democracy paves the way to disorder, fragmentation, and libertinage, giving rise to renewed pressures for authoritarianism or, perhaps, Fujimori-style strong government?

American foreign policy is based on the hopeful, perhaps wishful, premise that the democratic changes in Latin America are permanent. This is a very American assumption. Americans tend to assume that progress toward democracy is permanent, unilinear, irreversible, and inevitable. That, if given their choices, all right-thinking people will choose democracy, especially American-style democracy. That all good things (economic development, social change, democratization) go together.[48] And if all right-thinking people want democracy, then it follows in the American view that only evil people would want anything less than that—presumably oligarchs, unreformed militaries, and other reactionaries.

My research and earlier writings, a bit less ethnocentric than those described in the previous paragraph, one hopes, have supported the idea both that a democratic opening has occurred in Latin America and that it may be permanent.[49] This assessment was based not on wishful thinking or wishful sociology, however, but on the greater prosperity, growing size of the middle class, and greater institutionalization (filling the associational void) in Latin America in recent decades as compared with the earlier, largely unsuccessful decade of the 1960s. My analysis suggested that, although a reversion to authoritarianism may well appear in some of the weaker, less institutionalized countries, such a throwback was unlikely in the larger, better-endowed, better-institutionalized countries. I have, therefore, been critical of the cyclical theories, arguing that they ignore the significant social, economic, and political changes that have, in fact, in recent decades taken place in Latin America.[50]

But a new round of interviewing in 1997 among Latin American political elites in six countries suggests that perhaps the cyclical theory still has validity. If one asks these leaders why Latin America continues to have limited democracy, tutelary and controlled democracy, corporatist and Rousseauian democracy—that is, democracy with adjectives, again—the pragmatic answer is that anything more than that may trigger the overthrow of the area's still-fragile democracies. Recall that it was mainly the elites and not so much the popular masses who led the earlier democratic transitions, and they controlled the process, not letting it get out of control. But if democracy is allowed to go too far, if the "deepening" of democracy that the international community and some Latin Americans are calling for is actually carried out, it might still upset the democracy applecart. Or, should Latin American democracy, which so far has been moderate, reasonable, and centrist, take radical, populist, or left-wing directions (as seemed possible with Brazil's Lula, Mexico's Cárdenas, or some of the new left-wing popular fronts being formed), then the pressures for a reversal will also grow. As long as Latin American democracy remains under elite control, is limited, and does not go in radical populist-leftist directions, it will find acceptance, can survive and become better consolidated. But should the deepening process go too deep, then the cycle theory could yet come into play, and democracy itself would become more precarious and even a possible victim.[51]

Democracy's Problems

While many scholars as well as policy makers are reluctant, for obvious reasons, to reach the conclusion that democracy has failed in Latin America (a much too strong conclusion), they do tend to concentrate now on the obvious and manifold problems of the hemisphere. Replacing the euphoria and celebratory character of the early transitions to democracy literature has been a sobering reappraisal that emphasizes the immense problems that Latin American democracy must overcome if it is to not merely survive but flourish.

A partial listing of the problem areas includes the following:

- a system of income distribution and inequality that is the worst in the world;
- a judicial system that is woefully inadequate for today's needs and that is badly in need of top-to-bottom reform;
- endemic and large-scale corruption that not only poisons the domestic political process but discourages foreign investment as well;
- lack of accountability and transparency in public affairs and in the awarding of contracts;
- an inefficient state sector incapable of competing in today's world or of managing adequately the public accounts;
- weak civil society that must be strengthened if Latin American democracy is to be enhanced;
- weak local government and the absence of either decision-making or taxing authority at the local level;
- absence of credit, especially what has come to be called micro-credit, to help local, small-scale entrepreneurs;
- an inefficient, bloated, patronage-dominated bureaucracy that makes it all but impossible either to effect reforms or to carry out effective policies;
- drugs and narco-trafficking, which are corrupting whole societies as well as judicial systems and the political process;
- a military that is not fully subordinate to civilian authority and that in a number of countries continues to threaten democratic rule;
- rising crime and insecurity coupled with inadequate protection against them;
- weak political parties and party systems as agencies of representation and democratic governance;
- imbalanced interest group systems in which the elites are well organized and represented, while the majority, lower classes are ineffectively represented and must often rely on government handouts.

The list could go on and on.

A recent study by Douglas W. Payne, significantly entitled "Storm Watch: Democracy in the Western Hemisphere into the Next Century"[52] and conducted under the auspices of the Washington think tank Center for Strategic and International Studies, reached some surprisingly pessimistic conclusions. They were surprising because both Payne and the center have long championed the democratic cause in Latin America and have helped elevate the democracy agenda to high policy levels.[53]

Payne's study involved a survey of the state of democracy in every Latin American country. In reaching his assessments, Payne used four major criteria for measuring democracy:

- a true separation of powers that guarantees an independent, nondiscriminatory judiciary;
- representative and internally democratic political parties;
- a general acceptance of the rules of democracy within the political class and among ordinary citizens;
- a wide range of civil liberties guaranteed in law and practice and allowing for a vibrant civil society and reinforced accountability.

On these criteria, Payne judges Costa Rica to be the most democratic country in Latin America, followed by Uruguay and Chile. But no other country in the region has, in his words, "come even close" to establishing the democratic foundations necessary to withstand the domestic as well as international pressures currently straining Latin America. And even these three countries, the most democratic in Latin America, are by no means free of problems or even undemocratic tendencies.

Payne goes on to examine the state of democracy in each country, including the small island-states of the Caribbean. His survey presents a generally troubling and unsettled political picture. Democracy in most countries, he says, remains uncertain. He finds its prospects for sinking deeper roots extremely difficult, given the local and international (globalization) pressures upon it. He detects a striking lack of confidence in political parties, congresses, judicial systems, and public officials generally. He is alarmed by the enormous gaps between the numbers of people who prefer democracy to other systems (still over 60 percent in most countries) and the numbers who are satisfied with the workings of democracy in their own countries (27 percent overall). Only in Uruguay (52 percent) and Costa Rica (50 percent) is the satisfaction with democracy level at 50 percent or more. Payne's balanced account recognizes the factors strengthening democracy in Latin America and the plans under way to consolidate it, but he also notes that the record on turning rhetoric into effective action is uneven. His quite disturbing conclusion reads as follows:

The reality is that, with few exceptions, rule is still based more on power than on law. Judicial systems are less about justice than providing protection for those who can pay for it and punishing those who cannot. Militaries that gave way to civilian rule retain inordinate influence in a number of countries. Voters can change presidents and legislators through the ballot box in all but a few countries, but most Latin Americans remain inhabitants rather than citizens of their countries. In a number of countries, the problem is not simply corruption in the system but that corruption *is* the system. The gains that have been made since the 1980s are important and in many ways unprecedented, but the panorama remains one of inherent instability and uncertainty.

Toward a Balanced View

The comments offered above on democracy in Latin America and its problems and limits are quite fundamental. They challenge basic assumptions. Rather than the Panglossian view that Latin America and its people are all clamoring for democracy and moving steadily and inevitably forward, they suggest that Latin America may not want democracy all that much or want it in U.S. liberal form, that there are alternatives (strong government) out there, that Latin America often means something quite different by democracy than people in the United States do, that democratic institutions are exceedingly weak, that there are other priorities. These are uncomfortable facts, but they are facts nonetheless. They suggest that mere reform-mongering and tinkering by the United States may not be enough, that there are currents and traditions very deep and powerful in Latin America that are profoundly undemocratic, even antidemocratic. But if these intimations are true, U.S. democratic hopes and plans for the area may be in vain.

On the other hand, a number of new factors in Latin America today increase the prospects for not only the survival of democracy but also its consolidation. Today's Latin America is very different from the Latin America that many of us came to know in the 1960s, 1970s, and 1980s. Among the changes:

- the greater economic prosperity, dynamism, *movimiento,* and affluence now present in the region, the low inflation, and the solid prospect of continued investment, trade, and economic growth, all of which provide a stronger base for democracy;
- the significantly larger middle class, varying in size from country to country, which also lends a solider base for democracy;

339

the web of infrastructure, associational life, and institutions—
now stronger than ever before—that helps fill the organizational void that has always plagued the region;

- a military that has been discredited, is for the most part under
civilian control, and that is not, except under extreme circumstances, inclined to step into political power;
- a political culture that, even with all its reservations and misgivings, is now more supportive of democracy than in earlier
decades;
- greater, although still limited, pluralism;
- the end of the Cold War, which not only ended the superpower
rivalry in Latin America but enables the United States to move
away from the perverted no second Cuba strategy of the past and
to put its relations on a more normal basis; it also has meant the
decline of radical movements and destabilizing guerrilla campaigns—along with the right-wing responses to them—throughout the hemisphere;
- the decline of extremism and the discrediting of the other options: not only are Marxism-Leninism and blatant authoritarian-
corporatism discredited as manifest ideologies in Latin America
(leaving the field clear for democracy) but radical-right and
radical-left parties and movements are also in decline;
- Latin America wants democracy: although attitudes are still
often ambivalent or qualified, never before has the desire for democracy been so strong in Latin America—along with the institutional infrastructure to support it;
- the United States, human rights and other groups, and the international community all want democracy: while the Cold War
is over, the United States maintains a strong interest in Latin
America—and now sees democracy as the best way to guarantee
those interests; moreover, in contrast to earlier decades, external
support for Latin American democracy is bipartisan, cuts across
all interest groups, and is well-nigh universal.
- globalism *demands* democracy. This is the new factor. In the past,
the United States could present such issues as transparency, accountability, and democracy as options for Latin America. But
now democracy and these other changes are more than an option; they have become requirements. For if a regime is too corrupt, too inefficient, too dominated by patronage, then local
capital has the option to flee elsewhere, dragging down the
economy and, with it, the political system. Even more important, because of globalization, the lack of honesty in the public
accounts, the absence of decent educational and judicial systems, or the overthrow or malfunctioning of democracy will
oblige foreign capital to go elsewhere. Modern, extremely mo-

bile, electronically controlled capital has its choice of 200-odd countries in the world in which to invest; all it takes is a hint of instability, high-level corruption, or a possible democratic overthrow, and it will move elsewhere. Not only private investment will dry up, but also loans, grants, and assistance from foreign governments and the international lending agencies (World Bank, IMF, Interamerican Development Bank). Without this flow of capital and in an era of declining foreign aid, the local economy and its political system cannot survive.

So to the extent Latin American elites think rationally (most do, although some military officers and others may still have parochial views), coups, antidemocratic movements, and certainly the overthrow of democracy have been ruled out. At this stage, because the entire weight of global capitalism and international pressure would come down on the heads of the perpetrators, coups and antidemocratic movements would be downright irrational. Peru's Fujimori in 1992, Guatemala's Jorge Serrano in 1993, and Paraguay's Gen. Lino Oviedo in 1995 all found out rather quickly that antidemocratic steps cannot be countenanced in the present circumstances, although in 2000 Fujimori managed to commit apparent electoral fraud and get away with it. Democracy is, therefore, the only option—although it may come in modified, watered-down form; indeed, at this stage, given globalization, Latin America no longer has a choice in the matter: whether it wishes to have democracy or not, whether democracy is in accord with its history and traditions or not, democracy will rule.[54]

Options

Let us go back to the options and scenarios presented earlier in this chapter. If one accepts that the goal in Latin America is democracy—a goal now defined both by Latin Americans themselves as expressed in opinion surveys and other ways and by U.S. policy—then one has no choice but to go out and try to fix all the so-called second generation problems that exist in the area. That implies vast and very expensive, outside as well as domestic efforts to solve the problems of education, inequality, injustice, military reform, governmental reform, decentralization, privatization, drugs, unemployment, underdevelopment, the environment, corruption, inefficiency, and so forth. In 1998, the Santiago Summit of heads of state of the Americas identified no fewer than 170 such high-priority areas. But a list of priorities that long overloads the system. It is unrealistic. It cannot be done, certainly not in the short term and maybe not in the long. After all, two or three generations of change are called for here, change not just of institutions but of an entire history, culture, and political sociology as well. It is doubtful if any reform program can be consistently sustained over that period of time.

The second scenario calls for an examination of the goals themselves. The goals include full-fledged democracy, almost always defined and described with the U.S. model in mind and with free, unfettered, open markets. But is that to raise expectations too high? to raise expectations that Latin America at its present stage of development cannot fulfill and that lead mainly to disappointments and disillusionment in the region and in the United States? Such a view is not patronizing and certainly not racist, as has been alleged in some scurrilous reviews.[55] But it is to say that democracy does not and cannot emerge in a vacuum, without foundations, a solid base, and preparation. In Latin America, history has provided little grounding or preparation for democracy. There was little experience in self-government. The political culture, to say nothing of the sociopolitical power structure and the international environment (colonialism, dependency, the Cold War), has not long been supportive of democracy. The infrastructure, the associational life, the educational system, the organizational mores and effectiveness have simply not been at a high enough level to support functioning, stable, viable democracy. So scenario two would scale back the goals somewhat: to not expect some unrealistic model of a pure and pristine democracy to be fulfilled, to accept Latin America as it is and not as one might idealistically want it to be. That means acceptance of a limited democracy, a sometimes illiberal democracy, a number of halfway houses that fall short of full democracy—in other words, democracy with adjectives.

There is a third position, one that can be called the State Department position.[56] It combines elements of both the previous scenarios. It suggests that at the rhetorical level and in selling the policy to the Congress, the media, and the public, the United States should stand tall for democracy. Since that is its whole history and purpose as a nation (and also good politics), the United States should continue to be a beacon of light, a city on a hill, in favor of democracy, human rights, and social justice. Indeed, the American public will stand for nothing less than that from its government, and it is foolish to try to swim against these tides—which, actually, few people want to do. Hence, in presidential speeches, in testimony before Congress, and in its public utterances, the United States must continue to advance the cause of democracy. And it must have in place an array of public policies to implement these goals and to help nudge Latin America toward greater democracy.

But at the practical politics level, the United States also needs to be ready to compromise. To accept realistically at times solutions that are less than fully democratic. To accept the halfway houses and crazy-quilt patterns used previously as metaphors in this book. That is not to give up on the goal of full democracy but only to recognize that reaching the goal will take time, that sometimes there will be setbacks, that sometimes it is better to accept a glass that is half (or two-thirds or three-quarters or even one-quarter) full than one that is empty. One can think of numerous cases in Latin America in recent years in which the United States accepted such compromises—but nevertheless continued to stand for democracy and eventually saw its policies pay off as countries took greater steps toward democracy. Examples include Fujimori in Peru, Balaguer in the Dominican Republic, and the PRI in Mexico. Neither of these persons nor the political system represented by the PRI is or was exactly a pristine model of democracy. And yet by exercising patience and understanding as well as cajolery and strong pressure, by balancing carefully its interest in democracy with other legitimate interests (for example, stability), the United States has been able to coax these individuals or their countries toward greater democracy. I don't think these are bad compromises. And in a world of uncertainty and few moral absolutes, they are certainly better than a full-scale reversion to authoritarianism or, alternatively, a descent into chaos and ungovernability. For surely the situation of democracy and human rights in Latin America, even with all its limits and imperfections, is far better than it was two decades ago.[57] The United States needs to build realistically on that foundation.

Which Way Latin America?

The political theory and political tradition of Latin America, both reflecting and themselves influencing the class structure, the economy, and the political system, are very different from those of the United States. In this book we have traced, explained, and analyzed the origins and development of this theory and tradition, and explored its contemporary implications. The treatment here considers the theory and tradition of Latin America as both independent and dependent variable, both an important cause of Latin America's particular developmental pattern *and* a reflection of its underlying social, class, and institutional structures, with both of these mutually supporting each other in complex ways and with the relative weight of these explanatory factors varying over time.[1]

The intellectual roots of the American political system may be traced to the English common law tradition, the idea of limited government in John Locke, the focus on individual liberty in Thomas Jefferson, the checks and balances and concept of pluralism in Madison and Tocqueville, and the expansion of freedom and equality under Abraham Lincoln, Woodrow Wilson, and Franklin Delano Roosevelt. Although these concepts have not been uncontested in American history—above all in the Civil War—and though not all parts of the country,—for example, the pre–Civil War South—shared these values equally, the dominant tradition in the United States has long been, in Louis Hartz's term, liberal.[2] By that he means sharing a belief in representative and limited government, pluralism, equality, individualism, freedom, and the separation of Church and state. Virtually all Americans share these beliefs.

The political theory and tradition of Latin America, while similarly predominantly Western in origins, draw from ideas very different from those emphasized in the United States and gives them different meaning. Instead of Locke, Jefferson, and Madison, Latin America's political tradition draws from Aristotle, Plato, Roman law, Augustine, Thomas Aquinas, Spanish medievalism, sixteenth-century neoscholastics such as Suárez, Rousseau, Comte, Rodó, Hispanismo, and corporatism. And instead of liberty, equality, individualism, and pluralism, most of these writers tend to emphasize order, discipline, hierarchy, authority, non-equality, integralism, organicism, and the group or communal basis of society. All of these are fundamentally conservative values. They stand in marked contrast to the dominant political culture of the United States. If the dominant tradition, even ideology, of the United States is liberalism (Hartz) or perhaps interest group pluralism (Dahl, Lowi, and others),[3] the dominant tradition of Latin America, at least historically, may be termed Catholic-conservative or perhaps corporatist (my own term)[4] or organic-statist (Stepan).[5] Moreover, this tradition of thought and social organization in Latin America should not necessarily be seen as simply an "emerging" or "less-developed" version of the United States, fated inevitably to evolve in the American liberal, pluralist, democratic direction; instead, it is an alternative tradition within Western thought, with its own internal logic and political dynamics, often quite at variance with North American values and understandings.

Moreover, sociologically speaking, if the United States was, in Hartz's terms, "born free"—that is, without a feudal past (again, except in the South) and all the rigid, two-class features that accompany it—Latin America was "born feudal," and it stayed that way until recent decades. Latin America was a product of Spain and Portugal of 1500, of the late Middle Ages, of the premodern era. The conquest of Latin America during this period was an extension of the Reconquest of the Iberian peninsula from the Moors and of the feudal and medieval society that had emerged in the Iberian peninsula at that time: militaristic, absolutist, class-based, corporatist, rigidly Catholic and orthodox, crusading, inquisitorial, monolithic, mercantilist, and with land, peasants, wealth, and status tied to conquest. In the late Middle Ages there had been resistance to the Spanish and Portuguese crowns' centralizing and absolutist tendencies, as well as a nascent theory of contract and limited government; but these had been all but eliminated by Ferdinand and Isabella and their Hapsburg successors. Hence, it was the absolutist Hapsburgian model of political authority that was exported to Latin America in the sixteenth century, not the system of responsible monarchy held in check by customary law and group rights that had begun to emerge prior to the Catholic sovereigns.

The Hapsburgian model had an impact on all areas of Latin American life. The political system was top-down and authoritarian; at every level from king to viceroy to local official and landowner, it meant absolutist authority. The economy was similarly mercantilist, exploitive, and statist. Socially, the system was rigidly two-class and hierarchical, with each class in feudal fashion locked in place and obliged to accept its station in life. In terms of religion, the Spanish and Portuguese systems were similarly orthodox, absolutist, and monolithic, with the Church reinforcing and often functioning as an arm of royal authority, and counterreformationary Catholicism serving as the base of all social, political, economic, and cultural belief. Intellectually, the system was top-down, neoscholastic, based on rote memorization of Catholic precepts and deductive reasoning. The legal and educational precepts similarly followed from precepts of the Catholic faith.

These sets of traits were then transferred to Latin America, in which setting they not only persisted for centuries but actually received a renewed lease on life. For in the Americas the Spanish and Portuguese found new lands to conquer and subdue, vast territory for their quasi-feudal estates, and a ready-made peasantry in the form of the indigenous Indian population. Here the creoles could live in tropical feudal splendor, cut off and isolated from the main currents of modern Western civilization (the Protestant Reformation, the Enlightenment, the scientific revolution, the industrial revolution, and the revolution of limited government ushered in with John Locke and the English revolution), continuing in their feudal ways and institutions even while the rest of western Europe and North America were moving in a modern direction. Given the histories of the two mother countries to 1500, it should not be surprising that Latin America was established, a hundred years before the North American colonies, on this feudal or medieval basis; what is astounding is that the system lasted so long, not only through three centuries of colonial rule, but continuing through the independence period of the nineteenth century and on into the twentieth, and persisting in many particulars even to this day.

In the eighteenth century, rifts began to appear in this monolithic, very traditional, very conservative, very Catholic society. Enlightenment ideas began to filter in, more rationalist monarchs came to power in Spain and Portugal and introduced reforms, the Jesuits lost their monopoly and were expelled for a time, and Protestant notions in the form of Free Masonry infiltrated the army and the elite. There was also a social base to this split: the countryside remained traditional, conservative, and Catholic while the cities were more rationalist, liberal, and middle class. In the colonies the division between creoles and peninsulares added to the tensions, a split that would help lead a few decades later to independence. Nevertheless, unlike the North American colonies by 1776, Latin America throughout this period experienced only a modest strain of the liberal, rationalist, and Enlightenment ideas; at the level of the colonial power structure (military, Church, bureaucracy, landed elites) almost no effect was felt.

With the independence struggles from approximately 1807 to 1825, liberal and republican sentiment grew and frequently challenged the prevailing neoscholastic orthodoxy; in some countries liberalism even came to power temporarily. But within a few years of independence, conservative and reactionary forces staged a comeback and, with the independence armies stepping into the vacuum created by the withdrawal of the crown, dominated politics in most countries for the next thirty years or more. At that point and throughout the rest of the nineteenth century, liberal and conservative forces often contended for political power. But even then, liberalism remained a minority current; furthermore, Latin American liberalism took a form very different from that of U.S. liberalism: it was Rousseauian rather than Lockean; it continued to operate within a top-down, organic, elitist, and hierarchical structure; and it never fully developed a market or free enterprise economic underpinning. Never enjoying majoritarian support or legitimacy or showing the steady progress it did in England and the United States, democratic liberalism in Latin America died politically in the last decades of the nineteenth century and economically in the first decades of the twentieth.

In the political sphere, liberalism was largely supplanted or absorbed by positivism. Positivism took Latin America by storm, having far greater influence there than in the United States. Positivism was particularly attractive in Latin America for a number of reasons: (1) it was a total system of sociology, politics, and beliefs and thus served as a convenient, more secular and modern philosophy than the older Thomism; (2) it helped end the divisive nineteenth-century civil wars between liberals and conservatives by providing a belief system on which both sides could more or less agree; and (3) it represented an ide- **347** ology that appeared progressive but that could be readily adapted to Latin America's hierarchical, corporatist, and elitist tradition. Positivism swept Latin America and has a powerful influence even today; and with its state-led concept of change coming at precisely the time Latin America was beginning to industrialize, by about the time of World War I and in the interwar years, positivism was triumphant in the economic sphere, as it had earlier been in the intellectual and political. As statism and import substitution industrialization (ISI) spread and became the dominant economic philosophy, liberalism in its laissez-faire form was pronounced dead.[6]

Positivism enabled Latin America to adapt to change without actually changing very much in its fundamental structures. This is a classic Burkean conservative position: in order to remain the same, you have to be willing to change at least somewhat. The dominant positivist philosophy was then supplemented and strengthened by at least four other main currents that similarly had a profound impact on Latin America in the late nineteenth, early twentieth centuries. The first of these was nationalism, often associated with left-wing movements but in Latin America perhaps more important as a right-wing phenomenon. Second, Rodóism gave Latin America a similarly conservative sense of cultural nationalism, a way of resurrecting and glorifying the Hispanic past (including Catholicism) and of comparing Latin America favorably with the "barbaric" Yankees. Third and related, the concept and ideology of Hispanismo not only confirmed Latin America in its Catholic, conservative, non- (even anti-) liberal and antidemocratic position but gave that political position a pan-Hispanic or Ibero-American dimension. Fourth, corporatism represented an updated version of both the historic philosophy and contemporary political strategy: a way of organically coopting organized labor into the prevailing political system without implying profound alteration in the underlying sociopolitical or power structure.

Marxism grew in twentieth-century Latin America much like liberalism had in the nineteenth century: as a minority intellectual strain with dramatic moments but never a dominant mass philosophy. Indeed, liberalism and Marxism alike provoked widespread opposition precisely because they seemed so far from Latin America's dominant neoscholasticism and gave rise to strong reactions from conservative and Catholic elements that, in all but a few countries, prevented either liberalism or Marxism from definitively triumphing. In addition, both liberalism and Marxism, claiming universal validity, had trouble adapting their philosophies to Latin American realities and suffered in popularity because of it. On the other hand, part of Marxism's appeal in Latin America—following Octavio Paz's argument—was precisely that it seemed so close to the wholistic, total philosophy of Saint Thomas and Catholicism and, in a secular age, served as a convenient substitute, particularly among intellectuals, for these other beliefs.

Nevertheless, by the fifth or sixth decade of the twentieth century, a revived but often truncated form of liberalism and a Fidelista version of Marxism had taken their place in the pantheon of Latin American ideologies and political movements. Neither, except episodically, achieved definitive majority, let alone dominant, status, however. Instead, in leading countries like Chile, Argentina, perhaps Brazil and others, the Left (Marxism) could command from 15 to 30 percent of the vote; the Center (liberalism) could also get 25 to 30 percent; and the Right (corporatism, conservatism, authoritarianism) similarly commanded about one-third of popular sentiment. In country after country during the 1960s, this divide, the lack of majority support for any one political position, was producing paralysis, gridlock, fragmentation, a "conflict society" (Silvert), strife, and breakdown. The absence of consensus, the chaotic politics of the time, and the deep divisions in these societies helped produce a wave of military coups in the 1960s and early 1970s and ushered in the period referred to as either "bureaucratic-authoritarian" (O'Donnell),[7] "corporatist-authoritarian" (Malloy, Wiarda),[8] or "organic-statist" (Stepan).[9]

The military, bureaucratic-authoritarian, and corporatist regimes of the 1960s and 1970s eventually exhausted themselves and were discredited as well, even though at the time many scholars thought that authoritarianism, corporatism, and organic-statism might prove to be permanent features of the Iberian and Latin American political process. Thereafter, essentially all Latin American countries ushered in one form or another of what were called transitions to democracy.[10] These were often incomplete, however, in that they meant electoral democracy but not necessarily liberal democracy, the socioeconomic prerequisites for democracy were often weak, the institutional base (parties, parliament, and so on) for democracy was unsound, and the democracy that arrived in Latin America usually came with a variety of adjectives attached—tutelary, limited, controlled, delegative, Rousseauian, corporatist, elitist—that showed remarkable continuities with the area's past.

Moreover, after five hundred years of Latin American history but in most countries with no more than ten of them under democratic rule, the institutional, sociological, economic, political, and philosophical base for democracy remained fragile. Recent surveys, in addition, indicate that support for democracy is declining while sentiment for strong government is again on the rise. Is Latin America, therefore, about to begin a new cycle—one often present in the continent's past—in which well-meaning but weakly institutionalized democracies prove inept and unable to preside effectively over Latin America's divisive, invertebrate forces, producing ungovernability and again paving the way to renewed authoritarianism? Or is Latin American democracy now sufficiently established, consolidated, and institutionalized that it can survive and even flourish?

The preceding pages summarize some of the main themes of this book—what conclusions can be drawn from them? First, one must recognize that there is a very long and powerful tradition of political thought and ideology in Latin America. This finding flies in the face of oft-expressed views either that Latin America has no political or ideological tradition worth studying or that its politics are so chaotic and comic operatic as to defy serious consideration. The Iberian and Latin American tradition reaches all the way back to Greece, Rome, and the Bible. It finds particular inspiration in the Catholic-Christian tradition of Saint Augustine, Saint Thomas, and the Spanish neoscholastics (principally Suárez) of the sixteenth century. It also draws inspiration from the particular Spanish-Portuguese system of feudalism and the late Middle Ages, from the Reconquest and the sociopolitical conditions (large estates, two-class system, localism, segmented societies, corporatism, militarism, absolutism, etc.) it left in its wake, and from what we have here termed the "Hapsburg Model" of elitist, authoritarian, top-down rule. All of these features beginning in 1492 were transferred from the Old World of Spain and Portugal to the New World of the Americas.

Second, this tradition is continuous, a virtually unbroken string for more than two thousand years. The Latin American tradition may be traced linearly as follows: Greece, Rome, The Bible, Christianity, Augustine, Thomas, the Reconquest and the Iberian Middle Ages, Neoscholasticism and the Hapsburg Model, Rousseau, Comte, Rodó, *Hispanismo*, corporatism, bureaucratic-authoritarianism, limited democracy. This is a very conservative, conformist, and Catholic tradition; it was basically not affected by the great scientific, religious, economic, and political revolutions associated with the modern age. Indeed, for centuries Latin America was cut off from these modernizing currents and remained largely unaffected by them. In addition, neoscholastic political thought refused to separate politics from religion (as in the more secular West) and continued to insist that politics, education, economics, society, law, and so forth all be undergirded by right (Catholic) reason and morality.

This dominant tradition of thought was strongly challenged by liberalism in the nineteenth century, but it was not eliminated, and liberalism did not fully triumph; it was also challenged by Marxism in the twentieth century, but it survived that as well, in the form of bureaucratic-authoritarianism and corporatism. The current challenge to this historically dominant Latin American tradition could come from democratization, but the world will have to wait and see how that potential conflict unfolds: whether it will produce a real battle leading to fundamental change or if the historic tradition and ways of doing things will absorb this latest belief system as it has absorbed so many others in the past.

Third, this tradition affects all facets of existence. It infuses not just a set of political and religious beliefs but society, economy, law, education and intellectual life, and personal behavior as well. All endeavors, all areas of life come under the rubric of this longtime dominant, feudal-medieval, scholastic-Christian conception. No area of life is autonomous; instead, all are infused with Catholic-Christian beliefs. Social structure, economic behavior, the political system, the method of reasoning, religious and personal beliefs all stem from the same core values and assumptions; society and polity must be unified and harmonious in accord with this belief system rather than differentiated and pluralist. It is a total belief system.

Moreover, this total, neoscholastic belief system has numerous practical and this-worldly implications. It helps explain a myriad of phenomena: the dominance of mercantilism and statism throughout Latin American history and why privatization and the establishment of a laissez-faire free market economy are, even now, so difficult. It helps explain the dominance of centralism and executive-centered authority, and why the creation of stronger parliaments, judiciaries, and local government is so problematic. It helps explain the weaknesses of and skep-

ticism toward political parties as well as the system of still-limited pluralism and the constraints on American-style interest group lobbying.
It further helps explain the persistently corporatist (now often labeled
public-private partnerships) or group-centered, top-down, elite-man-
aged system of decision making in much of Latin America even in an
era of renewed democratization. It helps explain Latin America's persistent bureaucratic, state-centered poltics as distinct from the interest
group pluralism of the United States. It helps explain the persistence of
considerations of rank, place, hierarchy, and order in Latin America
that often fly in the face of democratic egalitarianism. It helps explain
the persistence, even rebirth, of neocorporatism (more democratic,
more pluralist) in Latin America even though the older ideological corporatism has by now been discredited. Indeed, in practically all areas
of national life one can find powerful echoes of Latin America's traditional past, currents of thought and action with practical applicability that have their origins in history and antiquity and that have
not been—and may never be—erased by the march of democracy and
modernization.

Fourth, not all of the ideologies traced in this book have had equal
influence. The dominant belief systems historically have been the
Thomistic and neoscholastic strains of Roman Catholicism. Positivism,
Rodóism, and corporatism were immensely influential in part because
they built on and extended these fundamental beliefs. In contrast, liberalism was never very popular in Latin America, but in its Rousseauian
version it could be accommodated to the prevailing beliefs. Marxism
made inroads in Latin America and even came to power for a time in
two or three countries, but it never gained widespread popular support
or adapted adequately to Latin American realities. Positivism and corporatism, in contrast, were both popular because they fit very well into
the Latin American ambiance and because they combined so many elements of the Latin American tradition: organicism, elitism, top-down
direction, a total system, authoritarianism, a way of managing change
without changing the fundamental power structure.

Fifth, it is striking that almost all of this tradition of political thought
in Latin America is derivative, secondhand, not homegrown. Almost all
of it comes from Europe, although after 1776 there is some American
influence, and in the twentieth century the United States has come
gradually to supplant Europe as the major source of outside influence
and ideas. Look at the political philosophies examined here: Thomism,

neoscholasticism, liberalism, positivism, nationalism, Hispanism, Marxism, corporatism, etc.—virtually all of them derived from the European context. Almost none of these ideologies (except Rodóism and Vasconcelos's "cosmic race" idea) could be said to be indigenous or home grown; nevertheless, as we see below, Latin America has shown a positive genius for adapting these outside-derived philosophies to its own conditions.

Sixth, Latin America's political tradition and ideology are mainly Western. The region has often fit uncomfortably into the Third World category; even less could it be considered non-Western.[11] From time to time Latin American writers have emphasized and sought to elevate their indigenous roots, and there have been various Indianist, African American, and black power movements; but the dominant strain has long been Western and Hispanic. It is remarkable how far down in the social scale of Latin America Hispanic values go, how successful the elites have been not only in hanging onto their values but in transferring them to the lower (indigenous and African American) classes. Of the philosophies and ideologies discussed here, virtually every one except indigenismo is, however tenuously from time to time, European or Western.

While mainly Western, seventh, Latin America represents a distinct tradition or fragment within the West,[12] one from the Middle Ages, feudalism, and a tradition of thought and ideology formed prior to 1500. Latin America never—until recently, and then only partially—accepted the notion of the separation of church and state; its social, economic, political, and educational institutions and practices continued to be infused with Catholic teachings and philosophy that had their origins in a premodern scholasticism. The landholding system, the role of the Church and the military, the tradition of political authoritarianism, the class and social systems, the mercantilist economic system all had their origins in this earlier, premodern time. Latin America was a fragment of the West of circa 1500 and remained locked into that premodern set of beliefs, just like South Africa's apartheid regime was a product of seventeenth-century Dutch Calvinism and it, too, remained, until recently, locked into that pattern. The question now is whether Latin America has changed enough to alter this historic pattern or if it still retains powerful vestiges of the past.

Eighth, Latin America's strength and originality have long lain in adapting its historic tradition to new contingencies. Indeed, Latin America has shown positive genius in absorbing, accommodating, and coopting new ideologies, pressures, and social movements to its dominant and often still prevailing historic political tradition. First business and commercial elements (through positivism), then the middle sectors (through more positivism, republicanism, Rodóism, and Hispanismo), then organized labor (through corporatism), and now women and indigenous elements (through neocorporatism, civil society, and cooptation) have been absorbed and accommodated to the political system. The traditional elitist systems of Latin America have bent but rarely broken; they have absorbed some change that they could control but resisted the rest; they have proved flexible and accommodative while retaining their traditional essence and its underlying power structure intact. Similarly, the ways in which some aspects of the Enlightenment, liberalism, positivism, corporatism, social democracy, and the market have been absorbed within the prevailing Latin American philosophy is nothing short of phenomenal. This has been a long-term fusion-absorption process, controlled by the elites, implying gradual but rarely radical change.

It is now known that the ability of traditional institutions to bend to and absorb change rather than cracking and disappearing under its pressures is not unique to Latin America. It includes most of the developing world. Consider the flexibility and staying power of the Confucian ethic in East Asia,[13] caste associations in India,[14] ethnicity and tribalism in Africa,[15] and political Islam in the Middle East.[16] All of these traditional institutions were once regarded by developmentalist theorists as hardened shells, doomed either to crack and disappear under the onslaught of modernization or to be swept away in revolution. But all of them have shown remarkable staying power, adapting to change instead of being overwhelmed by it. So Latin America's traditional Catholicism, elitism, patrimonialism, corporatism, and organicism: rather than standing against all change, these institutions have generally proved sufficiently flexible to absorb new, rising currents and coopt them in. That is why these institutions have survived so long, by being flexible on particulars but steadfast on the basics.[17]

While traditional institutions in Latin America often remain strong, they have now, ninth, been partially undermined and attenuated. The traditional landholding system and the two-class socioracial structure that went with it are now fading and changing as new kinds of economic enterprise come to the fore. The Catholic Church no longer

354

maintains its grip on the population as it once did, and the Church itself is undergoing profound change. Latin American political ideas and political culture—the focus of this book—are also changing as new ideologies and belief systems come in, as modern communications break down traditional isolation as socioeconomic development goes forward, and as the world culture of rock music, values, and mores challenges traditional beliefs. Literacy rates are rising; the hemisphere is more urban; and the middle class has become dominant in many areas. Globalization is changing the face of Latin America and putting new and all-but-irresistible pressures on it to change its traditional ways.

So not only are fundamental belief systems and ideologies changing but the socioeconomic bases of those beliefs are being altered as well. Nevertheless, the power of Latin American conservatism, corporatism, and neoscholasticism remains strong; while this is not your father's, let alone your grandfather's, Latin America anymore, traditional beliefs and the political candidates and movements they support can still in most countries command 30 or, depending on the political combinations and alliances, up to 50 or 60 percent of the population. In spite of all the modernization of recent decades, traditional forces and ideas in Latin America are still a power to be reckoned with—realistically and not merely by wishing them away.

And that helps explain, tenth, why societies respond to modernization in different and alternative ways and thus have divergent cultural, sociological, religious, political, historical, and economic experiences. They respond in many ways to the impulses that industrialization and overall modernization provide.[18] In the case of Latin America, we have emphasized, the dominant influences have been Catholicism in its medieval form, neoscholasticism, the experiences of Spain and Portugal in the late Middle Ages and then their encounter with the New World, the landholding and social class system, patrimonialism, organicism, persistent corporatism, and doubtless other features. These unique aspects of Latin America's history and background have shaped its system and mode of development continuing to this day. The result of these distinct experiences and backgrounds means that no two developing areas will modernize in the exact same way. There is no one, universal route to development but many diverse ones—even in the era of globalization. The image should be not of a single path to modernization but of a lattice, with multiple strands, numerous crosscutting pieces, and various branches for the flowers to climb on.[19] The philosophical tradition traced here provides a framework for the particular Latin American route to development, but in Africa, Asia, the Middle East, Europe, and North America there have been or will be other paths.

An eleventh and final issue involves the implications of the Latin American tradition for present-day democracy. On the face of it, the prospects do not appear good: Latin American elitism, authoritarianism, and monism seem to be incompatible with democracy. But recall also the definition of democracy in Latin America stemming from medieval Spain and, later, Rousseau and Comte, has always been organic, elitist, integralist, and monist or corporatist; perhaps this is not such a great barrier after all, at least to a limited form of democracy. At the same time, evidence presented in chapter 10 suggests that Latin America's commitment to democracy has already been hedged. The latest wave of democracy was ushered in by the elites on their conditions; it is constrained and circumscribed in various ways (electoral but not necessarily liberal democracy); it is a response in part to outside pressures (para inglés ver); it is a controlled and quite conservative form of democracy, still democracy with adjectives. In other words, it appears as if the elites are dealing with these newer pressures for democracy not very differently from the way they have dealt with numerous previous pressures and ideological challenges: by limiting and controlling the process, by absorbing limited change so as not to allow uncontrolled change that gets out of hand, by being flexible and bending to inevitable change rather than being submerged by it.

Obviously, this form of moderate, controlled, often top-down change will not satisfy democracy purists and idealists. It represents compromise, a glass that is only half full. What passes for Latin American democracy at this stage often includes various crazy-quilt patterns, halfway houses, mixed systems. But given their institutional deficiencies, their social and economic underdevelopment, and their historic associational vacuum, such mixed systems of democracy may be about all that many Latin American countries can handle at the present time. One needs to be pragmatic: a glass half full of democracy is better than an empty glass; democracy and human rights with modifiers are preferable to no democracy and no human rights at all. In addition, such partial or limited democracy establishes a platform on which greater democratic advances can be built in the future. The models used to interpret and to attempt to change Latin America thus need to reflect the complex, overlapping, multilayered realities of the area.

This is not a book primarily about policy, but it does have policy implications.[20] It suggests a number of things: for example, that movements and political parties that can build bridges between the traditional and the newer democratic movements in Latin America—for example, the Christian democrats in such countries as Chile, Venezuela, Costa Rica, El Salvador, the Dominican Republic, and Nicaragua—have a good chance at success. It suggests that elected presidents who are strong nationalists and paternalistic father figures—Carlos Menem in Argentina, Eduardo Frei in Chile, Alberto Fujimori in Peru, Joaquín Balaguer in the Dominican Republic, Hugo Chávez in Venezuela, the Mexican PRI presidents—are likely to achieve electoral and governmental success. It suggests that democratic and social-democratic movements will, if they are to achieve electoral and policy success, have to compromise with the more traditional ideas and forces in Latin America. It suggests that regimes like Brazil's which combine free markets with statist controls on prices for basics are likely to be successful. But it also suggests that overly strong U.S. efforts to push anticorruption policies, free markets, judicial restructuring (in the absence of knowledge about the code law systems of Latin America), civil society reforms (if the goal is American-style, unfettered pluralism), decentralization (given that the model of national administration in Latin America is France and its centralized ministries), and such a pure, pristine model of democracy and human rights that even the United States itself cannot live up to it are not likely to work—or will produce fragmentation and instability if pushed too hard and too quickly.

Latin America clearly wants democracy. At the same time, the status of democracy and human rights throughout the area, while obviously not perfect, is far better than it was two decades ago. But Latin America wants democracy in accord with its own priorities (including strong government and executive leadership) and on its own terms, which are likely to imply a more integralist, centralist, organic, paternalist, and corporatist conception than many North Americans would feel comfortable with. Latin America also wants a form of democracy within its range of realistic possibilities. Some idealistic textbook form that has no or little relation to Latin American realities will not do; for while their North American advisers can hop on the next plane and run away from the disasters their programs often produce, Latin Americans have to live with the consequences of these follies. That leads Latin America, knowing its own history, sociology, and possibilities far better than the Americans, to be understandably cautious and prudent about proceeding too far too fast down trails that have often in the past led to disaster. Quite frankly, if the United States were in their shoes, it would likely act the same way.

This is not a formula for inaction. But it is to say that the United States needs to be very careful before heavy-handedly mucking around in other people's countries. Not all democracies have to look exactly like the United States. I am content to see a variety of democracies in the world; moreover, I believe such institutional variety is healthy, not only for the individual countries but for democracy itself. Where the United States and other countries and international agencies can usefully help, let them help; however, where the United States or other outsiders, even with the best of intentions, could well destabilize an important country—Mexico is a case in point—by pushing for too much democracy before the country can handle it, it is better off letting the other country determine the pace and precise form of its transition. For American policy to get too far ahead or fall too far behind the country being assisted is a formula for disaster for both parties.

The United States can stand for and be a beacon of democracy in the world. But a detailed, thorough understanding of and empathy for the countries it seeks to assist are imperative. Lacking such comprehension of the dynamics and belief systems of other countries, U.S. policies are likely to be in vain or, worse, downright harmful, both to the countries involved and to U.S. policy. In the meantime, by advocating a prudent, measured policy that takes due account of local cultures and traditions, the United States lays the groundwork on which ever-higher levels of democracy may be constructed in the future.

Notes

Chapter 1. Foundations of Contrast

1. Irving Louis Horowitz, *Three Worlds of Development*, 2d ed. (New York: Oxford University Press, 1972).

2. Howard J. Wiarda, ed., *Nonwestern Theories of Development* (Fort Worth: Harcourt Brace, 1998).

3. Francis Fukuyama, *The End of History and the Last Man* (New York: Free Press, 1992).

4. Lucian Pye, *Aspects of Political Development* (Boston: Little, Brown, 1966).

5. The literature on political culture is both vast and rich, although still somewhat controversial. Among the better studies are Gabriel A. Almond and Sidney Verba, *The Civic Culture* (Boston: Little, Brown, 1965); Almond and Verba, eds., *The Civic Culture Revisited* (Boston: Little, Brown, 1980); A. H. Somjee, *Parallels and Actuals of Political Development* (London: Macmillan, 1986); Ronald Inglehart, *Culture Shift in Advanced Industrial Society* (Princeton: Princeton University Press, 1990); and Robert Putnam, *Making Democracy Work: Civic Traditions in Modern Italy* (Princeton: Princeton University Press, 1993). For Latin America, see, among others, Claudio Véliz, *The Centralist Tradition in Latin America* (Princeton: Princeton University Press, 1980); and Howard J. Wiarda, *Politics and Social Change in Latin America: Still a Distinct Tradition?* 3d ed. (Boulder: Westview, 1992). The analysis in my paragraph follows the argument of Paul Tolstoy, professor and chair, Department of Anthropology, University of Montreal, letter to *New York Times*, December 14, 1980.

6. For the United States, see Louis Hartz, *The Liberal Tradition in America* (New York: Harcourt, Brace, and World, 1955). For the contrasts, see Hartz, ed., *The Founding of New Societies* (New York: Harcourt Brace, 1964); Stephen Clissold, *Latin America: A Cultural Outline* (London: Hutchinson, 1965); Mariano Picón-Salas, *A Cultural History of Spanish America* (Berkeley: University of California Press, 1968); René Williamson, *Culture and Policy: The United States and the Hispanic World* (Knoxville: University of Tennessee Press, 1949); Octavio Paz, *The Labyrinth of Solitude* (New York: Grove Press, 1961); Angel del Rio, *The Clash and Attractions of Two Cultures: The Hispanic and Anglo-Saxon Worlds in America* (Baton Rouge: Louisiana State University Press, 1965); Glen Dealy, *The Public Man: An Interpretation of Latin American and Other Catholic Countries* (Amherst: University of Massachu-

setts Press, 1977); Emilio Willems, *Latin American Culture* (New York: Harper Row, 1975); Charles Wagley, *The Latin American Tradition* (New York: Columbia University Press, 1968).

7. Hartz, *The Liberal Tradition* and *The Founding of New Societies.* For the classic statement on and definition of the kind of democracy described here, see Robert Dahl, *A Preface to Democratic Theory* (Chicago: University of Chicago Press, 1956).

8. For elaboration, see Howard J. Wiarda and Harvey F. Kline, eds., *Latin American Politics and Development,* 4th ed. (Boulder: Westview, 1996).

9. Kalman H. Silvert, *The Conflict Society: Reaction and Revolution in Latin America,* rev. ed. (New York: Harper Row, 1968).

10. Charles W. Anderson, *Politics and Economic Change in Latin America: The Governing of Restless Nations* (Princeton: D. Van Nostrand, 1967).

11. Bernice Hamilton, *Political Thought in Sixteenth-Century Spain* (Oxford: Oxford University Press, 1963).

12. Octavio Paz, "Mexico and the U.S.: Ideology and Reality," *Time* (December 20, 1982), 42.

13. Howard J. Wiarda, *Ethnocentrism and Foreign Policy: Can We Understand the Third World?* (Washington, D.C.: American Enterprise Institute for Public Policy Research, 1985).

14. Cliffort Geertz, *The Interpretation of Cultures* (New York: Basic Books, 1973); Max Weber, *The Theory of Social and Economic Organization* (New York: Free Press, 1964).

15. More detailed historical and methodological treatment of the concept of political culture may be found in Howard J. Wiarda, *Introduction to Comparative Politics* (Fort Worth: Harcourt Brace, 1999); and Howard J. Wiarda, "Toward Consensus in Interpreting Latin American Politics: Developmentalism, Dependency, and 'The Latin American Tradition," *Studies in Comparative International Development* (2000); published also in *Journal of Intercultural Studies* 26 (1999): 147–62. But see also Marc Howard Ross, "Culture and Identity in Comparative Political Analysis," in Mark Lichbach and Alan S. Zuckerman, eds., *Comparative Politics: Rationality, Culture, and Structure* (Cambridge: Cambridge University Press, 1997); and Ruth Lane, "Political Culture: Residual Category or General Theory?" *Comparative Political Studies* 25 (2) (1992): 362–87.

16. Good, brief summaries of the Greek, Roman, and Christian conceptions may be found in George Sabine, *A History of Political Theory,* 3d ed. (New York: Holt, Rinehart and Winston, 1961); and Sheldon S. Wolen, *Politics and Vision* (Boston: Little, Brown, 1960).

17. Angus MacKay, *Spain in the Middle Ages: From Frontier to Empire, 1000–1500* (London: Macmillan, 1977).

18. Charles Gibson, *Spain in America* (New York: Harper and Row, 1967); C. H. Haring, *The Spanish Empire in America* (New York: Harcourt, Brace and World, 1963).

19. Tulio Halperin-Donghi, *The Aftermath of Revolution in Latin America* (New York: Harper Row, 1973); Guillermo Cespedes, *Latin America: The Early Years* (New York: Knopf, 1974).

20. Roberto Cortes Conde, *The First Stages of Modernization in Latin America* (New York: Harper Row, 1974); Ralph Lee Woodward, Jr., ed., *Positivism in Latin America* (Lexington, Mass.: D. C. Heath, 1971).

21. José Martí, *The America of José Martí*, trans. Juan de Onis (New York: Noonday, 1954); José Enrique Rodó, *Ariel*, trans. Margaret Sayers Peden (Austin: University of Texas Press, 1988); Fredrick Pike, *Hispanismo, 1898–1936: Spanish Liberals and Conservatives and Their Relations with Spanish America* (Notre Dame: University of Notre Dame Press, 1971).

22. Sheldon B. Liss, *Marxist Thought in Latin America* (Berkeley: University of California Press, 1984); Luis E. Aguilar, *Marxism in Latin America* (Philadelphia: Temple University Press, 1978).

23. Howard J. Wiarda, *Corporatism and National Development in Latin America* (Boulder: Westview, 1981); Wiarda, *Corporatism and Comparative Politics: The Other Great "Ism"* (New York: M. E. Sharpe, 1996).

24. Silvert, *Conflict Society*; Anderson, *Governing of Restless Nations*. For the varied solutions that come out of this era, see the magisterial work by Ruth Berins Collier and David Collier, *Shaping the Political Arena: Critical Junctures, the Labor Movement, and Regime Dynamics in Latin America* (Princeton: Princeton University Press, 1991).

25. My own, detailed analysis of this process in one country is Howard J. Wiarda, *Dictatorship, Development, and Disintegration: Politics and Social Change in the Dominican Republic* (Ann Arbor: Center for Latin American Studies, University of Massachusetts, Xerox University Microfilms Monograph Series, 1976).

26. Guillermo O'Donnell, *Modernization and Bureaucratic-Authoritarianism in Latin America* (Berkeley: Institute of International Studies, University of California, 1973).

27. Howard J. Wiarda, *The Democratic Revolution in Latin America: History, Politics, and U.S. Policy* (New York: Holmes and Meier, 1990); Roderic Ai Camp, ed., *Democracy in Latin America: Patterns and Cycles* (Wilmington, Del.: Scholarly Resources, 1996).

28. David Collier and Steven Levitsky, "Democracy with Adjectives: Conceptual Innovation in Comparative Politics," *World Politics,* 49 (3) (1997): 430–51.

Chapter 2. Origins

1. The term *Hispania* is the name given to the entire Iberian peninsula (encompassing both Spain and Portugal) by the Romans in the second century B.C. Hence, "Hispanic" or "Hispanic world" as used here refer to peoples and countries of both Iberia and Latin America, both Spain and Portugal, as well as to their former colonies in the Americas. See the Library of Congress *Gazette,* 1 (September 14, 1990), 1.

2. Louis Hartz, ed., *The Founding of New Societies* (New York: Harcourt, Brace Jovanovich, 1964). See especially Hartz's introduction as well as the chapter on Latin America by Richard Morse; see also the essays (including that by Morse) collected in Howard J. Wiarda, ed., *Politics and Social Change in Latin America,* 3d ed. (Boulder: Westview, 1992). More recently, consult Samuel P. Huntington, *The Clash of Civilizations* (New York: Simon and Schuster, 1996).

3. The phrase is Barbara Tuchman's from her study of premodern Europe, *The Proud Tower* (New York: Macmillan, 1962).

4. Aristotle, *The Politics.* In book 5 of *The Politics,* Aristotle analyzes change and revolution, but this aspect of his thought was never emphasized by Latin America's founding fathers.

5. For a fascinating study of the use of Greek philosophy by Spain to justify the enslavement of the indigenous peoples, see Lewis Hanke, *Aristotle and the American Indians* (Bloomington: Indiana University Press, 1970).

6. Plato, *The Republic*.

7. See Sidney Greenfield, "The Patrimonial State and Patron-Client Systems in the Fifteenth-Century Writings of the Infante Dom Pedro of Portugal," University of Massachusetts, Center for Latin American Studies, Occasional Papers Series, No. 1, 1976.

8. John R. Wallach, "Politics and the Division of Human Activity in Ancient Greek Political Theory," paper delivered at the Annual Meeting of the American Political Science Association, Washington, D.C., August 30–September 2, 1984.

9. George H. Sabine, *A History of Political Theory,* 3d ed. (New York: Holt, Rinehart and Winston, 1961), chaps. 1–7.

10. Glen Dealy, *The Public Man: An Interpretation of Latin American and Other Catholic Countries* (Amherst: University of Massachusetts Press, 1977).

11. See Sheldon S. Wolin, *Politics and Vision: Continuity and Innovation in Western Political Thought* (Boston: Little, Brown, 1960).

12. Robert F. Adie and Guy E. Poitras, *Latin America: The Politics of Immobility* (Englewood Cliffs: Prentice-Hall, 1974).

13. Wolin, *Politics and Vision,* chap. 2.

14. Donald C. Worcester, "Historical and Cultural Sources of Spanish Resistance to Change," *Journal of Inter-American Studies* 6 (April 1964): 173–80.

15. Frank Tannenbaum, *Ten Keys to Latin America* (New York: Vintage, 1962); and Roland H. Ebel, "The Development and Decline of the Central American City State," in Howard J. Wiarda, ed., *Rift and Revolution: The Central American Imbroglio* (Washington, D.C.: The American Enterprise Institute for Public Policy Research, 1984), 70–104.

16. Wolin, *Politics and Vision,* chap. 3.

17. Francisco José Moreno, *Legitimacy and Stability in Latin America* (New York: New York University Press, 1969).

18. Sabine, *A History of Political Theory,* chap. 8.

19. Moreno, *Legitimacy and Stability;* and John Henry Merryman, *The Civil Law Tradition* (Stanford: Stanford University Press, 1969).

20. Sabine, *A History of Political Theory,* chap. 9; Wolin, *Politics and Vision,* chap. 3. Cicero and his source Polybius believed in a popular element as part of the Roman "mixed" constitution, but he so qualified that argument as indicated here that in practice the aristocratic senate and, with it, top-down rule dominated.

21. Gabriel A. Almond and Sidney Verba, *The Civic Culture: Political Attitudes and Democracy in Five Nations* (Boston: Little, Brown, 1965).

22. Sabine, *A History of Political Theory,* chap. 9.

23. Ibid., 166–72.

24. W. W. Buckland and Arnold D. McNair, *Roman Law and Common Law: A Comparison in Outline* (Cambridge: Cambridge University Press, 1965), 54–59; W. W. Buckland, *A Text Book of Roman Law from Augustus to Justinian* (Cambridge: Cambridge University Press, 1966), 174–79, 292–93, 512-13.

25. Gaines Post, *Studies in Medieval Legal Thought: Public Law and the State, 1100–1322* (Princeton: Princeton University Press, 1964).

26. Worcester, "Historical and Cultural Sources," 173–74.

27. Lewis Hanke, *All Mankind Is One: A Study of the Disputation between Bartolomé de las Casas and Juan Ginés de Sepúlveda in 1550 on the Intellectual and Religious Capacity of the American Indians* (DeKalb: Northern Illinois University Press, 1974).

28. Elena Lourie, "A Society Organized for War: Medieval Spain," *Past and Present* 35 (December 1966): 54–76; also Claudio Sánchez-Albernoz, "The Frontier and Castilian Liberties," in Archibald R. Lewis and Thomas F. McGann, eds., *The New World Looks at Its History* (Austin: University of Texas Press, 1963), 27–46.

29. Charles Julian Bishko, "The Iberian Background of Latin American History," *Hispanic American Historical Review* 36 (February 1956): 50–80.

30. Moreno, *Legitimacy and Stability*.

31. Wolin, *Politics and Vision*, chap. 3.

32. Margaret Mott, "The Inquisition in New Spain: The Rule of Faith over Reason," *Journal of Church and State* 40 (Winter 1998): 57–81.

33. Sabine, *A History of Political Theory;* Wolin, *Politics and Vision*.

34. See especially Anton-Hermann Chroust, "The Corporate Idea and the Body Politic in the Middle Ages," *Review of Politics* 9 (October 1947): 423–52.

35. Wolin, *Politics and Vision*, chap. 4.

36. Stanley Payne, *A History of Spain and Portugal*, 2 vols. (Madison: University of Wisconsin Press, 1973).

37. Jacques Maritain, *St. Thomas Aquinas* (New York: Meridian Books, 1964); Bernice Hamilton, *Political Thought in Sixteenth-Century Spain* (London: Oxford University Press, 1963).

38. Quoted in Hamilton, *Political Thought*.

39. R. H. Tawney, *Religion and the Rise of Capitalism* (London: J. Murray, 1929).

40. Lawrence Littwin, *Latin America: Catholicism and Class Conflict* (Encino, Calif.: Dickmen, 1974); John A. McKay, *The Other Spanish Christ: A Study in the Spiritual History of Spain and South America* (London: Student Christian Movement Press, 1932).

41. Guenter Lewy, *Constitutionalism and Statecraft during the Golden Era of Spain* (Geneva: Droz, 1960). While there are glimmers of the need for consent, limited government, and constitutionalism in Aquinas, one should not read too much into these. First, his argument is overwhelmingly from the point of view of an authoritarian God and an authoritarian-hierarchical universe; second, Thomas wrote in a context and world in which, contrary to the modern secular view, power was spiritual, distant, and virtually unknowable; and third, the emphasis on consent in Thomas represents a twentieth-century effort to find the seeds of democracy in a philosophy that is, in its essentials, profoundly undemocratic. A close reading of Aquinas reveals models of government that are about piloting a ship, not about contractual relations nor representation. See Paul Sigmund, ed., *St. Thomas Aquinas on Politics and Ethics* (New York: Norton, 1988); and Jean Bethke Elshtain, *Augustine and the Limits of Politics* (Notre Dame: Notre Dame University Press, 1995).

Chapter 3. Medieval Iberia

1. Marc Bloch, *Feudal Society* (Chicago: University of Chicago Press, 1961).

2. Julian Marías, *Understanding Spain* (Ann Arbor: University of Michigan Press, 1990).

3. Américo Castro, *The Structure of Spanish History* (Princeton: Princeton University Press, 1954); John A. Crow, *Spain: The Root and the Flower* (Berkeley: University of California Press, 1985); Stanley Payne, *A History of Spain and Portugal* (Madison: University of Wisconsin Press, 1973).

4. W. Montgomery Watt, *A History of Islamic Spain* (Edinburgh: University of Edinburgh Press, 1965).

5. Claudio Sánchez-Albernoz, *La españa musulmana* (Madrid: Espasa Calpe, 1973); Harold Livermore, *The Origins of Spain and Portugal* (London: Allen and Unwin, 1971).

6. Charles Gibson, ed., *The Black Legend: Anti-Spanish Attitudes in the Old World and the New* (New York: Knopf, 1971).

7. Américo Castro, *The Spaniards* (Berkeley: University of California Press, 1971); and Claudio Sánchez-Albernoz, *España: Un enigma histórico* (Buenos Aires: Ed. Sudamericana, 1956).

8. Lyle N. McAlister, *Spain and Portugal in the New World, 1492–1700* (Minneapolis: University of Minnesota Press, 1984).

9. Richard M. Morse, "Some Characteristics of Latin American Urban History," *American Historical Review* 67 (January 1962): 317–38.

10. Gerald Brennan, *Spanish Labyrinth* (Cambridge: Cambridge University Press, 1971); and Archibald R. Lewis, *The Development of Southern French and Catalán Society, 718–1050* (Austin: University of Texas Press, 1975).

11. Cecil Roth, *The Spanish Inquisition* (New York: Norton, 1964); Margaret Mott, "The Inquisition in New Spain: The Rule of Faith over Reason," *Journal of Church and State* 40 (Winter 1998): 57–81.

12. Claudio Sánchez-Albernoz, "The Frontier and Castilian Liberties," in Archibald R. Lewis and Thomas F. McGann, eds., *The New World Looks at Its History* (Austin: University of Texas Press, 1963), 27–46.

13. John Henry Merryman, *The Civil Law Tradition* (Stanford: Stanford University Press, 1969); and Kenneth Karst and Keith Rosen, *Law and Development in Latin America* (Berkeley: University of California Press, 1975).

14. Ronald C. Newton, "Natural Corporatism and the Passing of Populism in Spanish America," *Review of Politics* 36 (January 1974): 34–51; Anton-Hermann Chroust, "The Corporate Idea and the Body Politic in the Middle Ages," *Review of Politics* 9 (October 1947): 423–52.

15. For the history and variations, see Howard J. Wiarda, *Corporatism and Comparative Politics: The Other Great "Ism,"* (Armonk, NY: M. E. Sharpe, 1997).

16. José Antonio Maravall, "The Origins of the Modern State," *Journal of World History* 6 (1961): 789–808.

17. Sánchez-Albernoz, "The Frontier"; Elena Lourie, "A Society Organized for War: Medieval Spain," *Past and Present* 35 (December 1966): 54–76.

18. The best study is Angus McKay, *Spain in the Middle Ages: From Frontier to Empire, 1000–1500* (London: Macmillan, 1977).

19. Excellent overviews are provided in Donald C. Worcester, "Historical and Cultural Sources of Spanish Resistance to Change," *Journal of Inter-American Studies* 6 (April 1964): 173–80; and "The Spanish American Past—Enemy of Change," *Journal of Inter-American Studies* 11 (January 1969): 66–75.

20. Chroust, "The Corporate Idea," 425; Glen Dealy, *The Public Man: An Interpretation of Latin American and Other Catholic Countries* (Amherst: University of Massachusetts Press, 1977).

21. Otto Gierke, *Political Theories of the Middle Ages* (Cambridge: Cambridge University Press, 1968); Gaines Post, *Studies in Medieval Legal Thought: Public Law and the State, 1100–1322* (Princeton: Princeton University Press, 1964).

22. Chroust, "The Corporate Idea"; Worcester, "Spanish American Past"; McKay, "Spain in the Middle Ages."

23. Gaines Post, "Roman Law and Early Representation in Spain and Italy, 1150–1250," *Speculum: A Journal of Medieval Studies* 18 (April 1943): 211–32; also McKay, "Spain in the Middle Ages."

24. Gaines Post, *Studies in Medieval Political Thought.* Iberian corporatism during this period, even though more militaristic, was not all that different from English corporatism. Corporatism could thus produce ambivalent results; it was not always or necessarily authoritarian, unitary, and nonparticipatory. As in England, corporatism can lead to legal and constitutional controls on the head by society's members and thus help produce the basis for a transition to democracy or, as in Sweden, democratic consultative mechanisms. But in Iberia and Latin America it was the authoritarian and top-down features of corporatism that won out.

25. Elena Lourie, "A Society Organized for War: Medieval Spain," *Past and Present* 35 (December 1966): 54–76; James F. Powers, "The Origins and Development of Municipal Military Service in the Leonese and Castilian Reconquest, 800–1250," *Traditio* 26 (1970): 91–111; and Powers, "Townsmen and Soldiers: The Interaction of Urban and Military Organization in the Militias of Medieval Castile," *Speculum* 46 (October 1971): 641–55. For the Latin America connection, see Lyle N. McAlister, *The "Fuero Militar" in New Spain, 1746–1800* (Gainesville: University of Florida Press, 1957).

26. The classic statement is E. H. Kontorowicz, *The King's Two Bodies: A Study in Medieval Political Theology* (Princeton: Princeton University Press, 1957); also Evelyn Stefanos Procter, *Curia and Cortes in Leon and Castile, 1072–1295* (Cambridge: Cambridge University Press, 1980). For the British contrast, see Brian Tierney, *Foundations of the Concilian Theory: The Contribution of the Medieval Canonists from Gratian to the Great Schism* (Cambridge: Cambridge University Press, 1955).

27. Sánchez-Albernoz, "The Frontier and Castilian Liberties," 36.

28. Julius Klein, *The Mesta: A Study in Spanish Economic History, 1273–1836* (Port Washington, N.Y.: Kennikat Press, 1964).

29. An extremely valuable study both empirically and theoretically is Anthony Black, *Guilds and Civil Society in European Political Thought from the Twelfth Century to the Present* (Ithaca: Cornell University Press, 1984).

30. Joseph F. O'Callaghan, "The Beginning of the Cortes of León-Castile," *American Historical Review* 74 (1969): 1503–37; Lesley Byrd Simpson, "The Cortes of Castile," *Americas* 12 (January 1956): 223–33; R. B. Merriman, "The Cortes of the Spanish Kingdoms in the Later Middle Ages," *American Historical Review* 16 (April 1911): 476–95; and Dámaso de Lario, *Los Parlamentos de España* (Madrid: Ed. Anaya, 1991).

31. Discussed in Howard J. Wiarda, *Corporatism and Development: The Portuguese Experience* (Amherst: University of Massachusetts Press, 1977).

32. De Lario, *Los Parlamentos;* Evelyn Proctor, "The Towns of León and Castile as Suitors before the King's Court in the Thirteenth Century," *English Historical Review* 290 (January 1959): 1–22; Joseph F. O'Callaghan, "The Cortes and Royal Taxation during the Reign of Alfonso X of Castile," *Traditio* 27 (1971): 379–98.

33. Howard J. Wiarda, *Politics in Iberia: The Political Systems of Spain and Portugal* (New York: Harper Collins, 1992); Wiarda, "State-Society Relations in Latin America: Toward a Theory of the Contract State," chap. 8 in *American Foreign Policy toward Latin America in the 80s and 90s: Issues and Controversies from Reagan to Bush* (New York: New York University Press, 1992).

34. Walter Opello, *Portugal's Political Development: A Comparative Approach* (Boulder: Westview, 1985).

35. Barbara Tuchman, *A Distant Mirror: The Calamitous 14th Century* (New York: Knopf, 1978), 17.

36. José Antonio Maravall, "Del régimen feudal al régimen corporativo en el pensamiento de Alfonso X," *Boletín de la Real Academia de la Historia* (Madrid) 157 (1958); Richard M. Morse, "Toward a Theory of Spanish American Government," *Journal of the History of Ideas* 15 (1964): 71–93.

37. De Lario, *Los Parlamentos;* McKay, *Spain in the Middle Ages.*

38. Claudio Véliz, *The Centralist Tradition in Latin America* (Princeton: Princeton University Press, 1980).

39. J. H. Mariejol, *The Spain of Ferdinand and Isabella* (New Brunswick: Rutgers University Press, 1961).

40. Antonio Domínguez Ortíz, *The Golden Age of Spain, 1516–1659* (London: Weidenfeld and Nicolson, 1971).

41. G. Griffiths, *Representative Government in Western Europe in the Sixteenth Century* (Oxford: Clarendon Press, 1963).

42. See Irving A. Leonard, "Science, Technology, and Hispanic America," *Michigan Quarterly Review* 2 (October 1963): 237–45.

Chapter 4. Spain and Portugal in America

1. The basic literature includes Mario Góngora, *El estado en el derecho indiano* (Santiago: University of Chile, 1951); Sergio Bagú, *Estructura social de la colonia* (Buenos Aires: El Ateneo, 1952); Américo Castro, *The Spaniards: An Introduction to Their History* (Berkeley: University of California Press, 1971); L. Cabat and R. Cabat, *The Hispanic World: A Survey of the Civilizations of Spain and Latin America* (New York: Oxford, 1961); George M. Foster, *Culture and Conquest: America's Spanish Heritage* (Chicago: Quadrangle, 1960); Charles Gibson, *Spain in America* (New York: Harper, 1966); O. H. Green, *Spain and the Western Tradition* (Madison: University of Wisconsin Press, 1963–66); C. H. Haring, *The Spanish Empire in America* (New York: Harcourt, Brace and World, 1963); H. B. Johnson, Jr., ed., *From Reconquest to Empire: The Iberian Background to Latin American History* (New York: Knopf, 1970); Mariano Picón-Sales, *Cultural History of Latin America* (Berkeley: University of California Press, 1968); Magali Sarfatti, *Spanish Bureaucratic-Patrimonialism in Latin America* (Berkeley: University of California, Institute of International Studies, 1966); Angel del Río, *The Clash and Attraction of Two Cultures: The Hispanic and Anglo-Saxon Worlds in America* (Baton Rouge: Louisiana University Press, 1965); Jaime Vicens Vives, *Approaches to the History of Spain* (Berkeley: University of California Press, 1970).

2. Luís Weckman, "The Middle Ages in the Conquest of America," in Lewis Hanke, ed., *History of Latin American Civilization: Sources of Interpretations,* vol. 1: *The Colonial Experience* (Boston: Little, Brown, 1967), 10–22.

3. Richard M. Morse, *New World Soundings: Culture and Ideology in the Americas* (Baltimore: Johns Hopkins University Press, 1989).

4. Johnson, *From Reconquest to Empire,* 43, 48.

5. Picón-Salas, *Cultural History,* 72.

6. Irving A. Leonard, "Science, Technology, and Hispanic America," *Michigan Quarterly Review* 2 (October 1963): 237–45. This superb essay is largely unknown in the literature, but it provides an excellent introduction to the philosophical bases of Hispanic America.

7. Marie R. Madden, *Political Theory and Law in Medieval Spain* (New York: Fordham University Press, 1930).

8. Leonard, "Science, Technology," 239.

9. Richard M. Morse, "The Heritage of Latin America," in Louis Hartz, ed., *The Founding of New Societies* (New York: Harcourt, Brace and World, 1964).

10. William Glade, *The Latin American Economies* (New York: American, 1969), a solid, balanced institutional history.

11. L. N. McAlister, "Social Structure and Social Change in New Spain," *Hispanic American Historical Review* 43 (August 1963): 349–70; also McAlister, *Spain and Portugal in the New World, 1492–1700* (Minneapolis: University of Minnesota Press, 1984).

12. McAlister, "Social Structure," 350; also McAlister, *The "Fuero Militar" in New Spain, 1746–1800* (Gainesville: University of Florida Press, 1957).

13. Ronald C. Newton, "On 'Functional Groups,' 'Fragmentation,' and 'Pluralism' in Spanish American Political History," *Hispanic American Historical Review* 50 (February 1970): 1–29; also by Newton, "Natural Corporatism and the Passing of Populism in Latin America," *Review of Politics* 36 (January 1974): 34–51.

14. Excellent summaries include Leonard, "Science, Technology"; and Morse, "Heritage."

15. Lewis Hanke, *The First Social Experiments in the Americas* (Cambridge: Harvard University Press, 1935).

16. The early conquests are well traced in Hubert Herring, *A History of Latin America,* 3d ed. (New York: Knopf, 1968); and Donald E. Worcester and Wendell G. Schaeffer, *The Growth and Culture of Latin America,* 2d ed. (New York: Oxford University Press, 1970).

17. The Brazilian tradition is best traced in Raymundo Faóro, *Os Donos do Poder: Formação do Patronato Político Brasileiro* (Rio de Janeiro: Ed. Globo, 1958). Faóro provides a rich scholarly interpretation linking Weberian patrimonialism with the development of Brazil.

18. Charles Julian Bishko, "The Iberian Background of Latin American History: Recent Progress and Continuing Problems," *Hispanic American Historical Review,* 36 (February 1956): 50–80.

19. Donald E. Worcester, "The Spanish American Past—Enemy of Change," *Journal of Inter-American Studies* 11 (January 1969): 66.

20. Octavio Paz, "Latin America and Democracy," in *Democracy and Dictatorship in Latin America* (New York: Foundation for the Independent Study of Social Ideas, 1982), 5–17.

21. Paz, "Latin America," 6.

22. O. Carlos Stoetzer, *The Scholastic Roots of the Spanish American Revolution* (New York: Fordham University Press, 1982). This excellent study richly documents the scholastic and Thomistic basis of the Spanish colonial system.

23. Howard J. Wiarda, ed., *Politics and Social Change in Latin America,* 3d ed. (Boulder: Westview, 1992); Wiarda, *Corporatism and National Development in Latin America* (Boulder: Westview, 1981); Octavio Paz, *The Labyrinth of Solitude* (New York: Grove, 1961); Richard Morse, *New World Soundings;* Glen Dealy, *The Public Man: An Interpretation of Latin American and Other Catholic Societies* (Amherst: University of Massachusetts Press, 1977). For a parallel perspective, albeit on another area, India, see Lloyd Rudolph and Susan Haeber Rudolph, *The Modernity of Tradition* (Chicago: University of Chicago Press, 1967).

24. Bernice Hamilton, *Political Thought in Sixteenth-Century Spain* (Oxford: Clarendon Press, 1963).

25. Beatríz Helena Domíngues Bitarello, "Iberian Modernity and the Scientific Revolution of the XVII Century," (Washington, D.C.: Library of Congress, Hispanic Division, June 14, 1994). This paper is based on a doctoral dissertation with the same focus.

26. Hamilton, *Political Thought in Sixteenth-Century Spain.*

27. Howard J. Wiarda, "State-Society Relations in Latin America: Toward a Theory of the Contract State," chap. 8 in the author's *American Foreign Policy toward Latin America in the 80s and 90s* (New York: New York University Press, 1992); elaborated further in Wiarda, *Politics in Iberia: The Political Systems of Spain and Portugal* (New York: Harper Collins, 1992).

28. Stoetzer, *Scholastic Origins.*

29. Joseph H. Fichter, S.J., *Man of Spain: Francis Suárez* (New York: Macmillan, 1940); Reijo Wilenius, *The Social and Political Theory of Francisco Suárez* (Helsinki: Societas Philosophica Fennica, 1963); Héctor José Tanzi, "La doctrina de los juristas hispanos sobre el poder político y su influencia en América," *Boletín Histórico,* no. 20 (September 1970): 328–49.

30. Fichter, *Man of Spain.* For a modern application, see Guillermo O'Donnell, "Delegative Democracy," *Journal of Democracy* 5 (January 1994): 55–69.

31. Wilenius, *Social and Political Theory,* 18.

32. J. H. Perry, *The Spanish Theory of Empire in the Sixteenth Century* (Cambridge: Cambridge University Press, 1940); Claudio Véliz, *The Centralist Tradition in Latin America* (Princeton: Princeton University Press, 1980).

33. Worcester and Schaeffer, *Growth and Culture.*

34. McAlister, "Social Structure," 353.

35. McAlister, *The "Fuero Militar."*

36. John Leddy Phelan, *The Kingdom of Quito in the Seventeenth Century: Bureaucratic Politics in the Spanish Empire* (Madison: University of Wisconsin Press, 1967), 57. Though dealing with a relatively small area and time period, this is one of the best and most insightful books written about Spanish colonial administration.

37. Góngora, *El Estado.*

38. The classic statement, a little romanticized, is Gilberto Freyre, *The Masters and the Slaves: A Study in the Development of Brazilian Civilization* (New York: Knopf, 1956).

39. For the comparison, see Vianna Moog, *Bandeirantes and Pioneers* (New York: George Braziller, 1964).

40. Faóro, *Os Donos do Poder.*

41. Louis de Vorsey, Jr., *Keys to the Encounter* (Washington, D.C.: Library of Congress, 1992); John R. Hebert, ed., *An Ongoing Voyage* (Washington, D.C.: Library of Congress, 1992).

42. Carefully balanced treatments may be found in Worcester and Schaeffer, *Growth and Culture;* Phelan, *The Kingdom;* McAlister, *Spain and Portugal.* By some accounts, the Indian population may have reached upward of ninety million.

43. For the diversity, see Friedrich Katz, *The Ancient American Civilizations* (New York: Praeger, 1974).

44. See especially Phelan, *The Kingdom.*

45. Murdo MacLeod, *Spanish Central America* (Berkeley: University of California Press, 1973).

46. Phelan, *The Kingdom.*

47. Lewis Hanke, *The Spanish Struggle for Justice in the Conquest of America* (Philadelphia: University of Pennsylvania Press, 1949).

48. Phelan, *The Kingdom,* 58.

49. Spain, Portugal, and their colonies treated new social groups in the same manner that they treated new philosophic ideas: by incorporating and adding them onto the traditional, neoscholastic structure but without in the process changing the fundamentals of the dominant tradition; for a modern expression of this process, see Charles W. Anderson, *Politics and Economic Change in Latin America: The Governing of Restless Nations* (Princeton: D. Van Nostrand, 1967), chap. 2.

50. Arthur Whitaker, ed., *Latin America and the Enlightenment* (Ithaca: Cornell University Press, 1961); and Kenneth Maxwell, *Pombal: Paradox of the Enlightenment* (Cambridge: Cambridge University Press, 1995).

51. A beautifully written account is Gerald Brennan, *The Spanish Labyrinth: An Account of the Social and Political Background of the Spanish Civil War* (Cambridge: Cambridge University Press, 1971); see also Howard J. Wiarda, *Corporatism and Development: The Portuguese Experience* (Amherst: University of Massachusetts Press, 1977).

52. Whitaker, *The Enlightenment;* also Irving Leonard, *Baroque Times in Old Mexico* (Ann Arbor: University of Michigan Press, 1959).

53. Worcester and Schaeffer, *Growth and Culture.*

54. Batia Siebzehner, *La Universidad Americana y la Ilustración* (Madrid: Editorial MAPFRE, 1994).

55. This is the main focus of O. Carlos Stoetzer's book *The Roots:* the argument that even the independence movements in Latin America had scholastic rather than liberal roots.

Chapter 5. Liberalism and the Latin American Independence Movements

1. For overviews, see E. Bradford Burns, *The Poverty of Progress: Latin America in the Nineteenth Century* (Berkeley: University of California Press, 1980); and David Bushnell and Neill Macaulay, *The Emergence of Latin America in the Nineteenth Century* (New York: Oxford University Press, 1994).

2. Richard M. Morse, *New World Soundings: Culture and Ideology in the Americas* (Baltimore: Johns Hopkins University Press, 1989).

3. Glen C. Dealy, "The Pluralistic Latins," *Foreign Policy* 57 (Winter 1984 – 85): 108 – 27.

4. Arthur P. Whitaker, ed., *Latin America and the Enlightenment* (Ithaca: Cornell University Press, 1961).

5. An excellent overview of the precursors is in Miguel Jorrín and John Martz, *Latin American Political Thought and Ideology* (Chapel Hill: University of North Carolina Press, 1970).

6. William Spence Robertson, *Rise of the Spanish-American Republics as Told in the Lives of Their Liberators* (New York: Collier Books, 1961).

7. Thomas Blossom, *Nariño: Hero of Colombian Independence* (Tucson: University of Arizona Press, 1967).

8. A pathbreaking volume is Joseph L. Love and Nils Jacobsen, eds., *Guiding the Invisible Hand: Economic Liberalism and the State in Latin American History* (New York: Praeger, 1988).

9. See Mariano Picón-Salas, *A Cultural History of Latin America from Conquest to Independence* (Berkeley: University of California Press, 1963).

10. The best study is by Charles Hale, *Mexican Liberalism in the Age of Mora, 1821–1853* (New Haven: Yale University Press, 1968).

11. Old but still good is Víctor Andrés Belaúnde, *Bolivar and the Political Thought of the Spanish American Revolution* (Baltimore: Johns Hopkins University Press, 1938).

12. The best overall study is Donald E. Worcester and Wendell G. Schaeffer, *The Growth and Culture of Latin America* (New York: Oxford University Press, 1970).

13. The best and most complete account is by O. Carlos Stoetzer, *The Scholastic Roots of the Spanish American Revolution* (New York: Fordham University Press, 1979).

14. Ibid., also Richard Konetzke, *La condición legal de los criollos y las causas de la independencia* (Seville, 1950).

15. Iêda Siqueira Wiarda, "Brazil: The Politics of 'Order and Progress' or Chaos and Retrogression," in Howard J. Wiarda and Harvey F. Kline, eds., *Latin American Politics and Development* (Boulder: Westview, 1996), 109–43.

16. Stoetzer, *Scholastic Roots,* conclusion.

17. Hale, *Mexican Liberalism.*

18. Robert Roswell Palmer, *The Age of the Democratic Revolutions* (Princeton: Princeton University Press, 1959).

19. Jorrín and Martz, *Latin American Political Thought;* Worcester and Schaeffer, *Growth and Culture;* Stoetzer, *Scholastic Roots.*

20. L. N. McAlister, *Spain and Portugal in the New World, 1492–1500* (Minneapolis: University of Minnesota Press, 1984).

21. Stoetzer, *Scholastic Roots;* Morse, *New World Soundings.*

22. Hale, *Mexican Liberalism.*

23. As it did in Cuba and Puerto Rico. For these exceptions, see Jorge Domínguez, *Cuba: Order and Revolution* (Cambridge: Belknap Press, 1978).

24. Charles A. Hale, *The Transformation of Liberalism in Late Nineteenth-Century Mexico* (Princeton: Princeton University Press, 1989).

25. Interested scholars might want to read the Italian philosopher Vilfredo Pareto, whose writings on the "circulation of elites" provides rich insights into Latin America.

26. The best study is by Glen Dealy, "Prolegomena on the Spanish American Political Tradition," *Hispanic American Historical Review* 48 (February 1968): 37–58.

27. Howard J. Wiarda, "Political Culture and the Attraction of Marxism-Leninism: National Inferiority Complexes as an Explanatory Factor," *World Affairs* 151 (Winter 1988–89): 143-50.

28. Claudio Véliz, *The Centralist Tradition in Latin America* (Princeton: Princeton University Press, 1980).

29. Charles W. Anderson, *Politics and Economic Change in Latin America: The Governing of Restless Nations* (Princeton: D. Van Nostrand, 1967), especially chap. 2, in which Anderson suggests that Latin America is a "living museum" of all these ideas.

30. The reference is to Arthur Schlesinger, *The Imperial Presidency* (Boston: Houghton Mifflin, 1989).

31. Frank Tannenbaum, *Ten Keys to Latin America* (New York: Vintage, 1961).

32. See the classic textbooks on Latin American politics: William S. Stokes, *Latin American Politics* (New York: Crowell, 1959); Harry Kantor, *Patterns of Politics and Political Systems of Latin America* (Chicago: Rand McNally, 1969); William Pierson and Federico G. Gil, *Governments of Latin America* (New York: McGraw-Hill, 1957); Peter G. Snow, *Government and Politics in Latin America* (New York: Holt Rinehart and Winston, 1967).

33. Glen Dealy, *The Public Man: An Interpretation of Latin America and Other Catholic Countries* (Amherst: University of Massachusetts Press, 1977); Véliz, *Centralist Tradition*.

34. Brian Loveman, *The Constitution of Tyranny: Regimes of Exception in Spanish America* (Pittsburgh: University of Pittsburgh Press, 1993).

35. Hale, *Transformation of Liberalism*.

36. The classic study is J. Lloyd Mecham, *Church and State in Latin America* (Chapel Hill: University of North Carolina Press, 1966).

37. Lyle N. McAlister, *The "Fuero Militar" in New Spain* (Gainesville: University of Florida Press, 1957).

38. Edwin Lieuwen, *Arms and Politics in Latin America* (New York: Praeger, 1961).

39. Frederick M. Nunn, *The Time of the Generals* (Lincoln: University of Nebraska Press, 1992).

40. Alfred Stepan, *The Military in Politics: Changing Patterns in Brazil* (Princeton: Princeton University Press, 1971).

41. Dirck Keyser, "Emilio Portes Gil and Mexican Politics, 1891–1978" (Ph.D. diss., University of Virginia, 1995), chaps. 1–2. This thesis is particularly useful for examining the long sweep of Mexican history in a corporatist perspective.

42. Dealy, "Prolegomena," 49; also Hale, *Transformation of Liberalism*.

43. John Henry Merryman, *The Civil Law Tradition* (Stanford: Stanford University Press, 1969); Kenneth L. Karst and Keith S. Rosenn, *Law and Development in Latin America* (Berkeley: University of California Press, 1975), part 1.

44. A revealing memoir, more scholarly than its dramatic title suggests, is James A. Gardner, *Legal Imperialism: American Lawyers and Foreign Aid in Latin America* (Madison: University of Wisconsin Press, 1980).

45. Karl W. Deutsch and William Foltz, eds., *Nation-Building* (New York: Atherton Press, 1966).

46. Worcester and Schaeffer, *Growth and Culture of Latin America,* vol. 2, parts 1, 2; Tulio Halperin-Donghi, *The Aftermath of Revolution in Latin America* (New York: Harper, 1973).

47. Hale, *Mexican Liberalism;* Burns, *Poverty or Progress;* Bushnell and Macauley, *The Emergence.*

48. Lieuwen, *Arms and Politics;* Eric R. Wolf and Edward C. Hansen, "Caudillo Politics: A Structural Analysis," *Comparative Studies in Society and History* 9 (January 1967): 168–79.

49. Howard J. Wiarda, "Contemporary Constitutions and Constitutionalism in the Dominican Republic: The Basic Law within the Political Process," *Law and Society Review* 2 (May 1968): 385–406.

50. Richard M. Morse, "Toward a Theory of Spanish American Government," *Journal of the History of Ideas* 15 (1964): 71–93; Roland H. Ebel, "Thomism and Machiavellianism in Central American Political Development," paper given at the 44th International Congress of Americanists, Manchester, England (September 5–10, 1982).

51. See the analysis and essays in Howard J. Wiarda, ed., *Politics and Social Change in Latin America,* 3d ed. (Boulder: Westview, 1992).

52. The classic statement is Wilfrid Hardy Callcott, *Liberalism in Mexico, 1857–1929* (Hamden, Conn.: Archon Books, 1965); more recently, Vincent C. Peloso and Barbara A. Tenenbaum, eds., *Liberals, Politics, and Power: State Formation in Nineteenth-Century Latin America* (Athens: University of Georgia Press, 1996); and Hale, *Transformation of Liberalism.*

Chapter 6. Positivism

1. Tulio Halperin-Donghi, *The Aftermath of Revolution in Latin America* (New York: Harper, 1973); David Bushnell and Neill Macaulay, *The Emergence of Latin America in the Nineteenth Century* (New York: Oxford University Press, 1994).

2. Roberto Cortes Conde, *The First Stages of Modernization in Spanish America* (New York: Harper, 1974); W. W. Rostow, *The Stages of Economic Growth* (Cambridge: Cambridge University Press, 1960).

3. Robert A. Potash, *Mexican Government and Industrial Development in the Early Republic: The Banco de Avío* (Amherst: University of Massachusetts Press, 1983).

4. Richard Graham, *Britain and the Onset of Modernization in Brazil, 1850–1914* (London: Cambridge University Press, 1968); and Harry Hoetink, *The Dominican People, 1850–1900* (Baltimore: Johns Hopkins University Press, 1982).

5. Miguel Jorrín and John Martz, *Latin American Political Thought and Ideology* (Chapel Hill: University of North Carolina Press, 1970), 87.

6. The analysis in this section relies on the pathbreaking work of ibid.; also W. Rex Crawford, *A Century of Latin American Thought* (New York: Praeger, 1961).

7. Jorrín and Martz, *Latin American Political Thought,* 89.

8. Charles A. Hale, *The Transformation of Liberalism in Nineteenth-Century Mexico* (Princeton: Princeton University Press, 1989), 173–77.

9. Fernando de Azevedo, *Brazilian Culture: An Introduction to the Study of Culture in Brazil* (New York: Macmillan, 1950).

10. Harvey F. Kline, *Colombia* (Boulder: Westview, 1995); Ronald H. McDonald and J. Mark Ruhl, *Party Politics and Elections in Latin America* (Boulder: Westview, 1989).

11. Paul Lewis, *Paraguay under Stroessner* (Chapel Hill: University of North Carolina Press, 1980).

12. Howard J. Wiarda, *Dictatorship and Development: The Methods of Control in Trujillo's Dominican Republic* (Gainesville: University of Florida Press, 1970), chap. 7.

13. James D. Henderson, *Conservative Thought in Twentieth-Century Latin America* (Athens: Ohio University Center for International Studies, Latin American Series Number 13, 1988).

14. The analysis follows those of Crawford, *A Century of Latin American Thought,* and Jorrín and Martz, *Latin American Political Thought.*

15. Charles A. Hale, *Mexican Liberalism in the Age of Mora, 1821–1853* (New Haven: Yale University Press, 1968).

16. Iván Jaksic, "Andrés Bello and the Problem of Order in Post-Independence Spanish America," *Working Papers on Latin America No. 97/98-1* (Rockefeller Center for Latin American Studies, Harvard University, 1998).

17. Jorrín and Martz, *Latin American Political Thought,* 106–09.

18. Ralph Lee Woodward, Jr., ed., *Positivism in Latin America, 1850–1900* (Lexington, Mass.: D. C. Heath, 1971), introduction.

19. Jorrín and Martz, *Latin American Political Thought,* 106–09.

20. Gertrud Lenzer, ed., *Auguste Comte and Positivism: The Essential Writings* (New York: Harper and Row, 1975).

21. Isaiah Berlin, "The Hedgehog and the Fox," in *Four Essays on Liberty* (New York: Oxford University Press, 1979).

22. Frederick M. Nunn, "An Overview of the European Military Missions in Latin America," *Military Affairs* 39 (February 1975): 1–7.

23. João Cruz Costa, *A History of Ideas in Brazil* (Berkeley: University of California Press, 1964).

24. Leopoldo Zea, *Positivism in Mexico* (Austin: University of Texas Press, 1974), xii.

25. See the excellent chapter 4 in Jorrín and Martz, *Latin American Political Thought.*

26. Hale, *The Transformation of Liberalism.*

27. Ibid.

28. Zea, *Positivism,* 71.

29. Quoted in ibid., 74.

30. Azevedo, *Brazilian Culture*

31. Cruz Costa, *History of Ideas.*

32. Steven Topik, *The Political Economy of the Brazilian State, 1889–1930* (Austin: University of Texas Press, 1982); Leonardo Trevisan, *A República Velha* (São Paulo: Global, 1982).

33. Euclydes da Cunha, *Rebellion in the Backlands (Os Sertões)* (Chicago: University of Chicago Press, 1944).

34. The analysis follows that of Jorrín and Martz, *Latin American Political Thought.*

35. Vincent C. Peloso and Barbara A. Tenenbaum, eds., *Liberals, Politics, and Power: State Formation in Nineteenth-Century Latin America* (Athens: University of Georgia Press, 1996), introduction.

36. Howard J. Wiarda, "Political Culture and the Attraction of Marxism-Leninism: National Inferiority Complexes as an Explanatory Paradigm," *World Affairs* 151 (Winter 1988–89): 143–56.

37. Jorrín and Martz, *Latin American Political Thought,* 122.

38. John Mander, *The Unrevolutionary Society: The Power of Latin American Conservatism in a Changing World* (New York: Knopf, 1969).

39. Jorrín and Martz, *Latin American Political Thought,* 126.

40. Warren Dean, *The Industrialization of São Paulo, 1880–1945* (Austin: University of Texas Press, 1969); Hoetink, *The Dominican People.*

41. Charles W. Anderson, *Politics and Economic Change in Latin America: The Governing of Restless Nations* (Princeton: D. Van Nostrand, 1967), chaps. 2–4.

42. See the more general and theoretical elaborations of this model in Howard J. Wiarda, ed., *Politics and Social Change in Latin America* (Boulder: Westview, 1992).

43. The conclusion here echoes that of Jorrín and Martz, *Latin American Political Thought,* 127.

44. Ibid., 152–53.

Chapter 7. Nationalism

1. Michael J. Kryzanek, *U.S.-Latin American Relations,* 3d ed. (Westport, Conn.: Praeger, 1996), part 1.

2. Howard J. Wiarda, ed., *The Iberian-Latin American Connection* (Boulder: Westview, 1986).

3. Gerhard Masur, *Nationalism in Latin America* (New York: Macmillan, 1966), ix.

4. Hans Kohn, *The Idea of Nationalism* (New York: Macmillan, 1960).

5. Carlton J. Hayes, *The Historical Evolution of Modern Nationalism* (New York: Macmillan, 1931).

6. Samuel L. Baily, ed., *Nationalism in Latin America* (New York: Knopf, 1971), introduction.

7. Barbarosa Lima Sobrinho, *Desde quando somos nacionalistas?* (Petropolis, Brazil: Vozes, 1995).

8. Arthur P. Whitaker and David C. Jordan, *Nationalism in Contemporary Latin America* (New York: Free Press, 1966).

9. Arthur P. Whitaker, *Nationalism in Latin America* (Gainesville: University of Florida Press, 1962).

10. Abraham F. Lowenthal, *Partners in Conflict: The United States and Latin America* (Baltimore: Johns Hopkins University Press, 1987); Norman A. Bailey, *Latin America in World Politics* (New York: Walker, 1967).

11. A balanced treatment is Federico G. Gil, *Latin American–United States Relations* (New York: Harcourt, Brace, Jovanovich, 1971).

12. Again, a good summary is Kryzanek, *U.S.-Latin American Relations.*

13. Hans J. Morgenthau, *In Defense of the National Interest* (New York: Knopf, 1951); Henry Kissinger, *Diplomacy* (New York: Simon and Schuster, 1994); and George Kennan, *American Diplomacy, 1900–1950* (Chicago: University of Chicago Press, 1951).

14. Bailey, *Latin America in World Politics;* G. Pope Atkins, *Latin America in the International Political System,* 2d ed. (Boulder: Westview, 1989).

15. Summaries of Martí's life and thought may be found in W. Rex Crawford, *A Century of Latin American Thought* (New York: Praeger, 1961), chap. 8; and Miguel Jorrín and John Martz, *Latin American Political Thought and Ideology* (Chapel Hill: University of North Carolina Press, 1970), chap. 5.

16. José Martí, *Martí on the USA* (Carbondale: Southern Illinois University Press, 1966), 41.

17. Peter Turton, *José Martí: Architect of Cuba's Freedom* (London: Zed Books, 1986), 120.

18. Ibid.

19. Ibid., 63.

20. Ibid.

21. Ibid., 2.

22. José Martí, *Our America* (New York: Monthly Review Press, 1977), 244.

23. Quoted in Turton, *José Martí*, 105.

24. Crawford, *A Century of Latin American Thought*, chap. 4; Jorrín and Martz, *Latin American Political Thought*, chap. 5.

25. For the English-language version, José Enrique Rodó, *Ariel* (Austin: University of Texas Press, 1988).

26. Howard J. Wiarda, *The Democratic Revolution in Latin America: History, Politics, and U.S. Policy* (New York: Holmes and Meier, 1990).

27. Rodó, *Ariel*, 78.

28. Ibid., 58.

29. Ibid., 63.

30. Ibid., 66.

31. Ibid., 82.

32. Ibid., 79.

33. Ibid., 82.

34. Ibid., 83.

35. Ibid., 82.

36. For a comprehensive survey, see Howard J. Wiarda, *The Iberian–Latin American Connection* (Boulder: Westview, 1986).

37. Frederick B. Pike, *Hispanismo, 1898–1936: Spanish Conservatives and Liberals and Their Relations with Spanish America* (Notre Dame: University of Notre Dame Press, 1971).

38. The history is traced in detail in Pike, *Hispanismo;* for the political theory, see Howard J. Wiarda, *Corporatism and Comparative Politics: The Other Great "Ism"* (New York: M. E. Sharpe, 1997).

39. See Pike, *Hispanismo*.

40. Richard M. Nuccio, "The Socialization of Political Values: The Content of Official Education in Spain" (Ph.D. diss., University of Massachusetts, 1977).

41. Wiarda, *Iberian–Latin American Connection*.

42. See, for instance, Andrés L. Mateo, *Mito y cultura en la era de Trujillo* (Santo Domingo: Lib. La Trinitaria e Instituto del Libro, 1993).

43. Wiarda, *The Iberian–Latin American Connection*.

44. Magnus Morner, ed., *Race and Class in Latin America* (New York: Columbia University Press, 1970).

45. Donald E. Worcester and Wendell G. Schaeffer, *The Growth and Culture of Latin America* (New York: Oxford University Press, 1971).

46. For example, Alcides Argüedas, *Pueblo infermo* (Barcelona: Vda. de L. Tasso, 1910). For several decades Argüedas's book was very influential.

47. See, for example, Bernardo Vega, *La agenda pendiente: Reformas, geopolítica, y frustración* (Santo Domingo: Fundación Cultural Dominicana, 1996), 26–29.

48. George Sabine, *A History of Political Theory,* 3d ed. (New York: Holt, Rinehart and Winston, 1961), 721–25.

49. Pike, *Hispanismo*.

50. Manuel Arturo Peña Batlle, *Contribución a una campaña (Cuatro discursos)* (Santiago: Ed. El Diario, 1942); Sandra McGee Deutsch and Ronald H. Dolkart, *The Argentine Right: Its History and Intellectual Origins, 1910 to the Present* (Wilmington, Del.: Scholarly Resources, 1993).

51. John J. Johnson, *Latin America in Caricature* (Austin: University of Texas Press, 1980); also Charles Gibson, ed., *The Black Legend: Anti-Spanish Attitudes in the Old World and the New* (New York: Knopf, 1971).

52. See, for example, the report of the president's brother, Milton S. Eisenhower, *The Wine Is Bitter: The United States and Latin America* (Garden City: Doubleday, 1963).

53. Mark Falcoff, *Small Countries, Large Issues: Studies in U.S.–Latin American Asymmetries* (Washington, D.C.: American Enterprise Institute for Public Policy Research, 1984).

54. An important summing up is Jorge Castañeda, *Utopia Unarmed: The Latin American Left after the Cold War* (New York: Knopf, 1993).

55. *The Economist.*

56. See Howard J. Wiarda, ed., *Non-Western Theories of Development* (Fort Worth: Harcourt Brace, 1998).

57. Donna Lee Van Cott, ed., *Indigenous Peoples and Democracy in Latin America* (New York: St. Martin's Press, 1995).

58. Donna Lee Van Cott, *Defiant Again: Indigenous Peoples and Latin American Security* (Washington, D.C.: Institute for National Strategic Studies, National Defense University, McNair Paper 53, 1996).

59. Pedro Andrés Pérez Cabral, *La Comunidad mulata: El caso socio-político de la República Dominicana* (Caracas: Gráficas Americana, 1967).

60. The most famous statement of this view is by former president Joaquín Balaguer, *La isla al revés: Haití y el destino dominicano,* 8th ed. (Santo Domingo: Fundación José Antonio Cano, 1994).

61. Anthony J. Spanakos, "Identity, Democracy, and Citizenship: The State of the Nation in the Dominican Republic and Brazil" (Ph.D. diss., University of Massachusetts, 1999).

62. José Vasconcelos, *La raza cósmica: Misión de la raza iberoamericana* (Paris: Agencia Mundial de Librerías, 1925).

63. Gilberto Freyre, *New World in the Tropics: The Culture of Modern Brazil* (New York: Random House, 1963).

64. A preliminary exploration is Howard J. Wiarda, *Democracy and Its Discontents: Development, Interdependence, and U.S. Policy in Latin America* (Lanham, Md.: Rowman and Littlefield, 1995).

Chapter 8. Marxism

1. Among the better studies are Luis E. Aguilar, ed., *Marxism in Latin America* (New York: Knopf, 1968); Robert J. Alexander, *Communism in Latin America* (New Brunswick: Rutgers University Press, 1960); Donald C. Hodges, *The Latin American Revolution* (New York: William Morrow, 1974); Sheldon B. Liss, *Marxist Thought in Latin America* (Berkeley: University of California Press, 1984); Michael Lowy, *Marxism in Latin America from 1909 to the Present* (Atlantic Highlands, N.J.: Humanities Press, 1992); Rollie Poppino, *International Communism in Latin America: A History of the Movement* (New York: Free Press, 1964).

2. Useful summaries and excerpts of Marx's thought can be found in Shlomo Avineri, ed., *Karl Marx on Colonialism and Modernization* (New York: Anchor, 1969); Carl Cohen, ed., *Communism, Fascism, and Democracy: The Theoretical Foundations* (New York: Random House, 1966); Robert C. Tucker, ed., *The Marx-Engels Reader* (New York: Norton, 1978); Robert Paul Wolff, *Understanding Marx: A Reconstruction and Critique* (Princeton: Princeton University Press, 1984).

3. Cohen's book is particularly useful in this regard, containing the original writings of Lenin, Stalin, Mao, and other important political figures.

4. Ché Guevara, *On Guerrilla Warfare* (New York: Praeger, 1961); Regis Debray, *Revolution in the Revolution* (New York: Grove Press, 1967).

5. *Sandinistas Speak* (New York: Pathfinder Press, 1982).

6. Octavio Paz, "Latin America and Democracy," in *Democracy and Dictatorship in Latin America* (New York: Foundation for the Independent Study of Social Ideas, 1982), 6.

7. Miguel Jorrín and John D. Martz, *Latin American Political Thought and Ideology* (Chapel Hill: University of North Carolina Press, 1970), 271.

8. Aguilar, *Marxism,* introduction; Jorrín and Martz, *Latin American Political Thought,* chaps. 6, 9.

9. Poppino, *International Communism,* 217.

10. The best treatment is Jorrín and Martz, *Latin American Political Thought,* chap. 6.

11. James L. Payne, "The Politics of Structured Violence," *Journal of Politics* 27 (May 1965): 362–74.

12. Jorrín and Martz, *Latin American Political Thought,* 183.

13. James L. Payne, *Labor and Politics in Peru: The System of Political Bargaining* (New Haven: Yale University Press, 1965).

14. Georges Sorel, *Reflections on Violence* (Glencoe: Free Press, 1950).

15. Robert J. Alexander, *Organized Labor in Latin America* (New York: Free Press, 1965); Victor Alba, *Politics and the Labor Movement in Latin America* (Stanford: Stanford University Press, 1968).

16. Jorrín and Martz, *Latin American Political Thought,* 181–96.

17. The analysis here derives from Aguilar, *Marxism;* Liss, *Marxist Thought;* Hodge, *The Latin American Revolution;* and Lowy, *Marxism.*

18. Avineri, *Karl Marx.*

19. The analysis here follows Aguilar, *Marxism,* introduction.

20. Richard J. Walter, *The Socialist Party of Argentina* (Austin: University of Texas Press, 1977).

21. Aguilar, *Marxism,* 11; Alexander, *Communism.*

22. Poppino, *International Communism;* Dorothy Dillon, *International Communism and Latin America* (Gainesville: University of Florida Press, 1962).

23. Aguilar, *Marxism,* 29.

24. Ronald M. Schneider, *Communism in Guatemala, 1944–1954* (New York: Praeger, 1959).

25. The best source is Harry Vanden, *National Marxism in Latin America: José Carlos Mariátegui's Thoughts and Politics* (Boulder: Lynne Rienner, 1986).

26. The best source is Harry Kantor, *The Ideology and Program of the Peruvian Aprista Movement* (Berkeley: University of California Press, 1953).

27. Charles Ameringer, *The Democratic Left in Exile: The Anti-Dictatorial Struggle in Latin America* (Miami: University of Miami Press, 1974).

28. Jerome Levinson and Juan de Onis, *The Alliance That Lost Its Way: A Critical Report on the Alliance for Progress* (Chicago: Quadrangle, 1970).

29. Guevara, *Guerrilla Warfare.*

30. Debray, *Revolution in the Revolution.*

31. Eudocio Ravines, *The Yenan Way* (New York: Scribner's, 1951).

32. Gustavo Gutiérrez, *A Theology of Liberation* (Maryknoll, N.Y.: Orbis, 1973).

33. There are several schools of dependency theory ranging from the Marxist-Leninist position of Andre Gunder Frank, *Capitalism and Underdevelopment in Latin America* (New York: Monthly Review Press, 1967); to the socialist position of Fernando Henrique Cardoso and E. Faletto, *Dependency and Development in Latin America* (Berkeley: University of California Press, 1978); to the pragmatic, non-ideological position of Theodore Moran, *Multinational Corporations and the Politics of Dependence* (Princeton: Princeton University Press, 1974).

34. Some of the better studies include Jorge Domínguez, *Cuba: Order and Revolution* (Cambridge: Belknap Press, 1978); Juan del Aguila, *Cuba: Dilemmas of a Revolution,* 3d ed. (Boulder: Westview, 1994); Andres Suárez, *Cuba: Castroism and Communism* (Cambridge: MIT Press, 1967); Ramón Ruiz, *Cuba: The Making of a Revolution* (New York: Norton, 1968); Hugh Thomas, *Cuba; or Pursuit of Freedom* (London: Eyre and Spottiswood, 1971); and Andres Oppenheimer, *Castro's Final Hour* (New York: Simon and Schuster, 1992).

35. On the spread of the Cuban revolution to other countries, see, among others, Hugo Blanco, *Land or Death: The Peasant Struggle in Peru* (New York: Pathfinder, 1972); Eduardo Galeano, *Guatemala: Occupied Country* (New York: Monthly Review Press, 1968); John Gerassi, *Venceremos! The Speeches and Writings of Ché Guevara* (New York: Macmillan, 1968); Richard Gott, *Guerrilla Movements in Latin America* (London: Nelson, 1970); Carlos Marighela, *For the Liberation of Brazil* (Baltimore: Penguin, 1971); Robert Moss, *Urban Guerrillas in Latin America* (London: Institute for the Study of Conflict, 1970).

36. Guillermo O'Donnell, *Modernization and Bureaucratic-Authoritarianism: Studies in South American Politics* (Berkeley: University of California, Institute of International Studies, 1973).

37. Howard J. Wiarda, *Dictatorship, Development, and Disintegration: Politics and Social Change in the Dominican Republic* (Ann Arbor: Xerox University Microfilms, Monograph Series, 1976).

38. Karl E. Meyer, "The Lesser Evil Doctrine," *New Leader* 46 (October 1963): 14.

39. The public opinion survey data indicate that in most Latin American countries support for Marxism-Leninism is down to its lowest point since World War II. The data come from the United States Information Agency and are discussed at length in Howard J. Wiarda, *The Democratic Revolution in Latin America* (New York: Holmes and Meier, 1990).

40. See, among others, Vladimir Tismaneanu, *The Crisis of Marxist Ideology in Eastern Europe* (London: Routledge, 1988); also Howard J. Wiarda and Vladimir Tismaneanu, eds., "The Vulnerabilities of Communist Regimes," *World Affairs* 150, Special Issue (Winter 1987–88).

41. Revelations since the collapse of the USSR have shown that the Soviet Union was an even worse violator of human rights and fomenter of bloody havoc than was thought before. See Steve D. Boilard, *Russia at the Twenty-First Century: Politics and Social Change in the Post-Soviet Era* (Fort Worth: Harcourt Brace, 1998).

42. Howard J. Wiarda, "The Future of Marxist-Leninist Regimes: Cuba in Comparative Perspective," in Sung Chul Yang, ed., *Democracy and Communism: Theory, Reality, and the Future* (Seoul: Korean Association of International Studies, 1995), 609–32.

43. For a recent, more realistic assessment by one of the Sandinista regime's early supporters, see Thomas W. Walker, ed., *Nicaragua without Illusions: Regime Transition and Structural Adjustment in the 1990s* (Wilmington, Del.: Scholarly Resources, 1997).

44. David Scott Palmer, ed., *Shining Path of Peru* (New York: St. Martin's, 1992); Harvey F. Kline, *Colombia: Democracy under Assault* (Boulder: Westview, 1995).

45. Jorge Castañeda, *Utopia Unarmed: The Latin American Left after the Cold War* (New York: Knopf, 1993).

46. "New Ideas for the Old Left," *Economist* (January 17, 1998), 29–30.

47. Jorge Castañeda and Roberto Unger, "Latin American Alternative," unpublished, 1997; also Mark Falcoff, "Latin America's Next Left," *Latin American Outlook* (April 1998).

Chapter 9. Corporatism

1. See, among others, Matthew H. Elbow, *French Corporative Theory, 1789–1948* (New York: Columbia University Press, 1983); Ralph Bowen, *German Theories of the Corporative State* (New York: McGraw Hill, 1947); and Howard J. Wiarda, *Corporatism and Comparative Politics: The Other Great "Ism"* (New York: M. E. Sharpe, 1997).

2. Andrew Cox and Noel O'Sullivan, eds., *The Corporate State: Corporatism and the State Tradition in Western Europe* (Cambridge: Cambridge University Press, 1988); Peter J. Williamson, *Corporatism in Perspective: An Introductory Guide to Corporatist Theory* (London: Sage, 1989).

3. Antony Black, *Guilds and Civil Society in European Political Thought from the Twelfth Century to the Present* (New York: Cornell University Press, 1984).

4. Carl Landauer, *Corporate State Ideologies: Historical Roots and Philosophical Origins* (Berkeley: University of California, Institute of International Studies, 1983).

5. Angus McKay, *Spain in the Middle Ages: From Frontier to Empire, 1000–1500* (London: Macmillan, 1977); see also the references cited in chapter 3.

6. Heinrich A. Rommen, *The State in Catholic Thought: A Treatise in Political Philosophy* (New York: Greenwood Press, 1969); Isaiah Berlin, "The Counter Enlightenment," in Berlin, *Against the Current: Essays in the History of Ideas* (New York: Viking, 1980), 1–24.

7. Elbow, *French Corporative Theory;* Bowen, *German Theories;* Landauer, *Corporative State Ideologies.*

8. On the atomizing effects of modernity, see Emile Durkheim, "The Solidarity of Occupational Groups," in Talcott Parsons, ed., *Theories of Society* (New York: Free Press, 1965).

9. José J. Azpiazu, *The Corporative State* (New York: Herder, 1951).

10. An analysis of the literature may be found in Howard J. Wiarda, *Corporatism and Development: The Portuguese Experience* (Amherst: University of Massachusetts Press, 1977).

11. Alfred Diamant, *Austrian Catholics and the First Republic* (Princeton: Princeton University Press, 1966); Elbow, *French Corporative Theory*.

12. Howard J. Wiarda, "Corporatist Theory and Ideology: A Latin American Development Paradigm," *A Journal of Church and State* 20 (Winter 1978): 29–56.

13. Joseph N. Moody, ed., *Church and Society: Catholic Social and Political Thought and Movements, 1789–1950* (New York: Arts, 1953).

14. Diamant, *Austrian Catholics;* Elbow, *French Corporative Theory;* for the activities of the early Workers' Circles, see Howard J. Wiarda, *The Brazilian Catholic Labor Movement* (Amherst: University of Massachusetts, Labor Relations and Research Center, 1969).

15. I am presently conducting research on the Protestant variations of corporatism focused particularly on the writings and political career of Abraham Kuyper of the Netherlands.

16. Andrew Shonfield, *Modern Capitalism* (London: Oxford University Press, 1965).

17. Raymond Aron, *Main Currents in Sociological Thought II: Durkheim, Pareto, Weber* (New York: Doubleday, 1970).

18. Stanley Payne, *Fascism: Comparisons and Definitions* (Madison: University of Wisconsin Press, 1980); Antonio Costa Pinto, *Salazar's Dictatorship and European Fascism* (New York: Columbia University Press, 1995).

19. G. Lowell Field, *The Syndical and Corporative Institutions of Italian Fascism* (New York: Columbia University Press, 1938); Roland Sarti, "Fascist Modernization in Italy: Traditional or Modern?" *American Historical Review* 75 (April 1970): 1029–45.

20. For a survey, see Wiarda, *Corporatism and Comparative Politics.*

21. Ibid., chap. 1.

22. Ronald C. Newton, "Natural Corporatism and the Passing of Populism in Latin America," *Review of Politics* 36 (January 1974): 34–51. This issue of the *Review of Politics* is devoted to corporatism and contains some seminal essays.

23. See the numerous references in chap. 4.

24. Charles Hale, *Mexican Liberalism in the Age of Mora, 1821–1853* (New Haven: Yale University Press, 1968); José Luis Romero, ed., *Pensamiento conservador, 1815–1898* (Caracas: Editorial Arte, 1978); James D. Henderson, *Conservative Thought in Twentieth-Century Latin America* (Athens: Ohio University, Monographs in International Studies, 1988); and especially Dirck Keyser, "Emilio Portes Gil and Mexican Politics, 1891–1978" (Ph.D. diss., University of Virginia, 1995).

25. Octavio Paz, "Latin America and Democracy," in *Democracy and Dictatorship in Latin America* (New York: Foundation for the Independent Study of Social Ideas, 1992), 5–17.

26. Richard M. Morse, *New World Soundings: Culture and Ideology in the Americas* (Baltimore: Johns Hopkins University Press, 1989).

27. Paz, "Latin America," 7.

28. O. Carlos Stoetzer, *The Scholastic Roots of the Spanish American Revolution* (New York: Fordham University Press, 1979).

29. Especially valuable is Keyser, "Emilio Portes Gil."

30. Keyser's analysis in ibid. is especially rich and valuable.

31. Octavio Paz, *The Labyrinth of Solitude* (New York: Grove, 1961), 11.

32. The analysis here follows that of Keyser, "Emilio Portes Gil"; also Evelyn Stevens, "Mexico: The Institutionalization of Corporatism," in James Malloy,

ed., *Authoritarianism and Corporatism in Latin America* (Pittsburgh: University of Pittsburgh Press, 1977).

33. The best study is George Grayson, *Mexico: From Corporatism to Pluralism?* (Fort Worth: Harcourt Brace, 1998).

34. Howard J. Wiarda, *Corporatism and National Development in Latin America* (Boulder: Westview, 1981).

35. Fredrick B. Pike, *The United States and the Andean Republics: Peru, Bolivia, and Ecuador* (Cambridge: Harvard University Press, 1977); see also his *Spanish America 1900–1970: Tradition and Social Innovation* (New York: Norton, 1973).

36. *New York Times* (August 7, 1941), 16.

37. Marie R. Madden, *Political Theory and Law in Medieval Spain* (New York: Fordham University Press, 1930).

38. Stoetzer, *Scholastic Roots;* Wiarda, *Corporatism and Development.*

39. Guenter Lewy, *Constitutionalism and Statecraft during the Golden Age of Spain* (Geneva: Droz, 1960); see also his *Religion and Revolution* (New York: Oxford University Press, 1974).

40. The arguments are detailed in Wiarda, *Corporatism and National Development;* also Malloy, *Authoritarianism and Corporatism.*

41. Philippe C. Schmitter, *Interest Conflict and Political Change in Brazil* (Stanford: Stanford University Press, 1971).

42. Robert J. Alexander, *The Perón Era* (New York: Columbia University Press, 1951); and George Blanksten, *Perón's Argentina* (New York: Russell and Russell, 1967).

43. Howard J. Wiarda, *The Corporative Origins of the Iberian and Latin American Labor Relations Systems* (Amherst: University of Massachusetts, Labor Relations and Research Center, 1976).

44. Carmelo Mesa Lago, *Social Security in Latin America: Pressure Groups, Stratification, and Inequality* (Pittsburgh: University of Pittsburgh Press, 1978).

45. Howard J. Wiarda, *Dictatorship and Development: The Methods of Control in Trujillo's Dominican Republic* (Gainesville: University of Florida Press, 1970); Wiarda, *The Brazilian Catholic Labor Movement, Corporatism and Development, Corporatism and National Development.*

46. For example, Manuel Arturo Peña Batlle, *Contribución a una campaña (Cuatro discursos)* (Santiago: Editorial El Diario, 1942).

47. Joaquín Balaguer, *Memorias de un cortesano de la era de Trujillo* (Santo Domingo: Editora Corripio, 1988).

48. Juan Linz, "An Authoritarian Regime: Spain," in E. Allardt and S. Rokkan, eds., *Mass Politics* (New York: Free Press, 1970), 251–83.

49. Mihail Manoilesco, *Le siècle du corporatisme* (Paris: Felix Alcan, 1936).

50. Wiarda, *Corporatism and Development.*

51. Samuel H. Beer, *Modern British Politics* (London: Faber and Faber, 1965); Diamant, *Austrian Catholics.*

52. Richard Metafora, "The Spirit of Corporatism and Catholic Social Welfare" (Ph.D. diss., University of Massachusetts, 1998).

53. Martin O. Heisler, *Politics in Europe* (New York: McKay, 1974); Philippe C. Schmitter and Gerhard Lehmbruch, eds., *Trends toward Corporatist Intermediation* (Beverly Hills: Sage, 1979).

54. Malloy, ed., *Authoritarianism and Corporatism.*

381

55. Kenneth P. Erickson, *The Brazilian Corporative State and Working-Class Politics* (Berkeley: University of California Press, 1977).

56. Charles W. Anderson, *Politics and Economic Change in Latin America: The Governing of Restless Nations* (Princeton: D. Van Nostrand, 1967). These themes are explored more fully in the following chapter.

57. Erickson, *Brazilian Corporative State;* Jerome Levinson and Juan de Onis, *The Alliance that Lost Its Way* (Chicago: Quadrangle, 1970).

58. Edward J. Williams, *Latin American Christian Democratic Parties* (Knoxville: University of Tennessee Press, 1967); also, Edward A. Lynch, "Catholic Social Thought in Latin America," *Orbis* 42 (Winter 1998): 105–18.

59. Guillermo O'Donnell, *Modernization and Bureaucratic-Authoritarianism* (Berkeley: Institute of International Studies, University of California, 1973).

60. José Ortega y Gasset, *Invertebrate Spain* (New York: Norton, 1937).

61. See Alfred Stepan, *The Military in Politics: Changing Patterns in Brazil* (Princeton: Princeton University Press, 1971), on the "moderative power" of the army.

62. Discussed in Howard J. Wiarda, ed., *The Iberian–Latin American Connection* (Boulder: Westview, 1986). As a scholar of corporatism, I was contacted during this period by the Argentine, Brazilian, and Chilean governments, which were looking for justifications for their rule.

63. Williams, *Latin American Christian Democratic Parties.*

64. Charles W. Anderson, *The Governing of Restless Nations;* Howard J. Wiarda, *Latin American Politics: A New World of Possibilities* (Fort Worth: Harcourt Brace, 1995).

65. William Glade, *The Latin American Economies: A Study of Their Institutional Evolution* (New York: American Book, 1969); also Howard J. Wiarda, "Economic and Political Statism in Latin America" in Michael Novak and Michael P. Jackson, eds., *Latin America: Dependency or Interdependence* (Washington, D.C.: American Enterprise Institute for Public Policy Research, 1985), 4–14.

66. Paul Sigmund, *Natural Law in Political Thought* (Cambridge, Mass.: Winthrop Publishers, 1971). See also Michael Novak, *The Spirit of Democratic Capitalism* (New York: Simon and Schuster, 1982).

67. David Scott Palmer, book review of Fredrick Pike, *The United States and the Andean Republics, American Political Science Review* 72 (December 1978): 1486–87.

68. Jorge Bustamante, *La república corporativa* (Buenos Aires: EMECE Editores, 1988). For a summary and analysis, see Howard J. Wiarda, "Dismantling Corporatism: The Problem of Modernization in Latin America," *World Affairs* 156 (Spring 1994): 199–203.

69. Mancur Olson, *The Rise and Decline of Nations* (New Haven: Yale University Press, 1982).

Chapter 10. The Conflict Society, 1930s–1980s

1. The main literature on these themes includes John Mander, *The Unrevolutionary Society: The Power of Latin American Conservatism in a Changing World* (New York: Knopf, 1969); Luis Mercier Vega, *Roads to Power in Latin America* (New York: Praeger, 1969); and two volumes edited by Claudio Véliz, *Obstacles to Change in Latin America* (New York: Oxford, 1965), and *The Politics of Conformity in Latin America* (New York: Oxford, 1967).

2. Howard J. Wiarda, *Critical Elections and Critical Coups: State, Society, and the Military in the Processes of Latin American Development* (Athens: Ohio University, Center for International Studies, 1979).

3. Joseph Maier and Alfred Weatherhead, eds., *The Twilight of the Middle Ages: The Politics of Change in Latin America* (New York: Praeger, 1964).

4. Kalman H. Silvert, *The Conflict Society: Reaction and Revolution in Latin America* (New York: Harper and Row, 1968).

5. Charles W. Anderson, *Politics and Economic Change in Latin America: The Governing of Restless Nations* (Princeton: D. Van Nostrand, 1967).

6. John C. Womack, *Zapata and the Mexican Revolution* (New York: Knopf, 1969).

7. Silvert, *The Conflict Society*.

8. Anderson, *Governing of Restless Nations*, chaps. 2–4.

9. David Collier and Ruth Berins Collier, *Shaping the Political Arena: Critical Junctures, the Labor Movement, and Regime Dynamics in Latin America* (Princeton: Princeton University Press, 1991).

10. John J. Johnson, *Political Change in Latin America: The Emergence of the Middle Sectors* (Stanford: Stanford University Press, 1958).

11. Howard J. Wiarda, ed., *Politics and Social Change in Latin America*, 3d ed. (Boulder: Westview, 1992).

12. For this and other elaborations of the Anderson model, see Howard J. Wiarda, *Latin American Politics: A New World of Possibilities* (Fort Worth: Harcourt Brace, 1995).

13. Perhaps the most complete study is Howard J. Wiarda, *Dictatorship, Development, and Disintegration: Politics and Social Change in the Dominican Republic* (Ann Arbor: Xerox University Microfilms, Monograph Series, 1976); a briefer and more accessible version by the same author is *The Dominican Republic: Nation in Transition* (New York: Praeger, 1969).

14. Jorge Bustamante, *La república corporativa* (Buenos Aires: EMECE Editores, 1988).

15. José Ortega y Gasset, *Invertebrate Spain* (New York: Norton, 1937).

16. Howard J. Wiarda, "Toward a Framework for the Study of Political Change in the Iberic-Latin Tradition: The Corporative Model," *World Politics* 25 (January 1973): 206–35.

17. Daniel Levine, *Religion and Politics in Latin America* (Princeton: Princeton University Press, 1981).

18. A useful overview as well as chapters on all the countries may be found in Howard J. Wiarda and Harvey F. Kline, eds., *Latin American Politics and Development*, 4th edition (Boulder: Westview, 1996).

19. Scott B. MacDonald and George A. Fauriol, *Fast Forward: Latin America on the Edge of the 21st Century* (New Brunswick: Transaction Books, 1997).

20. That is one of the conclusions of Howard J. Wiarda, *Corporatism and Development: The Portuguese Experience* (Amherst: University of Massachusetts Press, 1977).

21. Philippe C. Schmitter and Gerhard Lehmbruch, eds., *Trends toward Corporatist Intermediation* (Beverly Hills: Sage, 1979); Suzanne Berger, ed., *Organizing Interests in Western Europe* (Cambridge: Cambridge University Press, 1981).

22. Gabriel A. Almond and Sidney Verba, eds., *The Civic Culture* (Princeton: Princeton University Press, 1963).

23. Lloyd Rudolph and Susan H. Rudolph, *The Modernity of Tradition* (Chicago: University of Chicago Press, 1967).

24. Howard J. Wiarda, *Dictatorship and Development: The Methods of Control in Trujillo's Dominican Republic* (Gainesville: University of Florida Press, 1970).

25. Wiarda, *The Dominican Republic; Dictatorship, Development, and Disintegration.*

26. Thomas Skidmore, *Politics in Brazil, 1930–64: An Experiment in Democracy* (New York: Oxford University Press, 1967).

27. See the individual country chapters in Wiarda and Kline, eds., *Latin American Politics and Development.*

28. Harvey F. Kline, *Colombia: Democracy under Assault* (Boulder: Westview, 1995).

29. David Scott Palmer, *Peru: The Authoritarian Tradition* (New York: Praeger, 1980); Kevin J. Middlebrook and D. S. Palmer, *Military Government and Corporatist Political Development* (Beverly Hills: Sage, 1975).

30. James M. Malloy and Eduardo A. Gamarra, *Reaction and Revolution: Bolivia, 1964–85* (New Brunswick: Transaction, 1988).

31. George Grayson, *Mexico: From Corporatism to Pluralism?* (Fort Worth: Harcourt Brace, 1998).

32. Philip B. Taylor, *Government and Politics of Uruguay* (New Orleans: Tulane Studies in Political Science, 1962).

33. Martin Weinstein, *Uruguay: Democracy at the Crossroads* (Boulder: Westview, 1988).

34. Paul E. Sigmund, *The Overthrow of Allende and the Politics of Chile, 1964–76* (Pittsburgh: University of Pittsburgh Press, 1977).

35. Frederick Nunn, *The Military in Chilean History* (Albuquerque: University of New Mexico Press, 1976).

36. Peter H. Smith, *Argentina and the Failure of Democracy: Conflict among Political Elites* (Madison: University of Wisconsin Press, 1976).

37. Bustamante, *La república corporativa.*

38. Mancur Olson, *The Rise and Decline of Nations* (New Haven: Yale University Press, 1982).

39. Argentina was the main focus of the last section of my "Corporatist Framework" article cited previously, in which I talk about the disintegration of corporatist systems.

40. Samuel P. Huntington, *The Third Wave: Democratization in the Late Twentieth Century* (Norman: University of Oklahoma Press, 1991).

41. Howard J. Wiarda, ed., *The Continuing Struggle for Democracy in Latin America* (Boulder: Westview, 1980).

42. The distinction is from Alfred Stepan, *The State and Society: Peru in Comparative Perspective* (Princeton: Princeton University Press, 1978).

43. Guillermo O'Donnell, *Modernization and Bureaucratic Authoritarianism* (Berkeley: Institute of International Studies, University of California, 1973). A devastating critique is David Collier, ed., *The New Authoritarianism in Latin America* (Princeton: Princeton University Press, 1979).

44. José Nun, "The Middle Class Military Coup" in Véliz, ed., *Politics of Conformity;* also Wiarda, *Dominican Republic.*

45. Quoted in Howard J. Wiarda, "The Latin American Development Process and the New Developmental Alternatives: Military 'Nasserism' and 'Dictatorship with Popular Support,'" *Western Political Quarterly* 25 (September 1972): 464–90.

46. For example, Middlebrook and Palmer, *Military Government and Corporatist Political Development*.

47. Howard J. Wiarda, ed., *The Iberian–Latin American Connection* (Boulder: Westview, 1986).

48. See Linz, "Spain: An Authoritarian Regime"; James M. Malloy, ed., *Authoritarianism and Corporatism in Latin America* (Pittsburgh: University of Pittsburgh Press, 1977); Schmitter and Lehmbruch, *Trends toward Corporatist Interest Intermediation;* Stepan, *State and Society;* and Wiarda, *Corporatism and National Development in Latin America* (Boulder: Westview, 1981).

49. I have tried to wrestle with these themes in *Transcending Corporatism: The Portuguese Corporative System and the Revolution of 1974* (Columbia: University of South Carolina, Institute of International Studies, 1976); *Politics in Iberia: The Political Systems of Spain and Portugal* (New York: Harper Collins, 1992); and *Iberia and Latin America: New Democracies, New Policies, New Models* (Lanham, Md.: Rowman and Littlefield, 1996).

Chapter 11. Transitions to Democracy

1. See both the "Declaration of Principles" and the "Plan of Action" that emerged from the Summit of the Americas held in Miami in 1994. Among the books and studies expressing optimism on Latin America of the early 1990s are Inter-American Dialogue, *Convergence and Community: The Americas in 1993* (Washington, D.C.: Inter-American Dialogue, 1993); Abraham Lowenthal and Gregory Treverton, eds., *Latin America in a New World* (Boulder: Westview, 1994); and Howard J. Wiarda, *Latin American Politics: A New World of Possibilities* (Belmont, Calif.: Wadsworth Publishers, 1994).

2. Among the exceptions, Martin C. Needler, "The Military Withdrawal from Power in South America," *Armed Forces and Society* 6 (Summer 1980); and Talukder Maniruzzaman, *Military Withdrawal from Politics: A Comparative Study* (Cambridge, Mass.: Ballinger, 1987).

3. Among the better studies are Edwin J. Lieuwen, *Arms and Politics in Latin America* (New York: Praeger, 1961); Lyle N. McAlister, *The "Fuero Militar" in New Spain* (Gainesville: University of Florida Press, 1962); Frederick Nunn, *The Military in Chilean History* (Albuquerque: University of New Mexico Press, 1976); and Alfred Stepan, *The Military in Politics: Changing Patterns in Brazil* (Princeton: Princeton University Press, 1971).

4. Lyle N. McAlister et al., *The Military in Latin American Sociopolitical Evolution* (Washington, D.C.: Center for Research in Social Systems, 1970).

5. José Nun, "The Middle Class Military Coup" in Claudio Véliz, ed., *The Politics of Conformity in Latin America* (London: Oxford University Press, 1967), 66–118.

6. See the author's earlier analysis of the military's withdrawal from politics in *The Democratic Revolution in Latin America* (New York: Holmes and Maier, 1990), chap. 3.

7. Maniruzzaman, *Military Withdrawal*.

8. Wiarda, *The Democratic Revolution*.

9. Douglas A. Chalmers and Craig H. Robinson, "Why Power Contenders Choose Liberalization: Perspectives from Latin America." Paper presented at the Annual Meeting of the American Political Science Association, Washington, D.C., August 28–31, 1980.

10. Samuel P. Huntington, *The Third Wave: Democratization in the Late Twentieth Century* (Norman: University of Oklahoma Press, 1991).

11. Wiarda, *The Democratic Revolution.*

12. For example, in Guillermo O'Donnell, Philippe C. Schmitter, and Lawrence Whitehead, eds., *Transitions from Authoritarian Rule* (Baltimore: Johns Hopkins University Press).

13. Enrique Baloyra, "The Salvadoran Elections of 1982–1991," *Studies in Comparative International Development* 28, 3 (1993): 4–31; and William A. Douglas, *La democracia en los países en desarrollo* (San José, Costa Rica: Libro Libre, 1985).

14. More extensive country-by-country treatments can be found in Howard J. Wiarda and Harvey F. Kline, *Latin American Politics and Development,* 4th ed. (Boulder: Westview, 1996).

15. Michael J. Kryzanek, "The 1978 Election in the Dominican Republic: Opposition Politics, Intervention, and the Carter Administration," *Caribbean Studies* 19, nos. 1, 2 (1979): 51–73.

16. George Grayson, *Mexico: From Corporatism to Pluralism?* (Fort Worth: Harcourt Brace, 1998).

17. Jennifer McCoy et al., eds., *Venezuelan Democracy under Stress* (New Brunswick: Transaction Books, 1995); Daniel C. Hellinger, *Venezuela: Tarnished Democracy* (Boulder: Westview, 1991).

18. See the comments of the Brazilian social scientist and minister of culture Francisco Weffort in "Culture, Politics, and Greed: The Complexity of Anti-Corruption Policies in Latin America," Washington, D.C.: Latin America Program of the Woodrow Wilson Center, *Noticias* (1998).

19. See Howard J. Wiarda, ed., *New Directions in Comparative Politics* (Boulder: Westview, 1991).

20. Arend Lijphart, *Democracies* (New Haven: Yale University Press, 1984).

21. Larry Diamond, *Promoting Democracy in the 1990s* (Washington, D.C.: Carnegie Commission, 1995); Fareed Zakaria, "The Rise of Illiberal Democracy," *Foreign Affairs* 76 (November–December 1997): 22–43. See also Howard J. Wiarda, *Cracks in the Consensus: Debating the Democracy Agenda in U.S. Foreign Policy* (Westport, Conn.: Center for Strategic and International Studies and Praeger Publishers, 1997).

22. See, for example, Antonio H. de Oliveira Marques, *A History of Portugal* (New York: Columbia University Press, 1972).

23. See Wiarda, *The Democratic Revolution in Latin America.*

24. Ronald H. McDonald and J. Mark Ruhl, *Party Politics and Elections in Latin America* (Boulder: Westview, 1989); Scott Mainwaring and Timothy R. Scully, eds., *Building Democratic Institutions: Party Systems in Latin America* (Stanford: Stanford University Press, 1995).

25. See the formulation of limited pluralism by Juan Linz, "An Authoritarian Regime: Spain," in E. Allardt and Stein Rokkan, eds., *Mass Politics* (New York: Free Press, 1970).

26. Glen Dealy, *The Public Man: An Interpretation of Latin American and Other Catholic Countries* (Amherst: University of Massachusetts Press, 1977); more recently, Dealy, *The Latin Americans.*

27. For the history, see Magali Sarfatti, *Spanish Bureaucratic-Patrimonialism in America* (Berkeley: Institute of International Studies, University of California,

1966); also Raymundo Faóro, *Os Donos do Poder: Formação do Patronato Político Brasileiro* (Puerto Alegre, Brazil: Globo, 1976).

28. Based on my fieldwork in Latin America; parallel conclusions were reached by Richard Feinberg in his report on the Summit of the Americas in Chile (1998), "The Santiago Summit of the Americas: A First-Hand Report," presented at the Institute on Global Conflict and Cooperation, University of California Washington Center, Washington, D.C., April 20, 1998.

29. Howard J. Wiarda, "After Miami: The Summit, the Peso Crisis, and the Future of U.S.–Latin American Relations," *Journal of Interamerican Studies and World Affairs* 37 (Spring 1995): 43–68.

30. The reference is to Samuel P. Huntington, *The Third Wave*.

31. Maniruzzaman, *Military Withdrawal;* also Guillermo O'Donnell et al., *Transitions from Authoritarian Rule*.

32. Chalmers and Robinson, "Why Power Contenders Choose Liberalization."

33. The survey results are reported in Wiarda, *The Democratic Revolution*.

34. Natalio R. Botana, "New Trends in Argentine Politics," paper presented at the Seminar on the Southern Cone, the Argentine–American Forum, Washington, D.C., June 5–6, 1983.

35. Tina Rosenberg, "Latin America's Magical Liberalism," *Washington Quarterly* (Autumn 1992): 58–74.

36. Ibid., 61.

37. See the surveys of eleven Latin American countries reported in *Cambio 16* [Madrid] (July 19, 1993); see also the surveys of the Chilean polling agency Latinobarómetro of seventeen Latin American countries. United States Information Agency (USIA) polls on Latin American attitudes toward democracy provide strikingly similar results.

38. Reported in Wiarda, *The Democratic Revolution*.

39. The results of a more recent Latinobarómetro survey is reported in *The Economist* (April 4, 1998), 38.

40. Consultores 21, *Cultura democrática en Venezuela: Informe analítico de resultados* (Caracas, 1996).

41. The analysis here and in the following paragraph is based on the Latinobarómetro surveys, cited above.

42. The phrase is Botana's, "New Trends."

43. Luís J. Oropeza, *Tutelary Pluralism: A Critical Approach to Venezuelan Democracy* (Cambridge: Harvard University, Center for International Affairs, 1983).

44. Guillermo O'Donnell, "Delegative Democracy," *Journal of Democracy* 5 (January 1995): 55–69.

45. Diamond, *Promoting Democracy in the 1990s;* Zakaria, "Rise of Illiberal Democracy."

46. Robert Kaplan, "The Coming Anarchy," *Atlantic Monthly* (February 1994), 44–76.

47. See the comments in *Washington Quarterly* (Autumn 1992); also Wiarda, *Democracy and Its Discontents: Development, Interdependence, and U.S. Policy in Latin America* (Lanham, Md.: Rowman and Littlefield, 1995).

48. See the powerful critique of developmentalist assumptions in Samuel P. Huntington, *Political Order in Changing Societies* (New Haven: Yale University Press, 1968).

49. Wiarda, *The Democratic Revolution; Democracy and Its Discontents.*

50. Roderic Ai Camp, *Democracy in Latin America: Patterns and Cycles* (Wilmington, Del.: Scholarly Resources, 1996); and James M. Malloy and Mitchell A. Seligson, eds., *Authoritarian and Democratic: Regime Transitions in Latin America* (Pittsburgh: University of Pittsburgh Press, 1987).

51. Peter Smith, "On Democracy and Democratization," in Howard J. Wiarda, ed., *Politics and Social Change in Latin America: Still a Distinct Tradition,* 3d ed. (Boulder: Westview, 1992).

52. Douglas W. Payne, *Storm Watch: Democracy in the Western Hemisphere into the Next Century* (Washington, D.C.: Center for Strategic and International Studies, Policy Papers on the Americas, 1998); also Anthony Faiola, "Some in Latin America Recall the Good Side of Dictatorship," *Washington Post* (May 31, 1998), A24.

53. See especially the CSIS Western Hemisphere Election Studies carried out by the Americas Program, Georges Fauriol, Director.

54. I am grateful to my CSIS colleagues Lowell Fleischer and Sidney Weintraub for insisting that I understand the political effects of globalization; a major book on these themes is Thomas Friedmann, *The Lexus and the Olive Tree* (New York: Farrar, Straus, and Giroux, 1999).

55. Martin C. Needer, *The Problem of Democracy in Latin America* (Lexington, Mass.: Lexington Press, 1987).

56. Based both on interviews with Department of State officials and on my own participation in a number of these policy discussions, specifically relating to the Dominican Republic, Venezuela, and Mexico but with broader policy implications as well. For the background of the policy debates, see Howard J. Wiarda, "The 1996 Dominican Republic Elections" (Washington, D.C.: Western Hemisphere Election Studies Series, Americas Program, Center for Strategic and International Studies, 1966); and Wiarda, "U.S. Policy and Democracy in the Caribbean and Latin America," Policy Papers on the Americas (Washington, D.C.: CSIS, 1995).

57. Compare Howard J. Wiarda, ed., *The Continuing Struggle for Democracy in Latin America* (Boulder: Westview, 1977) with Wiarda, *The Democratic Revolution: Democracy and Its Discontents,* or *Latin American Politics: A New World of Possibilities* (Belmont, Cal.: Wadsworth, 1995).

Chapter 12. Which Way Latin America?

1. For astute reflections on these themes of distinct explanatory variables in the process of development, see David Landes, *The Wealth and Poverty of Nations* (New York: Norton, 1998).

2. Louis Hartz, *The Liberal Tradition in America* (New York: Harcourt Brace, 1955).

3. Robert Dahl, *A Preface to Democratic Theory* (Chicago: University of Chicago Press, 1956); Theodore Lowi, *The End of Liberalism* (New York: Norton, 1969).

4. Howard J. Wiarda, *Corporatism and National Development in Latin America* (Boulder: Westview, 1981).

5. Alfred Stepan, *State and Society: Peru in Comparative Perspective* (Princeton: Princeton University Press, 1978).

6. Vincent C. Peloso and Barbara A. Tenenbaum, eds., *Liberals, Politics, and*

Power: State Formation in Nineteenth-Century Latin America (Athens: University of Georgia Press, 1996), introduction.

7. Guillermo O'Donnell, *Modernization and Bureaucratic-Authoritarianism: Studies in South American Politics* (Berkeley: Institute of International Studies, University of California, 1973).

8. James Malloy, ed., *Authoritarianism and Corporatism in Latin America* (Pittsburgh: University of Pittsburgh Press, 1977); Wiarda, *Corporatism*.

9. Stepan, *State and Society*.

10. Guillermo O'Donnell, Philippe C. Schmitter, and Lawrence Whitehead, eds., *Transitions from Authoritarian Rule: Prospects for Democracy* (Baltimore: Johns Hopkins University Press, 1986); Howard J. Wiarda, *The Democratic Revolution in Latin America* (New York: Holmes and Maier, 1990).

11. See Lucian W. Pye, "The Non-Western Political Process," *Journal of Politics* 20 (August 1958): 468–86.

12. Louis Hartz, ed., *The Founding of New Societies* (New York: Harcourt Brace Jovanovich, 1964).

13. Peter R. Moody, Jr., *Tradition and Modernization in China and Japan* (Belmont, Calif.: Wadsworth, 1995).

14. Lloyd Rudolph and Suzanne Rudolph, *The Modernity of Tradition* (Chicago: University of Chicago Press, 1967).

15. Okwudiba Nnoli, *Ethnicity and Development in Nigeria* (Aldershot: Avebury, 1995).

16. Anwar Syed, *Pakistan: Islam, Politics and National Solidarity* (Lahore: Vanguard, 1983).

17. An excellent analysis of traditional and modern tendencies in Latin America is H. C. F. Mansilla, *Tradición autoritaria y modernización imitativa: Dilemas de la identidad colectiva en America Latina* (La Paz: Plural Editores, 1997).

18. Howard J. Wiarda, ed., *Non-Western Theories of Development* (Fort Worth: Harcourt Brace, 1998).

19. Philippe C. Schmitter, "Paths to Political Development in Latin America," in Douglas Chalmers, ed., *Changing Latin America* (New York: Academy of Political Science, Columbia University Press, 1972).

20. Recent efforts by the author include *American Foreign Policy: Actors and Processes* (New York: Harper, Collins, 1996); and *Democracy and Its Discontents: Development, Interdependence, and U.S. Policy in Latin America* (Lanham, Md.: Rowman and Littlefield, 1995).

Select Bibliography

Adie, Robert F., and Poitras, Guy E. *Latin America: The Politics of Immobility*. Englewood Cliffs: Prentice-Hall, 1974.

Agüero, Felipe, and Jeffrey Stark, eds. *Fault Lines of Democracy in Post-Transition Latin America*. Miami: North/South Center Press, University of Miami, 1998.

Aguilar, Luís E., ed. *Marxism in Latin America*. New York: Knopf, 1968.

Ai Camp, Roderic. *Democracy in Latin America: Patterns and Cycles*. Wilmington, Del.: Scholarly Resources, 1996.

Alba, Víctor. *Politics and the Labor Movement in Latin America*. Stanford: Stanford University Press, 1968.

Alexander, Robert J. *Communism in Latin America*. New Brunswick: Rutgers University Press, 1960.

——. *Organized Labor in Latin America*. New York: Free Press, 1965.

——. *The Perón Era*. New York: Columbia University Press, 1951.

Almond, Gabriel, and Sidney Verba. *The Civic Culture: Political Attitudes and Democracy in Five Nations*. Boston: Little, Brown, 1965.

Ameringer, Charles. *The Democratic Left in Exile: The Anti-Dictatorial Struggle in Latin America*. Miami: University of Miami Press, 1974.

Anderson, Charles W. *Politics and Economic Change in Latin America: The Governing of Restless Nations*. Princeton: D. Van Nostrand, 1967.

Argüedas, Alcides. *Pueblo infermo*. Barcelona: Vda. de L. Tasso, 1910.

Aristotle. *The Politics*.

Aron, Raymond. *Main Currents in Sociological Thought II: Durkheim, Pareto, Weber*. New York: Doubleday, 1970.

Atkins, G. Pope. *Latin America in the International Political System*. 2d ed. Boulder: Westview, 1989.

Avineri, Shlomo, ed. *Karl Marx on Colonialism and Modernization*. New York: Anchor Books, 1969.

Azevedo, Fernando de. *Brazilian Culture: An Introduction to the Study of Culture in Brazil*. New York: Macmillan, 1950.

Azpiazu, José J. *The Corporative State*. New York: Herder, 1951.

Bagú, Sergio. *Estructura social de la colonia*. Buenos Aires: El Ateneo, 1952.

Bailey, Norman A. *Latin America in World Politics*. New York: Walker, 1967.

Baily, Samuel L., ed. *Nationalism in Latin America*. New York: Knopf, 1971.

Balaguer, Joaquín. *La isla al revés: Haití y el destino dominicano*. 8th ed. Santo Domingo: Fundación José Antonio Cano, 1994.

——. *Memorias de un cortesano de la era de Trujillo*. Santo Domingo: Editora Corripio, 1988.

Baloyra, Enrique. "The Salvadoran Elections of 1982–1991." *Studies in Comparative International Development* 28, 3 (1993): 4–31.

Beer, Samuel H. *Modern British Politics*. London: Faber and Faber, 1965.

Belaúnde, Víctor Andrés. *Bolívar and the Political Thought of the Spanish American Revolution*. Baltimore: Johns Hopkins University Press, 1938.

Berlin, Isaiah. "The Counter Enlightenment," 1–24. In *Against the Current: Essays in the History of Ideas*. New York: Viking, 1980.

——. "The Hedgehog and the Fox." In *Four Essays on Liberty*. New York: Oxford University Press, 1979.

Berger, Suzanne, ed. *Organizing Interests in Western Europe*. Cambridge: Cambridge University Press, 1981.

Bishko, Charles Julian. "The Iberian Background of Latin American History: Recent Progress and Continuing Problems." *Hispanic American Historical Review* 36 (February 1956): 50–80.

Bitarello, Beatriz Helena Domíngues. "Iberian Modernity and the Scientific Revolution of the XVII Century." Washington, D.C.: Library of Congress, Hispanic Division, June 14, 1994.

Black, Anthony. *Guilds and Civil Society in European Political Thought from the Twelfth Century to the Present*. Ithaca: Cornell University Press, 1984.

Blanco, Hugo. *Land or Death: The Peasant Struggle in Peru*. New York: Pathfinder, 1972.

Blanksten, George. *Perón's Argentina*. New York: Russell and Russell, 1967.

Bloch, Marc. *Feudal Society*. Chicago: University of Chicago Press, 1961.

Blossom, Thomas. *Nariño: Hero of Colombian Independence*. Tucson: University of Arizona Press, 1967.

Boilard, Steve D. *Russia at the Twenty-First Century: Politics and Social Change in the Post-Soviet Era*. Fort Worth: Harcourt Brace, 1998.

Botana, Natalio R. "New Trends in Argentina Politics." Paper presented at the Seminar on the Southern Cone, the Argentine-American Forum, Washington, D.C., June 5–6, 1983.

Brennan, Gerald. *The Spanish Labyrinth: An Account of the Social and Political Background of the Spanish Civil War*. Cambridge: Cambridge University Press, 1971.

Buckland, W. W. *A Text Book of Roman Law from Augustus to Justinian.* Cambridge: Cambridge University Press, 1966.

Buckland, W. W., and Arnold D. McNair. *Roman Law and Common Law: A Comparison in Outline.* Cambridge: Cambridge University Press, 1965.

Burns, E. Bradford. *The Poverty of Progress: Latin America in the Nineteenth Century.* Berkeley: University of California Press, 1980.

Bushnell, David, and Neill Macaulay. *The Emergence of Latin America in the Nineteenth Century.* New York: Oxford University Press, 1988.

Bustamante, Jorge. *La república corporativa.* Buenos Aires: EMECE Editores, 1988.

Cabat, L., and Cabat, R. *The Hispanic World: A Survey of the Civilizations of Spain and Latin America.* New York: Oxford, 1961.

Callcott, Wilfrid Hardy. *Liberalism in Mexico, 1857–1929.* Hamden, Conn.: Archon Books, 1965.

Cardoso, Fernando Henrique, and E. Faletto. *Dependency and Development in Latin America.* Berkeley: University of California Press, 1978.

Castro, Américo. *The Spaniards: An Introduction to Their History.* Berkeley: University of California Press, 1971.

———. *The Structure of Spanish History.* Princeton: Princeton University Press, 1954.

Castañeda, Jorge. *Utopia Unarmed: The Latin American Left after the Cold War.* New York: Knopf, 1993.

Castañeda, Jorge, and Roberto Unger. "Latin American Alternative." Unpublished, 1997.

Cespedes, Guillermo. *Latin America: The Early Years.* New York: Knopf, 1974.

Chalmers, Douglas A., and Craig H. Robinson. "Why Power Contenders Choose Liberalization: Perspectives from Latin America." Paper presented at the Annual Meeting of the American Political Science Association, Washington, D.C., August 28–31, 1980.

Chroust, Anton-Hermann. "The Corporate Idea and the Body Politic in the Middle Ages." *Review of Politics* 9 (October 1947): 423–52.

Cohen, Carl, ed. *Communism, Fascism, and Democracy: The Theoretical Foundations.* New York: Random House, 1966.

Collier, David, ed. *The New Authoritarianism in Latin America.* Princeton: Princeton University Press, 1979.

Collier, David, and Ruth Berins Collier. *Shaping the Political Arena: Critical Junctures, the Labor Movement, and Regime Dynamics in Latin America.* Princeton: Princeton University Press, 1991.

Consultores 21. *Cultura democrática en Venezuela: Informe analítico de resultados.* Caracas, 1996.

Conde, Roberto Cortes. *The First Stages of Modernization in Spanish America.* New York: Harper, 1974.

Cox, Andrew, and Noel O'Sullivan, eds. *The Corporate State: Corporatism and the State Tradition in Western Europe*. Cambridge: Cambridge University Press, 1988.

Costa, João Cruz. *A History of Ideas in Brazil*. Berkeley: University of California Press, 1964.

Crow, John A. *Spain: The Root and the Flower*. Berkeley: University of California Press, 1985.

Crawford, W. Rex. *A Century of Latin American Thought*. New York: Praeger, 1961.

Cunha, Euclydes da. *Rebellion in the Backlands (Os Sertões)*. Chicago: University of Chicago Press, 1944.

Dahl, Robert. *A Preface to Democratic Theory*. Chicago: University of Chicago Press, 1956.

Dealy, Glen C. "The Pluralistic Latins." *Foreign Policy* 57 (Winter 1984–85): 108–27.

——. "Prolegomena on the Spanish American Political Tradition." *Hispanic American Historical Review* 48 (February 1968): 37–58.

——. *The Public Man: An Interpretation of Latin American and Other Catholic Countries*. Amherst: University of Massachusetts Press, 1977.

Dean, Warren. *The Industrialization of São Paulo, 1880–1945*. Austin: University of Texas Press, 1969.

del Aguila, Juan. *Cuba: Dilemmas of a Revolution*. 3d ed. Boulder: Westview, 1994.

de Lario, Dámaso. *Los Parlamentos de España*. Madrid: Ed. Anaya, 1991.

del Río, Angel. *The Clash and Attraction of Two Cultures: The Hispanic and Anglo-Saxon Worlds in America*. Baton Rouge: Louisiana University Press, 1965.

Deutsch, Karl W., and William Foltz, eds. *Nation-Building*. New York: Atherton Press, 1966.

Deutsch, Sandra McGee, and Ronald H. Dolkart. *The Argentine Right: Its History and Intellectual Origins, 1910 to the Present*. Wilmington, Del.: Scholarly Resources, 1993.

Diamant, Alfred. *Austrian Catholics and the First Republic*. Princeton: Princeton University Press, 1966.

Diamond, Larry. *Promoting Democracy in the 1990s*. Washington, D.C.: Carnegie Commission, 1995.

Dillon, Dorothy. *International Communism and Latin America*. Gainesville: University of Florida Press, 1962.

Domínguez Ortiz, Antonio. *The Golden Age of Spain, 1516–1659*. London: Weidenfeld and Nicolson, 1971.

Domínguez, Jorge. *Cuba: Order and Revolution*. Cambridge: Belknap Press, 1978.

Douglas, William A. *La democrácia en los países en desarrollo*. San José, Costa Rica: Libro Libre, 1985.

Durkheim, Emile. "The Solidarity of Occupational Groups." In *Theories of Society*, edited by Talcott Parsons. New York: Free Press, 1965.

Ebel, Roland H. "The Development and Decline of the Central American City State." In *Rift and Revolution: The Central American Imbroglio*, 70–104, edited by Howard J. Wiarda. Washington, D.C.: American Enterprise Institute for Public Policy Research, 1984.

——. "Thomism and Machiavellianism in Central American Political Development." Paper given at the 44th International Congress of Americanists, Manchester, England, September 5–10, 1982.

Eisenhower, Milton S. *The Wine Is Bitter: The United States and Latin America*. Garden City: Doubleday, 1963.

Elbow, Matthew H. *French Corporative Theory, 1789–1948*. New York: Columbia University Press, 1983.

Erickson, Kenneth P. *The Brazilian Corporative State and Working Class Politics*. Berkeley: University of California Press, 1977.

Falcoff, Mark. *Small Countries, Large Issues: Studies in U.S.–Latin American Asymmetries*. Washington, D.C.: American Enterprise Institute for Public Policy Research, 1984.

Faóro, Raymundo. *Os Donos do Poder: Formação do Patronato Político Brasileiro*. Rio de Janeiro: Ed. Globo, 1958.

Fichter, Joseph H., S.J. *Man of Spain: Francis Suárez*. New York: Macmillan, 1940.

Field, G. Lowell. *The Syndical and Corporative Institutions of Italian Fascism*. New York: Columbia University Press, 1938.

Foster, George M. *Culture and Conquest: America's Spanish Heritage*. Chicago: Quadrangle, 1960.

Freyre, Gilberto. *The Masters and the Slaves: A Study in the Development of Brazilian Civilization*. New York: Knopf, 1956.

——. *New World in the Tropics: The Culture of Modern Brazil*. New York: Random House, 1963.

Fukuyama, Francis. *The End of History and the Last Man*. New York: Free Press, 1992.

Galeano, Eduardo. *Guatemala: Occupied Country*. New York: Monthly Review Press, 1968.

Gardner, James. *Legal Imperialism: American Lawyers and Foreign Aid in Latin America*. Madison: University of Wisconsin Press, 1980.

Geertz, Clifford. *The Interpretation of Cultures*. New York: Basic Books, 1973.

Gerassi, John. *Venceremos! The Speeches and Writings of Ché Guevara*. New York: Macmillan, 1968.

Gibson, Charles, ed. *The Black Legend: Anti-Spanish Attitudes in the Old World and the New*. New York: Knopf, 1971.

———. *Spain in America*. New York: Harper, 1966.

Gierke, Otto. *Political Theories of the Middle Ages*. Cambridge: Cambridge University Press, 1968.

Gil, Federico G. *Latin American–United States Relations*. New York: Harcourt, Brace, Jovanovich, 1971.

Glade, William. *The Latin American Economies: A Study of Their Institutional Evolution*. New York: American Book, 1969.

Góngora, Mario. *El estado en el derecho indiano*. Santiago: University of Chile, 1951.

Gott, Richard. *Guerrilla Movements in Latin America*. London: Nelson, 1970.

Graham, Richard. *Britain and the Onset of Modernization in Brazil, 1850–1914*. London: Cambridge University Press, 1968.

Grayson, George. *Mexico: From Corporatism to Pluralism?* Fort Worth: Harcourt Brace, 1998.

Green, O. H. *Spain and the Western Tradition*. Madison: University of Wisconsin Press, 1963–66.

Greenfield, Sidney. "The Patrimonial State and Patron-Client Systems in the Fifteenth-Century Writings of the Infante Dom Pedro of Portugal." Occasional Papers Series, No. 1, University of Massachusetts, Center for Latin American Studies, 1976.

Griffiths, G. *Representative Government in Western Europe in the Sixteenth Century*. Oxford: Clarendon Press, 1963.

Guevara, Ché. *On Guerrilla Warfare*. New York: Praeger, 1961.

Gutiérrez, Gustavo. *A Theology of Liberation*. Maryknoll, N.Y.: Orbis Books, 1973.

Hale, Charles A. *Mexican Liberalism in the Age of Mora, 1821–1853*. New Haven: Yale University Press, 1968.

———. *The Transformation of Liberalism in Late Nineteenth-Century Mexico*. Princeton: Princeton University Press, 1989.

Hamilton, Bernice. *Political Thought in Sixteenth-Century Spain*. Oxford: Clarendon Press, 1963.

Halperin-Donghi, Tulio. *The Aftermath of Revolution in Latin America*. New York: Harper, 1973.

Hanke, Lewis. *All Mankind Is One: A Study of the Disputation between Bartolomé de las Casas and Juan Ginés de Sepúlveda in 1550 on the Intellectual and Religious Capacity of the American Indians*. DeKalb, Ill.: Northern Illinois University Press, 1974.

———. *Aristotle and the American Indians*. Bloomington: Indiana University Press, 1970.

——. *The First Social Experiments in the Americas*. Cambridge: Harvard University Press, 1935.

——. *The Spanish Struggle for Justice in the Conquest of America*. Philadelphia: University of Pennsylvania Press, 1949.

Haring, C. H. *The Spanish Empire in America*. New York: Harcourt, Brace, and World, 1963.

Hartz, Louis, ed. *The Founding of New Societies*. New York: Harcourt, Brace, Jovanovich, 1964.

——. *The Liberal Tradition in America*. New York: Harcourt, Brace, 1955.

Hayes, Carlton J. *The Historical Evolution of Modern Nationalism*. New York: Macmillan, 1931.

Hebert, John R., ed. *An Ongoing Voyage*. Washington, D.C.: Library of Congress, 1992.

Heisler, Martin O. *Politics in Europe*. New York: McKay, 1974.

Hellinger, Daniel C. *Venezuela: Tarnished Democracy*. Boulder: Westview, 1991.

Henderson, James D. *Conservative Thought in Twentieth-Century Latin America*. Latin American Series Number 13. Athens: Ohio University Center for International Studies, 1998.

Herring, Hubert. *A History of Latin America*. 3d ed. New York: Knopf, 1968.

Hodges, Donald C. *The Latin American Revolution*. New York: William Morrow, 1974.

Hoetink, Harry. *The Dominican People, 1850–1900*. Baltimore: Johns Hopkins University Press, 1982.

Horowitz, Irving Louis. *Three Worlds of Development*. 2d ed. New York: Oxford University Press, 1972.

Huntington, Samuel P. *Political Order in Changing Societies*. New Haven: Yale University Press, 1968.

——. *The Third Wave: Democratization in the Late Twentieth Century*. Norman: University of Oklahoma Press, 1991.

Inglehart, Ronald. *Cultural Change in Advanced Industrial Society*. Princeton: Princeton University Press, 1990.

Inter-American Dialogue. *Convergence and Community: The Americas in 1993*. Washington, D.C.: Inter-American Dialogue, 1993.

Johnson, Jr., H. B., ed. *From Reconquest to Empire: The Iberian Background in Latin American History*. New York: Knopf, 1970.

Johnson, John J. *Latin America in Caricature*. Austin: University of Texas Press, 1980.

——. *Political Change in Latin America: The Emergence of the Middle Sectors*. Stanford: Stanford University Press, 1958.

Jorrín, Miguel, and John Martz. *Latin American Political Thought and Ideology*. Chapel Hill: University of North Carolina Press, 1970.

Kantor, Harry. *The Ideology and Program of the Peruvian Aprista Movement.* Berkeley: University of California Press, 1953.

———. *Patterns of Politics and Political Systems of Latin America.* Chicago: Rand McNally, 1969.

Karst, Kenneth, and Keith Rosen. *Law and Development in Latin America.* Berkeley: University of California Press, 1975.

Katz, Friedrich. *The Ancient American Civilizations.* New York: Praeger, 1974.

Keyser, Dirck. "Emilio Portes Gil and Mexican Politics, 1891–1978." Ph.D. dissertation, University of Virginia, 1995.

Kicza, John E., ed. *The Indian in Latin American History.* Wilmington, Del.: Scholarly Resources, 1993.

Klein, Julius. *The Mesta: A Study in Spanish Economic History, 1273–1836.* Port Washington, N.Y.: Kennikat Press, 1964.

Kline, Harvey F. *Colombia: Democracy under Assault.* Boulder: Westview, 1995.

Kohn, Hans. *The Idea of Nationalism.* New York: Macmillan, 1960.

Konetzke, Richard. *La condición legal de los criollos y las causas de la independencia.* Seville, 1950.

Kontorowicz, E. H. *The King's Two Bodies: A Study in Medieval Political Theology.* Princeton: Princeton University Press, 1957.

Kryzanek, Michael J. *U.S.–Latin American Relations.* Part I. 3rd ed. Westport, Conn.: Praeger, 1996.

Landauer, Carl. *Corporate State Ideologies: Historical Roots and Philosophical Origins.* Berkeley: University of California, Institute of International Studies, 1983.

Landes, David. *The Wealth and Poverty of Nations.* New York: Norton, 1998.

Lenzer, Gertrude, ed. *Auguste Comte and Positivism: The Essential Writings.* New York: Harper and Row, 1975.

Leonard, Irving A. *Baroque Times in Old Mexico.* Ann Arbor: University of Michigan Press, 1959.

———. "Science, Technology, and Hispanic America." *Michigan Quarterly Review* 2 (October 1963): 237–45.

Levine, Daniel. *Religion and Politics in Latin America.* Princeton: Princeton University Press, 1981.

Levinson, Jerome, and Juan de Onis. *The Alliance that Lost Its Way: A Critical Report on the Alliance for Progress.* Chicago: Quadrangle, 1970.

Lewis, Archibald R. *The Development of Southern French and Catalan Society, 718–1050.* Austin: University of Texas Press, 1975.

Lewis, Paul. *Paraguay under Stroessner.* Chapel Hill: University of North Carolina Press, 1980.

Lewy, Guenter. *Constitutionalism and Statecraft during the Golden Era of Spain.* Geneva: Droz, 1960.

——. *Religion and Revolution*. New York: Oxford University Press, 1974.

Lieuwen, Edwin. *Arms and Politics in Latin America*. New York: Praeger, 1961.

Lijphart, Arend. *Democracies*. New Haven: Yale University Press, 1984.

Linz, Juan. "An Authoritarian Regime: Spain." In *Mass Politics*, 251–83, edited by E. Allardt and S. Rokkan. New York: Free Press, 1970.

Liss, Sheldon B. *Marxist Thought in Latin America*. Berkeley: University of California Press, 1984.

Littwin, Lawrence. *Latin America: Catholicism and Class Conflict*. Encino, Calif.: Dickmen, 1974.

Livermore, Harold. *The Origins of Spain and Portugal*. London: Allen and Unwin, 1971.

Lourie, Elena. "A Society Organized for War: Medieval Spain." *Past and Present* 35 (December 1966): 54–76.

Love, Joseph L., and Nils Jacobsen, eds. *Guiding the Invisible Hand: Economic Liberalism and the State in Latin American History*. New York: Praeger, 1988.

Loveman, Brian. *The Constitution of Tyranny: Regimes of Exception in Spanish America*. Pittsburgh: University of Pittsburgh Press, 1993.

Lowenthal, Abraham F. *Partners in Conflict: The United States and Latin America*. Baltimore: Johns Hopkins University Press, 1987.

Lowenthal, Abraham, and Gregory Treverton, eds. *Latin America in a New World*. Boulder: Westview, 1994.

Lowi, Theodore. *The End of Liberalism*. New York: Norton, 1969.

Lowy, Michael. *Marxism in Latin America from 1909 to the Present*. Atlantic Highlands, N.J.: Humanities Press, 1992.

MacDonald, Scott B., and George A. Fauriol. *Fast Forward: Latin America on the Edge of the 21st Century*. New Brunswick: Transaction Books, 1997.

MacLeod, Murdo. *Spanish Central America*. Berkeley: University of California Press, 1973.

Madden, Marie R. *Political Theory and Law in Medieval Spain*. New York: Fordham University Press, 1930.

Maier, Joseph, and Alfred Weatherhead, eds. *The Twilight of the Middle Ages: The Politics of Change in Latin America*. New York: Praeger, 1964.

Malloy, James M., ed. *Authoritarianism and Corporatism in Latin America*. Pittsburgh: University of Pittsburgh Press, 1977.

Malloy, James M., and Mitchell A. Seligson, eds. *Authoritarians and Democrats: Regime Transitions in Latin America*. Pittsburgh: University of Pittsburgh Press, 1987.

Malloy, James M., and Eduardo A. Gamarra. *Reaction and Revolution: Bolivia, 1964–85*. New Brunswick: Transaction, 1988.

Mander, John. *The Unrevolutionary Society: The Power of Latin American Conservatism in a Changing World*. New York: Knopf, 1969.

Maniruzzaman, Talukder. *Military Withdrawal from Politics: A Comparative Study*. Cambridge, Mass.: Ballinger, 1987.

Manoilesco, Mihail. *Le siècle du corporatisme*. Paris: Felix Alcan, 1936.

Maravall, José Antonio. "The Origins of the Modern State." *Journal of World History* 6 (1961): 789–808.

———. "Del régimen feudal al régimen corporativo en el pensamiento de Alfonso I." *Boletín de la Real Academia de la Historia* (Madrid) 157 (1958).

Marías, Julian. *Understanding Spain*. Ann Arbor: University of Michigan Press, 1990.

Mariejol, J. H. *The Spain of Ferdinand and Isabella*. New Brunswick: Rutgers University Press, 1961.

Marighela, Carlos. *For the Liberation of Brazil*. Baltimore: Penguin, 1971.

Maritain, Jacques. *St. Thomas Aquinas*. New York: Meridan Books, 1964.

Marques, Antonio H. de Oliveira. *A History of Portugal*. New York: Columbia University Press, 1972.

Martí, José. *Martí on the USA*. Carbondale: Southern Illinois University Press, 1966.

———. *Our America*. New York: Monthly Review Press, 1977.

Masur, Gerhard. *Nationalism in Latin America*. New York: Macmillan, 1966.

Mateo, Andres L. *Mito y cultura en la era de Trujillo*. Santo Domingo: Lib. La Trinitaria e Instituto del Libro, 1993.

Maxwell, Kenneth. *Pombal: Paradox of the Enlightenment*. Cambridge: Cambridge University Press, 1995.

McAlister, Lyle N. *The "Fuero Militar" in New Spain, 1746–1800*. Gainesville: University of Florida Press, 1957.

———, et al. *The Military in Latin American Sociopolitical Evolution*. Washington, D.C.: Center for Research in Social Systems, 1970.

———. "Social Structure and Social Change in New Spain." *Hispanic American Historical Review* 43 (August 1963): 349–70.

———. *Spain and Portugal in the New World, 1492–1700*. Minneapolis: University of Minnesota Press, 1984.

McCoy, Jennifer, et al., eds. *Venezuelan Democracy under Stress*. New Brunswick: Transaction Books, 1995.

McDonald, H., and J. Mark Ruhl. *Party Politics and Elections in Latin America*. Boulder: Westview, 1989.

McKay, Angus. *Spain in the Middle Ages: From Frontier to Empire, 1000–1500*. London: Macmillan, 1977.

McKay, John A. *The Other Spanish Christ: A Study in the Spiritual History of Spain and South America*. London: Student Christian Movement Press, 1932.

Mecham, J. Lloyd. *Church and State in Latin America*. Chapel Hill: University of North Carolina Press, 1966.

Mercier Vega, Luis. *Roads to Power in Latin America*. New York: Praeger, 1969.

Merryman, John Henry. *The Civil Law Tradition*. Stanford: Stanford University Press, 1969.

Mesa Lago, Carmelo. *Social Security in Latin America: Pressure Groups, Stratification, and Inequality*. Pittsburgh: University of Pittsburgh Press, 1978.

Merriman, R. B. "The Cortes of the Spanish Kingdoms in the Later Middle Ages." *American Historical Review* 16 (April 1911): 476–95.

Metafora, Richard. "The Spirit of Corporatism and Catholic Social Welfare." Ph.D. dissertation, University of Massachusetts, 1998.

Meyer, Karl E. "The Lesser Evil Doctrine." *New Leader* 46 (October 1963): 14.

Middlebrook, Kevin J., and D. S. Palmer. *Military Government and Corporatist Political Development*. Beverly Hills: Sage, 1975.

Moody, Joseph N., ed. *Church and Society: Catholic Social and Political Thought and Movements, 1789–1950*. New York: Arts, 1953.

Moody, Jr., Peter R. *Tradition and Modernization in China and Japan*. Belmont, Calif.: Wadsworth, 1995.

Moog, Vianna. *Bandeirantes and Pioneers*. New York: George Braziller, 1964.

Moran, Theodore. *Multinational Corporations and the Politics of Dependence*. Princeton: Princeton University Press, 1974.

Moreno, Francisco José. *Legitimacy and Stability in Latin America*. New York: New York University Press, 1969.

Morner, Magnus, ed. *Race and Class in Latin America*. New York: Columbia University Press, 1970.

Morse, Richard M. "The Heritage of Latin America." In *The Founding of New Societies*, edited by Louis Hartz. New York: Harcourt, Brace and World, 1964.

——. *New World Soundings: Culture and Ideology in the Americas*. Baltimore: Johns Hopkins University Press, 1989.

——. "Some Characteristics of Latin American Urban History." *American Historical Review* 67 (January 1962): 317–38.

——. "Toward a Theory of Spanish American Government." *Journal of the History of Ideas* 15 (1964): 71–93.

Moss, Robert. *Urban Guerrillas in Latin America*. London: Institute for the Study of Conflict, 1970.

Mott, Margaret. "The Inquisition in New Spain: The Rule of Faith over Reason." *Journal of Church and State* 40 (Winter 1998): 57–81.

Needler, Martin C. "The Military Withdrawal from Power in South America." *Armed Forces and Society* 6 (Summer 1980).

——. *The Problem of Democracy in Latin America*. Lexington, Mass.: Lexington Press, 1987.

Newton, Ronald C. "On 'Functional Groups,' 'Fragmentation,' and 'Pluralism' in Spanish American Political History." *Hispanic American Historical Review* 50 (February 1970): 1–29.

———. "Natural Corporatism and the Passing of Populism in Spanish America." *Review of Politics* 36 (January 1974): 34–51.

Naoli, Okwidiba. *Ethnicity and Development in Nigeria.* Aldershot: Avebury, 1995.

Nuccio, Richard M. "The Socialization of Political Values: The Content of Official Education in Spain." Ph.D. dissertation, University of Massachusetts, 1977.

Nun, José. "The Middle Class Military Coup." In *Politics of Conformity,* edited by Claudio Véliz.

Nunn, Frederick M. *The Military in Chilean History.* Albuquerque: University of New Mexico Press, 1976.

———. "An Overview of the European Military Missions in Latin America." *Military Affairs* 39 (February 1975): 1–7.

———. *The Time of the Generals.* Lincoln: University of Nebraska Press, 1992.

O'Callaghan, Joseph F. "The Beginning of the Cortes of Leon-Castile." *American Historical Review* 74 (1969): 1503–37.

———. "The Cortes and Royal Taxation during the Reign of Alfonso I of Castile." *Traditio* 27 (1971): 379–98.

O'Donnell, Guillermo. "Delegative Democracy." *Journal of Democracy* 5 (January 1994): 55–69.

———. *Modernization and Bureaucratic-Authoritarianism: Studies in South American Politics.* Berkeley: University of California, 1973.

O'Donnell, Guillermo, Philippe C. Schmitter, and Lawrence Whitehead. *Transitions from Authoritarian Rule.* Baltimore: Johns Hopkins University Press, 1986.

Olson, Mancur. *The Rise and Decline of Nations.* New Haven: Yale University Press, 1982.

Opello, Walter. *Portugal's Political Development: A Comparative Approach.* Boulder: Westview, 1985.

Oropeza, Luís J. *Tutelary Pluralism: A Critical Approach to Venezuelan Democracy.* Cambridge: Harvard University Press, 1983.

Oppenheimer, Andrés. *Castro's Final Hour.* New York: Simon and Schuster, 1992.

Ortega y Gasset, José. *Invertebrate Spain.* New York: Norton, 1937.

Palmer, David Scott. Review of *The United States and the Andean Republics,* by Fredrick Pike. *American Political Science Review* 72 (December 1978): 1486–87.

———, ed. *Shining Path of Peru.* New York: St. Martin's, 1992.

Palmer, Robert Roswell. *The Age of the Democratic Revolutions.* Princeton: Princeton University Press, 1959.

Payne, Douglas W. *Storm Watch: Democracy in the Western Hemisphere into the Next Century.* Policy Papers on the Americas. Washington, D.C.: Center for Strategic and International Studies, 1998.

Payne, James L. *Labor and Politics in Peru: The System of Political Bargaining*. New Haven: Yale University Press, 1965.

——. "The Politics of Structured Violence." *Journal of Politics* 27 (May 1965): 362–74.

Payne, Stanley. *Fascism: Comparisons and Definitions*. Madison: University of Wisconsin Press, 1980.

——. *A History of Spain and Portugal*. 2 vols. Madison: University of Wisconsin Press, 1973.

Paz, Octavio. *The Labyrinth of Solitude*. New York: Grove, 1961.

——. "Latin America and Democracy." In *Democracy and Dictatorship in Latin America*, 5–17. New York: Foundation for the Independent Study of Social Ideas, 1982.

——. "Mexico and the U.S.: Ideology and Reality." *Time*, December 20, 1982, 42.

Peloso, Vincent C., and Barbara A. Tenenbaum, eds. *Liberals, Politics, and Power: State Formation in Nineteenth-Century Latin America*. Athens: University of Georgia Press, 1996.

Peña Batlle, Manuel Arturo. *Contribución a una campaña (Cuatro discursos)*. Santiago: Ed. El Diario, 1942.

Pérez Cabral, Pedro Andrés. *La Comunidad mulata: El caso socio-político de la República Dominicana*. Caracas: Gráficas Americana, 1967.

Perry, J. H. *The Spanish Theory of Empire in the Sixteenth Century*. Cambridge: Cambridge University Press, 1940.

Phelan, John Leddy. *The Kingdom of Quito in the Seventeenth Century: Bureaucratic Politics in the Spanish Empire*. Madison: University of Wisconsin Press, 1967.

Picón-Salas, Mariano. *A Cultural History of Latin America from Conquest to Independence*. Berkeley: University of California Press, 1963.

Pierson, William, and Federico G. Gil. *Governments of Latin America*. New York: McGraw-Hill, 1957.

Pike, Frederick B. *Hispanismo, 1898–1936: Spanish Conservatives and Liberals and Their Relations with Spanish America*. Notre Dame: University of Notre Dame Press, 1971.

——. *The United States and the Andean Republics: Peru, Bolivia, and Ecuador*. Cambridge: Harvard University Press, 1977.

——. *Spanish America 1900–1970: Tradition and Social Innovation*. New York: Norton, 1973.

Pinto, Antonio Costa. *Salazar's Dictatorship and European Fascism*. New York: Columbia University Press, 1995.

Plato. *The Republic*.

Poppino, Rollie. *International Communism in Latin America: A History of the Movement*. New York: Free Press, 1964.

Post, Gaines. "Roman Law and Early Representation in Spain and Italy, 1150–1250." *Speculum: A Journal of Medieval Studies* 18 (April 1943): 211–32.

———. *Studies in Medieval Legal Thought: Public Law and the State, 1100–1322.* Princeton: Princeton University Press, 1964.

Potash, Robert A. *Mexican Government and Industrial Development in the Early Republic: The Banco de Avio.* Amherst: University of Massachusetts Press, 1983.

Powers, James F. "The Origins and Development of Municipal Military Service in the Leonese and Castilian Reconquest, 800–1250." *Traditio* 26 (1970): 91–111.

———. "Townsmen and Soldiers: The Interaction of Urban and Military Organization in the Militias of Medieval Castile." *Speculum* 46 (October 1971): 641–55.

Proctor, Evelyn Stefanos. *Curia and Cortes in León and Castile, 1072–1295.* Cambridge: Cambridge University Press, 1980.

Proctor, Evelyn. "The Towns of León and Castile as Suitors before the King's Court in the Thirteenth Century." *English Historical Review* 290 (January 1959): 1–22.

Putnam, Robert. *Making Democracy Work: Civic Traditions in Modern Italy.* Princeton: Princeton University Press, 1993.

Ravines, Eudocio. *The Yenan Way.* New York: Scribner's, 1951.

Robertson, William Spence. *Rise of the Spanish-American Republics as Told in the Lives of Their Liberators.* New York: Collier Books, 1961.

Rodó, José Enrique. *Ariel.* Austin: University of Texas Press, 1988.

Romero, José Luís, ed. *Pensamiento conservador, 1815–1898.* Caracas: Editorial Arte, 1978.

Rommen, Heinrich A. *The State in Catholic Thought: A Treatise in Political Philosophy.* New York: Greenwood Press, 1969.

Rosenberg, Tina. "Latin America's Magical Liberalism." *Washington Quarterly* (Autumn 1992): 58–74.

Rostow, W. W. *The Stages of Economic Growth.* Cambridge: Cambridge University Press, 1960.

Roth, Cecil. *The Spanish Inquisition.* New York: Norton, 1964.

Rudolph, Lloyd, and Susan Hoeber Rudolph. *The Modernity of Tradition.* Chicago: University of Chicago Press, 1967.

Ruíz, Ramón. *Cuba: The Making of a Revolution.* New York: Norton, 1968.

Sabine, George H. *A History of Political Theory.* 3d ed. New York: Holt, Rinehart, and Winston, 1961.

Sánchez-Albernoz, Claudio. *La españa musulmana.* Madrid: Espasa Calpe, 1973.

———. *España: Un enigma histórico.* Buenos Aires: Ed. Sudamericana, 1956.

———. "The Frontier and Castilian Liberties." In *The New World Looks at Its History*, 27–46, edited by Archibald R. Lewis and Thomas F. McGann. Austin: University of Texas Press, 1963.

Sarfatti, Magali. *Spanish Bureaucratic-Patrimonialism in Latin America*. Berkeley: University of California, 1966.

Sarti, Roland. "Fascist Modernization in Italy: Traditional or Modern?" *American Historical Review* 75 (April 1970): 1029–45.

Schlesinger, Arthur. *The Imperial Presidency*. Boston: Houghton Mifflin, 1989.

Schmitter, Philippe C. *Interest Conflict and Political Change in Brazil*. Stanford: Stanford University Press, 1971.

———. "Paths to Political Development in Latin America." In *Changing Latin America*, edited by Douglas Chalmers. New York: Columbia University Press, 1972.

Schmitter, Philippe C., and Gerhard Lehnbruch, eds. *Trends toward Corporatist Intermediation*. Beverly Hills: Sage, 1979.

Schneider, Ronald M. *Communism in Guatemala, 1944–1954*. New York: Praeger, 1959.

Scully, Timothy R., and Scott Mainwaring, eds. *Building Democratic Institutions: Party Systems in Latin America*. Stanford: Stanford University Press, 1995.

Shonfield, Andrew. *Modern Capitalism*. London: Oxford University Press, 1965.

Siebzehner, Batia. *La universidad americana y la ilustración*. Madrid: Editorial MAPFRE, 1994.

Sigmund, Paul E. *Natural Law in Political Thought*. Cambridge, Mass.: Winthrop Publishers, 1971.

———. *The Overthrow of Allende and the Politics of Chile, 1964–76*. Pittsburgh: University of Pittsburgh Press, 1977.

Silvert, Kalman. *The Conflict Society: Reaction and Revolution in Latin America*. New York: Harper, 1968.

Simpson, Lesley Byrd. "The Cortes of Castile." *Americas* 12 (January 1956): 113–33.

Skidmore, Thomas. *Politics in Brazil, 1930–64: An Experiment in Democracy*. New York: Oxford University Press, 1967.

Smith, Peter H. *Argentina and the Failure of Democracy: Conflict among Political Elites*. Madison: University of Wisconsin Press, 1976.

———. "On Democracy and Democratization." In *Politics and Social Change in Latin America: Still a Distinct Tradition*, 3d ed., edited by Howard J. Wiarda. Boulder: Westview, 1992.

Snow, Peter G. *Government and Politics in Latin America*. New York: Holt, Rinehart, and Winston, 1967.

Sobrinho, Barbarosa Lima. *Desde quando somos nacionalistas?* Petropolis, Brazil: Vozes, 1995.

Somjee, A. H. *Parallels and Actuals of Political Development.* London: Macmillan, 1986.

Sorel, Georges. *Reflections on Violence.* Glencoe, Ill.: Free Press, 1950.

Spanakos, Anthony J. "Identity, Democracy, and Citizenship: The State of the Nation in the Dominican Republic and Brazil." Ph.D. dissertation, University of Massachusetts, 1999.

Stepan, Alfred. *The Military in Politics: Changing Patterns in Brazil.* Princeton: Princeton University Press, 1971.

———. *The State and Society: Peru in Comparative Perspective.* Princeton: Princeton University Press, 1978.

Stevens, Evelyn. "Mexico: The Institutionalization of Corporatism." In *Authoritarianism and Corporatism in Latin America,* edited by James Malloy. Pittsburgh: University of Pittsburgh Press, 1977.

Stoetzer, O. Carlos. *The Scholastic Roots of the Spanish American Revolution.* New York: Fordham University Press, 1982.

Stokes, William S. *Latin American Politics.* New York: Crowell, 1959.

Suárez, Andres. *Cuba: Castroism and Communism.* Cambridge: MIT Press, 1967.

Syed, Anwar. *Pakistan: Islam, Politics and National Solidarity.* Lahore: Vanguard, 1983.

Tannenbaum, Frank. *Ten Keys to Latin America.* New York: Vintage, 1962.

Tanzi, Héctor José. "La doctrina de los juristas hispanos sobre el poder político y su influencia en América." *Boletín Histórico* 20 (September 1970): 328–38.

Tawney, R. H. *Religion and the Rise of Capitalism.* London: J. Murray, 1929.

Taylor, Philip B. *Government and Politics of Uruguay.* New Orleans: Tulane Studies in Political Science, 1962.

Thomas, Hugh. *Cuba, or Pursuit of Freedom.* London: Eyre and Spottiwood, 1971.

Tismaneanu, Vladimir. *The Crisis of Marxist Ideology in Eastern Europe.* London: Routledge, 1988.

Topik, Steven. *The Political Economy of the Brazilian State, 1889–1930.* Austin: University of Texas Press, 1982.

Trevisan, Leonardo. *A República Velha.* São Paulo: Global, 1982.

Tuchman, Barbara. *A Distant Mirror: The Calamitous 14th Century.* New York: Knopf, 1978.

———. *The Proud Tower.* New York: Macmillan, 1962.

Tucker, Robert C., ed. *The Marx-Engels Reader.* New York: Norton, 1978.

Turton, Peter. *José Martí: Architect of Cuba's Freedom.* London: Zed Books, 1986.

Van Cott, Donna Lee. *Defiant Again: Indigenous Peoples and Latin America's Security.* McNair Paper 53. Washington, D.C.: Institute for National Strategic Studies, National Defense University, 1996.

———, ed. *Indigenous Peoples and Democracy in Latin America.* New York: St. Martin's Press, 1995.

Vasconcelos, José. *La raza cósmica: Misión de la raza iberoamericana.* Paris: Agencia Mundial de Librerias, 1925.

Vanden, Harry. *National Marxism in Latin America: José Carlos Mariátegui's Thoughts and Politics.* Boulder: Lynne Rienner Publishers, 1986.

Vega, Bernardo. *La agenda pendiente: Reformas, geopolítica, y frustración.* Santo Domingo: Fundación Cultural Dominicana, 1996.

Véliz, Claudio. *The Centralist Tradition in Latin America.* Princeton: Princeton University Press, 1980.

———. *Obstacles to Change in Latin America.* New York: Oxford, 1965.

———. *The Politics of Conformity in Latin America.* New York: Oxford, 1967.

Vives, Jaime Vicens. *Approaches to the History of Spain.* Berkeley: University of California Press, 1970.

Vorsey, Louis de, Jr. *Keys to the Encounter.* Washington, D.C.: Library of Congress, 1992.

Wagley, Charles. *The Latin American Tradition.* New York: Columbia University Press, 1968.

Walker, Thomas W., ed. *Nicaragua without Illusions: Regime Transition and Structural Adjustment in the 1990s.* Wilmington, Del.: Scholarly Resources, 1997.

Wallach, John R. "Politics and the Division of Human Activity in Ancient Greek Political Theory." Paper presented at the Annual Meeting of the American Political Science Association, Washington, D.C., August 30–September 2, 1984.

Walter, Richard J. *The Socialist Party of Argentina.* Austin: University of Texas Press, 1977.

Watt, W. Montgomery. *A History of Islamic Spain.* Edinburgh: University of Edinburgh Press, 1965.

Weber, Max. *The Theory of Social and Economic Organization.* New York: Free Press, 1964.

Weckman, Luís. "The Middle Ages in the Conquest of America." In *History of Latin American Civilization: Sources of Interpretations.* Volume 1: *The Colonial Experience,* 10–22, edited by Lewis Hanke. Boston: Little, Brown, 1967.

Weffort, Francisco. "Culture, Politics, and Greed: The Complexity of Anti-Corruption Policies in Latin America." *Noticias.* Washington, D.C.: Latin American Program of the Woodrow Wilson Center, 1998.

Weinstein, Martin. *Uruguay: Democracy at the Crossroads.* Boulder: Westview, 1998.

Whitaker, Arthur P. *Nationalism in Latin America*. Gainesville: University of Florida Press, 1962.

———, ed. *Latin America and the Enlightenment*. Ithaca: Cornell University Press, 1961.

———, and David C. Jordan. *Nationalism in Contemporary Latin America*. New York: Free Press, 1966.

Wiarda, Howard J. "After Miami: The Summit, the Peso Crisis, and the Future of U.S.–Latin American Relations." *Journal of Interamerican Studies and World Affairs* 37 (Spring 1995): 43–68.

———. *American Foreign Policy: Actors and Processes*. New York: Harper, Collins, 1996.

———. *The Brazilian Catholic Labor Movement*. Amherst: University of Massachusetts, Labor Relations and Research Center, 1969.

———. *Corporatism and Comparative Politics: The Other Great "Ism."* New York: M. E. Sharpe, 1997.

———. *Corporatism and Development: The Portuguese Experience*. Amherst: University of Massachusetts Press, 1977.

———. *Corporatism and National Development in Latin America*. Boulder: Westview, 1981.

———. "Corporatist Theory and Ideology: A Latin American Development Paradigm." *Journal of Church and State* 20 (Winter 1978): 29–56.

———. *The Corporative Origins of the Iberian and Latin American Labor Relations Systems*. Amherst: University of Massachusetts, 1976.

———. *Cracks in the Consensus: Debating the Democracy Agenda in U.S. Foreign Policy*. Westport, Conn.: Praeger, 1997.

———. *Critical Elections and Critical Coups: State, Society, and the Military in the Processes of Latin American Development*. Athens: Ohio University Press, 1979.

———. *Democracy and Its Discontents: Development, Interdependence, and U.S. Policy in Latin America*. Lanham, Md.: Rowman and Littlefield, 1995.

———. *The Democratic Revolution in Latin America: History, Politics, and U.S. Policy*. New York: Holmes and Meier, 1990.

———. *Dictatorship and Development: The Methods of Control in Trujillo's Dominican Republic*. Gainesville: University of Florida Press, 1970.

———. "Dismantling Corporatism: The Problem of Modernization in Latin America." *World Affairs* 156 (Spring 1994): 199–203.

———. "Economic and Political Statism in Latin America." In *Latin America: Dependency or Interdependence*, 4–14, edited by Michael Novak and Michael P. Jackson. Washington, D.C.: American Enterprise Institute for Public Policy Research, 1985.

———. *Ethnocentrism and Foreign Policy: Can We Understand the Third World?* Washington, D.C.: American Enterprise Institute for Public Policy Research, 1985.

———. "The Future of Marxist-Leninist Regimes: Cuba in Comparative Perspective." In *Democracy and Communism: Theory, Reality, and the Future,* 609–32, edited by Sung Chul Yang. Seoul: Korean Association of International Studies, 1995.

———. *Iberia and Latin America: New Democracies, New Policies, New Models.* Lanham, Md.: Rowman and Littlefield, 1996.

———. *Introduction to Comparative Politics.* Belmont: Wadsworth, 1993.

———. "The Latin American Development Process and the New Developmental Alternatives: Military 'Nasserism' and 'Dictatorship with Popular Support'." *Western Political Quarterly* 25 (September 1971): 464–90.

———. *Latin American Politics: A New World of Possibilities.* Fort Worth: Harcourt Brace, 1995.

———. "Political Culture and the Attraction of Marxism-Leninism: National Inferiority Complexes as an Explanatory Factor." *World Affairs* 151 (Winter 1988–89): 143–50.

———. *Politics in Iberia: The Political Systems of Spain and Portugal.* New York: Harper Collins, 1992.

———. "State-Society Relations in Latin America: Toward a Theory of the Contract State." Chapter 8 in *American Foreign Policy toward Latin America in the 80s and 90s: Issues and Controversies from Reagan to Bush.* New York: New York University Press, 1992.

———. "Toward Consensus in Interpreting Latin American Politics: Developmentalism, Dependency, and 'The Latin American Tradition'." *Studies in Comparative International Development,* 2000.

———. "Toward a Framework for the Study of Political Change in the Iberic-Latin Tradition: The Corporative Model." *World Politics* 25 (January 1973): 206–35.

———. *Transcending Corporatism: The Portuguese Corporative System and the Revolution of 1974.* Columbia: University of South Carolina Press, 1976.

———, ed. *The Continuing Struggle for Democracy in Latin America.* Boulder: Westview, 1980.

———, ed. *The Iberian–Latin American Connection.* Boulder: Westview, 1986.

———, ed. *New Directions in Comparative Politics.* Boulder: Westview, 1991.

———, ed. *Non-Western Theories of Development.* Fort Worth: Harcourt Brace, 1998.

———, ed. *Politics and Social Change in Latin America.* 3d ed. Boulder: Westview, 1992.

———, and Harvey F. Kline, eds. *Latin American Politics and Development.* 4th ed. Boulder: Westview, 1996.

———, and Vladimir Tismaneanu, eds. "The Vulnerabilities of Communist Regimes." Special issue, *World Affairs* 150 (Winter 1987–88).

Wiarda, Iêda Siqueira. "Brazil: The Politics of 'Order and Progress' or Chaos and Retrogression." In *Latin American Politics and Development,* 109–143, edited by Howard J. Wiarda and Harvey F. Kline. Boulder: Westview, 1996.

Wilenius, Reijo. *The Social and Political Theory of Francisco Suárez.* Helsinki: Societas Philosophica Fennica, 1963.

Willems, Emilio. *Latin American Culture.* New York: Harper Row, 1975.

Williams, Edward J. *Latin American Christian Democratic Parties.* Knoxville: University of Tennessee Press, 1967.

Williamson, Peter J. *Corporatism in Perspective: An Introductory Guide to Corporatist Theory.* London: Sage, 1989.

Williamson, René. *Culture and Policy: The United States and the Hispanic World.* Knoxville: University of Tennessee Press, 1949.

Wolf, Eric R., and Edward C. Hansen. "Caudillo Politics: A Structural Analysis." *Comparative Studies in Society and History* 2 (January 1967): 168–79.

Wolff, Robert Paul. *Understanding Marx: A Reconstruction and Critique.* Princeton: Princeton University Press, 1984.

Wolin, Sheldon S. *Politics and Vision: Continuity and Innovation in Western Political Thought.* Boston: Little, Brown, 1960.

Womack, John C. *Zapata and the Mexican Revolution.* New York: Knopf, 1969.

Woodward, Ralph Lee, Jr., ed. *Positivism in Latin America, 1850–1900.* Lexington, Mass.: D. C. Heath, 1971.

Worcester, Donald C. "Historical and Cultural Sources of Spanish Resistance to Change." *Journal of Inter-American Studies* 6 (April 1964): 173–80.

——. "The Spanish American Past: Enemy of Change." *Journal of Inter-American Studies* 11 (January 1969): 66–75.

——, and Wendell G. Schaeffer. *The Growth and Culture of Latin America.* 2nd ed. New York: Oxford University Press, 1970.

Zakaria, Fareed. "The Rise of Illiberal Democracy." *Foreign Affairs* 76 (November–December 1997): 22–43.

Zea, Leopoldo. *Positivism in Mexico.* Austin: University of Texas Press, 1974.

Index

absolute monarchy, 70
absolutism, 98
Adams, John, 7
Africa, 354
Agency for International Development (AID), 318
agrarian reform, 289
agrarian-socialists, 234
Alberdi, Juan Bautista, 154, 168, 200
Alemán, Arnoldo, 242
Alfonsín, Raúl, 313
Alfonso X, 69
Allende, Salvador, 301
Alliance for Progress, 127, 273, 275, 304
Almagro, Diego de, 86
Alvarado, Pedro de, 85
American foreign policy, 127
American Popular Revolutionary Alliance (APRA), 225, 267
anarchism, 216, 219, 233
anarcho-syndicalism, 221
Anderson, Charles W., 283
Andersonian model, 283, 333
anticommunism, 226
Apristas, 234, 267
Aquinas, Thomas, Saint, 6, 44, 60, 69, 126, 129, 136, 265, 290, 305, 308, 345, 350,
Aragon, 71
Argentina, 153ff., 167, 169, 177, 201, 205, 218, 219, 221, 237, 244, 275, 291, 301, 303, 306, 311, 316, 349; Communist Party, 225; Socialist Party, 223
Arias, Arnulfo, 267
Ariel, 187, 236
arielismo, 264
Aristide, Jean-Bertrand, 316
aristocratic ethos, 21
Aristotle, 21, 345
armed forces, 134, 146, 272, 276, 310. *See also* military
army, 140
Arosemena, Otto, 190
Atahualpa, 86
Athens, 26
Augustine, Saint, 6, 39, 42, 345
authoritarianism, 17, 33, 58, 60, 79, 98, 146, 197, 275, 289, 303ff., 313, 332
autonomy, 67
Aztecs, 105

Báez, Buenaventura, 140
Bakunin, Michael, 219
Balaguer, Joaquín, 277, 297, 316, 343, 357
Barbusse, Henri, 227
Barreda, Gabino, 163, 226n
Barreto, Tobias, 223
Batista, Fulgencio, 197, 202, 272
Batlle y Ordoñez, José, 168, 300
Belgrano, Manuel, 116

Index

Bello, Andrés, 153
Benavides, Oscar, 267
Bentham, Jeremy, 147
Betancourt, Rómulo, 232
Bible, 37, 350
black legend, 53
Blaine, James, 185
Bolívar, Simón, 114, 118ff., 129
Bolivia, 127, 168, 219, 267, 299, 316, 332
Bolshevik Revolution, 224, 253
Bosca, Giuseppe, 249
Bosch, Juan, 232, 238, 297
Bourbon royal family, 107, 120
Brazil, 87, 102, 123, 127, 139, 149, 166, 169, 209, 237, 244, 298, 305, 306, 316, 329, 332, 349, 357
Buenos Aires, 86
bureaucracy, 146
bureaucratic-authoritarianism, 275, 304, 308, 349
business groups, 256, 288
Bustamante, Jorge, 279, 291, 302

cabildos, 98
Cabral, Pedro Alvares, 87
Caldera, Rafael, 277
Calderon Guardía, Rafael, 226n
Calhoun, John, 8
Calles, Pultarco, 262
capital, foreign, 145
captains general, 98
Cárdenas, Cuauhtemoc, 235, 243, 336
Cárdenas, Lázaro, 263
Cardoso, Fernando Henrique, 244
Carías Andino, Tiburcio, 197
Carta del Lavoro, 268
Carter, Jimmy, 127, 313
Castañeda, Jorge, 245
caste associations, 354
caste system, 100
Castile, 71
Castro, Fidel, 206, 216, 232, 244
Castroism, 313
Catholic orthodoxy, 79
Catholicism, 246, 352. See also Roman Catholic Church
caudillo, 43, 142
caudilloism, 146
Central America, 127, 168, 314, 332
Central American Confederation, 26, 177
centralism, 51
Chapelier Law, 133, 248

Charles I, 73, 95
charters, 58
Chávez, Hugo, 29, 329, 357
Chile, 138, 139, 143, 153, 168, 201, 218, 219, 221, 225, 237, 278, 301, 303, 306, 316, 331, 338, 349
Christian community, 40, 42
Christian democrats, 274, 357
Christian kingdoms, 59
Christianity, 36, 37ff.
Church, the, 101, 132, 140. See also Roman Catholic Church
Cicero, 30
científicos, 164
city-states, 26
civil society, 312, 319, 354
class struggle, 214
class system, 56
clientelism, 31
Clinton, Bill, 335
Coimbra, University of, 95
Cold War, 179, 226, 314
Colombia, 138, 150, 242, 244, 298, 304, 316, 333
Columbus, Christopher, 83
Comintern, 224
"common good, the," 136
communist parties, 224
communists, 233
Comte, Auguste, 6, 157, 200, 345
concordats, 273
"conflict society," 5, 16, 281ff.
Confucianism, 354
Congress, U.S., 131, 318
conquest, political theory of, 88
consent, theory of, 96
conservatism, 143
conservatives, 108, 110, 124, 126, 139, 150, 195
Constant Betelho de Magolhães, Benjamin, 166
constitutionalism, 50, 67
constitutions, 127, 131, 141
containment, 226
contract theory, 93, 96
corporate groups, 65, 68, 151, 290, 306
corporations, 132
corporatism, 6, 15, 17, 23, 33, 58, 61, 246ff., 288, 307, 312, 345, 348, 352, 359; ideological, 257; natural, 257; origins, 247; State, 270
corporatist democracy, 334, 349
corporative organization of society, 93, 95, 101, 135, 304

412

corruption, 319
cortes, 58, 65, 82
Cortés, Hernán, 84
"cosmic race," 228
Costa Rica, 143, 169, 201, 304, 316, 331, 338
Council of the Indies, 98
Council of Trade, 98
courts, 131
Cousin, Victor, 149
Covadonga, 55
creoles, 108, 121, 124, 128
crises of the system, 292
Crown, the, 82
Cuba, 14, 168, 180, 183ff., 210, 216, 219, 225, 315, 317; Revolution, 232ff.
cuerpos, 260
culture studies, 2
Cunha, Euclydes da, 167

Dark Ages, 43
Darwin, Charles, 157, 189, 201
Debray, Régis, 232
Decurtins, Kaspar, 249
"delegative democracy," 334
demes, 23
democracy, 17, 50, 113, 128; attacks on, 188; consolidation of, 323; definitions of, 67, 133, 287, 321, 328, 334; transitions to, 304, 309ff., 323
democratic caesarism, 32, 334
dependency theory, 235
development, idea of, 320
dialectic, 214
Diamond, Larry, 321, 334
Díaz, Porfirio, 29, 164, 261
Dickens, Charles, 213
dictatorship of the prolatariat, 215
divine-right monarchy, 46
Dominican Republic, 138, 168, 170, 180, 199, 204, 209, 219, 275, 288, 297, 316, 333
donatario, 102
Donoso Cortés, Juan Francisco, 151, 249
Durkheim, Emile, 250
Dutch, 103

Echevarría, Esteban, 153
economic determinism, 214
economic growth, 145
Ecuador, 275, 299, 316, 332, 333
Eisenhower, Dwight, 204
ejidos, 100, 107, 155

elite democracy, 334
elites, 31, 60, 96, 132, 172, 174, 289, 305, 327
elitist, 33
El Salvador, 169, 242, 298, 316
encomienda, 57, 98
Engels, Friedrich, 214
enlightened despotism, 32
Enlightenment, 114
entitlements, 279, 302
estates, landed, 34; medieval, 65, 8
eugenics, 202
executive authority, 130

Fabian socialism, 216
Falklands/Malvinas War, 311
fascism, 255
federalism, 131
Ferdinand, 71, 95, 345
Ferdinand VII, 120, 122, 260
feudalism, 3, 50, 56, 77, 346, 350
Fidelistas, 234
Figueras, José, 232
Flores Magón brothers, 221
foco theory, 233
Ford Foundation, 318
Franco, Francisco, 29, 196, 198, 254, 270, 305
free trade, 309
Frei, Eduardo, 357
French Revolution, 133, 248
Frondizi, Arturo, 232
fueros, 57, 62, 73, 81, 83, 93, 120, 122, 123
Fujimori, Alberto, 29, 96, 132, 244, 329, 333, 341, 343, 357
functional groups, 25, 46, 81
functional representation, 256

Geertz, Clifford, 9
Generation of, 98, 194
Ghioldi, Américo, 223
globalization, 325
Gómex, Juan Vicente, 169
Gómez, Laureano, 197, 267
González Prada, Manuel, 231
Good Neighbor Policy, 127, 179
Gospels, 40
Goulart, João, 298, 305
government, systems of, 36
Gramsci, Antonio, 227
Gran Colombia, 26
"great chain of being," 41, 60, 93
Great Depression, 197

Index

Greece, influence of, 20ff., 350
gridlock, 303
group rights, 58, 62, 68, 346
Guatemala, 209, 226, 242, 275, 298, 316
guerrilla groups, 242
Guevara, Ché, 206, 216, 237
guilds, 61, 64, 101, 248
Gumplowicz, Ludwig, 254

Haiti, 170, 199, 316
Hapsburg model, 71, 74, 281, 305, 345, 350
harmony, in society, 23
Haya de la Torre, Víctor Raúl, 230
"hedgehogs," 158
Hegel, Friedrich, 250
Hernández Martínez, Maximiliano, 197, 267
Heureaux, Ulises, 169
Hidalgo, Miguel, 117, 119
hierarchy, 21, 32, 60, 93, 290
Hispania, 28
Hispaniola, 83
Hispanismo, 15, 193ff., 202, 209, 264, 345, 348
Hobbes, Thomas, 72, 89
Honduras, 150, 169, 275, 316
Hostos, Eugenio María de, 168
human rights, 313, 315
Huntington, Samuel P., 304

Ibáñez, Carlos, 197, 267
Iberia, history, 19ff. See also Spain; Portugal
"ideal types," 11
idealism, 148
imperialism, 216
import substitution industrialization (ISI), 304, 348
Incas, 106, 208, 228
independence, 110, 112ff.
Indian communities, 100, 104, 228
indianism, 228
indigenous groups, 104, 354
individualism, 188
industrialization, 212
Inquisition, the, 57, 60, 72
Institute for Hispanic Cooperation, 198
Institute for Hispanic Culture, 196
intendant, 109
Inter-American Development Bank (IADB), 213

Inter-American Dialogue, 318
inter-American system, 179
International Monetary Fund (IMF), 213
"invertebrate society," 275, 303
Isabella, Queen, 71, 95, 345
Islam, 51, 354
Iturbide, Agustín, 125, 135, 261

Jefferson, Thomas, 6, 155, 290
Jesuits, 107
Jews, 53
jihad, 51
João VI, 123
Johnson, Lyndon B., 190
Juárez, Benito, 162
juridical personality, 33, 80, 287
jurists, 93
justicialismo, 268
Justo, Juan B., 223

Kennedy, John F., 127, 273, 304
kingdoms, of Iberia, 65
Krause, Christian Friedrich, 148
Krausism, 148
Kuyper, Abraham, 249

labor, organized, 256
labor, theory of value, 214
La Farrell, François, 250
landholding, 56
Las Casas, Bartolomé de, 84
Lastarría, José Victorino, 168
Latinobarómetro, 332
law, 29
League of Nations, 182
League of Popular Parties, 229, 232
left groups, 243
legal culture, 137, 324
legal system, 137
Lenin, Vladimir, 216
Leo XIII, Pope, 251
Leoni, Raúl, 232
"lesser evil doctrine," 239
Letelier, Valentín, 168
Ley Lerdo, 155
liberalism, 17, 112ff., 138, 143, 155, 246, 321, 347
liberals, 150, 195
liberation theology, 235, 274, 294
liberties, 57
Linz, Juan, 270
"living museum," 5, 16, 283

local government, 131, 319
localism, 51
Locke, John, 5, 89, 96, 155, 346

Machiavelli, 71, 89, 142
machismo, 52
Madden, Marie R., 265
Madison, James, 6, 155, 290
"magical liberalism," 330
Maistre, Joseph de, 151, 248
Manning, Cardinal Henry, 249
Manoilesco, Mihail, 271
Mao Zedong, 216
Mariátegui, José Carlos, 227
Marines, U.S., 169
Maritain, Jacques, 274
Martí José, 14, 183ff., 223
Marx, Karl, 231, 222
Marxism, 7, 15, 212ff., 348; crisis of, 239; indigenous, 227; varieties of, 233;
Marxism-Leninism, 238, 243
Maryknoll Order, 293
materialism, 214
Mayans, 105, 208
medievalism, 3, 50, 76, 90, 345
Menem, Carlos, 29
mercantilism, 80, 319
MERCOSUR, 182
mesta, 64
Mexican-American War, 175, 180
Mexican Revolution, 155, 230
Mexico, 14, 31, 84, 96, 138, 143, 162, 209, 244, 260, 280, 287, 299, 312, 316, 325
Michels, Roberto, 254
militarism, 56
military, 100, 132, 305, 327; *See also* armed forces
military *fuero*, 140, 310
military orders, 60, 63, 72, 247
military regimes, 306
Mill, James, 147
Mill, John Stuart, 157, 290
Minas Gerais, 167
Miranda, Francisco de, 114
"moderative power," 310
modernization, 1, 91
monism, 324
Monroe Doctrine, 179
Montesquieu, 6, 114, 155
Montezuma, 85
Moors, 43, 50
Mora, José María Luís, 133, 152

Morelos, Father José María, 117, 119
Moreno, Mariano, 116, 134
Mosca, Gaetano, 254
Mun, Albert de, 249
Muñoz Marín, Luís, 232
Mussolini, Benito, 254, 255

Napoleon I, 120, 260
Napoleonic Code, 137
Nariño, Antonio, 115
National Endowment for Democracy (NED), 127
National Revolutionary Movement (MNR-Bolivia), 267, 299
nationalism, 175ff., 348
Nazi Germany, 225, 255
neocorporatism, 270, 280, 354
neoliberalism, 17, 325, 326. *See also* liberalism
neoscholastics, 92, 345
Nicaragua, 170, 216, 242, 275, 288, 298, 317
Nixon, Richard, 204
nobility, 100
nongovernmental organizations (NGOs), 312, 324

obedience, obligation to, 39
O'Donnell, Guillermo, 304, 334
oligarchy, 57, 72, 133, 140, 189
Olney, Richard, 180
Olson, Mancur, 303
open markets, 309
order, 25
organic state, 345, 349
organicism, 23, 58, 93, 95, 324, 345
Organization of American States (OAS), 182
Ortega, Daniel, 242
Ortega y Gasset, José, 194, 275
Os Sertões, 167
Oviedo, Lino, 341
Owen, Robert, 147

Palacios, Alfredo, 223
pan-Americanism, 15
Panama, 170, 180, 306, 317
Paraguay, 107, 169, 268, 317
Pareto, Vilfredo, 254
Partido Revolucionario Institucional (PRI), 96, 197, 262, 343, 357
patria chica, 26, 178
patriarchal, 132
patrimonialist, 87, 120, 319

Index

patronage, 290
Paul, Saint, 40
Payne, Douglas, W., 337
Paz, Octavio, 9, 258
Peace Corps, 293
peasants, 289
Pedro I (Brazil), 123
Pedro II (Brazil), 166
Pelloutier, Ferdinand, 221
Peña Gómez, José Francisco, 201
peninsulars, 108
Pérez, Carlos Andrés, 232
Pérez-Jiménez, Marcos, 204, 226n, 267, 273
Perón, Juan, 29, 197, 202, 267, 268, 272, 273, 302, 329
Peru, 86, 168, 169, 221, 231, 242, 244, 299, 306, 317, 333
Philip II (Spain), 95
philosopher kings, 22
Pinochet, Augusto, 278, 301, 308
Pizarro brothers, 86
Plato, 22, 24, 345
Platt Amendment, 184
political culture, 12ff.
political parties, 15
political process, 285
political system, 66, 82, 98
Pombal, Marques de, 107
Ponce deLeón, Juan, 85
populist nationalism, 244
Portugal, 19ff., 50ff., 71, 102, 108, 175, 193, 308, 313
positivism, 14, 145ff., 264, 347, 352
Pottiers, Antoine, 249
presidency, powers of, 130
Prestes, Luis Carlos, 225
Primo de Revera, 255
privatization, 325
procuradores, 66
Protestant Reformation, 4, 45, 79, 346
Proudhon, Pierre-Joseph, 218
Puerto Rico, 168, 170
pyramidal, 290

Quadragesimo Anno, 255
Quadros, Janio, 298
Quijote, Don, 36

racism, 198ff.
Radical parties, 288
reactionaries, 139
Reagan administration, 314
Reconquest, 50, 54, 345, 350

regionalism, 51
religious orders, 63, 72
Repetto, Nicolás, 223
republicanism, 128, 166
Rerum Novarum, 252
Riego revolt, 122
rights, 50, 62, 330
Rio Treaty, 225
Roca, Blas, 225
Rodó, José, 15, 187ff., 200, 236, 345, 348, 352
Roland legends, 53
Roman Catholic Church, 60, 63, 99, 151, 155, 274, 312
Roman Empire, 28
Roman law, 61
Romans, St. Paul's letters to the, 38
Rome, influence of, 27ff., 345, 350
Roosevelt, Franklin F., 127, 179
Roosevelt, Teddy, 180
Roosevelt Corollary to the Monroe Doctrine, 180
Rosas, Manuel de, 140
Rosenberg, Tina, 330
Rousseau, Jean-Jacques, 6, 114, 115, 116, 119, 126, 129, 130, 136, 155, 236, 330, 345
Rousseauian democracy, 334, 347
royal absolutism, 70, 79
royal authority, 68
rulers, 29
Russia, 320

Saint-Simon, Henri, 147, 218, 250
Salamanca, University of, 95
Salazar, Antonio, 196, 254, 270
Salisbury, John of, 41
sandinismo, 234, 313
Sandinistas, 216
Santa Anna, Antonio López de, 140, 155, 261
Santana, Pedro, 140
Sanz del Rio, Julián, 148
São Paulo, 167
Sarmiento, Domingo, 154, 168, 200
scholasticism, 92
scientific revolution, 82
Sendero Luminoso, 228
Seneca, 31, 69
Serrano, Jorge, 341
Sierra Justo, 165
Siete Partidas, 69, 125, 137
Silva, Luis Inacio da ("Lula"), 235, 243, 336

Silvert, Kalman H., 282
slavery, in Brazil, 166
social democracy, 230
social democrats, 226
social movements, 312
"social question," 15, 246
Socialist International (SI), 231
socialists, 226, 233
Society of Jesus, 109
sociopolitical structure, 99
Somoza, Anastasio, 197, 202, 298
Sorel, Georges, 221, 254
Soto, Hernando de, 85
Soviet Union, collapse of, 240
Spain, 19ff., 50ff., 73, 108, 175, 183, 193, 306, 308, 313
Spanish-American War, 176
Sparta, 26
Spencer, Herbert, 157, 189, 201
spiritualism, 149
Stalin, Joseph, 216, 224
Stalinist, 238
state, 33, 59, 96, 133, 290
State Department, 342
state-society relations, 95, 129
statism, 319
Stoics, 28
Stroessner, Alfredo, 151, 197, 267
student revolt, 228
Suárez, Francisco, 6, 92ff., 103, 120, 121, 125, 259, 265, 305, 308, 345
Symington, James W., 190
syndicalism, 34, 220

tequila effect, 326
Third International, 224
"Third Wave" of democratization, 304, 313
Thomistic, 139, 142, 274. See also Aquinas
totalitarianism, 255
Tour du Pin, La, 249
towns, 63, 72, 248
trade unions, 212, 253, 291
traditional institutions, 296
Treaty of Tordesillas, 87, 103
Trotsky, Leon, 216

Trotskyite, 233
Trujillo, Rafeal, 33, 151, 197, 202, 267, 273, 297
Tupamaros, 300
two swords, doctrine of, 40

Ubico, Jorge, 197, 202, 267, 272
Unger, Roberto, 245
United Nations (UN), 182
United States, 3, 175, 225, 297, 304, 318, 342
unity, 129, 130
Uruguay, 143, 168, 201, 218, 221, 237, 300, 303, 306, 317, 329, 331, 338
utilitarianism, 147
utopian socialism, 147, 218

Valdivia, Pedero de, 86
Vargas, Getulio, 197, 267, 268, 271, 272, 273, 329
Varona, Enrique José, 228
Vasconcelos, José, 228
Vatican II, 274
Velasco Ibarra, José María, 197
Venezuela, 204, 280, 299, 304, 317, 332
verba, 279
viceroyalties, 98
Villedo Morales, Ramón, 297
Visigoths, 43, 50
Vogelsang, Karl van, 249
Voltaire, 114

War of Texas Independence, 175
warrior caste, 35
"Washington consensus," 309
Weber, Max, 9
Wilson, Woodrow, 127, 180
women, 52, 354
workerpriests, 274
Workers' Party (Brazil), 235
working class, 288
Working Men's Circles, 251
World Bank, 213
"world culture," 2

Zakaria, Fareed, 334
Zapatistas, 312